"Covid-19," Psychological Operations, and the War for Technocracy

"David Hughes masterfully details history in the making by implicitly asking the reader to ponder and answer two questions: *How did we get here? How did we let this happen?* His perspectives and methods are unique in that they allow, or rather insist, that the reader be a participant in the narrative rather than be cognitively passive, as just a hobbyist or voyeur of humanity. Reading this book forces deep reflection on the trajectory of our personal lives and the extent to which we allow others to influence and control what we do, think, and permit. When the World survives this attack, and there is time to reflect on its events, this book will be a prerequisite for any and all discussions seeking truth. Dr. Hughes does not seek consensus and he does not provide answers; he provides a forensic set of tools for the reader to do that job independently. In this sense, he is helping to describe the problem twice."

—Matt Taylor, *Forensic Electrical Engineer (Ecuador)*

"Bold and moved by an unwavering love of the truth, David Hughes demolishes a mass of clever mis-directions, cunning lies and half-truths serving to prop up the false promises of an emerging technocratic age. This new book probes the history of the movement towards technocracy, the seedy streams of funding, forms of political and societal capture, usurpation of science, and the weaponization of medicine all in service to the perverse inhuman logic characteristic of the present late stage of the fiat system. This scholarly and meticulous deconstruction of the major narratives reshaping much of the world in the image of the transnational order will clear the vision of many eyes still partly mesmerized by Covid-19 theatre."

—Dr. Daniel Broudy, *Professor of Applied Linguistics, Okinawa Christian University (Japan)*

"The most pressing issue today is for people to become cognizant of the deliberate drive for a global technocratic dictatorship. Dr. David Hughes lays bare, with great scholarly skill, how the architects of the "COVID-19" menticidal dictatorship are slowly ensnaring humanity in a dystopian totalitarian future. Hughes presses the point that our current predicament is not due to an ill-judged reaction to a respiratory disease, where people have fallen into wrong-think or collective delusion; what we are experiencing is due to real perpetrators waging war against humanity. In *"Covid-19," Psychological Operations, and the War for*

Technocracy, Dr. Hughes stands out as a rare, brave, academic, who is willing to go where few are willing to tread. Therefore, Dr. Hughes' book is a must read for our times."

—Dr. Bruce Scott, Psychoanalyst and author of *Gulag Caledonia* (Scotland)

"Whether you want to understand world events in terms of geopolitics, history, or your own psychological experience, *"Covid-19," Psychological Operations, and the War for Technocracy* is for you. Scholarly and accessible, Dr. David Hughes' meticulously researched book digs tirelessly beneath the surface of received wisdom on subjects ranging from world wars to global finance to leading psychiatric institutes and their methods. Laypeople and experts alike will be taken on an extensively documented voyage beyond what they thought they knew of the status quo, even within their own areas of expertise.

The multiple converging strands of evidence laid out by Hughes lead readers time and again to the same place: a precipice of global technocratic totalitarianism and biodigital enslavement, being pushed by the wealthiest 0.001 percent upon the rest of humanity. Hughes' book lights the paths laid here by decades of mind control, both psychological and technobiological. It is impossible to overstate the contribution that this volume makes to the literatures on psychology and governance, and humanity's trajectory into World War III. While sober and sobering, if Hughes' lucid and unflinching approach to academic scholarship catches on, humanity might just stand a chance, armed with insight and understanding."

—Valerie Kyrie, Ph.D. (Psychology), *author and Associate Researcher with the Working Group on Propaganda and the 9/11 Global 'War on Terror'*

David A. Hughes

“Covid-19,” Psychological Operations, and the War for Technocracy

Volume 1

palgrave
macmillan

David A. Hughes
School of Social and Political Sciences
University of Lincoln
Lincoln, UK

ISBN 978-3-031-41849-5 ISBN 978-3-031-41850-1 (eBook)
https://doi.org/10.1007/978-3-031-41850-1

Cover illustration: @ Alex Linch shutterstock.com

This Palgrave Macmillan imprint is published by the registered company Springer Nature Switzerland AG
The registered company address is: Gewerbestrasse 11, 6330 Cham, Switzerland

Paper in this product is recyclable.

Dedicated to all who are actively resisting the global technocratic coup

Legal Disclaimer

This book provides scholarly analysis of the tectonic shifts that have been taking place in the global political economy since 2020. The information it provides is for educational and research purposes only. The views it contains are solely those of the author.

Neither the author nor the publisher may be held responsible by any person or entity for any action or claim, loss, injury, damage, or inconvenience caused, or alleged to be caused, directly or indirectly, as the result of information contained within this book or its listed sources or any errors or omissions.

Although every care has been taken to ensure that the information contained within this book is accurate at the time of publication, no representation or warranties, either express or implied, are made with respect to the accuracy, completeness, currency, reliability, or usefulness of the information contained in this book.

Any errors will be corrected in subsequent editions.

Contents

CHAPTER 1

Permanent Counterrevolution, Technocracy, and World War III

An undeclared global class war was initiated in 2020, whose aim is the controlled demolition of liberal democracy and the institution of global technocracy—a novel, biodigital form of totalitarianism that threatens to lead to the irreversible enslavement of humanity. World War III looks nothing like its two predecessors and is waged by the transnational deep state against populations using the novel methods of Omniwar, i.e. war waged in every domain, but clandestinely, so that the public does not recognise it as such. The opening campaign of World War III involved the largest psychological warfare operation in history, which I call the "'Covid-19' operation." This was intended to demoralise, disorientate, and debilitate the public, thus weakening its resistance to the intended transition to technocracy. Historically, psychological warfare has served as the prelude to physical war, raising the alarm concerning what is to come.

Introduction

With the World Health Organization's declaration of the "Covid-19 pandemic" on March 11, 2020, an undeclared global class war was initiated, aimed at the controlled demolition of liberal democracy and the institution of global technocracy, a novel, biodigital form of totalitarianism. The largest psychological warfare operation in history was waged transnationally against unwitting populations to cripple their resistance to the intended transition to technocracy. That psychological operation,

D. A. Hughes, *"Covid-19," Psychological Operations, and the War for Technocracy*, https://doi.org/10.1007/978-3-031-41850-1_1

which I refer to as the "'Covid-19" operation, is the subject of the two volumes of this book. This volume explores various techniques for attacking the mind and psychologically breaking down the victim—"menticide," to borrow the term coined by Joost Meerloo in *The Rape of the Mind. The Psychology of Thought Control, Menticide, and Brainwashing* (1956). Volume 2 deals with the "brainwashing" part of Meerloo's title, i.e. means of reprogramming the mind with desired thoughts, attitudes, and behaviours.

If successfully implemented, technocracy will be worse than anything imaginable by Hitler or Stalin, because it amounts to the biodigital *enslavement* of humanity through biometric technologies, the "Internet of Bodies," constant surveillance and monitoring, central bank digital currencies, and a Chinese-style social credit system (Davis, 2022; Broudy & Kyrie, 2021; Wood, 2022). Moreover, if allowed to happen, such a control system could prove irreversible. Technocracy has been incubated for decades in China with the support of the Rockefellers and various technology transfers, and, with proof of concept having been established, the aim is now to roll it out in the West (Corbett, 2014, 2019a; Wood, 2018; Davis, 2022).

The decision by a numerically tiny transnational ruling class to use its control over the means of production to wage war against the rest of humanity is as desperate as it is audacious, and can only be understood in the context of 150 + years of transnational class conflict. The rise of international socialism in the nineteenth and early twentieth centuries was met with ruthless methods of suppression, including world war, paramilitary brutality, fascism, and totalitarianism (van der Pijl, 2015, 2019; Sutton, 2016). After World War II, similarly ruthless methods were used to crush any sign of emergent socialism in "Third World" countries under the pretext of fighting a "Cold War" against the Soviet Union (McCoy, 2015; Ahmed, 2012, pp. 70–1; Hughes, 2022b). Social tensions mounted in the West, and following May 1968, when France was brought to the brink of revolution, low-level counterinsurgency methods came to be deployed against Western populations (Minnicino, 1974; Ganser, 2005; Hughes, 2022b). From that point on, it was clear that an ongoing, transnationally coordinated effort to suppress class conflict had to take precedence over rivalries between different ruling classes and that, ultimately, only a global scientific dictatorship can prevent worldwide social revolution. The ARPANET (the military precursor of the internet, created in 1969) has since evolved into a global surveillance dragnet collecting data on everyone for counter-revolutionary purposes (van der Pijl, 2022, p. 73). The "War on Terror" was used to normalise the invocation of emergency powers (Agamben, 2005), militarise the domestic environment (Valentine, 2017), and hollow out liberal democracy.

The transnational ruling class now seeks to replace liberal democracy with technocracy. Historically, such fundamental sociopolitical and economic change has only been possible through world war. Thus, the global class war is synonymous with World War III, which, however, looks nothing like the two previous world wars, just as they did not resemble anything seen before (J. Corbett, 2020a). World War III is waged using the novel methods of Omniwar (see below), i.e. war waged across every domain, but clandestinely, so that the public does not recognise it as such. It amounts to a global counterinsurgency campaign, with dissidents replacing "terrorists" as the enemy using the infrastructure established through the "War on Terror" (cf. Valentine, 2017, p. 64). Deception is fundamental: the public must not get wise to what is happening, lest there be a surge in revolutionary activity. So far, physical fighting has not broken out, however, the largest psychological warfare operation in history—the "Covid-19" operation—has been waged against the public, and historically, psychological warfare serves as the prelude to physical war.

The proximate triggers for the global class war were: (i) the failure of the previous security paradigm—the so-called "War on Terror"—to contain increasingly progressive forms of social movements in 2019 (van der Pijl, 2022, 54–58); (ii) clear warning signs in 2019 that the international monetary and financial system was on the brink of collapse (BlackRock, 2019; Wolff, 2021); and (iii) a crisis of the Western propaganda system (see below). A new paradigm of social control was needed, the pretext for which was provided by "Covid-19," whether "real or simulated" (Agamben, 2021, p. 7). Indeed, it is conspicuous that once the dominant security paradigm shifted from the "War on Terror" to biosecurity in 2020, major terrorist attacks in the West declined markedly.

After decades of laying the groundwork for global technocracy, low-intensity operations against Western populations gave way in March 2020 to full-frontal psychological warfare. All meaningful semblance of liberal democracy disappeared as governments and major media corporations around the world, acting in coordination at the behest of the transnational deep state (Hughes, 2022b), resorted to menticidal techniques against the public, a phenomenon previously only seen under totalitarianism (Meerloo, 1956, p. 35). Quite apart from its demoralising, disorienting, and debilitating functions, the "Covid-19" operation was used to coerce populations into taking the "vaccine," a physical measure whose most likely purpose, in the context of war, is as a weapons platform (see Chaps. 6 and 8).

Permanent Counterrevolution: A Brief History

Contrary to the clichéd image in IR realism, war is not simply fought "horizontally," between nation-states. More fundamentally, it is also fought "vertically," between classes, putting aside national differences. This first became evident in 1871, when the Paris Commune was crushed by a combination of French and German forces, even though Bismarck had only just prevailed in the Franco-Prussian War. Marx's *The Civil War in France* recognises the international character of class rule revealed in this event: "Class rule is no longer able to disguise itself in a national uniform; the national governments are one as against the proletariat" (cited in Epp, 2017, 87). Proletarian internationalism thus derived from "the likelihood of a common response by European exploiting classes, bourgeois and aristocratic, to a revolutionary threat affecting any one of them" (Gilbert, 1981, p. 149).

Bismarck sought to placate the rising socialist movement in Germany by creating the world's first welfare state in the 1880s. With international socialism continuing to rise, however, working-class energies were channelled into programmes of imperialist expansion, in line with Cecil Rhodes' 1895 idea of imperialism as a means of avoiding civil war: "In order to save the forty million inhabitants of the United Kingdom from a bloody civil war, we colonial statesmen must acquire new lands to settle surplus population, to provide new markets for the goods produced by them in the factories and mines" (cited in Lenin, 1987, p. 229). The crisis of capitalism at home, in other words, had to be externalised.

In 1905, following Russia's defeat in its war with Japan, mass political and social unrest spread throughout the Russian Empire, involving worker strikes, peasant unrest, and military mutinies. German Emperor Wilhelm II apparently understood the warning signs, telling the Chancellor, Bernhard von Bülow: "shoot, decapitate, and break the socialists, if necessary with a bloodbath [...] After that, war abroad; but not before [...]." This was, as van der Pijl (2015, pp. 76–77) notes, a considerable departure from Bismarck's reforms, representing nothing less than "war against the working class." It clearly shows that class war is more fundamental than wars against foreign enemies.

With a "counterrevolutionary capitalist bloc" underwritten by Anglo-American power seeking to suppress the rise of "contender states" as well as prevent civil war at home (van der Pijl, 2019, pp. 1275–6), World War I saw the working classes of different countries turned against one another and submerged in what German militarists called "a bath of steel." But popular revulsion against imperialism and war in turn led to the October Revolution and the widespread emergence of Communist parties at the war's end. The Revolution symbolised a threat to ruling classes everywhere; for decades, U.S. leaders were "more afraid of the implicit and indirect challenge of the revolution than they were of the actual power of the Soviet Union" (Williams, 1972, pp. 105–106).

The Allies' intervention against the Red Army, which was intended to "protect their commercial, industrial and financial interests, and to defeat the communist threat" (Abramovici, 2014, p. 115), offers another example of separate ruling classes uniting to protect their shared interests. The communist threat was violently put down in country after country. In Germany, most notably, the crushing of the Bavarian Soviet Republic and the assassination of Rosa Luxemburg and Karl Liebknecht by the paramilitary Freikorps in 1919 were followed by the founding of the NSDAP in 1920.

There are important lessons to be learned from these events when it comes to understanding war from a class perspective. As van der Pijl (2015, p. 77) explains:

> [There] developed a silent collective will among the rival ruling classes to deal with their working populations by turning [Trotsky's] "permanent revolution" into a "permanent counterrevolution" through imperialism and war [...A]cross the entire ruling class spectrum there was agreement that the rise of the socialist labour movement had to be met one way or the other, with war as the common denominator of the different responses [...] against a class which under unchanged conditions was on the way to gaining the upper hand. Only through war could the combined ruling classes, nominal enemies no doubt, deal with the tectonic tensions between the growth of productive forces and the political-economic structure in which these had developed so far.

Thus, for well over a century, there has been a shared understanding among the ruling classes of different countries that their mutual interests are best served by uniting to crush class conflict—if necessary, by war.

In the post-World War I era, Anglo-American power, focused on the City of London and Wall Street, coordinated its designs for the world via the Royal Institute of International Affairs (Chatham House, founded 1920) and the Council on Foreign Relations (1921). Montagu Norman, Governor of the Bank of England, helped to manoeuvre Hitler and the Nazis into power, as did Henry Ford and Wall Street (Sutton, 2016). Having subverted the Bolshevik Revolution and turned the Soviet Union into a giant opportunity to acquire financial control over nationalised industries on a model previously established in Latin America (Sutton, 1981), Wall Street looked to do the same in Germany. National Socialism, and Roosevelt's New Deal were all forms of "corporate socialism," in which the power of the state is made available to big business, thus eliminating competition to an oligarchy of large corporations financed (and thus ultimately directed) by the major investment banks (Sutton, 2016, pp. 50, 121).

Had the "Business Plot" of 1933/34 (an attempted coup d'état by Wall Street financiers and wealthy industrialists) not been foiled by its intended leader, General Smedley Butler, the United States would likely have followed Nazi Germany and the Soviet Union on the path to totalitarianism—and with it, perhaps, the world. This demonstrates the ruthlessness to which the ruling class is willing to resort to keep the working class in check, particularly during moments of acute capitalist crisis, such as the aftermath of the 1929 Wall Street crash. Once again, world war proved to be the means of resolving the crisis in favour of the ruling class. Wall Street and Henry Ford profited from backing both sides (Sutton, 2016), while millions of working-class lives were lost; in Germany and Japan, it did not take long before the leading industrialists of old were back in positions of power after 1945 (Hughes, 2022b).

The "Cold War," though marked by geopolitical rivalry at one level, was also marked by a more fundamental collaboration between the West and the USSR to suppress international class conflict (Hughes, 2022b). For example, the East German uprising of 1953 was not only crushed by Soviet tanks, but "to make sure that it did not spread, the western powers of England, France and the United States built a wall of police and military might to prevent West Berlin workers from marching to join their brothers and sisters in the East" (Glaberman & Faber, 2002, pp. 171–2). Similarly, when Soviet tanks rolled into Hungary in 1956 to crush the uprising there, "the Eisenhower administration loudly protested the Soviet action, but did not intervene militarily. Liberation was exposed as a sham" (Wilford, 2008, p. 49).

Revolutionary activity in the "Third World" was met by 104 covert operations in eight years under President Eisenhower, followed by 163 covert operations in only three years under President Kennedy (McCoy, 2015). Such operations were used to force open markets and establish client regimes facilitating Western capital penetration and labour dispossession (Ahmed, 2012, pp. 70–1). McCoy (2015) describes a "'reverse wave' in the global trend towards democracy from 1958 to 1975, as coups—most of them U.S.-sanctioned—allowed military men to seize power in more than three-dozen nations, representing a quarter of the world's sovereign states." The permanent counter-revolution entailed subversion in any country where socialism threatened to gain a foothold. Socialist movements were ruthlessly crushed using methods derived from the Nazis, including death squads, torture, false flag terrorism, biochemical warfare, surveillance-based targeting of political opponents, and the mass killing of civilians (Hughes, 2022b).

The transnationalisation of resistance in the 1960s, which culminated in President de Gaulle being forced to flee France in May 1968, led to the permanent counterrevolution assuming the form of low-level counterinsurgency operations against Western *domestic* populations, modelled on Kitson's (1971, pp. 52–53) "stability operations," which are "as much concerned with organising the population as they are with fighting battles." Tavistock-inspired psychological operations involving the application of shock and stress to entire populations (see Chap. 2) fit this model, as does NATO's covert paramilitary false flag terrorism of the 1970s and 1980s (Ganser, 2005; Hughes, 2022b).

When the domestic population is seen as the object of counterinsurgency, it becomes the enemy in a clandestine war waged by the transnational deep state (Hughes, 2022b). As Minnicino (1974, p. 37) realises, the ultimate direction of travel is martial law, or "direct military takeover in the advanced capitalist sector." A transnationally coordinated effort to keep a rapidly growing population in check at this point becomes more fundamental to global political economy than rivalries between different ruling classes, geopolitics, and inter-state competition. Wars of course persist, but in the final analysis, "the only war that is left [is] the world revolution" (Minnicino, 1974, p. 51). Globally, the ruling classes have no choice but to join forces and push for a world state/global dictatorship, while the rest of humanity has no choice but worldwide social revolution if it wishes to avoid permanent subjugation and enslavement.

With the end of the Soviet Union, a new pretext (other than fighting "communism") had to be found for the capitalist oligarchy to maintain its violent rule. Carter et al. (1998, p. 81) envisaged a "transforming event" that would, "like Pearl Harbor [...] divide our past and future into a before and after," involving "loss of life and property unprecedented in peacetime," and necessitating "draconian measures, scaling back civil liberties, allowing wider surveillance of citizens, detention of suspects, and use of deadly force." Similarly, the Project for a New American Century (2000) claimed that rebuilding America's defences would be a drawn-out affair "absent some catastrophic and catalyzing event—like a new Pearl Harbor."

"9/11" was duly used as the pretext, not only for continuing imperialist wars abroad, but also for militarising the domestic environment under the banner of the "War on Terror" (Hughes, 2022b). The ensuing "permanent state of emergency" (Agamben, 2005, p. 2) meant, in the words of Jeff Halper, that war was "rendered endemic, since it is neither possible nor desirable to end the 'permanent emergency'" from a ruling-class perspective; "pacifying humanity becomes the only way to remove war, but that endeavour itself becomes a violent, never-ending totalitarian project" (cited in van der Pijl, 2022, p. 61). As Orwell (1984, p. 329) predicted, the ruling classes are "not fighting against one another at all. The war is waged by each ruling group against its own subjects, and the object of the war is not to make or prevent conquests of territory, but to keep the [class] structure of society intact."

The dress rehearsal for "9/11" was the Oklahoma City bombing in 1995, whose provenance is dubious (Corbett, 2015). Senator Joe Biden introduced the Omnibus Counterterrorism Act two months before the bombing that enabled its passage, and it served as the template for the USA PATRIOT Act that was hurriedly passed into law in 2001. In 2002, Biden reflected that the 1995 legislation was intended to alter the 1878 *Posse Comitatus* Act, which prevents the military from exercising police powers within the United States, to allow the military to intervene in incidents involving WMD ("Biden backs letting soldiers arrest civilians," 2002). General Ralph Eberhart, who presided over NORAD's catastrophic failure to prevent the "9/11" attacks and who lied under oath to the 9/11 Commission (Griffin & Woodworth, 2018, Chap. 37), was made the inaugural head of U.S. Northern Command, which asserts military jurisdiction over the U.S. domestic arena. Eberhart agreed that "*Posse Comitatus* and other laws" needed to be reviewed.

In words that seem prescient considering the "9/11" attacks, Hoffman (1998, p. 385) writes in his book on the OKC bombing:

> The Shadow Government's willingness to kill large numbers of foreigners in its bloody wars and covert operations is now being extended to the American people, as its goals shift from controlling third-world populations to controlling American citizens [...] It is a short leap from rationalizing the killing of hundreds of thousands or even millions of foreigners to killing a few hundred or a few thousand Americans, if the policy objectives deem it necessary.

The 3000 lives lost in the attacks of September 11, 2001, enabled the transnational deep state (Hughes, 2022b) to pull off a covert *coup d'état*, and Western democracy was replaced by a new mode of governance modelled on the Italian Strategy of Tension (Ganser, 2005), though its outward trappings remained. This involves normalising emergency powers through a never-ending series of manufactured threats (terrorism, financial crisis, the "climate emergency," disease outbreaks, etc.) to keep the public fearful, shocked, duped, and willing to cede its liberties in the name of dealing with those threats. Western societies have thereby been manoeuvred in an increasingly authoritarian direction, which Hoffman (1998, p. 391) calls "worldwide fascism."

Western populations, subjected to military-grade psychological operations, not only failed to see that they were the quarry after "9/11," but were also manipulated into *defending* official narratives, and, through Pavlovian conditioning, were trained to attack anyone who questions those narratives as a "conspiracy theorist." Meanwhile, the architecture of their oppression was invisibly scaffolded around them, not least via "smart" technologies and social media that create the digital gulag harvesting everyone's personal information for surveillance and control purposes as part of "permanent surveillance and information warfare" (van der Pijl, 2022, p. 76). Worse still, during this entire period (since before "9/11"), a revolution in warfare, based on "convergent technologies" in the "IT/Bio/Nano" era, was being worked on behind the scenes, and a potentially highly advanced weapons system, for use against the public, may now be in the process of installation (see Chap. 8). The permanent counterrevolution now stands on the brink of irreversible triumph—the technocratic enslavement of humanity—that only worldwide social revolution can prevent.

The "Covid-19" Operation: Proximate Triggers

By 1968 at the latest, the logic of an increasingly transnational class struggle meant that the ultimate outcome would either be a global dictatorship (the fulfilment of permanent counterrevolution) or world socialism (the fulfilment of Trotsky's permanent revolution, requiring the expropriation of the means of production by the working class and the just redistribution of wealth and opportunity on a worldwide scale). The transnational ruling class, while using low-level counterinsurgency and psychological warfare techniques against Western populations since 1968, has been carefully laying the groundwork for the inevitable global class war for over half a century, buying time until the necessary revolution in warfare could be covertly achieved.

As explained in Chap. 8, a timeline involving the years 2020, 2025, and 2030 was framed as early as 2001, but even so, the "Covid-19" operation was in many ways rushed and botched, as though rolled out ahead of schedule. It is hard to avoid the impression that the ruling class wanted longer to prepare. This section lays out three reasons why the "Covid-19" operation was launched earlier than planned, namely: (i) worldwide social protests in 2019; (ii) the crisis of the international monetary and financial system in 2019; and (iii) the crisis of the Western propaganda system.

Worldwide Social Protests

In keeping with the global Strategy of Tension outlined above, a spate of terrorist attacks in France between 2015 and 2017 resulted in the introduction of a state of emergency, renewed five times since, seeing 10,000 troops deployed on French streets under the *Sentinelle* anti-terrorism operation (van der Pijl, 2022, p. 64). However, if such actions, in France and elsewhere, were intended to quell social unrest by moving societies ever further in the direction of police states, the effort failed, as conspicuously expressed by the rise of the Yellow Vests in France in 2018, as well as mass uprisings in Chile and India (van der Pijl, 2022, pp. 54–58). Those social movements assumed a socially progressive form not easily assimilated by populism, "instilling fear in the ruling classes the world over" (van der Pijl, 2022, p. 3). In 2019, following a decade of austerity, a "tsunami of protests" erupted in one in five countries, "unleashing public fury on a global scale," and reflecting "unprecedented political mobilization" (Wright, 2019). It seemed that "every corner of the globe" was being "rocked by an explosion of unrest" and that "the Old World Order of neoliberal globalism under Pax Americana [was] finally coming apart at the seams" (Corbett, 2019b). These uncontainable social tensions, according to van der Pijl (2022, p. 72), were what triggered the "Covid-19" counterrevolution in 2020, "the signs of revolution [being] too serious" for the transnational ruling class to ignore.

Crisis in the International Monetary and Financial System

The acute crisis of capitalism in 2019 was also reflected in warning signs regarding the international monetary and financial system (IMFS). In May 2019, the yield curve on U.S. treasuries inverted, historically a harbinger of recession (Jones, 2019). The S&P price/earnings ratio in 2019 was the second highest of all time, even higher than in 1929 and 2007, again indicative of a coming recession (Bourbon Financial Management, 2019). CEOs obviously knew that trouble lay ahead, with record numbers resigning (Atkinson, 2019).

This was not to be just any recession, however. This was, potentially, to be a system-destroying recession (Wolff, 2021). The storm clouds had been gathering for some time, viz. the Long-Term Capital Management crisis (1998), the "global" financial crisis of 2007/8 (more accurately described as a crisis of the "Atlantic banking community" [Nesvetailova & Palan, 2008]), and the Eurozone debt crisis. First, the banks had to bail out a hedge fund; then, the public had to bail out the banks; then, sovereign nation-states went bankrupt. Since 2008, the system had been on artificial life support in the form of "quantitative easing" plus near-0% interest rates. The next major crisis always had the potential to prove fatal (Wolff, 2021).

The erstwhile Bank of England Governor, Mark Carney, warned at a meeting of the world's most senior figures in international finance in Jackson Hole, Wyoming, in August 2019 that "the deficiencies of the IMFS have become increasingly potent. Even a passing acquaintance with monetary history suggests that this centre won't hold" (Carney, 2019).

The previous week, BlackRock had published a seminal report arguing that conventional monetary and fiscal policies will not be enough to deal with the next economic downturn (BlackRock, 2019). The report proposes completely remaking the financial system based on the idea of "going direct," i.e. abolishing the split-circuit system that keeps central bank reserves and retail money separate (as is necessary for a democratic system of "no taxation without representation") and instead establishing a direct connection between central banks and individuals' private accounts.

This is what the drive towards central bank digital currencies (CBDC, cf. Strohecker, 2023) is all about, with the public having been primed for the rollout of digital currency via the cryptocurrency mania of the 2010s (the crucial difference being that CBDC will be centralised rather than decentralised). If implemented, central banks will be able to freeze individuals' bank accounts, or take money out of them, or impose conditions on the way that "money" (just a voucher system by this point) is spent, and no financial transaction anymore will be private (Davis, 2023). Put bluntly, it is a system of financial enslavement, more "direct" than "debt slavery." Dissidents will be financially outcast, as already indicated by the abortive move to freeze Canadian truckers' bank accounts and those of their supporters in January 2022.

On September 17, 2019, a crisis in the U.S. repo market saw the secured overnight lending rate briefly hit 10% (vs. its prior 2019 rate of 2–3%), prompting the Federal Reserve to step in and provide additional liquidity. As Titus (2021) demonstrates based on Federal Reserve activity, this was the moment when the decision was made to put the "Going Direct" plan into action, and with it the entire manufactured "Covid-19" crisis: "It's easy if not trivial to look at a timeline of monetary events and see that the official monetary response to the 'coronavirus pandemic' went into effect *before* there even was a pandemic."

Crisis of the Western Propaganda System

Propaganda has long served an essential function in the maintenance and management of U.S. liberal democracy. Lippmann (1925, p. 145), for instance, writes that the public is "necessarily ignorant, usually irrelevant and often meddlesome," and so, through propaganda, "must be put in its place [...] so that each of us may live free of the trampling and the roar of the bewildered herd." Bernays (1928, p. 1) writes in the famous opening lines of *Propaganda* that "The conscious and intelligent manipulation of the organized habits and opinions of the masses is an important element in democratic society" and those who do this constitute "an invisible government which is the true ruling power of our country." Lippmann (1922, p. 248) coins the phrase "the manufacture of consent," and Bernays (1947) uses the term "engineering of consent." Donald Slesinger, a participant in a 1939 Rockefeller seminar on communications, uses the phrase "dictatorship-by-manipulation" when objecting to Lippmann's ideas (cited in Simpson, 1994, p. 23). According to *Fortune* magazine in 1949, "It is as impossible to imagine a genuine democracy without the science of persuasion as it is to think of a totalitarian state without coercion," leading Chomsky (1982, p. 67) to infer: "indoctrination is to democracy what coercion is to dictatorship." In neither system is there real freedom.

Soviet communism and Western liberal democracy had a shared interest in censorship: direct political censorship in the case of the former, censorship through "the concentration of communication power in the hands of a few big concerns" in the case of the latter (Huxley, 1958, p. 35). Centralisation of media ownership is one of five "filters" identified by Herman and Chomsky (1988, p. 2) in their propaganda model of the Western media. The others include advertising revenue, reliance on information provided by government and business, "flak" as a means of disciplining those who step out of line, and the dominant ideology of the time. The net result is a highly sophisticated propaganda system, often reliant on self-censorship by those who have internalised its workings, which gives the lie to the liberal model of the media as an obstreperous "Fourth Estate."

The U.S. propaganda system enables "brainwashing under freedom," whereby the most egregious human rights abuses by U.S. imperialism go virtually unnoticed by a population indoctrinated to believe that U.S. foreign policy is fundamentally about safeguarding freedom and other higher values (Herman and Chomsky, 1979, p. 67). "To achieve this result without explicit government censorship," the authors note, "is the genius of the Western way."

Wolin (2008) uses the term "inverted totalitarianism" to describe the United States. No national institution in the USA can properly be regarded as democratic, he claims, pointing to "the highly managed, money-saturated elections, the lobby-infested Congress, the imperial presidency, the class-biased judicial and penal system, or, least of all, the media" (2008, p. 105). This system, in Wolin's view, represents "the antithesis of constitutional power," constantly projecting power upwards while seeking to keep the citizenry off balance and passive (Hedges, 2015). The "genius" of the "totalizing system" in the USA, Wolin writes, "lies in wielding total power without appearing to, without establishing concentration camps, or enforcing ideological uniformity, or forcibly suppressing dissident elements so long as they remain ineffectual" (2008, p. 57). "The government does not need to stamp out dissent," he argues, because "the uniformity of imposed public opinion through the corporate media does a very effective job" (cited in Hedges, 2015).

Yet, the rise of social media, independent media, and citizen journalism during a period of relative internet freedom up to 2020 posed an increasing threat to the "genius" of the Western propaganda system. More and more people, waking up to the extent to which their previous worldview had been manipulated through propaganda, came to see through that system and to lose trust in liberal democracy. Should the population, steadily stripped of its rights and freedoms, grow restive and refuse to play along in the illusion of democracy, Wolin warns, it can expect a response familiar from past systems of totalitarianism (in Hedges, 2015).

Since March 2020, a transnational deep state operation (Hughes, 2022b) has been underway to institute a novel, technocratic form of totalitarianism. In many ways, we are still at the thin edge of the wedge, but the warning signs are undeniable. Although, in the West, we may not yet find ourselves "under the yoke of totalitarian regimes comparable to those we know so well from the twentieth century, there is no doubt that we are faced with a global paradigm that brings forth steadily expanding totalitarian tendencies [...]" (Alting von Geusau, 2021). However, Alting von Geusau is wrong to claim that those tendencies are not "planned intentionally or maliciously." They are by design, instigated by a transnational ruling class seeking recourse to totalitarianism in response to an acute crisis of capitalism—the same principle as in the 1930s. Then, as now, totalitarianism did not simply spring, fully formed, into existence. The descent into its worst horrors took place over many years. The origins of Nazi genocide, for instance, can be traced back to earlier euthanasia programmes, making the reappearance of state-sponsored euthanasia since 2020 deeply troubling (Hughes et al., 2022).

Further similarities between the "Covid-19" era and Nazi Germany include: the surrendering of liberties in the name of "the greater good"

(Agamben, 2021, p. 17), use of propaganda to induce ideological conformity, the telling of Big Lies (see Chap. 6), widespread order following ("following Government guidelines"), mass psychosis (see Chap. 2), dehumanisation of outgroups as spreaders of disease (e.g. Jews, the "pandemic of the unvaccinated"), the descent of civilised society into harmful and irrational behaviour (see Chap. 7), forcing health services to comply with government dictats (viz. the "'Nazification' of the NHS" [Corbett, 2021]), experimenting on human beings without their informed consent (Hughes et al., 2022), eugenics themes involving the same actors active in Nazi Germany (Ehret, 2021), censorship and silencing of dissent that belong "firmly in the realms of a totalitarian Nazi dystopia" (Polyakova, 2021), legislation that pushes in the direction of dictatorship (Davis, 2021e), a fascistic fusion of the state and Big Business (today's "global public–private partnership" [Davis, 2021b]), and the promotion of ecopolitics (cf. Brüggemeier et al., 2005; Biehl & Staudenmaier, 2011). These continuities are explored in greater detail in Hughes (2024).

Technocracy: A Brief History

Technocracy: Origins

Technocracy originated on the campus of Columbia University in 1932 as the brainchild of Howard Scott, who went on to found Technocracy, Inc. with M. King Hubbert (later proponent of "peak oil" theory) in 1934. Their *Technocracy Study Course* (1934) characterises technocracy as "dealing with social phenomena in the widest sense of the word; this includes not only actions of human beings, but also everything which directly or indirectly affects their actions," including biology, the climate, and natural resources (Technocracy Inc., 2005, p. v). Their magazine, *The Technocrat*, defines technocracy as "the science of social engineering, the scientific operation of the entire social mechanism to produce and distribute goods and services to the entire population" (cited in Wood, 2018, p. 10). In other words, technocracy is about the scientific management of everyone and everything.

Writing during the Great Depression, Scott and Hubbert were looking for an alternative economic system to capitalism. Technocracy represents a centrally managed system based on energy rather than money. Instead of market forces of supply and demand determining price, citizens are to receive a quota of energy certificates to be spent on goods and services priced according to the energy cost of production (Technocracy Inc., 2005, p. 230; cf. Wood, 2018, p. 13). The efficiencies achieved will, in Scott and Hubbert's vision, lead to material abundance alongside increased leisure time. The technology required to fulfil this vision, which essentially requires the constant monitoring and control of everything, was not available in the 1930s, but it is now (under the label "smart").

Technocracy is hostile to human freedom. At the apex of its power structure (the Technate) stand the technocrats, who control everyone and everything. It is they who get to manage and distribute resources, right down to the individual level (Davis, 2022). Paraphrasing Wood (2018, pp. 14–15), technocracy implies:

- eradication of private property, for everything is owned by the Technate;
- dependence on the Technate for all basic needs, e.g. food, housing, healthcare, transportation (all vehicles, for instance, must be rented, with ride sharing as the norm);
- inability to save for future needs, since energy certificates expire at the end of an accounting period;
- abolition of all previous political systems, including democracy;
- education as a form of conditioning to prepare people for the career path chosen for them by the Technate.

Technocracy thus inaugurates a new form of totalitarianism facilitated by scientific advances that could in principle be used for human emancipation, were the relevant technologies expropriated from the ruling class.

The "Scientific Dictatorship" and the "Technetronic Era"

Mid-twentieth-century thinkers also recognised the prospect of using science for purposes of total social control. Russell (1952, pp. 30–54), for instance, envisages a "scientific dictatorship" in which access to the relevant scientific knowledge will be "rigidly confined to the governing class. The populace will not be allowed to know how its convictions were generated." Not only "the art of persuasion" (propaganda), but also diet, injections, and education will combine to render "any serious criticism of the powers that be [...] psychologically impossible," immunising the ruling class against revolution. After a single generation needed to perfect such techniques, the scientific dictatorship will no longer require physical forms of coercion (police forces and armies) to control its subjects.

According to Huxley (1958, p. 118), "Under a scientific dictator education will really work – with the result that most men and women will grow up to love their servitude and will never dream of revolution." Huxley envisages "a new kind of non-violent totalitarianism," not based on terror and coercion, in which the trappings of democracy (e.g., elections, parliaments, and the rhetoric of freedom) remain while "the ruling oligarchy and its highly trained elite of soldiers, policemen, thought-manufacturers and mind-manipulators will quietly run the show as they see fit" (1958, pp. 110–11). The "final revolution" (or, better, counter-revolution) will be a "dictatorship without tears, so to speak, producing a kind of painless concentration camp for entire societies" (Huxley, 1959, p. 226). In 1962, Huxley spent a semester at Berkeley as a Ford research professor. Evidently attracted by his ideas, the Ford Foundation threw enormous sums of money at behavioural science research in the 1960s.

Brzezinski (1970, p. 10) argues that social change is being driven by the advent of "technetronic society," present only in the USA at the time, characterised by the pervasive "impact of technology and electronics – particularly in the area of computers and communications," with the ARPANET having come online in November 1969. Technetronic society represents a "more controlled and directed society," dominated by

> an elite whose claim to political power would rest on allegedly superior scientific know-how. Unhindered by the restraints of traditional liberal values, this elite would not hesitate to achieve its political ends by using the latest modern techniques for influencing public behaviour and keeping society under close surveillance and control. (Brzezinski, 1970, p. 97)

This requires nothing less than a "redefinition of the American system" (Brzezinski, 1970, p. 66) and leans in the direction of totalitarianism. In fact, Brzezinski (1970, p. 34) cites Teilhard de Chardin: "monstrous as it is, is not modern totalitarianism really the distortion of something magnificent, and thus quite near to the truth?"

China: The World's First Technate

In Brzezinski's words, Henry Kissinger and President Nixon "initiated a kind of secret collaboration or even perhaps you could call it an alliance" with China in the early 1970s (cited in Corbett, 2014), paving the way for David Rockefeller's trip to China in 1973. Signalling his eagerness to collaborate with China, Rockefeller (1973) wrote in the *New York Times*: "The social experiment in China under Chairman Mao's leadership is one of the most important and successful in human history"—ignoring the tens of millions of people who starved to death during the "Great Leap Forward" (1958–1962). In 1979, Rockefeller met with Rong Yiren, chairman of China International Trust Investment Corporation (CITIC). An agreement was reached between CITIC, Chase, and the Bank of China to "identify and define those areas of the Chinese economy most susceptible to American technology and capital infusion" (Chossudovsky, 1986, p. 140).

China's remarkable annual GDP growth rate since 1978, averaging just under 10%, flows from the "opening up" to Western investment. Thus, Corbett (2014) remarks, "the Chinese industrial juggernaut did not just spring up overnight"; rather, it was "carefully and deliberately constructed by wealth transfers, banking agreements, R&D investments, military technology 'leaks' and offshoring of manufacturing over the course of several decades." Particularly interesting is the boom in research and development funding since the 1990s, which is not about exploiting cheap Chinese labour. Rather, a deliberate technology transfer has taken place, akin to that identified by Sutton (1981, 2016) with respect to U.S. transfers to the Soviet Union and Nazi Germany. This includes military technology transfers (Corbett, 2019a). Sutton (2002, p. 135) predicted in 1983 that by 2000, "communist China will be a 'superpower' built by American technology and skill." Contrary to the realist image of "great power competition" (Layne, 2018), the West and China have, for decades, been collaborating in the development of new technologies capable of making technocracy workable.

By 2010, while the "global" financial crisis of 2007/8 had prompted a perilous cycle of "austerity" and "quantitative easing" in the West, China was still enjoying significant annual GDP growth. Around this time, Chinese authoritarianism began to be promoted as a potential global template. The Rockefeller Foundation and Global Business Network (2010, p. 18), in their infamous "lockstep" scenario, contrast the "deadly leniency" of the U.S. response to a fictional pandemic with the Chinese government's "quick imposition and enforcement of mandatory quarantine for all citizens," which "saved millions of lives," enabling a "swifter post-pandemic recovery."

Corbett (2014) notes the praise heaped on China by representatives of the transnational ruling class in the years around 2010, including George Soros, Evelyn de Rothschild, Richard Rockefeller, and Henry Kissinger. Corbett (2022a) also notes the open affinities of Western political leaders with China, including Justin Trudeau ("There's a level of admiration I actually have for China, because their basic dictatorship is allowing them to turn their economy around on a dime"), Angela Merkel (described as an "old friend" by Xi Jinping), Joe Biden (who calls Xi a "bright and really tough guy"), and Boris Johnson (who claims to be "fervently Sinophile").

Klaus Schwab's son Olivier married a Chinese woman and has led the World Economic Forum (WEF) office in Beijing since 2011. Chinese officials of increasing importance have attended the WEF since 2009, including Xi Jinping in 2017. Schwab claims that the West needs to adopt the kinds of technologies introduced in China (Velázquez, 2020).

Wood (2018, p. 125) warns of the dangers of the Chinese social credit system (SCS), noting that those with a higher score "will have travel freedoms, will attend better schools and get better jobs. Low SCS holders will not be allowed to have travel passes, live in better housing, get into better schools and will be left with less desirable work conditions." The social credit scoring system was then extended to companies in China—a precursor of the "Environmental Sustainability Goals" metrics currently being introduced to score companies worldwide and thereby manipulate their activities. Wood (2018, p. 125) also cites a BBC experiment conducted in Guiyang to test how long it would take for police to locate and apprehend a reporter randomly present in a population of 3.5 million people. The answer: just seven minutes. Whereas "pre-crime" was science fiction in Philip K. Dick's 1956 novella *The Minority Report* (Dick, 2002), Chinese pre-crime algorithms based on social data, which will inevitably be used to target dissidents, are a reality and have been exported to multiple U.S. cities despite being illegal and unconstitutional—"scientific dictatorship, pure and simple" (Wood, 2018, pp. 126–7).

China as "the world's first Technate" (Davis, 2022) or first "full-blown Technocracy" was only made possible via the "clever manipulation and support of Western elites like the Trilateral Commission" (Wood, 2022). Now that technocracy has proven feasible as a means of controlling the world's most populous country, the aim is to roll it out in the West and elsewhere (Wood, 2018, p. 73). China's "intentional Technocracy," Wood (2022) warns, is "spreading like a cancer" to other nations worldwide. The goal all along was to use technology to implement global scientific dictatorship.

To see where it leads, one need only consider the Shanghai "lockdown" in April 2022. 25 million people were confined to their homes, policed by drones using facial recognition software and broadcasting the message "Control your soul's desire for freedom" (Browning, 2022). Amidst conditions of food deprivation, inability to help vulnerable loved ones, and a brute display of power by the government, harrowing videos emerged of people screaming from their high-rise balconies, some jumping to their deaths. In May 2022, China announced that it would "strictly limit non-essential outbound travel activities by Chinese citizens," i.e. prevent its own citizens from leaving the country (George, 2022). Lest such things be deemed unimaginable in the West, remember that Canada did not allow "unvaccinated" people to board commercial planes or trains between October 2021 and June 2022.

World War III

World War as an Instrument of Social Engineering

In the context of an inevitable worldwide eruption of class conflict caused by "a dangerously lopsided, oligarchic capitalism in terminal decline" (van der Pijl, 2020), and with conditions of class compromise having irreversibly broken down, a numerically tiny transnational ruling class went to war against the rest of humanity in 2020 in a desperate attempt to prevent its own demise by issuing in a system of global technocracy. As Davis (2021a) writes, "The *pseudopandemic* was the opening salvo in a global *coup d'état*." The "real battle," James Corbett (2020) notes, is "between the banksters and would-be societal engineers and the mass of humanity." The Atlantic ruling class has a track history of using world war to remake society in its desired image. Prior to World War I, for instance, social engineers saw war, all of its attendant horrors, as "the easiest way to demolish the old traditions and beliefs that lay between them and their goals" (Corbett, 2018).

Lest "war" seem too strong a term for what is happening, consider what ruling-class representatives have told us in their own words. The

WEF (2019) argued pre-Covid that a "new global architecture" must be created, much as "after the Second World War, leaders worked together to develop new institutional structures and governance frameworks." UN Secretary General António Guterres described Covid-19 as "the most challenging crisis we have faced since the Second World War" (Guterres, 2020). Angela Merkel called "coronavirus" the greatest challenge since the Second World War (Lawler, 2020). Klaus Schwab told the WEF on June 3, 2020: "It is obvious that we are in the middle of the most severe crisis that the world has experienced since World War II" (cited in Poona, 2021, p. 14). IMF head Kristalina Georgieva (2020) announced a "new Bretton Woods moment" on October 15, 2020. Bill Gates claimed that "Covid-19 vaccine" production was "similar to how, during World War II, the U.S. ramped up its manufacturing capacity at a mind-blowing rate" (Gates, 2020). These powerful figures are tacitly acknowledging that the radical, systemic changes they want to make only occur because of world war. Their slogan "Build back better" is analogous to postwar reconstruction after 1945, although the destruction wrought under the banner of "Covid-19" results from the policies of governments enacted against their own citizens, and not from the actions of official enemies.

These repeated invocations of World War II by ruling class representatives raise the very real possibility that we are now in World War III. If so, then, like previous world wars, World War III will look nothing like what went before (J. Corbett, 2020a). World War I, for instance, introduced machine guns, no man's land, and mass mechanised slaughter. World War II introduced bombers, submarine warfare, nuclear weapons, and the targeting of civilians. The aims, strategies, tactics, and weapons systems in World War III will not resemble those of the two previous world wars. Yet, the outcomes, in terms of large numbers of lives lost and the manifestation of previously unimaginable horrors (see Chap. 8), are sure to be the same, unless those behind the war can be stopped.

Wars typically kill large numbers of people. According to the Office for National Statistics (ONS, 2023a, Fig. 1), all-cause mortality in England and Wales has exceeded the five-year average most weeks since the start of the "pandemic" and many of those deaths are "deaths not involving Covid-19"; in Week 16 of 2023—not in the winter, and measured against a five-year average including deaths in the previous three years, it hit 22% (ONS, 2023b). In the United States, excess mortality has been consistently above the five-year average since March 2020 (U.S. Mortality, n.d.). Across the European Union between 2020 and 2022, excess mortality trended mostly within a 6–27% range (spiking to 40% in November 2020), before dropping to ca. 3–4% in 2023 (eurostat, n.d.). In Australia, the death rate for 2022 was 15.3% higher than the "historical average" (Australian Bureau of Statistics, 2023). In New Zealand the death rate in 2022 was 10.4% higher than in 2021 (Gabel & Knox, 2023), and between July 2022 and June 2023 it was 14% higher than in the corresponding period in 2018/19, the last available pre- "pandemic" data (Hatchard, 2023). The step change in the number of people dying in the West since March 2020 (which can be explored further via www.mortality.watch/explorer) offers *prima facie* evidence that a war is indeed taking place, with most excess deaths being "induced by the government measures," according to detailed analysis by Rancourt et al. (2021, pp. 115, 35–6). The outlier is Sweden, which did not "lock down" in 2020, and where deaths per 1000 people have held steady between 8.52 and 9.93 every year since 2009 (peaking at 9.48 during the "pandemic") (Official Statistics of Sweden, n.d.).

How Can the Few Wage War Against the Many?

How is it possible for a numerically miniscule ruling class to wage war against the rest of humanity? Let us consider some numbers. The richest 10% of the world's population controls 76% of the wealth and receives 52% of the total income, whereas the poorest 50%—half of humanity—only accounts for 2% of the wealth and 8.5% of the income, notwithstanding variations between countries and regions (Chancel et al., 2022, p. 10). We might, therefore, speculate that the top 10% is afraid of the remaining 90% pressing its claims for a more just world, and is certainly afraid of the revolutionary power of the bottom 50%, which, having been completely fleeced, has virtually nothing to lose and the whole world to win.

Another way of thinking about the numbers is in terms of millionaires. There are 62.2 million people in the world with a fortune of $1 million or over—a meagre 0.8% of a global population of ca. eight billion (Chancel et al., 2022, p. 20). So, when talking about "the 1%," we are effectively dealing with the millionaire class. Between 1995 and 2021, the richest 1% captured 38% of global wealth growth, with 21% of that growth going to the top 0.001% consisting of 76,460 people with a fortune of over $100 million (Chancel et al., 2022, pp. 15, 20). To be clear, over a fifth of global wealth growth in the last quarter of a century has been captured by one one-hundred-thousandth of the global population. Phillips (2018), focusing mainly on Europe and America, argues that the "global power elite" consists of just a few hundred named actors. Seen in these terms, it is clear where the root of the world's problems lies, as well as the focus of any potential solutions.

How, then, can a ruling class whose wealth accrues almost exponentially in the top 1%, the top 0.1%, the top 0.01%, the top 0.001%, etc. hope to win a war against the rest of humanity? True, it can count on the support of the richest 10% that has so much to lose, as well as further layers that see their interests best served by aligning with power. It also has control over the means of production on its side, including the power to magic money out of thin air (Werner, 2014), global communications flows (most importantly the "news"), the food supply, consumer products (including "smart" devices for connection to the technocratic control grid), and all military technologies (including black technologies). Nevertheless, coercing populations worldwide to accept a system of technocratic enslavement—the war aim—without reaping the whirlwind of revolution poses seemingly insuperable challenges.

Clearly, the solution does not lie in the centuries-long development of ever more destructive technologies that used to win wars. Ever since General MacArthur's thwarted desire to use nuclear weapons during the Korean War in 1950, or the Second Taiwan Strait Crisis of 1958, when President Eisenhower refused to authorise nuclear weapons usage against China for fear of galvanising national liberation movements (Hanania, 2017, pp. 78–80), it has been evident that nuclear weapons usage risks catalysing massive transnational opposition to the aggressor state. In any case, nuclear weapons are "totally unsuitable for dealing with insurgents" (Kitson, 1971, p. 28), and the war for global technocracy amounts to a global counterinsurgency campaign.

Nor can advanced technologies such as drones and Boston Dynamics robots (whose military potential is obvious) be deployed against entire populations, not only for reasons of scale, but also because it would be obvious that the government had openly declared war on the people, inviting revolution. An overt war of any kind against the people additionally risks soldiers, police officers, and state officials defecting once they realise what it is they are part of.

To prevail against overwhelming numerical odds in World War III, the ruling class must revolutionise the nature of warfare. It will have spent over half a century (since 1968 at least) covertly working on ways of doing so. The key elements of the new way of war will, of necessity, remain classified, but there is nevertheless much that can be worked out based purely on the logic of the situation. For the first time in history, a numerically tiny proportion of the world's population seeks to wage war on the overwhelming majority. That peculiar situation dictates the fundamentals of both the war's aims and how the war must be fought.

The most fundamental principle is deception: the public must not be allowed to know that war is being waged against it. Sun Tzu (1963, p. 66) famously claimed that "All warfare is based on deception." The Mossad motto reads: "By way of deception, thou shalt do war." Much as the United States has not formally declared war since 1941, despite being almost continually at war ever since, particularly through covert operations, so World War III is undeclared and is waged by stealth. Deception must be carried to the extreme in World War III, for if the public gets wise to what is happening before the technocratic architecture of its oppression reaches maturity, worldwide social revolution becomes a realistic possibility. Therefore, the war must be waged pre-emptively, to preclude revolution, and it must remain "invisible" to the extent that its weapons are not immediately obvious and it is concealed by a highly advanced propaganda system.

No war has ever been won through purely psychological means, however, and the point will inevitably come when public consciousness starts to align with the objective reality of the global class war. At that point, the war could turn physical in ways that it has not already. In that respect, it is troubling that the injections reportedly administered to over 5.55 billion people (Holder, 2023) turn out to have been a military operation from start to finish (see Chap. 6). Moreover, they demonstrably contain an array of undisclosed ingredients (Hughes, 2022c), apparently including EMF-responsive self-assembling and disassembling nanotechnologies (Hughes, 2023, 50:25). Coupled with the simultaneous 5G rollout (the Secure 5G and Beyond Act of 2020 was passed into U.S. law on March 23, 2020), we must take seriously the possibility that a weapons system is being installed that would allow human bodies to be targeted via remote administration of particular frequencies (see Chap. 8). This, in the final analysis, is how a tiny cabal of technocrats could fight and win a war against the rest of humanity.

In the longer term, the precipitous declines in birth rates since the "Covid-19 vaccine" rollout (Pfeiffer, 2022; Bujard & Andersson, 2022;

Swiss Policy Research, 2022; Naked Emperor, 2023) could prove consistent with a global depopulation agenda dating back to 1968, the year the ruling classes of the world found confirmation that their position was endangered by a growing and restive global population. Hardin (1968) argues that "a finite world can support only a finite population; therefore, population growth must eventually equal zero." The Club of Rome, founded in 1968, published its *Limits to Growth* report in 1972 (Meadows et al., 1972), premised on the same flawed Malthusian logic. The Rockefeller Commission Report on *Population and the American Future* (Centre for Research on Population & Security, 1972) argues that "no substantial benefits would result from continued growth of the nation's population." *National Security Memorandum 200*, aka the Kissinger Report, states: "it is urgent that measures to reduce fertility be started and made effective in the 1970s and 1980s," and proposes "constructive action to lower fertility rates in selected developing countries" (National Security Council, 1974). Since 1968, the global fertility rate (number of children per woman) has halved (United Nations, 2022a) and is now at or below the 2.1 replacement rate in all regions apart from Africa (United Nations, 2022b).

Omniwar

Contemporary developments in warfare are sometimes described in terms of "fifth-generation warfare" (Abbott, 2010; Qureshi, 2019; Krishnan, 2022). Isolated from the context of global class relations, however, that term is unhelpful. There is much confusion in the literature as to what "fifth-generation warfare" is supposed to mean, how to recognise it, how it differs from hybrid warfare and grey-zone conflict, and whether it exists at all. It has been associated, *inter alia*, with not "fighting a defined adversary in a defined battlespace for a defined period of time" (2018, p. 4) and with "wars of perception [...], with information being the weapon, [including] deception and propaganda" (Qureshi, 2019, p. 210). Perhaps most significantly, the targets of "5GW" may not even realise there is a war going on, or that they are combatants in that war; the secrecy of such warfare then makes it "the most dangerous warfare generation of all time" (Qureshi, 2019, p. 209).

The 5GW literature fails to get to grips with who is waging war against whom and for what purpose. For example, the idea of "unrestricted warfare" (Liang & Xiangsui, 1999) is often associated with an alleged plan by China to undermine and destroy the United States. It is, thus, just a more sophisticated version of geopolitics, played "horizontally" on the global chessboard. The more fundamental war—i.e. global class war, waged "vertically"—goes missing. Corbett (2022b) provides a much-needed rectification:

> Fifth-generation warfare is an all-out war that is being waged against all of us [...] right now, and it is a battle for full-spectrum dominance over every single aspect of your life: your movements and interactions, your transactions, even your innermost thoughts and feelings and desires. Governments the world over are working with corporations to leverage technology to control you down to the genomic level, and they will not stop until each and every person who resists them is subdued or eliminated.

This is an apt description of the global class war, though Corbett's anarchism makes him reluctant to frame it in the language of class and edges him in the direction of parallel societies rather than revolution.

A better term than "fifth-generation warfare," I propose, is "Omniwar." The key thing to understand is that the transnational ruling class has weaponised *everything* against the population, as indeed it must to subdue billions of people. The war is being waged in every conceivable domain, yet in ways that are intended to remain concealed as far as possible. Corbett (2022b), for instance, discusses information warfare (cf. Webb, 2020, 2022; Turley, 2022; Shir-Raz et al., 2022), neurological warfare (cf. Giordano, 2017, 2018), biological warfare, and economic warfare, and notes the "wider operation to manipulate, control and weaponize all aspects of our environment, our food supply [cf. Corbett, 2023] and even our genome itself for the purposes of the ruling oligarchs." To this list we might add:

- psychological warfare (Scott, 2021a);
- the "necrosecurity" (Lincoln, 2022) of the "lockdowns," which medical doctors Dan Erickson and Artin Massihi immediately warned would create "millions of casualties" (Stringham, 2020), which 500 + doctors branded a "mass casualty incident" ("A Doctor a Day Letter," 2020), and which have caused immeasurable harm (Bardosh, 2023; Harrison, 2023);
- 5G (rolled out despite lack of adequate safety testing and known harms to human health [Burdick, 2023; Jamieson, 2023]);

- deprivation of necessary healthcare (Triggle & Jeavans, 2021; Spectator, n.d.) in the name of reconfiguring health services (Stevens & Pritchard, 2020) to deal with "the virus" (public health as death by stealth);
- bioweapons masquerading as vaccines (Latypova, 2022; Ponton, 2023); and
- stratospheric aerosol injection (Freeland, 2018).

When Goebbels spoke in 1943 of "a war more total and radical than anything that we can even imagine today" (cited in Moorhouse, 2010, p. 339), Omniwar fits the bill. Yet, with most people still thinking of war in terms of nation-state standing armies, foreign enemies, guerrilla warfare, counter-terrorism operations, etc., it never occurs to them that they themselves are now combatants in the undeclared Omniwar being waged against *them*.

Information Warfare

To give one obvious example of how free humanity finds itself in the crosshairs, consider the UK Ministry of Defence's (2020) *Integrated Operating Concept* (IOC), announced as "the most significant change in UK military thought in several generations." According to the IOC, "The old distinction between foreign and domestic defence is increasingly irrelevant" when it comes to misinformation and disinformation, which can stoke "confusion, disagreement and doubt in our societies," meaning "home" no longer represents a "secure sanctuary" (2020, p. 7). Here, a militarised domestic environment is treated as threatening, because of the free flow of information and the possibility of disagreement and doubt, which are fundamental to liberal societies. The IOC proposes to "drive the conditions and tempo of strategic activity, rather than responding to the actions of others"—implying permanent counterrevolution in the information space. Accordingly, organisations such as the 77th Brigade and the 13th Signal Regiment were deployed alongside GCHQ to combat online "anti-vaccine propaganda" (Fisher & Smyth, 2020).

Omniwar thus includes a war on free speech and a drive to censor dissident voices, consistent with emergent totalitarianism. The U.S. National Security Commission on Artificial Intelligence, headed by former Google/Alphabet CEO Eric Schmidt, advises on "countering disinformation" online, including the use of A.I. to identify which accounts to censor and deplatform (Webb, 2022). Sean Gourley, who created A.I. programmes allowing the military to track insurgents in Iraq, proposes a "Manhattan Project for truth" that will enable intelligence agencies to determine what is true or not (Webb, 2020). "Unless you hear it from us [the Government], it is not the truth," claimed New Zealand Prime Minister, Jacinda Ardern, in March 2020; "we will continue to be your single source of truth" (cited in Haynes, 2021). In 2022, Ardern called internet freedom a "weapon of war," claiming that "rules" must be introduced to make sure that people do not "take up arms" and "threaten the security of others" by questioning official narratives (cited in Turley, 2022).

Certain fabricated narratives on which the transnational ruling class depends—always involving a global crisis, the myth of "settled science," and the need for a global solution based on ceding power to authorities at ever higher levels (Hudson, 2023)—are not allowed to be questioned. In this environment, Webb (2022) reflects, "journalism is becoming less of a profession and more of a war zone. Indeed the difference between journalism and 'information warfare' is becoming increasingly difficult to pinpoint." The information landscape is just one of many battlefields in the unfolding Omniwar.

The "Covid-19" Operation

This book focuses on one element of the Omniwar in particular, namely, the psychological warfare operation launched in 2020, which I call the "Covid-19 operation." To be clear, there was no viral "pandemic" in 2020 (see Chap. 6). Rather, what took place was what Devlin (2021, p. 2) calls "the psy-op to end all psy-ops," i.e. "the culmination of many, many decades of slow and methodical planning with the aim of completely enslaving and subjugating humanity into a technocratic control grid."

That war aim, which defines victory for the ruling class in World War III, cannot be achieved overnight. Replacing the fiat currency system with biometric IDs and CBDC (Hughes, 2022a, 234; Davis, 2023); rolling out social credit scoring and an environmental, social, and governance (ESG) framework for corporations (Davis, 2021d); scaffolding a global health dictatorship through the WHO Pandemic Treaty and amendments to the 2005 International Health Regulations (Kheriaty, 2022); creating the Internet of Bodies in which we are all hooked up to the technocratic control grid (Kyrie & Broudy, 2022)—all of this architecture of oppression takes years to put in place, although the would-be global technocrats are clearly moving as fast as they can, with the initial injection rollout already pushed as far as it could go, the Pandemic Treaty touted for 2024 (World Health Organisation [WHO], 2023) and CBDC in Britain by 2025 (Taaffe-Maguire, 2023). The World Bank's (2020) $6 billion "Covid-19 Strategic Preparedness and Response Programme" has a closing date of March 31, 2025.

These gruesome measures, intended to enslave the human race through biodigital means, would never be accepted by a healthy, confident, free-thinking population. The population must, therefore, be rendered sick, demoralised, and psychologically incapacitated before the main fighting breaks out. This, it seems, was the whole point of the "Covid-19" operation. For if "man can be so utterly demoralised that he accepts any political system" (Meerloo, 1956, p. 132), then technocracy can be rolled out once the population's will to resist has been broken. "War is an affair of morale," Rees (1945, p. 81) writes, "and all weapons have, or should have, a morale-destroying effect."

Historically, psychological warfare aims precisely to break the opponent's will to fight. During World War II, for instance, William Donovan, the head of the Office of Strategic Services (the forerunner to the CIA), described psychological warfare as "the coordination and use of all means [...] which tend to destroy the will of the enemy to achieve victory [...]" (cited in Roosevelt, 1976, p. 99). According to the Nuremberg Tribunal Prosecutor in 1946, "Before every major aggression, [the Nazis] initiated a press campaign calculated to weaken their victims [...] In the propaganda system, it was the daily press and the radio that were the most important weapons" (Office of United States Chief of Counsel for Prosecution of Axis Criminality, 1946, p. 1041). "If a period of peace can be used to soften up a future enemy," Meerloo (1956, p. 100) writes, "the totalitarian armies may be able in time of war to win a cheap and easy victory. Totalitarian psychological warfare is [...] an effort to propagandize and hypnotize the world into submission." According to Valley and Aquino (1980, pp. 5–6), "If we do not attack the enemy's will until he reaches the battlefield, his nation will have strengthened it as best it can. We must attack that will before it is thus locked in place. We must instil in it a predisposition to inevitable defeat."

"Psychological warfare" is a slippery concept that has "multilayered, often contradictory meanings" (Simpson, 1994, p. 41). First used in

English in 1941 with reference to Nazi propaganda, terror, and fifth-column activities, the term was broadened during World War II to include ideological training of friendly forces and boosting morale and discipline on the home front (Simpson, 1994, p. 11). Subsequent U.S. military and NATO manuals include propaganda, covert operations, guerrilla warfare, and public diplomacy under "psychological warfare," a term used interchangeably with "psychological operations." Always deployed to achieve certain ideological, political, or military objectives, psychological warfare can work through non-physical means, such as mass communications, as well as through selective applications of violence (e.g. sabotage, assassination, and counter insurrection) (Simpson, 1994, p. 11). Psychological warfare can be brutal and overt, as in totalitarian menticide (Meerloo, 1956), "shock and awe" operations, and barbarous counterinsurgency methods (see Chap. 8). Or it may be more subtle, operating through applied behavioural psychology, mass hypnosis, neurolinguistic programming, etc. (see Volume 2 of this book). Officially, psychological warfare is reserved for foreign enemies and populations (viz. National Security Council, 1947; Joint Chiefs of Staff, 2010, § 2.2.a), yet psychological operations have been waged against Western populations for a very long time: "the targets of U.S. psychological warfare" between 1945 and 1960, for instance, were "not only the 'enemy,' but also the people of the United States and its allies" (Simpson, 1994, p. 13). During the Gulf War and 2003 Iraq War, "extreme PSYOP" targeted public opinion in both Iraq and the United States (Aquino, 2003, p. 3).

In March 2020, a ferocious, transnationally coordinated campaign of psychological warfare was unleashed by governments against their own citizens, on behalf of the transnational ruling class—what Scott (2021b) calls a "menticidal assault" that was "planned and [...] firmly on the side of evil." Elsewhere, Scott (2022) observes that governments, whose first obligation used to be to protect their own citizens, have instead deployed tactics "used to confuse us, terrorise us, manipulate us, and change our minds and behaviour against our will and consent." According to a U.S. observer, "The unpredictable and abusive psychological attacks by our government and military on American citizens is similar to the brainwashing techniques used on prisoners of war, hostages, and cult members" and is designed to leave the population "battle-fatigued" (K, 2021). Potts (2020) claims, without exaggeration, that the controllers of society have "locked down people's minds. The ramifications of that psychological murder will last a lot longer than destroyed businesses." For

Broadberry (2022), "There's a war raging, alright, but you will find its theatre of operations inside the human psyche. It is a war on consciousness," involving an "atrophy of culture" and "the spiritual malaise of humanity."

Following over a century of development in different forms, in different historical contexts, psychological warfare has become highly advanced in its methods and applications, which is why this book requires two volumes to do justice to the complexity and sophistication of the "Covid-19" operation. Those behind the operation clearly spent years assimilating every possible method—from Nazi Germany, the Soviet Union, the Western propaganda system, the Tavistock Institute, CIA trauma-based mind control experiments and developments in torture, cults, the psychology of evil (Zimbardo, 2007), applied behavioural psychology (Dolan et al., 2010), hypnosis and neurolinguistic programming, etc.—*and then deployed all of those methods at once* against an unsuspecting public in the most comprehensive and vicious psychological operation of all time.

Seen in its entirety, the levels of premeditation, transnational coordination, and attention to detail are chilling. The planning required must go back a very long way, possibly to before "9/11" (see Chap. 8). Those who think that no conspiracy could be planned on such a scale and in such detail not only ignore the role of compartmentalisation (only the most senior board-level executives of global corporations, for instance, have oversight of the operation as a whole [Davis, 2021c]), but they also radically underestimate (and are probably ignorant of) a transnational deep state dating at least as far back as the late 1940s (Hughes, 2022b). True, there are tensions and rivalries within and between different ruling classes and class fractions (van der Pijl, 1998, p. 3), but when it comes to suppressing the international working class, they act as one, and have done so of necessity since 1968.

This volume deals with psychological warfare techniques used to attack the mind and impair its healthy functioning. Chapter 2 explores the use of shock for social control purposes, including the influence of the Tavistock Institute, Klein's (2007) "shock doctrine," and the shock and awe tactics deployed during the first "lockdown." Chapter 3 is about trauma-based mind control, involving psychological torture techniques, trauma bonding, and false rescue of an infantilised population by transnational power. Chapter 4 addresses the role of fear and imaginary existential threats in rendering the public susceptible to psychological manipulation, discussing multiple ways in which the threat of the "pandemic" was wildly exaggerated via propaganda, manipulated statistics, face masks, PCR tests, new variants, "long Covid," etc. Chapter 5 deals with cognitive attack, i.e. means of making the world not make sense, including weaponised confusion, deliberately absurd "countermeasures," unpredictability of treatment, mixed messaging, and abuse of language. Chapter 6, on deception, draws on the Big Lie concept and argues that probably *everything* we were told about "Covid-19" was false—but that cognitive dissonance renders most people psychologically incapable of engaging with the truth. Chapter 7 looks at the social division manufactured through mass paranoia, weaponised guilt, scapegoating of dissidents, mask mandates as tools of segregation, hate speech, snitching, priming the public for violence, dehumanisation, and media incitement of hatred against "the unvaccinated." Chapter 8 returns to the theme of global class war and argues that in the context of the "IT/Bio/Nano" era planned for since 2001, the "vaccines" could be a form of military hardware aimed at connecting human bodies to a technocratic control grid—but also that the controlled demolition of liberal democracy presents a moment of worldwide revolutionary potential.

Readers will notice that many terms in this book are placed in inverted commas/scare quotes: "pandemic," "Covid-19," "SARS-CoV-2," "Covid-19 vaccine," etc. This is because, in the Omniwar, language itself has been weaponised and deceit is ubiquitous. For reasons given in Chaps. 5 and 6, it seems doubtful that any of these things exist in a credible scientific sense. Planting an alien vocabulary of trigger words at a moment of traumatic rupture, on the other hand, is a known tactic of psychological warfare, which is why Curtin (2016) proposes not using weaponised terms such as "9/11" and instead finding a "new vocabulary to speak of these terrible things." We could, for instance, refer to the vaccine-free rather than "the unvaccinated": freedom is positive, whereas "un" is always negative. The power of propaganda, however, means that the dominant discourse is all-pervasive, and particularly when trying to engage those who use the buzzwords uncritically, it seems necessary to speak a common language, or at least to appear to do so (though I refuse to write "COVID-19" in all caps that aggressively leap off the page for impact). In this book, I have retained the dominant terms, but placed them in inverted commas/scare quotes to indicate a critical distance from them. The extent to which I have done so merely reflects how automatically they are used in society (a form of Pavlovian conditioning; people unwittingly using the terms of their own oppression).

This book serves, as much as anything else, as a project of anamnesis. It provides a historical record of the phenomenal psychological abuse that was inflicted upon the public through the "Covid-19" operation. A key part of that abuse was the intentional infliction of trauma (see Chap. 3), and as Mary Holland recognises, "Anyone alive today may be forgiven for experiencing PTSD (Post-Traumatic Stress Disorder) about all things COVID [...] After three years of horror, it is only human to want to put this behind us and to forget" (Doctors for COVID Ethics, 2023, p. xiii). This psychological defence mechanism, however, is precisely what keeps victims locked in the orbit of their abusers. The abuse is blanked out/suppressed/buried, and patterns of abuse are allowed to repeat. Holland understands, in this context, that the "undeclared war against humanity is not over, and we must arm ourselves with knowledge," not least of the enemy's methods. Recognising the nature of the abuse that has taken place is the first step towards pulling free from it and beginning the process of healing, which may involve "deep grieving over the abuse of trust, over the betrayals, over the intentionality of the trauma bonding and the set-ups" (Svali, 2000, p. 4). Reading this book may, therefore, prove to be an emotionally challenging experience and is not something that should be entered into lightly. On the other hand, when survivors can "recall everything about any contact with their abusers, including the sites of the abuse and the identities of the perpetrators," there is genuine jeopardy for the latter (Lacter, 2011). In that sense, anamnesis is a prerequisite for defeating the vicious transnational cabal that has demonstrated its willingness to go any lengths to enslave humanity.

The contents of this book may prove shocking to many readers. Nevertheless, the evil that is at work in the world must be squarely faced if it is to be confronted and vanquished. Make no mistake: the war for technocracy means that human freedom is now under very real threat. Readers who may be sceptical of my position should consider Yeadon's (2023) advice concerning asymmetry of risk. If the argument made in this book is correct, then sceptics stand to lose their liberty and would be unwise to resort to the usual thought-terminating clichés and system-justifying responses to avoid serious debate and discussion. On the other hand, if readers are inclined to agree with the argument made here, and it is one day disproven, what is the worst that can happen? As Yeadon (2023) recognises, "These options aren't faintly balanced. A rational actor should cease believing what we're being told. It's not a safe position, keeping your counsel and your head down. It's the most dangerous thing you could do." Totalitarianism comes for everyone in the end, which is why the global technocratic coup must be put down before it is too late.

References

360iSR. (2018). *Fifth generation warfare: The brave new world. The changing shape of the Fifth Generation Mission Space*. https://irp-cdn.multiscreensite.com/26db15ee/files/uploaded/5GW%20Section1.pdf.

Abbott, D. (Ed.). (2010). *The handbook of 5GW*. Nimble Books.

Abramovici, P. (2014). The World anti-communist league: Origins, structures and activities. In L. Dongen, S. Roulin, & G. Scott-Smith (Eds.), *Transnational anti-communism and the cold war* (pp. 113–129). Palgrave Macmillan.

A doctor a day letter. (2020, May 19). Retrieved December 31, 2023, from https://www.scribd.com/document/462319362/A-Doctor-a-Day-Letter-Signed.

Agamben, G. (2005). *State of exception* (Trans. K. Attell). Chicago University Press.

Agamben, G. (2021). *Where are we now?* Rowman and Littlefield.

Ahmed, N. M. (2012). Capitalism, covert action and state terrorism: Toward a political economy of the dual state. In E. Wilson (Ed.), *The dual state: Parapolitics, Carl Schmitt, and the national security complex* (pp. 171–192). Routledge.

Alting von Geusau, C. W. J. M. (2021, November 17). Totalitarianism and the five stages of dehumanization. *Brownstone Institute*. https://brownstone.org/articles/totalitarianism-and-the-five-stages-of-dehumanization/.

Aquino, M. (2003). Introduction. In P. Valley, & M. Aquino (Eds.) *From psyop to mind war: The psychology of victory* (pp. 1–3). Presidio of San Francisco.

Atkinson, C. (2019, November 6). Why have more than 1300 CEOs left their posts in the past year? *NBC News*. https://www.nbcnews.com/business/business-news/why-have-more-1-000-ceos-left-their-post-past-n1076201.

Australian Bureau of Statistics. (2023). *Provisional mortality statistics*. https://www.abs.gov.au/statistics/health/causes-death/provisional-mortality-statistics/jan-dec-2022.

Bardosh, K. (2023). How did the Covid pandemic response harm society? A global evaluation and state of knowledge review (2020–21). Preprint retrieved from https://doi.org/10.2139/ssrn.4447806.

Bernays, E. (1928). *Propaganda*. Horace Liveright.

Bernays, E. (1947). The engineering of consent. *The Annals of the American Academy of Political and Social Science, 250*(1), 113–120.

Biden backs letting soldiers arrest civilians. (2002, July 22). *Washington Times*. https://www.washingtontimes.com/news/2002/jul/22/20020722-034620-9653r/.

Biehl, J. & Staudenmaier, P. (Eds.). (2011). *Ecofascism revisited: Lessons from the German experience*. New Compass.

BlackRock. (2019, August 15). *Dealing with the next downturn*. https://www.blackrock.com/corporate/insights/blackrock-investment-institute/publications/global-macro-outlook/august-2019.

Bourbon Financial Management. (2019). *Highest P/E ratios at all U.S. market peaks prior to recessions*. https://www.bourbonfm.com/blog/highest-pe-ratios-all-us-market-peaks-prior-recessions.

Broadberry, D. (2022, May 7). Revelation of the method. *OffGuardian*. https://off-guardian.org/2022/05/07/revelation-of-the-method/.

Browning, O. (2022, April). Drone flying over Shanghai tells residents on balconies to comply with Covid lockdown. *The Independent*. https://www.independent.co.uk/tv/news/shanghai-china-covid-lockdown-drone-b2055301.html.

Brzezinski, Z. (1970). *Between two ages: America's role in the technetronic era*. Viking Press.

Broudy, D., & Kyrie, V. (2021). Syllogistic reasoning demystifies evidence of Covid-19 vaccine constituents. *International Journal of Vaccine Theory, Research, and Practice*, *2*(1), 149–171. https://doi.org/10.56098/ijvtpr.v2i1.32.

Brüggemeier, F. –J., Cioc, M., & Zeller, T. (Eds.). (2005). *How green were the Nazis? Nature, environment, and nation in the Third Reich*. Ohio University Press.

Bujard, M., & Andersson, G. (2022). Fertility declines near the end of the Covid-19 pandemic: Evidence of the 2022 birth declines in Germany and Sweden. Preprint retrieved from https://su.figshare.com/articles/preprint/Fertility_declines_near_the_end_of_the_COVID-19_pandemic_Evidence_of_the_2022_birth_declines_in_Germany_and_Sweden/20975611.

Burdick, S. (2023, February 23). 5G towers can make healthy people sick, two case reports show. *The Defender*. https://childrenshealthdefense.org/defender/5g-cell-towers-microwave-syndrome/.

Carney, M. (2019, August 23). The growing challenges for monetary policy in the current international monetary and financial system. *Bank of England*. https://www.bankofengland.co.uk/speech/2019/mark-carney-speech-at-jackson-hole-economic-symposium-wyoming.

Carter, A. B., Deutsch, J., & Zelikow, P. (1998). Catastrophic terrorism: Tackling the new danger. *Foreign Affairs*, *77*(6), 80–94. https://www.foreignaffairs.com/articles/united-states/1998-11-01/catastrophic-terrorism.

Centre for Research on Population and Security. (1972). *Population and the American future*. https://www.population-security.org/rockefeller/001_population_growth_and_the_american_future.htm.

Chancel, L., Piketty, T., Saez, E., & Zucman, G. (2022). *World Inequality Report 2022*. https://www.cadtm.org/IMG/pdf/summary_worldinequalityreport2022_english.pdf.

Chomsky, N. (1982). *Towards a new Cold War*. Pantheon Books.

Chossudovsky, M. (1986). *Towards capitalist restoration?* St. Martin's Press.

Corbett, J. (2014). Episode 297—China and the new world order. *The Corbett Report*. https://www.corbettreport.com/episode-297-china-and-the-new-world-order/.

Corbett, J. (2015). Episode 305—The secret life of Timothy McVeigh. *The Corbett Report*. https://www.corbettreport.com/episode-305-the-secret-life-of-timothy-mcveigh/.

Corbett, J. (2018). Episode 348—The WWI conspiracy—part two: The American front. *The Corbett Report*. https://www.corbettreport.com/episode-348-the-wwi-conspiracy-part-two-the-american-front/.

Corbett, J. (2019a, April 21). China's suspiciously American arsenal: a closer look. *The Corbett Report*. https://www.corbettreport.com/chinas-suspiciously-american-arsenal-a-closer-look/.

Corbett, J. (2019b, November 16). Your guide to a world on fire. *Steemit*. https://steemit.com/news/@corbettreport/your-guide-to-a-world-on-fire.

Corbett, J. (2020a, March 21). World War III has begun. *The International Forecaster*. https://theinternationalforecaster.com/topic/international_forecaster_weekly/wwiii_has_begun.

Corbett, J. (2022a, March 14). It's confirmed: Tyrants love China! …but why? *The Corbett Report*. https://corbettreport.substack.com/p/its-confirmed-tyrants-love-china.

Corbett, J. (2022b, March 28). Your guide to fifth-generation warfare. *The Corbett Report*. https://corbettreport.substack.com/p/your-guide-to-fifth-generation-warfare.

Corbett, J. (2023, March 6). Episode 438—The future food false flag. *The Corbett Report*, 6 March. https://www.corbettreport.com/foodfalseflag/.

Corbett, K. P. (2021, August 7). The "'Nazification" of the NHS. *The Light Paper*. https://thelightpaper.co.uk/assets/pdf/Light-12h.pdf.

Curtin, E. (2016). Why I don't speak of 9/11 anymore. *Journal of 9/11 Studies*. http://www.journalof911studies.com/why-i-dont-speak-of-911-anymore/.

Davis, I. (2021a). *Pseudopandemic*. Independently published.

Davis, I. (2021b, October 6). What is the global public-private partnership? *Iain Davis*. https://iaindavis.com/what-is-the-global-public-private-partnership/.

Davis, I. (2021c, October 12). Seizing everything: The theft of the global commons—part 1. *Iain Davis*. https://in-this-together.com/global-commons-part-1/.

Davis, I. (2021d, November 7). Seizing everything: The theft of the global commons—part 2. *Iain Davis*. https://in-this-together.com/global-commons-part-2/.

Davis, I. (2021e, December 14). The UK new normal dictatorship. *UK Column*. https://www.ukcolumn.org/article/the-uk-new-normal-dictatorship.

Davis, I. (2022, February 22). Technocracy: The operating system for the new international rules-based order. *Unlimited Hangout*. https://unlimitedhangout.com/2022/02/investigative-reports/technocracy-the-operating-system-for-the-new-international-rules-based-order-1/.

Davis, I. (2023, March 7). Central bank digital currency is the endgame—part 1. *OffGuardian*. https://off-guardian.org/2023/03/07/central-bank-digital-currency-is-the-endgame-part-1/.

Devlin, M. (2021). *Musical truth, volume 3*. aSys Publishing.

Dick, P. K. (2002). *Minority report*. Gollancz.

Doctors for Covid Ethics. (2023). *mRNA Vaccine Toxicity*. https://doctors4covidethics.org/mrna-vaccine-toxicity/.

Dolan, P., Hallsworth, M., Halpern, D., King, D., & Vlaev, I. (2010). *MINDSPACE: Influencing behaviour through public policy*. Cabinet Office and Institute for Government. https://www.instituteforgovernment.org.uk/sites/default/files/publications/MINDSPACE.pdf.

Ehret, M. (2021, March 16). Nazi healthcare revived across the Five Eyes: Killing useless eaters and Biden's covid relief bill." *OffGuardian*. https://off-guardian.org/2021/03/16/nazi-healthcare-revived-across-the-five-eyes-killing-useless-eaters-and-bidens-covid-relief-bill/.

Epp, R. (2017). Mastering the mysteries of diplomacy: Karl Marx as international theorist. *Socialist Studies*, *12*(1), 78–96. https://doi.org/10.18740/S4VP8J.

eurostat. (n.d.). *Excess mortality by month* . https://ec.europa.eu/eurostat/databrowser/view/DEMO_MEXRT__custom_309801/bookmark/line?lang=en&bookmarkId=26981184-4241-4855-b18e-8647fc8c0dd2.

Fisher, L., & Smyth, C. (2020, November 9). GCHQ in cyberwar on anti-vaccine propaganda. *The Times*. https://www.thetimes.co.uk/article/gchq-in-cyberwar-on-anti-vaccine-propaganda-mcjgjhmb2.

Freeland E. (2018). *Under an Ionized Sky: From Chemtrails to Space Fence Lockdown*. Feral House.

Gabel, J., & Knox, C. (2023, February 20). New Zealand records biggest increase in registered deaths in 100 years. *nzherald*. https://www.nzherald.co.nz/nz/new-zealand-records-biggest-increase-in-registered-deaths-in-100-years/BQERSTKIANCKRNNA7IL42RD52U/.

Ganser, D. (2005). *NATO's secret armies. Operation Gladio and terrorism in Western Europe*. Frank Cass.

Gates, B. (2020, December 22). These breakthroughs will make 2021 better than 2020. *GatesNotes*. https://www.gatesnotes.com/About-Bill-Gates/Year-in-Review-2020.

George, L. (2022, May 12). China to "strictly limit" citizens from leaving the country. *American Military News*. https://americanmilitarynews.com/2022/05/china-to-strictly-limit-citizens-from-leaving-the-country/.

Georgieva, K. (2020, October 15). A new Bretton Woods moment. *International Monetary Fund*. https://www.imf.org/en/News/Articles/2020/10/15/sp101520-a-new-bretton-woods-moment.

Gilbert, A. (1981). *Marx's politics: Communists and citizens*. Rutgers University Press.

Giordano, J. (2017, August 29). *Brain science from bench to battlefield: The realities—and risks—of neuroweapons*. Centre for Global Security Research seminar, Lawrence Livermore National Laboratory. https://cgsr.llnl.gov/event-calendar/2017/2017-06-12.

Giordano, J. (2018, September 25). *The brain is the battlefield of the future*. Modern War Institute, West Point. https://mwi.usma.edu/mwi-video-brain-battlefield-future-dr-james-giordano/.

Glaberman, M., & Faber, S. (2002). Back to the future: The continuing relevance of Marx. *Critique: Journal of Socialist Theory*, *30*(1), 167–177. https://doi.org/10.1080/03017600508413479.

Griffin, D. R., & Woodworth, E. (2018). *9/11 unmasked: An international review panel investigation*. Olive Branch.

Guterres, A. (2020, April 15). Message by António Guterres on Covid-19 and misinformation. *United Nations Indonesia*. https://indonesia.un.org/en/92948-message-antonio-guterres-covid-19-and-misinformation.

Hanania, R. (2017). Tracing the development of the nuclear taboo: The Eisenhower administration and four crises in East Asia. *Journal of Cold War Studies*, *19*(2), 43–83. https://doi.org/10.1162/JCWS_a_00740.

Hardin, G. (1968). The tragedy of the commons. *Science*, *162*(3859), 1243–1248. https://doi.org/10.1126/science.162.3859.1243.

Harrison, N. (2023, December 7). Lockdowns: A study of the harms. *UK Column*. https://www.ukcolumn.org/article/lockdowns-a-study-of-the-harms.

Hatchard, G. (2023, September 1). Deaths up 14%. Births down 28%. Disability up 37%. Wake up, politicians! *TCW*. https://www.conservativewoman.co.uk/deaths-up-14-births-down-28-disability-up-37-wake-up-politicians/.

Haynes, M. (2021, July 16). Flashback: New Zealand PM told public "we are your single source of truth." *LifeSite News*. https://www.lifesitenews.com/news/flashback-new-zealand-pm-told-public-we-are-your-single-source-of-truth/.

Hedges, C. (2015, November 2). Sheldon Wolin and inverted totalitarianism. *truthdig*. https://www.truthdig.com/articles/sheldon-wolin-and-inverted-totalitarianism/.

Herman, E., & Chomsky, N. (1979). *The political economy of human rights, volume 1: The Washington connection and Third World fascism*. South End Press.

Herman, E., & Chomsky, N. (1988). *Manufacturing consent: The political economy of the mass media*. Pantheon.

Hoffman, D. (1998). *The Oklahoma City bombing and the politics of terror*. Feral House.

Holder, J. (2023, March 13). Tracking coronavirus vaccinations around the world. *New York Times*. https://www.nytimes.com/interactive/2021/world/covid-vaccinations-tracker.html.

Hudson, N. (2023, June 23). Fabricated global crises are provoking centralized global control. *PANDA*. https://pandata.org/fabricated-global-crises-are-provoking-centralized-global-control-nick-hudson-panda/.

Hughes, D. A. (2022a). "Covid-19 vaccines" for children in the UK: A tale of establishment corruption. *International Journal of Vaccine Theory, Practice, and Research*, *2*(1), 209–247. https://doi.org/10.56098/ijvtpr.v2i1.35.

Hughes, D. A. (2022b, July 29). Wall Street, the Nazis, and the crimes of the deep state. *Propaganda in Focus*. https://propagandainfocus.com/wall-street-the-nazis-and-the-crimes-of-the-deep-state/.

Hughes, D. A. (2022c). What is in the so-called Covid-19 "vaccines"? Part 1: Evidence of a global crime against humanity. *International Journal of Vaccine Theory, Practice, and Research*, *2*(2), 455–586. https://doi.org/10.56098/ijvtpr.v2i2.52.

Hughes, D. A. (2023, April 14). *We are in a global class war* [Video]. Bitchute. https://www.bitchute.com/video/ZPHbyPe04Yc0/.

Hughes, D. A. (2024). *Wall Street, the Nazis, and the crimes of the deep state*. Skyhorse.

Hughes, D. A., Kyrie, V., & Broudy, D. (2022, November 29). Covid-19: Mass formation or mass atrocity? *Unlimited Hangout*. https://unlimitedhangout.com/2022/11/investigative-reports/covid-19-mass-formation-or-mass-atrocity/.

Huxley, A. (1958). *Brave new world revisited*. Harper & Row.

Huxley, A. (1959). The final revolution. In A. Simon & R. M. Featherstone (Eds.), *A pharmacologic approach to the study of the mind* (pp. 216–228). University of California Medical School.

Jamieson, G. (2023, February 1). How safe really is 5G? *The Daily Sceptic*. https://dailysceptic.org/2023/02/01/how-safe-really-is-5g/.

Joint Chiefs of Staff. (2010). *Psychological operations*. Joint Publication 3–13.2. https://irp.fas.org/doddir/dod/jp3-13-2.pdf.

Jones, C. (2019, December 31). 2019's Yield Curve Inversion means a Recession could hit in 2020. *Forbes*. https://www.forbes.com/sites/chuckjones/2020/12/31/2019s-yield-curve-inversion-means-a-recession-could-hit-in-2020/.

K, A. (2021, October 27). Covid-19: A psychological military operation—part I. *Allan's Newsletter*. https://allank.substack.com/p/covid-19-a-psychological-military.

Kheriaty, A. (2022, May 24). The WHO treaty is tied to a global digital passport and ID system. *Brownstone Institute*. https://brownstone.org/articles/who-treaty-tied-to-digital-passport-id-system/.

Kitson, F. (1971). *Low intensity operations*. Stackpole Books.

Klein, N. (2007). *The shock doctrine*. Metropolitan Books.

Krishnan, A. (2022). Fifth generation warfare, hybrid warfare and gray zone conflict: A comparison. *Journal of Strategic Security, 15*(4), 14–31. https://doi.org/10.5038/1944-0472.15.4.2013.

Kyrie, V., & Broudy, D. (2022). Cyborgs R us: The bio-nano panopticon of injected bodies? *International Journal of Vaccine Theory, Practice, and Research, 2*(2), 355–383. https://doi.org/10.56098/ijvtpr.v2i2.49.

Lacter, E.P. (2011, May 11). Ritual abuse and torture-based mind control: Reducing and preventing re-contact with abusers. *End Ritual Abuse*. https://endritualabuse.org/ritual-abuse-and-torture-based-mind-control-reducing-and-preventing-re-contact-with-abusers/.

Latypova, S. (2022, December 13). Intent to harm. *Due Diligence and Art*. https://sashalatypova.substack.com/p/intent-to-harm.

Lawler, D. (2020, March 18). Coronavirus is the greatest challenge since World War II, Merkel warns. *Axios*. https://www.axios.com/2020/03/18/angela-merkel-germany-coronavirus-lockdown-wwii.

Layne, C. (2018). The US–Chinese power shift and the end of the pax Americana. *International Affairs, 94*(1), 89–111. https://doi.org/10.1093/ia/iix249.

Lenin, V.I. (1987). *Essential works of Lenin* (H.M. Christman, Ed., 2nd ed.). Dover Publications.

Liang, Q., & Xiangsui, W. (1999). *Unrestricted warfare*. PLA Literature and Arts Publishing House.

Lincoln, M. (2022, September 7). The years of magical thinking: Pandemic necrosecurity under Trump and Biden. *Bill of Health*. https://blog.petrieflom.law.harvard.edu/2022/09/07/the-years-of-magical-thinking-pandemic-necrosecurity-under-trump-and-biden/.

Lippmann, W. (1922). *Public Opinion*. Harcourt, Brace, and Company.

Lippmann, W. (1925). *The Phantom Public*. Transaction Publishers.

McCoy, A. (2015, February 26). The real American exceptionalism. *truthdig*. https://www.truthdig.com/articles/the-real-american-exceptionalism/.

Meadows, D. H., Meadows, D. L., Randers, J., & Behrens, III, W.W. (1972). *The limits to growth*. Potomac Associates.

Meerloo, J. A. (1956). *The rape of the mind. The psychology of thought control, menticide, and brainwashing*. World Publishing Company.

Ministry of Defence. (2020). *Integrated operating concept*. https://www.gov.uk/government/publications/the-integrated-operating-concept-2025.

Minnicino, M. (1974). Low intensity operations: The Reesian theory of war. *The Campaigner, 7*(6), 37–55.

Moorhouse, R. (2010). *Berlin at war*. Basic Books.

Naked Emperor. (2023, March 4). Number of births in England falls by 11.9% in 2022. *The Daily Sceptic*. https://dailysceptic.org/2023/03/04/number-of-births-in-england-falls-by-11-9-in-2022/.

National Security Council. (1947). *NSC-4*. https://irp.fas.org/offdocs/nsc-hst/nsc-4.htm.

National Security Council. (1974). *National security study memorandum 200*. https://pdf.usaid.gov/pdf_docs/PCAAB500.pdf.

Nesvetailova, A., & Palan, R. (2008). A very North Atlantic credit crunch: Geopolitical implications of the global liquidity crisis. *Journal of International Affairs, 62*(1), 165–185.

Office for National Statistics. (2023a). *Deaths registered weekly in England and Wales, provisional*. https://www.ons.gov.uk/peoplepopulationandcommunity/birthsdeathsandmarriages/deaths/bulletins/deathsregisteredweeklyinenglandandwalesprovisional/latest.

Office for National Statistics. (2023b). *Deaths registered weekly in England and Wales, provisional: week ending 21 April 2023*. https://www.ons.gov.uk/peoplepopulationandcommunity/birthsdeathsandmarriages/deaths/bulletins/deathsregisteredweeklyinenglandandwalesprovisional/weekending21april2023.

Office of United States Chief of Counsel for Prosecution of Axis Criminality. (1946). *Nazi Conspiracy and Aggression, Volume II*. United States Government Printing Office.

Official Statistics of Sweden. (n.d.). *Mortality rate per 1000 of the mean population by age, sex and year*. https://www.statistikdatabasen.scb.se/pxweb/en/ssd/START__BE__BE0101__BE0101I/Dodstal/table/tableViewLayout1/.

Orwell, G. (1984). *Nineteen eighty-four*. Oxford University Press.

Pfeiffer, M.B. (2022, November 28). The missing babies of Europe. *RESCUE with Michael Capuzzo*. https://rescue.substack.com/p/the-missing-babies-of-europe?utm_campaign=post.

Phillips, P. (2018). *Giants*. Seven Stories Press.

Pijl, K. van der. (1998). *Transnational classes and international relations*. Routledge.

Pijl, K. van der. (2015). The uneven and combined development of international historical sociology". In R. Desai (Ed.), *Theoretical engagements in geopolitical economy* (pp. 45–83). Emerald Group.

Pijl, K. van der. (2019). The Russian revolution at 100: The Soviet experience in the mirror of permanent counterrevolution. *Third World Quarterly, 41*(8), 1272–1288. https://doi.org/10.1080/01436597.2019.1665462.

Pijl, K. van der. (2020, April 27). Health emergency or seizure of power? The political economy of Covid-19. *New Cold War*. https://newcoldwar.org/health-emergency-or-seizure-of-power-the-political-economy-of-covid-19/.

Pijl, K. van der. (2022). *States of emergency. Keeping the global population in check*. Clarity Press.

Polyakova, K. (2021). Do doctors have to have the Covid-19 vaccine? *BMJ*, 372, Article n810. https://doi.org/10.1136/bmj.n810.

Ponton, F. (2023, February 1). Are Covid-19 "vaccines" a military biodefense response gone terribly wrong? *21st Century Wire*. https://21stcenturywire.com/2023/02/01/covid-19-vaccine-a-military-response-to-a-public-health-threat/.

Poona, K. (2021, November). Climate change and Covid-19—How Covid-19 has made us aware of the necessity of a great reset. *The Meath Herald*. https://issuu.com/meathherald.com/docs/the_meath_herald_november_2021.

Potts, S.C. (2020, June 9). The cult of the mask. *The Remnant*. https://remnantnewspaper.com/web/index.php/articles/item/4927-the-cult-of-the-mask#_ftnref1.

Project for a New American Century. (2000, September). *Rebuilding America's Defences*. Retrieved June 13, 2023, from https://resistir.info/livros/rebuilding_americas_defenses.pdf.

Qureshi, W. A. (2019). Fourth- and fifth-generation warfare: Technology and perceptions. *San Diego International Law Journal, 21*(7), 187–216.

Rancourt, D., Baudin, M., & Mercier, J. (2021). *Nature of the Covid-era public health disaster in the USA, from all-cause mortality and socio-geo-economic and climatic data*. https://denisrancourt.ca/uploads_entries/1635189453861_USA%20ACM%20into%202021%20-%20article----12d.pdf.

Rees, J. R. (1945). *The shaping of psychiatry by war*. W.W. Norton & Company.

Rockefeller, D. (1973, August 10). From a China traveller. *The New York Times*. https://www.nytimes.com/1973/08/10/archives/from-a-china-traveler.html.

Rockefeller Foundation and Global Business Network. (2010, May). *Scenarios for the future of technology and international development*. Retrieved June

13, 2023, from https://archive.org/details/scenarios-for-the-future-of-technology-and-international-development-rockefeller-foundation-2010.

Roosevelt, K. (Ed.). (1976). *War report of the OSS, volume I*. Walker and Company.

Russell, B. (1952). *The impact of science on society*. Simon and Schuster.

Scott, B. (2021a, January 3). Psychological attack on the UK. *UK Column*. https://www.ukcolumn.org/article/psychological-attack-uk.

Scott, B. (2021b, October 13). Beyond a state of fear: Menticide and schizogenesis. *Borderline*. https://dr-bruce-scott.com/2021/10/13/beyond-a-state-of-fear-menticide-and-schizogenesis/.

Scott, B. (2022, July 26). Menticide 101 and the brainwashing of a world: Part I—the biosecurity state. *UK Column*. https://www.ukcolumn.org/article/menticide-101-and-the-brainwashing-of-a-world-part-i-the-biosecurity-state.

Shir-Raz, E.E., Martin, B., Ronel, N., & Guetzkow, J. (2022, November 1). Censorship and suppression of Covid-19 heterodoxy: Tactics and counter-Tactics. *Minerva*. https://doi.org/10.1007/s11024-022-09479-4.

Simpson, C. (1994). *Science of coercion: Communication research and psychological warfare, 1945–1960*. Oxford University Press.

Spectator (n.d.). *Data tracker—NHS*. Retrieved July 15, 2023, from https://data.spectator.co.uk/nhs.

Stevens, S. & Pritchard, A. (2020, March 17). *Important and urgent—next steps on NHS response to Covid-19. Letter to: Chief executives of all NHS trusts and foundation trusts, CCG accountable officers, GP practices and primary care networks, and providers of community health services*. https://www.england.nhs.uk/coronavirus/wp-content/uploads/sites/52/2020/03/urgent-next-steps-on-nhs-response-to-covid-19-letter-simon-stevens.pdf.

Stringham, E.P. (2020, April 26). Open up society now, say Dr. Dan Erickson and Dr. Artin Massihi. *American Institute for Economic Research*. https://www.aier.org/article/open-up-society-now-say-dr-dan-erickson-and-dr-artin-massihi/.

Strohecker, K. (2023, July 10). Twenty-four central banks will have digital currencies by 2030, survey shows. *Reuters*. https://www.reuters.com/markets/currencies/twenty-four-central-banks-will-have-digital-currencies-by-2030-bis-survey-2023-07-10/.

Sutton, A. C. (1981). *Wall Street and the Bolshevik Revolution*. Veritas Publishing.

Sutton, A. C. (2002). *America's secret establishment: An introduction to the order of Skull & Bones* (3rd ed.). TrineDay.

Sutton, A.C. (2016). *Wall Street and the rise of Hitler* (5th ed.). Clairview.

Svali. (2000, October 12). *Trauma bonding: The pull to the perpetrator*. https://www.dougriggs.org/Trauma_Bonding.pdf.

Swiss Policy Research. (2022, June). *Covid vaccines and fertility (2022)*. https://swprs.org/covid-vaccines-and-fertility/.

Taaffe-Maguire, S. (2023, February 7). Britcoin digital pound decision due by 2025. *Sky News*. https://news.sky.com/story/britcoin-digital-pound-decision-to-be-made-by-2025-12804842.

Technocracy, Inc. (2005). *Technocracy study course*. https://www.technocracyinc.org/wp-content/uploads/2015/07/Study-Course.pdf.

Titus, J. (2021). The going direct reset. *The Solari Report*. https://goingdirect.solari.com/the-going-direct-reset/.

Triggle, N., & Jeavans, C. (2021, May 13). The NHS Covid legacy—long waits and lives at risk. *BBC News*. https://www.bbc.co.uk/news/health-57092797.

Turley, J. (2022, September 27). New Zealand Prime Minister calls for a global censorship system. *ZeroHedge*. https://www.zerohedge.com/geopolitical/new-zealand-prime-minister-calls-global-censorship-system.

Tzu, S. (1963). *The art of war* (S.B. Griffith, Trans.). Oxford University Press.

United Nations. (2022a). *World Population Prospects (global)*. https://ourworldindata.org/grapher/children-per-woman-UN?tab=chart.

United Nations. (2022b). *World Population Prospects (by region)*. https://ourworldindata.org/grapher/children-per-woman-UN?tab=chart&country=Asia+%28UN%29~Africa+%28UN%29~Europe+%28UN%29~Latin+America+and+the+Caribbean+%28UN%29~Oceania+%28UN%29~Northern+America+%28UN%29.

U.S. Mortality (n.d.). *Weekly all-cause excess mortality (percentage)*. https://www.usmortality.com/excess-mortality/percentage.

Valentine, D. (2017). *The CIA as organized crime*. Clarity Press.

Velázquez, A. (2020, November 28). *China and the "Great Reset."* Substack. https://ayavela.substack.com/p/coming-soon.

Valley, P. E., & Aquino, M. A. (1980). *From psyop to mind war: The psychology of victory*. Presidio of San Francisco.

Webb, W. (2020, September 25). Engineering contagion: UPMC, corona-thrax and "the darkest winter." *The Last American Vagabond*. https://www.thelastamericanvagabond.com/engineering-contagion-upmc-corona-thrax-darkest-winter/.

Webb, W. (2022, October 27). They may deplatform the truth, but their lies and distortions will never replace it. *The Defender*. https://childrenshealthdefense.org/defender/whitney-webb-government-truth-distortions/.

Werner, R. A. (2014). Can banks individually create money out of nothing? *International Review of Financial Analysis, 36*, 1–19. https://doi.org/10.1016/j.irfa.2014.07.015.

Wilford, H. (2008). *The mighty Wurlitzer: How the CIA played America*. Harvard University Press.

Williams, W. A. (1972). *The tragedy of American diplomacy*. W.W. Norton & Company.

Wolff, E. (2021, September 20). The master plan behind the Covid crisis. *TCW*. https://www.conservativewoman.co.uk/the-master-plan-behind-the-covid-crisis/.

Wolin, S. S. (2008). *Democracy incorporated*. Princeton University Press.

Wood, P. (2018). *Technocracy: The hard road to world order*. Coherent Publishing.

Wood, P. (2022, December 19). "Day 7: China is a Technocracy." *Technocracy News & Trends*. https://www.technocracy.news/day-7-china-is-a-technocracy/.

World Bank. (2020). *Covid-19 strategic preparedness and response program and proposed 25 projects under phase 1*. https://documents1.worldbank.org/curated/en/993371585947965984/pdf/World-COVID-19-Strategic-Preparedness-and-Response-Project.pdf.

World Economic Forum. (2019). *Globalization 4.0. Shaping a new global architecture in the age of the fourth industrial revolution*. https://www3.weforum.org/docs/WEF_Globalization_4.0_Call_for_Engagement.pdf.

World Health Organisation. (2023). *Countries begin negotiations on global agreement to protect world from future pandemic emergencies*. https://www.who.int/news/item/03-03-2023-countries-begin-negotiations-on-global-agreement-to-protect-world-from-future-pandemic-emergencies.

Wright, R. (2019, December 30). The story of 2019: Protests in every corner of the globe. *The New Yorker*. https://www.newyorker.com/news/our-columnists/the-story-of-2019-protests-in-every-corner-of-the-globe.

Yeadon, M. (2023, March 22). Why I don't believe there ever was a Covid virus. *TCW*. https://www.conservativewoman.co.uk/why-i-dont-believe-there-ever-was-a-covid-virus/.

Zimbardo, P. (2007). *The Lucifer effect: Why good people turn evil*. Random House.

CHAPTER 2

Shock and Stress

Ever since it became clear that victims of shell shock in World War I displayed increased psychological malleability, social engineers have sought to exploit the application of shock and stress for social control purposes. Experiments on POWs and other test subjects in the 1950s showed that it was possible to "depattern" the human mind and to reprogramme behaviour. The Tavistock Institute, which took control of the mental health profession after 1945, weaponised psychiatry and found ways of applying shock and stress techniques to entire societies, facilitating what Klein (2007) calls the "shock doctrine," i.e. systematic exploitation of public disorientation following a moment of collective shock. The "lockdowns" in 2020 were a shock and awe operation, and other techniques associated with "depatterning" the mind were additionally deployed, including disruption of behavioural patterns, isolation, and defamiliarisation. The moment of shock was used to implant trigger words and images for purposes of trauma-based mind control.

Shocking the Mind

The Tavistock Institute of Medical Psychology (usually referred to as the Tavistock Clinic) was founded in 1920 by Hugh Crichton-Miller, who worked with shell-shocked soldiers during and after World War I. One of its practitioners, John Rawlings Rees, had studied war neuroses in France during World War I; he came to believe that, "under controlled

D. A. Hughes, *"Covid-19," Psychological Operations, and the War for Technocracy*, https://doi.org/10.1007/978-3-031-41850-1_2

conditions, neurotic behaviour could be induced, and, through these methods, individual behaviour could be absolutely controlled" (Wolfe, 1996b, p. 25). After ousting Crichton-Miller in 1933/34, Rees, with immediate Rockefeller funding, oversaw work at the Clinic using electro-convulsive shock, barbiturates, and hypnosis in brainwashing experiments (Minnicino, 1974, p. 39). In 1940, he recruited Eric Trist, who had also been researching drug and hypnosis-induced abreaction as a Rockefeller Foundation Medical Fellow at an English hospital. Rees' primary interest was never in therapy in a positive, health-restoring sense. Rather, it was in psychiatry as a means of social control.

Meanwhile, in the Soviet Union, physiologist/psychologist Ivan Pavlov was making similar discoveries. 30 days of modern warfare, Pavlov found, pushed most men beyond the limits of psychological endurance, and similar, breakdown-inducing stress could be artificially produced through other means (as cited in Huxley, 1958, pp. 59–61). As in dogs, a political prisoner subjected to just the "right" of amount of stress (i.e., just before breaking point) becomes unusually suggestible, and at that point, new behaviour patterns can be installed.

Thus, the lesson of World War I, for both Rees and Pavlov, was that shell shock/combat fatigue/continuous high-level stress is enough to break down an individual to the point where their behaviour can be reliably controlled/reprogrammed.

Orwell writes in *Nineteen Eighty-Four* (1984, p. 389): "Power is in tearing human minds to pieces and putting them together again in new shapes of your own choosing." One of the key principles established in psychological warfare research of the 1950s is that the mind must first be "depatterned" before it can be reprogrammed. In Pavlovian conditioning, for example, "First the old patterns have to be broken down in order to build up new conditioned reflexes" (Meerloo, 1956, p. 45). In Chinese "thought reform" techniques, there was, according to CIA Director Allen Dulles (1953, p. 20), "a 'brain washing' which 'cleansed the mind of the old and evil thoughts spawned by imperialists of the West,' [followed by] a 'brain changing' which implanted the 'new and glorious thoughts of the Communist Revolution.'"

Dulles himself, however, was presiding over experiments to achieve a very similar result. Tavistock's Ewen Cameron, the Scottish-born U.S. citizen who had risen to become the president of the American Psychiatric Association, president of the Canadian Psychiatric Association, and president of the World Psychiatric Association, performed mind control experiments for the CIA in the 1950s, which involved the use of electroshock and drugs to "depattern" victims and put them into an "almost vegetative state" in which they could do nothing but listen to pre-recorded messages "for sixteen to twenty hours a day for weeks; in one case, Cameron played a message continuously for 101 days" (Klein, 2007, pp. 30–32). Cameron called this "psychic driving."

In a variation on Machiavelli's advice that injuries should be inflicted "all at once," Klein describes depatterning as "attacking the brain with everything known to interfere with its normal functioning—all at once," the aim being to make prisoners "so regressed and afraid that they can no longer think rationally or protect their own interests" (Klein, 2007, pp. 7, 31, 16). In such a state of shock, prisoners will typically give their interrogators whatever they want.

MKULTRA and other CIA mind control programmes in the 1950s and 1960s yielded the *KUBARK [CIA] Manual* (1963), intended as a guide to "interrogation" (torture). In order to break down a prisoner, the *Manual* claims, it is necessary to apply "a kind of psychological shock or paralysis. It is caused by a traumatic or sub-traumatic experience which explodes, as it were, the world that is familiar to the subject as well as his image of himself within that world" (CIA, 1963, p. 66).

Tavistock Influence

Psychiatry as a Means of Social Control

Psychiatry as a means of social control was the ethos of the Tavistock Institute, whose methods after World War II would become "the means of class war" (Minnicino, 1974, p. 52), i.e. "a weapon of the ruling class" (Marcus, 1974, p. 22), intended to "guide the population into accepting the policy designs of […] a small Anglo-American international financial establishment, centered in London and its extension, Wall Street" (Wolfe, 1996b, p. 28).

Lamenting that it would be difficult in peacetime to arrange the kind of psychological experiments that Tavistock psychiatrists had carried out on service personnel during World War II, Rees (1945, pp. 52, 120) proposes "legislation that will make it possible for people of every social group to have treatment when they need it, even though they do not wish it, without the necessity to invoke the law"—in other words, an extralegal means of coercing psychiatric "treatment"/experimentation.

This, presumably, will be targeted along eugenics lines at the "constitutionally inferior group, the psychopathic tenth of the community," the "dullards" that form a "social problem group," reproducing "defective children" (Rees, 1945, pp. 43–45). In order to implement this, Rees (1945, pp. 133–134) calls for "shock troops," i.e. "mobile teams of well-selected, well-trained psychiatrists, who are free to move around and make contacts with the local situation in their particular area," but whose loyalty lies with the network and not local institutions. Achieving this would require support both from the "great foundations" and the state.

The Rockefeller Memorandum of 1946 led to the formation of a new institution, the Tavistock Institute of Human Relations, which, though initially constituted as a division of the Tavistock Clinic, was spun off in 1947. In return for offering up his network, now several hundred strong (Wolfe, 1996b, p. 24), to the Rockefeller family, Rees was rewarded with a new appointment in 1948. Stepping down from the Tavistock Institute, he became President of the UN World Federation of Mental Health, founded by former Bank of England Governor Montagu Norman and resurrected from a previous Rockefeller front organisation, the International Committee for Mental Hygiene (Minnicino, 1974, p. 43). Also in 1948, Rees' ally, Brock Chisholm, was appointed as the first Director-General of the World Health Organization, confirming the founding connection between the WHO and the Rockefeller-Rees axis. From his dominant position, Rees was able to plant his protégés in key positions (Marcus, 1974, p. 23), grow a transnational network of influential practitioners and research labs—over three dozen affiliated organisations—and thereby dominate the postwar mental health profession (Minnicino, 1974, p. 42; Wolfe, 1996a, p. 25). In the United States, Rees' influence expanded into the National Institute of Health and the National Institute of Mental Health, complementing Rockefeller control over the American Medical Association and American Psychiatric Association (Marcus, 1974, p. 23).

These institutional origins of the mental health profession, rooted in the Reesian idea of psychiatry as a means of social control, raise serious questions about that profession. For example, to what extent is the routine prescription of antidepressants really intended to treat depression, and to what extent is it about facilitating social control via biochemical means? Is mental illness deliberately inculcated within the population, so that such "treatments" can be prescribed? It has been suggested that psychiatry could be used to "neutralise" dissidents: "The 'brainwashed' dissident is mentally murdered in fact; [and] provided the Rockefeller forces control the majority of the psychiatric profession, especially the state-controlled psychiatric institutions, a fairly efficient form of murder can be perpetrated [...]" (Marcus, 1974, p. 18). This is not so very different from the Soviet abuse of psychiatry for political purposes (see Chap. 5).

Tavistock Methods of Counterinsurgency

Winston Churchill claimed in 1943: "The empires of the future are the empires of the mind" (cited in Alkon, 2006, p. 93). The battlefield would, thus, shift "away from control of territory, to control of the minds, not merely of the colonial peoples, but of the United States and the rest of the Western world" (Wolfe, 1996b, p. 24).

In terms of counterinsurgency, Tavistock's three "primary weapons against the working class" were food control, resettlement, and counter-gangs (Minnicino, 1974, p. 50). The first two make people more susceptible to behaviour modification, while the latter is used to infiltrate and subvert resistance movements. From the resultant psychological wreckage, new leaders based on "weak ego" types can be "selected out" and controlled by Western intelligence (Minnicino, 1974, p. 42).

In Malaya, for example, where a pro-communist labour movement swept the peninsula after 1945, threatening to hand control of the strategically vital Straits of Malacca to the Soviet Union, British intelligence not only infiltrated the communist armed guerrillas, but also destroyed the rice crop and punctured food cans, sending the population into near starvation. This false flag operation was blamed on the guerrillas, and the population was told it could obtain food by resettling to "New Villages" set up by the government. More than half a million Malayans (a tenth of the population) were resettled, by force if necessary (Minnicino, 1974, p. 48). In the "psychologically manipulated environment of the camps," it was possible to "profile the population, and select out the future Malaysian Government and Civil Service," passing political control of the country to Western intelligence (Minnicino, 1974, pp. 49, 52).

In Kenya, the Mau Mau rebellion (1952–1960) was met with similar tactics, i.e. food control and resettlement, in a process called 'villagization." The insurgency was infiltrated using what Brigadier Frank Kitson referred to as "counter-gangs," i.e. British intelligence-controlled units, comprised of brainwashed prisoners from POW camps, used to penetrate national liberation movements so that their leaders could be murdered, ostensibly by rival factions (Wolfe, 1996a, p. 26). The British experience in Malaya and Kenya confirmed the viability of such tactics to the CIA (Minnicino, 1974, p. 46).

When the CIA brought in Sir Robert Thompson, who had served in the Malayan operation, to help with the Vietnam War, Thompson renamed the resettlement camps "strategic hamlets." The Taylor-Staley strategic hamlet programme in South Vietnam, as it became known, resulted in 13 million farmers and workers being forcibly relocated to 12,000 "fortified villages, surrounded by barbed wire fences and ditches fortified with bamboo spikes" (Schlesinger Jr., 1965, p. 549). Food control was applied to the camps in an attempt to "psychologically smash" their inhabitants, with a view to selecting out future leaders to replace the ineffectual Diem regime (Minnicino, 1974, p. 50).

Counterinsurgency against the Domestic Population

As years of mounting social tensions in the West reached a climax in 1967/68, counterinsurgency methods started to be deployed at home as well as abroad, as recommended by the American Institute of Research, a CIA think tank, in 1967 (Minnicino, 1974, p. 51). This was most evident in the treatment of the African-American population, "by far the one group that throughout the twentieth century kept alive a spirit of resistance and rebelliousness" (Wolin, 2008, p. 58).

The purpose of Operation Phoenix was to "neutralize" civilian members of the revolutionary underground in South Vietnam (Valentine, 2017, p. 24). The same "neutralisation" tactic was deployed against effective black organisers in the United States. An FBI memo dated March 4, 1968, states: "Through counterintelligence, it should be possible to pinpoint potential troublemakers and neutralize them […]" (Glick, 1989, p. 78). On April 4, 1968, Martin Luther King Jr. was assassinated. On December 4, 1969, Fred Hampton and Mark Clark were murdered in a "gestapo-style attack set up by the FBI" (Chomsky, 2015).

The difference between Vietnam and the United States, Marcus (1974, p. 18) notes, is that the political climate in the latter does not "yet permit open deployment of Special Forces-type assassination teams against civilian populations generally." But, he argues, CIA infiltration of courts, prosecutor's offices and police forces can be used for frame-up purposes, which are no less effective in eliminating political opponents—and the corporate media can be expected to cover it up. Provoking violence that can be prosecuted then becomes a domestic counterinsurgency tactic: "Much of the violence in which U.S. radicals have become involved turns out to have been the responsibility of the FBI or police," with infiltrators and covert operations being used (Glick, 1989, p. 66). Kitson's "counter-gang" concept, deploying mind-controlled operatives to infiltrate and subvert foreign resistance movements, here enters the domestic arena.

Tavistock was also the "driving force" behind the drugs counterculture of the late 1960s (Wolfe, 1996b, p. 28), aimed at neutering youth resistance. This grew naturally out of the role of Tavistock's Ewen Cameron and William Sargant in MKULTRA experiments involving psychotropic drugs and mind control. The function of drugs, according to the *KUBARK Manual*, "is to cause capitulation, to aid in the shift from resistance to cooperation" (CIA, 1963, p. 99). In Huxley's *Brave New World*, first published in 1932, the use of the drug soma provides a "holiday from reality" without side effects (Huxley, 1956, p. 65). Huxley promotes mescaline in *Doors of Perception* (1954), and in *Brave New World Revisited* (1958, pp. 70, 73) discusses adrenochrome, serotonin, and LSD-25. The U.S. college students who had engaged in various forms of direct action against the system in the 1960s were, by the end of the decade, "a collection of doped-up zombies, 'change agents,' and shock-troops for Tavistock's Brave New World" (Wolfe, 1996b, p. 28).

The concept of "medication into submission," so as to "prepare the pattern of mental submission so beloved by the totalitarian brainwasher" (Meerloo, 1956, pp. 55, 60), also goes some way to explaining the CIA's notorious history of bringing narcotics into the United States (Scott & Marshall, 1991; Scott 2003) and releasing them particularly in black communities. It is also worth asking critical questions about the escalating use of prescription medications since the early 1960s, given that "vast swaths of the [population] have been rendered docile and comfortably numb, silenced, sedated and marginalised over decades of 'massive over-prescription'" (Broudy & Arakaki, 2020).

The Quest for Mass Suggestibility.

The ultimate goal for Tavistock operatives was finding ways of applying the mind control techniques inflicted on individuals in CIA and similar experiments to societies at large. Shock and stress were the key factors. After 1945, the Tavistock Institute routinely sent flying squads to war-torn areas and disaster zones, with a view to learning more about the potential for manipulating shocked and stressed populations (Minnicino, 1974, p. 44).

Kurt Lewin, building on Rees' work on controlling neurotic individuals, sought to "develop methods for inducing controlled, irrational behavior by groups of people" (Wolfe, 1996b, p. 25). The idea was to induce the "breakdown of moral and social capacity," not by totalitarian terror (involving the threat of direct violence), but via large group manipulation (Wolfe, 1996a, p. 23). Lewin's Research Centre for Group Dynamics (MIT), which moved to the University of Michigan as the Institute for Social Research following his death in 1947 (where the journal *Human Relations* was founded), as well as the spin-off National Training Laboratories, were all established in the second half of the 1940s, with funding coming from "royal family-sponsored charitable trusts, as well as from the Rockefellers, the Mellons, and the Morgans" (Wolfe, 1996b, p. 25)—further evidence of the Establishment's investment in psychological means of social control.

Tavistock psychiatrist William Sargant writes in *Battle for the Mind* that the same principles of mind control applicable to individuals can also be applied to groups. Fear, anger, and excitement can be used to impair judgement and heighten suggestibility, allowing "various types of belief" to be "implemented in many people." The resulting group manifestations are witnessed "most spectacularly in wartime, during severe epidemics, and in all similar periods of common danger" (Sargant, 1997, p. 151). The mass fear principle was already operative in the 1950s via apocalyptic propaganda about nuclear war (see Chapter 4), and the references to wars and epidemics (Sargant was writing at the time of the so-called "Asian flu pandemic") anticipate the "War on Terror" and "Covid-19" decades later.

Tavistock's Fred Emery and Eric Trist (editor of *Human Relations*) gave a paper to a select Tavistock audience in 1963 outlining a new paradigm of "permanent social turbulence," whereby "a series of sharp and universal, cathartic shocks would destabilise a targeted population, plunging a whole society into a form of managed psychosis" (Wolfe, 1996a, p. 24). Shocks repeated over the course of years would cause the population to adopt "more infantile forms of reasoning" (cf. Chapter 3) and to accept as normal what was once considered abnormal. With the widespread acquiescence to deprivation of civil liberties after "9/11" and the draconian "new normal" in 2020, accepting "the unthinkable" (a term deliberately propagated both times) was witnessed in spectacular style.

In May 1967, the Conference on Transatlantic Technological Imbalance and Collaboration, held in Deauville, France, brought together Tavistock representatives Fred Emery and Harland Cleveland, Willis Harm of the Tavistock-connected Stanford Research Institute, Zbigniew Brzezinski, the British Government's Chief Scientific Adviser, Solly Zuckerman, and future sustainability champions Aurelio Peccei and Sir Alexander King (Wolfe, 1996a, 5–24). Here we see a convergence of Tavistock, technocracy, and sustainability. Emery (1977, p. 18) would later reflect that the 1967–1969 period "marked the undenied significance of 'turbulence' in Western societies," though he neglects to add: in response to the class struggle.

The "Tavistock brainwashers," as Wolfe (1996b, p. 28) refers to them, envisaged a "period of successive social, economic, political, and cultural shocks" that would lead to "maladaptive responses" that are "present in the society at the same time, interacting with each other, to produce neurotic behaviors on a grand scale." By such means, Wolfe (1996b, pp. 26–28) argues, could populations be manipulated into accepting the transition to a "post-industrial" model that would prevent industrialising non-Western societies from "catching up" with their Western counterparts.

Alvin Toffler in *Future Shock* (1970, pp. 2, 15) describes the transition from industrial to "super-industrial" society in terms of "the shattering stress and disorientation that we induce in individuals by subjecting them to too much change in too short a time." Wood (2018, p. 123) paraphrases Toffler by writing that "excessively rapid change induces a state of shock that interferes with normal mental and emotional processes." Digital Citizen (2003), referencing the work of Trist and Emery, notes that society can be shocked by energy shortages, economic and financial crises, and terrorist attacks, and that a series of shocks delivered with increasing intensity can drive society into a state of mass psychosis. A "turbulent environment," according to Emery and Emery (1976, p. 64), creates a "dissociative mode within individuals and societies," rendering social interactions unpredictable and undesirable. Thus, society becomes atomised, with the television playing an important role in conditioning maladaptation to stress (Emery & Emery, 1976, Chapter 8).

Energy shortages, economic and financial instability, and terrorist attacks were indeed the means by which Western societies were shocked into accepting the "post-industrial" transition in the 1970s. The decoupling of the U.S. dollar from gold in 1971, for instance, ushered in a "new era of instability in the global economy" (Ravenhill, 2020, p. 18) and "the most turbulent period in international finance since the 1930s" (Strange, 1997, p. vii), characterised by decades of escalating financial crises worldwide. The 1973 oil price shock, which saw the price of oil quadruple within a matter of days, led to a major drop in industrial activity throughout the world in 1974/75 (not unlike the impact of "Covid-19" in 2020), plus steep increases in bankruptcies and unemployment, while consolidating the power of Wall Street, the City of London, and the Seven Sisters (Engdahl, 2004, pp. 139–140).

As Strange (1997, pp. 2–71) recognises, the 1973 oil price shock should not be lazily attributed to "exogenous" factors. According to Engdahl (2004, pp. 130, 135), the May 1973 Bilderberg meeting—five months *before* the oil price shock—planned for "how to manage the about-to-be-created flood of oil dollars" arising from the petrodollar arrangements to be put in place following the Yom Kippur war, which was "secretly orchestrated by Washington and London." The oil price shocks and consequent oil shortages were, in Marcus' (1974, p. 7) view, "artificially created" and the result of "Rockefeller rigging of the October Arab–Israeli war." Their purpose was to undermine industrial growth in the "Third World" and to "tilt the balance of power back to the advantage of Anglo-American financial interests" (Engdahl, 2004, p. 135). In keeping with Hitler's (1939, p. 183) concept of the "grossly impudent lie" (see Chapter 6), the Anglo-American financial establishment used its clout "in a manner no one could imagine possible. The very outrageousness of their scheme was to their advantage, they clearly reckoned" (Engdahl, 2004, p. 135).

Terrorism added to the "social turbulence." In 1969/70, Kitson's "counter-gang" concept spawned a raft of militant organisations willing to kill civilians in pursuit of their objectives, e.g. the Provisional IRA which Kitson helped to set up (Wolfe, 1996b, p. 26), the Weather Underground, the Black September Organisation, the Red Brigades, and the Red Army

Faction. In Minnicino's (1974, p. 51) judgement, "every 'underground' terrorist group in the world is either a counter-gang or so infiltrated by operatives and psychologically manipulated victims that it is, except in the case of individual members, impossible to make the distinction." One key purpose of these counter-gangs was to syphon off vulnerable workers into violent, myopic, self-destructive forms of "radicalism" that undermine the class struggle.

In the case of the clandestine NATO networks spread across Europe, referred to in shorthand as Operation Gladio after the Italian network that was exposed in the 1990s, the purpose was to implement the "Strategy of Tension." As one of the perpetrators, Vincenzo Vinciguerra, testified in 1984, this involved attacking innocent civilians, including women and children, in order to make the public think that a state of emergency could be declared at any time, thus making people willing to "trade part of their freedom" for greater security (cited in Davis, 2018). Here, "social turbulence" is created by the shocks of terrorist attacks that leave society feeling insecure and willing to accept a more authoritarian political climate. The fact that many of the attacks were deceptively blamed on "far left" groups was another effective tactic for undermining the class struggle. The "Strategy of Tension" was later globalised through the "War on Terror" (Hughes, 2022).

Emery and Trist both seek to camouflage the artificially induced nature of "social turbulence." Emery (1977, p. 67), for instance, claims that "Massive unpredictable changes appear to arise out of the causal texture of the environment itself and not just as planned, controlled actions, not even those of the superstates or the multinational corporations." Trist (1997, p. 519), in an article first published in 1979, reflects: "All of these events, and there are many others, came as surprises. They were not predicted. They are not understood. For this reason they create bewilderment, raising levels of anxiety and suspicion. Such is the experience of turbulence and loss of the stable state." In reality, "social turbulence" is *designed* to create bewilderment and anxiety.

The Shock Doctrine

Klein (2017, p. 2) uses the term "shock doctrine" to describe "the quite brutal tactic of systematically using the public's disorientation following a collective shock—wars, coups, terrorist attacks, market crashes, or natural disasters—to push through radical pro-corporate measures, often called 'shock therapy.'" Here, the use of shock tactics against the public enters the era of neoliberalism and goes hand in hand with what Klein calls "disaster capitalism," i.e. "orchestrated raids on the public sphere in the wake of catastrophic events, combined with the treatment of disasters as exciting market opportunities" (2007, p. 22). Milton Friedman's "free market" capitalism has, Klein argues, always relied on disasters to progress—the facilitating disasters "getting bigger and more shocking" over time (2007, p. 9). The key principle is that "only a great rupture—a flood, a war, a terrorist attack—can generate the kind of vast, clean canvases" that social engineers require to "begin their work of remaking the world," i.e. "malleable moments, when we are psychologically unmoored and physically uprooted" (Klein, 2007, p. 21).

Klein (2007, p. 10) identifies three categories of shock prior to 9/11. The first involves acts aimed at "terrorizing the public." Terror, for instance, was integral to the Pinochet dictatorship in Chile following the CIA coup in 1973 that laid the foundation for the first experiment in neoliberal economics. Similarly in Argentina during Operation Condor, the forced disappearance of 30,000 mostly left activists went hand in hand with the imposition of Chicago School policies. The Tiananmen Square massacre, followed by the arrest of tens of thousands of activists in 1989, enabled the CCP to "convert much of the country into a sprawling export zone, staffed with workers too terrified to demand their rights." In Russia in 1993, the fire-sale privatisation that saw most of the country's wealth transferred into the hands of a few dozen "oligarchs" (so-called "shock therapy") followed Boris Yeltsin's decision to use tanks to fire on the parliament building and lock up opposition leaders. The second category of shock involves war. The Falklands War, for instance, enabled Margaret Thatcher, riding a wave of nationalist sentiment, to crush the UK miners' strike and "launch the first privatisation frenzy in a Western democracy." The Kosovo War of 1999 created the conditions for rapid privatisation ("shock therapy") in the former Yugoslavia. The third category of shock is financial. In the 1980s, Latin American and African debt crises and hyperinflation were leveraged to force privatisation. The Asian financial crisis of 1997–8 forced open the markets of the "Asian Tigers."

Klein posits "9/11" as the traumatic moment when the shock doctrine "finally had its chance to come home" to the United States, allowing the Bush administration to "wage privatized wars abroad and build a corporate security complex at home" (2007, pp. 12, 16). Even though Klein (2007, pp. 11–16) places the origins of the shock doctrine with CIA torture experiments in the 1950s and later the CIA coup in Chile; claims that "For three decades, Friedman and his followers had methodically exploited moments of shock in other countries," calling these "foreign equivalents of 9/11"; notes that neoconservatives were "calling for a shock therapy-style economic revolution in the U.S." in the mid-1990s; observes that "When the September 11 attacks hit, the White House was packed with Friedman's disciples, including his close friend Donald Rumsfeld [and] veterans of earlier disaster capitalism experiments in Latin America and Eastern Europe"; and presents "the shock of 9/11" as "the clearest example" of "attempting [implying intent] to achieve on a mass scale what torture does one on one in the interrogation cell," she avoids any suggestion that 9/11 may have been deliberately orchestrated by deep state actors. Instead, 9/11 appears almost as an act of God in Klein's book, the answer to the prayers of key figures in the administration who prayed for crisis "the way Christian-Zionist end-timers pray for the Rapture." To underscore the point, Klein titles a later section of her book "No Conspiracies Required."

Although Klein does not say so explicitly (and includes a section titled "The Big Lie" that has nothing to do with Hitler), the shock doctrine has a Nazi heritage. It always requires a "major collective trauma that either temporarily suspend[s] democratic practices or block[s] them entirely," allowing for "iron-fisted leadership" (Klein, 2007, p. 11). The Schmittian overtones of a state of exception allowing the dictator to rule by decree are palpable here. The line which Klein refuses to cross is that such means of bypassing democracy have been artificially manufactured through mass trauma events.

Klein (2007, p. 17) highlights the way in which the shock doctrine can be exploited to strip back civil liberties: "Like the terrorized prisoner who gives up the names of comrades and renounces his faith, shocked societies often give up things they would otherwise fiercely protect." In a state of shock, she notes, "a great many people become vulnerable to authority figures telling us to fear one another and relinquish our rights for the greater good" (2017, p. 7)—words which resonate in the context of the "Covid-19" operation.

The Shock of "Covid-19"

"Lockdown" as Shock and Awe Operation

"Shock and Awe," write Ullman et al., (1996, p. 110) "are actions that create fears, dangers, and destruction that are incomprehensible to the people at large." Their objective is to "control the adversary's will, perceptions, and understanding and literally make an adversary impotent to act or react" (Ullman et al., 1996, p. xxviii). Similarly, in "shock and awe" terrorism, "the more instantly shocking and disgraceful the action, the more completely defeated is the will of the opposition and thus the more effective is the action" (de Lint, 2021, p. 60).

In 1999, Joseph Cyrulik of the Centre for Strategic and International Studies, a CIA partner think tank, contemplated the possibility of a "decisive attack against the political will of an entire populace," which would involve "killing and wounding people, damaging and destroying their homes and communities, disrupting their jobs and economic livelihoods, and undermining their confidence and sense of security" (1999, pp. 3, 6). Such an attack could "destroy the people's faith in their government, in their military and in themselves," and would thus be an effective precursor to regime change. The methods described by Cyrulik sound like a fitting description of the "Covid-19 lockdowns" and are consistent with the attempted transnational regime change from liberal democracy to technocracy.

The "lockdowns" were a "shock and awe" deployment by governments, which are controlled by a transnational capitalist oligarchy, against their own citizens, and were aimed at crippling public resistance to the intended transition to technocracy. In that respect, they were hugely successful in the short term: the social response to "Covid-19" countermeasures was marked by an astonishing level of obedience and conformity. Agamben (2021, p. 17) observes that people accepted the new "lockdown" arrangement "as if it were obvious, being "ready to sacrifice practically everything—their life conditions, their social relationships, their work, even their friendships, as well as their religious and political convictions." This is reminiscent of the "millions in [Nazi] Germany [who] were as eager to surrender their freedom as their fathers were to fight for it" (Fromm, 1960, p. 2). In most countries, van der Pijl (2022, p. 26) observes, "the bulk of the population so far has remained largely passive in this upheaval and submits to the revolution from above," notwithstanding the millions of protestors worldwide who marched against the "Covid-19 countermeasures."

The WEF's "Great Reset" agenda is consistent with Klein's (2007, p. 21) notion of a "great rupture" allowing social engineers to remake the world while the population is "psychologically unmoored." For example, the logic of the shock doctrine is evident in Schwab and Malleret's advice to decision-makers to "take advantage of the shock inflicted by the pandemic" to implement radical, long-lasting, systemic change (2020, pp. 58–59, 102). "The shock that the pandemic has inflicted on the global economy," they write, "has been more severe and has occurred much faster than anything else in recorded economic history" (2020, p. 23). They frame the "extreme shock" of the "pandemic" in terms of a line from Camus' *The Plague* (1947): "Yet all these changes were, in one sense, so fantastic and had been made so precipitately that it wasn't easy to regard them as likely to have any permanence" (2020, p. 10). They neglect to mention that Camus' novel is an allegory of the Nazi occupation of France.

According to the CIA, "rapid exploitation at the moment of shock" is required to achieve objectives (1983, § J-2). This is one reason, for instance, why the UK Coronavirus Act, like the USA PATRIOT Act after "9/11," was rushed through a disoriented legislature answerable to a shocked and terrified public before it could be properly read or debated.

Consistent with the "shock doctrine," the "Covid-19" operation hit the public with the gamut of psychological warfare techniques—all at once. The scale, intensity, and coordination of the operation are testament to the transnational deep state behind it (Hughes, 2022). Though many techniques will be unravelled over the course of subsequent chapters, for now it suffices to highlight four which were deployed in the early stages of the operation, namely: disruption of behavioural patterns, isolation, defamiliarisation, and implantation of triggers.

Disruption of Behavioural Patterns

The shock to the prisoner's mind begins with the moment of arrest. Preferably, according to the *KUBARK Manual*, the arrest should be carried out to achieve "surprise, and the maximum amount of mental discomfort in order to catch the suspect off balance and to deprive him of the initiative," hence the rationale for dawn raids (1963, p. 85).

It is fair to say that no one, other than those responsible for them, saw the global "lockdowns" of March 2020 coming. Healthy people had never been quarantined *en masse*, nor was there any recognised scientific reason for doing so (WHO, 2019, p. 16). In Britain, the government had insisted upon a "policy" of natural herd immunity right up until the "lockdown" announcement on March 23. For example, Chief Scientific Adviser, Patrick Vallance, claimed on March 13, 2020: "because the vast majority of people get a mild illness, [our aim is] to build up some kind of herd immunity so more people are immune to this disease and we reduce the transmission, at the same time we protect those who are most vulnerable to it" (cited in Stewart & Busby, 2020). Not even Neil Ferguson's infamous "Report 9" of March 16, for all its fear-mongering usage of statistics, advocates for full "lockdown" measures including the closing of businesses (Ferguson et al., 2020). The Prime Minister's father, Stanley Johnson, publicly called for letting pubs carry on business as usual on March 17 (Child, 2020). The Scientific Advisory Group for Emergencies (SAGE) was then effectively "closed" for the March 19–22 period, whereupon followed "the single most important science-followed decision since the Manhattan Project," i.e. to "lock down," which SAGE minutes from March 23 do not even record (Chaplin, 2020). Out of the blue, on March 23, the United Kingdom was told to suspend its normal operations at a moment's notice, for no discernible or good reason.

The implications of this are worth reflecting on. If neither the Government's Chief Scientific Adviser, nor a "lead" modeller, nor SAGE recommended full "lockdown," then who exactly decreed it, and on what basis? This is a classic example of the transnational deep state exercising veto power over normal democratic/parliamentary processes (Tunander, 2016, pp. 171, 186). The transnationally coordinated decision to "lock down" was evidently taken at a higher level than national governments. This fact alone is enough to sound the death knell of liberal democracy and ideas about national sovereignty.

In their new environment, according to the torture manuals, prisoners "should not be provided with any routine to which [they] can adapt [...] Constantly disrupting patterns will cause [the prisoner] to become disoriented and to experience feelings of fear and helplessness" (CIA, 1983, § K-5). Schwab and Malleret (2020, p. 150) seem strangely familiar with this principle in the "Covid-19" context: "Psychologically, the most important consequence of the pandemic is to generate a phenomenal amount of uncertainty that often becomes a source of angst. We do not know what tomorrow will bring [...] and such a lack of surety makes us uneasy and troubled" (2020, p. 150). Multiple passages in their book, published within just three months of the WHO "pandemic" declaration, read like a blueprint for how to use a "pandemic" for psychological warfare purposes, rather than as an authentic commentary on events, and their use of "we" and "our" seems stilted and disingenuous given that human beings are often presented in detached, anthropological terms.

One of the key ways in which prisoners' routines are disrupted is through changes to their temporal rhythms. Ellul (1965, p. 311) for example, references windowless incarceration with "irregular hours for meals, sleep, interrogations, and so on," which work to destroy the prisoner's sense of time and habitual patterns. Techniques documented by the CIA (1983, § K-2, E-3, H-6) similarly include disrupting sleep and mealtimes and blocking out natural light to disrupt the prisoner's sense of night and day, to "reduce his capacity for resistance." Correspondingly, Schwab and Malleret (2020, p. 167) draw on the experience of "prisoners who face the harshest and most radical form of confinement" to describe the "Covid-19 lockdowns," which, they claim, "altered our sense of time," which became "amorphous and undifferentiated, with all the markers and normal divisions gone." No evidence is presented to support this claim, which reads more like a planned outcome, with the jarring use of the past tense to describe ongoing events recalling "pandemic preparedness" scenario planning documents (cf. Rockefeller Foundation & Global Business Network, 2010). WEF agenda contributor Ruth Ogden (2020) nevertheless concurs that "there was widespread distortion [of] time during lockdown."

Isolation

Pavlovian conditioning teaches that "isolation and the patient repetition of stimuli are required to tame wild animals," and the same is true of humans: "the totalitarians have followed this rule. They know that they can condition their political victims most quickly if they are kept in isolation" (Meerloo, 1956, p. 43). Arendt (1962, pp. 123–124) writes that the loyalty required from totalitarian subjects can only come from "the completely isolated human being who, without any other social ties to family, friends, comrades, or even mere acquaintances, derives his sense of having a place in the world only from his belonging to a movement, his membership in the party."

CIA researchers found in the 1950s that "the subject's susceptibility to propaganda" increases markedly in isolation (cited in McCoy, 2007, p. 41). McGill University's Donald O. Hebb discovered that "the effect of isolation on the brain function of the prisoner is much like that which occurs if he is beaten, starved, or deprived of sleep" (cited in McCoy, 2007, p. 42). Cornell's Lawrence Hinkle, also working for the CIA, drew on Hebb's findings to describe isolation as "the ideal way of 'breaking down' a prisoner" and increasing their "malleability" (cited in McCoy, 2007, p. 33). The *Human Resource Exploitation Training Manual* (adapted from the *KUBARK Manual*) recommends that "Isolation, both physical and psychological, must be maintained from the moment of apprehension" (CIA, 1983, § F-2). Isolation is also the first step on Biderman's 1957 "Chart of Coercion," with variants ranging from "complete solitary confinement" and "complete isolation" to "semi-isolation" and "group isolation" (Amnesty International, 1973, p. 49).

Isolation robs the prisoner of their usual support structures. According to Biderman, isolation "deprives [the] victim of all social support of his ability to resist" (Amnesty, 1973, p. 49). The idea is to throw the prisoner back onto their "own unaided internal resources" (CIA, 1983, § K-5). This is why guards tell prisoners: "You are alone. Your friends on the outside don't know whether you're alive or dead. Your fellow prisoners don't even care"; the calculated result is "[unbearable] uncertainty and hopelessness" for the prisoner (Meerloo, 1956, p. 80). According to Zimbardo (2005, p. 131), "being part of a social support network is the most effective prophylaxis against mental and physical illnesses. Anything that isolates us from our kin kills the human spirit." Abusers like to isolate their victims in order to exert more effective control over them (Anthony & Cullen, 2021).

Isolation was a key feature of the "Covid-19" operation, viz. the stay-at-home orders, enforced working from home, "self-isolation," and mandatory isolation in hotels for some travellers. The prolonged isolation and chronic social deprivation imposed by the "lockdowns" served to "exacerbate the desire for social connection and group belonging, potentially fuelling susceptibility to group-based psychology and tribal identification, with all the propaganda vulnerabilities that entails" (Kyrie & Broudy, 2022).

According to the British Prime Minister in June 2020, "There is one certainty: the fewer social contacts you have, the safer you will be" (Prime Minister's Office, 2020a). When announcing the second national "lockdown" on October 31, 2020, he told the clinically vulnerable to "minimise their contact with others and not to go to work if they are unable to work from home" (Prime Minister's Office, 2020b). Yet, isolation meant that ordinary people saw their usual support mechanisms, such as being able to visit friends and family, see the doctor/dentist, go to church, attend local clubs, etc. stripped back. Loneliness and despair afflicted large numbers of people. Bill Gates, in December 2021, was aware that "stress and isolation have triggered far-reaching impacts on mental health" (Gates & Gates, 2021). In the United States, suicide calls and overdoses rose steeply during the "lockdowns," as did suicide rates among young people (Farah et al., 2023; Salai, 2023).

Isolating people is psychologically harmful, because it deprives them of the social interaction necessary for mental wellbeing: "Social intercourse, our continual contact with our colleagues, our work, the newspapers, voices, traffic, our loved ones and even those we don't like—all are daily nourishment for our senses and minds"; without them, one's "entire personality may change" (Meerloo, 1956, p. 78). The "lockdowns" resulted in a sharp decrease in social interaction, with predictable effects on the public's mental health. The UK Government knew in February 2021, for instance, that "Restrictions on socialising have had an adverse impact on people's wellbeing and mental health with nearly half of adults (49%) reporting boredom, loneliness, anxiety or stress arising due to the pandemic" (Cabinet Office, 2021). Regardless, the Government maintained the third national "lockdown" until July 19, 2021.

Isolation leads to introspection, which in turn can lead to delusion. For example, "Solitary confinement acts on most persons as a powerful stress. A person cut off from external stimuli turns his awareness inward and projects his unconscious outward"; this can result in "superstition, intense love of any other living thing, perceiving inanimate objects as alive, hallucinations, and delusions" (CIA, 1983, § K-6). Biderman's "Chart of Coercion" recommends methods that "foster introspection" (Amnesty International, 1973, p. 49). According to Meerloo (1956, p. 78), a person closed off from the outside world may find repressed memories and anxieties coming to the surface and assuming "gigantic proportions" as that person is unable to "evaluate or check his fantasies against the events of his ordinary days." In the "Covid-19" context, Schwab and Malleret write, "Existential crises like the pandemic confront us with our own fears and anxieties and afford great opportunities for introspection" (2020, p. 94). The pattern is, thus, quite deliberate, and designed to produce dissociation and psychosis.

Defamiliarisation

According to the *KUBARK Manual*, it is important to create a sense of radical defamiliarisation within the prisoner: "the circumstances of detention are arranged to enhance within the subject his feelings of being cut off from the known and the reassuring, and of being plunged into the strange" (CIA, 1963, § 86). This principle appears to be based on tactics deployed in communist and Nazi regimes:

> All of the victims of deliberate menticide – the P.O.W.'s in Korea, the imprisoned "traitors" to the dictatorial regimes of the Iron Curtain countries, the victims of the Nazi terror during the Second World War – are people whose ways of life had been suddenly and dramatically altered. They had been torn from their homes, their families, their friends, and thrown into a frightening, abnormal atmosphere [in which] breakdown is almost sure to follow. (Meerloo, 1956, pp. 4–73)

Ellul (1965, p. 311) remarks of Chinese brainwashing techniques: "The individual is cut off from everything, from his former social milieu, from news and information. This can be done only if he is placed in a prison cell or a camp. The individual is totally uprooted." The idea of "resettlement" in Tavistock counterinsurgency operations serves a similar purpose (Minnicino, 1974, p. 50).

Covid-era psychological warfare involved similar techniques of defamiliarisation, applied to entire societies. According to Schwab and Malleret (2020, p. 8), for instance, "the world as we knew it in the early months of 2020 is no more, dissolved in the context of the pandemic." The same tactic was used with "9/11," the shock of which "exploded 'the world that is familiar' and opened up a period of deep disorientation and regression that [was] expertly exploited" (Klein, 2007, p. 16). The idea is always the same: to create a moment of rupture in which "everything changes," such that all the old rules can be done away with and a new regime of control can be introduced. The shock of the "lockdowns" in March 2020 was a success in that respect: "Intricate webs of well-established projects and pastimes were suddenly suspended or lost. Work stopped or changed radically. Over the ensuing months, our everyday habits of life were replaced with something new and unfamiliar" (Kidd & Ratcliffe, 2020).

The change was encapsulated in the idea of the "new normal," which, in the "Covid-19" context, "relies essentially on the same principles and outcomes [as those described above] to induce disorientation and loss of cognitive function" (van der Pijl, 2022, p. 29). The WHO's Maria van Kerkhove explained in July 2020: "Our new normal includes physical distancing from others. Our new normal includes wearing masks where appropriate. Our new normal includes us knowing where this virus is each and every day, where we live, where we work, where we want to travel" ("What the New Normal looks like after Covid-19," 2020). In other words, the "new normal" reflects an alien, dehumanised biodigital surveillance state that only a shocked public would accept.

The mask mandates turned the social environment into something profoundly unfamiliar and disturbing, perhaps even resembling an LSD trip in keeping with some of the early MKULTRA experiments (McCoy, 2007, pp. 27–31, 46). If this sounds exaggerated, consider some accounts by those who have taken LSD. Alfred Hoffmann, who pioneered LSD in 1943, recounts: "the faces of those around me appeared as grotesque, colored masks" (cited in Campbell, 1971, p. 67). For others, "Other people's faces seem to have become changing masks [...] People's faces are grotesque" (cited in Dobkin de Rios & Janiger, 2003, p. 38). According to the Beatles' assistant Mal Evans, an LSD trip created the hallucination of "thousands and thousands of people all wearing masks" (in Grelsamer, 2010, p. 190). Another LSD account claims: "Faces turned into lurid masks" (Whitaker, 1969, p. 119). It does not seem to be uncommon for those tripping on LSD to see other people's faces as lurid and grotesque masks. Compare this to the grotesque, dehumanised, masked world of "Covid-19," as shown in the stunning photograph taken by Jose Carlos Fajardo, reproduced in Scott (2020). The "brave new normal," as Scott calls it, thus resembles an LSD trip.

Implanting Triggers

Pavlovian conditioning in the USSR worked to degrade language, such that words came to act as behavioural triggers, rather than as bearers of meaning. Losing their communicative function, words formed "slowly hypnotizing slogans" and worked as "commanding signs, triggering off reactions of fear and terror" (Meerloo, 1956, p. 136). Language in a totalitarian system is weaponised and used to control the population. Propaganda terms, repeated over and over, are used to trigger fear-based behaviour, train obedience, and cripple independent thinking.

The *Human Resource Exploitation Training Manual* states that the interrogatee "experiences a kind of psychological shock, which may only last briefly, but during which he is far more open to suggestion and far likelier to comply, than he was before he experienced the shock" (CIA, 1983, § J-2). It is at this moment of shock, with the victim's suggestibility heightened, that key triggers words, sounds, and images can be implanted. Once implanted, triggers can continue to trigger subconscious associations with the original trauma long after the event, perhaps even for decades (Lacter, 2007).

"9/11" is a trigger word designed to reactivate trauma, associated as it is with the emergency number 911 and the traumatic events of September 11, 2001. Key messages were implanted during the moment of shock. Fox News (2016), for example, pinned the blame on Osama bin Laden just 33 seconds after the South Tower was hit, a theme which talking heads on the day were quick to seize upon and implant in the minds of their shocked audience. Quoting Mao, Klein (2007, p. 16) argues that viewers' minds were turned into a blank slate by the shock—"a clean sheet of paper" on which "the newest and most beautiful words can be written," such as "clash of civilizations," "Axis of evil," "Islamo-fascism," and "homeland security." MKULTRA-style programming was thus applied via the media to entire populations. Other trigger words such as "terrorism," "bin Laden," "Al Qaeda," etc. were endlessly repeated by politicians and in the media, searing the new "reality" into the minds of the public.

When "Covid-19" hit and "lockdowns" were announced, complete with demands for "self-isolation," "social distancing," "contact tracing," a "new normal," etc. in the bid to "flatten the curve" and "stop the spread" of "SARS-CoV-2," an alien lexicon of trigger words was injected into everyday discourse at the moment of shock and would forever be subliminally associated with the original trauma. Their calculated repetition ad nauseam by mainstream journalists, politicians, and talking heads was just like after 9/11, etching trigger words (and images like the ubiquitous computer-generated simulation of the "SARS-CoV-2" virion) into public consciousness so that trauma-based mind control could be exercised (see Chapter 3).

Mass Psychosis

The last century has witnessed the development of ever more cunning, complex, and large-scale applications of shock and stress in order to induce maladaptive responses among populations, such as neurosis or psychosis, which create mass suggestibility to propaganda and official narratives without relying on methods of terror familiar from totalitarian regimes of old. Those methods, during the "Covid-19" operation, were geared to the mass administration of injections allegedly intended to deliver an "artificial shock" to the human body in the name of mounting an effective immune response (Broudy & Kyrie, 2021, p. 152).

According to Versluis (2006, p. 143), "the totalitarian systems of the twentieth century represent a kind of collective psychosis." Jung (1961, p. 212) describes the Hitler years as "the first outbreak of epidemic insanity," in which millions of people were "swept into the blood-drenched madness of a war of extermination. No one knew what was happening to [them], least of all the Germans, who allowed themselves to be driven to the slaughterhouse by their leading psychopaths like hypnotized sheep." This "mass psychosis," Jung (1961, p. 236) adds, was evident from the moment Hitler seized power, yet "I could not help telling myself that this was after all Germany, a civilized European nation with a sense of morality [...]."

The parallels between what Jung describes and life in the "civilized West" today are ominous. "Covid-19" was indeed an epidemic—an epidemic of insanity produced through all the deliberately absurd "measures" with which the public humiliatingly played along. Most of the population continues to get swept along, unaware, by propaganda for whatever the "current thing" is: support for Ukraine (despite political opposition being banned there [Rahman, 2022] and Nazi elements operating within the Armed Forces [News Wire, 2022]), reverence for the Royal Family (despite its dark history and proven close ties to Jimmy Savile and Jeffrey Epstein [Corbett, 2022]), the trans agenda (linked to the Tavistock Clinic), and so on. Today's "leading psychopaths" (Jung, 1961, p. 212) are apparently driving the "hypnotized sheep" wherever they like, and the last time this occurred it ended in the worst horrors of World War II.

Pace Desmet (2022), totalitarian mass psychosis does not arise organically or spontaneously out of the social environment (a similar mode of argument to that of Emery [1977, p. 67] and Trist [1997, p. 519] with respect to "social turbulence"). Rather, it is deliberately inculcated by the ruling class. The real lesson from Nazi Germany is that

> [m]ass delusion can be induced. It is simply a question of organizing and manipulating collective feelings in the proper way. If one can isolate the mass, allow no free thinking, no free exchanges, no outside corrective, and can hypnotize the group daily with noises, with press and radio and television, with fear and pseudo-enthusiasms, any delusion can be instilled. People will begin to accept the most primitive and inappropriate acts. (Meerloo, 1956, p. 157)

These techniques—isolation, monopolisation of perception, fear-mongering, etc.—were integral to the "lockdowns" and explain the willingness of the deluded masses to adopt the most primitive, inappropriate, and harmful of behaviours, such as mask wearing (see Chapter 3; Children's Health Defence [n.d.]) and neurotically avoiding other people.

When there is a "fear of daily existence," Meerloo (1956, p. 89) writes, "the mind can retreat into delusion" and "fantasy begins to prevail over reality, and soon assumes a validity which reality never had." In 2020, psychiatrist Mark McDonald correspondingly identified "a delusional psychosis that has taken over where people are [...] impervious to reason, to logic, to education at this point. They are psychotically managed by their fear" (in Tapscott, 2020). Those caught up in mass psychosis do not realise that they are, for "delusional thinking doesn't know the concept of delusional thinking" (Meerloo, 1956, p. 156). It was similarly observed with respect to "Covid-19" that "people generally find it very difficult to recognise the delusional nature of a totalitarian master narrative" (Scott, 2020) and "those suffering from a mass psychosis are unaware of what is occurring" (Academy of Ideas, 2021). This creates an extremely dangerous situation where large numbers of people—most of society, in fact—are unaware of how irrationally they are behaving and how thoroughly manipulated their thoughts and behaviours are.

Since 2020, "social turbulence" has intensified: the shocks are coming thicker and faster than ever before. First it was "Covid-19," a two-year psychological operation of unprecedented impact, complexity, and malice, keeping populations disoriented and demoralised. Around 16 months in, inflation began to soar, as was inevitable after historically unprecedented levels of quantitative easing in 2020 (cf. BlackRock, 2019), threatening hyperinflation, as was manufactured by the CIA in Chile in the 1970s to institute a new economic model (Klein, 2007, p. 7; see Chapter 8). Then came artificially manufactured energy shortages, not least owing to the US-led NATO sabotage of the Nord Stream pipeline (Ponton, 2023), recalling the artificially created oil shortages of 1973 (Marcus, 1974, p. 7). Widespread disruption to food security in the United States (Hoft, 2022), at a time when Bill Gates became the largest owner of farmland there (Shapiro, 2021), threatens to result in food shortages, an early Tavistock tactic (Minnicino, 1974, pp. 6–45, 52).

Some commentators, such as Adam Tooze, fear that the confluence of such crises is creating a "polycrisis" whose danger is greater than the sum of its parts, possibly threatening nuclear war (Mercola, 2022). Seen through the lens of "social turbulence," however, this seems unlikely, given that the whole point is to keep the population shocked, suggestible, and thereby herdable. The transition to technocracy must be managed, and the demolition of liberal democracy must be controlled. Things must not be allowed to spin out of control, although it helps with the production of stress and anxiety (see Chapter 4) if the population thinks that chaos could ensue at any moment.

The effects of shock do wear off, however. The rapid-fire sequence of shocks since 2020 may itself be a sign that the population is starting to develop immunity to shock and stress tactics as more and more people come to recognise them for what they are. It is also possible that too many shocks will cease to be shocking. If so, then the would-be global technocrats may have no choice but to resort to old-fashioned terror tactics (secret police, round-ups, massacres of dissidents, concentration camps, etc.). The warning signs are already present, with a wide variety of measures, some of them harsh, having been used to silence dissent against the "Covid-19" narrative (Liester, 2022; Doctors For Covid Ethics, 2023). Against an enlightened and restive global population that wants no repeat of the worst horrors of the twentieth century, however, such a move could prove fatal unless a revolution in warfare can give the transnational ruling class the decisive advantage (see Chapter 8).

References

Academy of Ideas. (2021, April 24). *The manufacturing of a mass psychosis—can sanity return to an insane world?* https://academyofideas.com/2021/04/manufacturing-of-a-mass-psychosis-can-sanity-return-to-an-insane-world/.

Agamben, G. (2021). *Where are we now?* Rowman and Littlefield.

Alkon, P. H. (2006). *Winston Churchill's imagination*. Bucknell University Press.

Amnesty International. (1973). *Report on torture*. Duckworth.

Anthony, J., & Cullen, D. (2021, January 6). Breaking the Covid trance: How the Irish people were psychologically manipulated [Speech transcript]. *UK Column*. https://www.ukcolumn.org/article/breaking-covid-trance-how-irish-people-were-psychologically-manipulated.

Arendt, H. (1962). *The origins of totalitarianism*. The World Publishing Company.

BlackRock. (2019, August 15). *Dealing with the next downturn*. https://www.blackrock.com/corporate/insights/blackrock-investment-institute/publications/global-macro-outlook/august-2019.

Broudy, D., & Arakaki, M. (2020). Who wants to be a slave? The technocratic convergence of humans and data. *Frontiers in Communication, 5*(37), 1–9. https://doi.org/10.3389/fcomm.2020.00037.

Broudy, D., & Kyrie, V. (2021). Syllogistic reasoning demystifies evidence of Covid-19 vaccine constituents. *International Journal of Vaccine Theory, Research, and Practice, 2*(1), 149–171. https://doi.org/10.56098/ijvtpr.v2i1.32.

Cabinet Office. (2021, February 22). *Covid-19 response—spring 2021*. https://www.gov.uk/government/publications/covid-19-response-spring-2021/covid-19-response-spring-2021.

Campbell, R. (1971). The chemistry of madness. *LIFE Magazine, 71*(22), 68–86.

Camus, A. (1947). *La Peste*. Gallimard.

Central Intelligence Agency. (1963). *KUBARK counterintelligence interrogation*. https://nsarchive2.gwu.edu/NSAEBB/NSAEBB27/docs/doc01.pdf.

Central Intelligence Agency. (1983). *Human resource exploitation training manual*. https://nsarchive2.gwu.edu/NSAEBB/NSAEBB122/#hre.

Chaplin, P. (2020). Lockdown Boris violated SAGE advice. *Paul Chaplin*. https://www.paulchaplin.life/blog-original/lockdown-boris-violated-sage-advice.

Child, D. (2020). Boris Johnson's dad Stanley refuses to rule out pub visit despite government advice. *Evening Standard*. https://www.standard.co.uk/news/uk/boris-johnson-dad-stanley-coronarvirus-pub-a4389601.html.

Children's Health Defence. (n.d.). *The science of masks*. https://childrenshealthdefense.org/the-science-of-masks/.

Chomsky, N. (2015, April 15). We're facing a new Cold War. *Salon*. https://www.salon.com/2015/04/15/noam_chomsky_were_facing_a_new_cold_war_partner/.

Corbett, J. (2022, September 11). The dark history of the Royals. *The Corbett Report*. https://www.corbettreport.com/the-dark-history-of-the-royals/.

Cyrulik, J. C. (1999). Asymmetric Warfare and the threat to the American homeland. *Association of the United States Army Landpower Essay Series*, *99*(8), 1–12. https://www.ausa.org/sites/default/files/LPE-99-8-Asymmetric-Warfare-and-the-Threat-to-the-American-Homeland.pdf.

Davis, I. (2018, May 12). Operation Gladio—hard evidence of government sponsored false flag terrorism. *Iain Davis*. https://iaindavis.com/operation-gladio-false-flag-evidence/.

de Lint, W. B. (2021). *Blurring intelligence crime: A critical forensics*. Springer.

Desmet, M. (2022). *The psychology of totalitarianism*. Chelsea Green Publishing.

Digital Citizen. (2003, September 25). 9/11 official theory. Are you brainwashed? *Phil Taylor's Papers*. https://universityofleeds.github.io/philtaylorpapers/vp01eff8.html.

Dobkin de Rios, M., & Janiger, O. (2003). *LSD spirituality and the creative process*. Park Street Press.

Doctors For Covid Ethics. (2023, January). *D4CE 5th symposium—session IV understanding tactics of oppression*. https://doctors4covidethics.org/session-iv-understanding-tactics-of-oppression-2/.

Dulles, A. (1953). How the communists "wash brains." *United States Army Combat Forces Journal*, July: 20–21.

Ellul, J. (1965). *Propaganda: The formation of men's attitudes*. Knopf.

Emery, F. (1977). *Futures we are in*. Martinus Nijhoff.

Emery, F., & Emery, M. (1976). *A choice of futures*. Martinus Nijhoff.

Engdahl, F.W. (2004). *A century of war. Anglo-American oil politics and the new world order* (2nd ed.). Pluto Press.

Farah, R., Rege, S. V., Cole, R. J., & Holstege, C. P. (2023). Suspected suicide attempts by self-poisoning among persons aged 10–19 years during the Covid-19 pandemic—United States, 2020–2022. *MMWR Morbidity and Mortality Weekly Report*, *72*(6), 426–430. https://doi.org/10.15585/mmwr.mm7216a3.

Ferguson, N. M, Laydon, D., Nedjati-Gilani, G., Imai, N., Ainslie, K., Baguelin, M., Bhatia, S., Boonyasiri, A., Cucunubá, Z., Cuomo-Dannenburg, G., Dighe, A., Dorigatti, I., Fu, H., Gaythorpe, K., Green, W., Hamlet, A., Hinsley, W., Okell, L. C., van Elsland, S., Ghani, A. C., et al. (2020). *Report 9: Impact of non-pharmaceutical interventions (NPIs) to reduce Covid-19 mortality and healthcare demand*. https://www.imperial.ac.uk/media/imperial-college/medicine/sph/ide/gida-fellowships/Imperial-College-COVID19-NPI-modelling-16-03-2020.pdf.

Fox News. (2016, March 17). *Original news broadcast on 9/11/01* [Video]. https://www.foxnews.com/video/1153066443001#sp=show-clips.
Fromm, E. (1960). *Fear of freedom*. Routledge and Kegan Paul.
Gates, B., & Gates, M. (2021, January 27). The year global health went local. *GatesNotes*. https://www.gatesnotes.com/2021-Annual-Letter.
Glick, B. (1989). *War at home: Covert action against U.S. activists and what we can do about it*. South End Press.
Grelsamer, R. P. (2010). *Into the sky with diamonds*. Authorhouse.
Hitler, A. (1939). *Mein Kampf* (Trans. James Murphy). Hurst and Blackett.
Hoft, J. (2022, June 23). Interactive map details destruction of numerous U.S. food manufacturing plants, grocery stores, etc.—compares U.S. incidents to global trends. *Gateway Pundit*. https://www.thegatewaypundit.com/2022/06/interactive-map-details-destruction-numerous-us-food-manufacturing-plants-compares-us-incidents-global-trends/.
Hughes, D.A. (2022, July 29). Wall street, the Nazis, and the crimes of the deep state. *Propaganda in Focus*. https://propagandainfocus.com/wall-street-the-nazis-and-the-crimes-of-the-deep-state/.
Huxley, A. (1954). *Doors of perception*. Harper and Row.
Huxley, A. (1956). *Brave new world*. The Modern Library.
Huxley, A. (1958). *Brave new world revisited*. Harper and Row.
Jung, C. G. (1961). *Collected works, volume X: Civilization in transition* (H. Read, Ed., R.F.C. Hull, Trans., 2nd ed.). Routledge.
Kidd, I. J., & Ratcliffe, M. (2020, November). Welcome to Covidworld. *The Critic*. https://thecritic.co.uk/issues/november-2020/welcome-to-covidworld/.
Klein, N. (2007). *The shock doctrine*. Metropolitan Books.
Klein, N. (2017). *No is not enough*. Knopf.
Kyrie, V., & Broudy, D. (2022, September 22). The Covid-19 concoction: A recipe for successful psychological operations. *Propaganda in Focus*. https://propagandainfocus.com/the-covid-19-concoction-a-recipe-for-successful-psychological-operations/.
Lacter, E. P. (2007, June 29). Relationships between mind control programming and ritual abuse. *End Ritual Abuse*. http://www.whale.to/b/lacter2.html.
Liester, M. B. (2022). The suppression of dissent during the Covid-19 pandemic. *Social Epistemology Review and Reply Collective, 11*(4), 53–76. https://wp.me/p1Bfg0-6Jw.
Marcus, L. (1974). The real CIA—the Rockefellers' fascist establishment, a polemic. *The Campaigner, 7*(6), 5–34.
McCoy, A. (2007). *A question of torture: CIA interrogation, from the Cold War to the War on Terror*. Henry Holt and Company.
Meerloo, J. A. (1956). *The rape of the mind. The psychology of thought control, menticide, and brainwashing*. World Publishing Company.

Mercola, J. (2022, July 14). "Polycrisis of doom": Technocracy's mother of all wars to conquer the world. *Technocracy News*. https://www.technocracy.news/polycrisis-of-doom-technocracys-mother-of-all-wars-to-conquer-the-world/.

Minnicino, M. (1974). Low intensity operations: The Reesian theory of war. *The Campaigner, 7*(6), 37–55.

News Wire. (2022, June 1). Ukraine's Azov battalion removes Nazi insignias in effort to rescue damaged reputation. *21st Century Wire*. https://21stcenturywire.com/2022/06/01/ukraines-azov-battalion-removes-nazi-insignias-in-effort-to-rescue-damaged-reputation/.

Ogden, R. (2020, December 28). A year of blursdays: How coronavirus distorted our sense of time in 2020. *The Conversation*. https://theconversation.com/a-year-of-blursdays-how-coronavirus-distorted-our-sense-of-time-in-2020-151512.

Orwell, G. (1984). *Nineteen eighty-four*. Oxford University Press.

Pijl, K. van der. (2022). *States of emergency. Keeping the global population in check*. Clarity Press.

Ponton, F. (2023, May 3). Part 2—smoking guns: Nord Stream sabotage 'secret teams' revealed. *21st Century Wire*. https://21stcenturywire.com/2023/05/03/part-2-smoking-guns-nord-stream-sabotage-secret-teams-revealed/.

Prime Minister's Office. (2020a, June 23). *Prime Minister's statement on coronavirus (Covid-19): 23 June 2020*. https://www.gov.uk/government/speeches/prime-ministers-statement-to-the-house-on-covid-19-23-june-2020.

Prime Minister's Office. (2020b, October 31). *Prime Minister's statement on coronavirus (Covid-19): 31 October 2020*. https://www.gov.uk/government/speeches/prime-ministers-statement-on-coronavirus-covid-19-31-october-2020.

Rahman, A. (2022, March 24). Opposition political parties banned in Ukraine and "unified information policy" imposed. *Monthly Review*. https://mronline.org/2022/03/24/opposition-political-parties-banned-in-ukraine-and-unified-information-policy-imposed/.

Ravenhill, J. (2020). *Global political economy*. Oxford University Press.

Rees, J. R. (1945). *The shaping of psychiatry by war*. W.W. Norton and Company.

Rockefeller Foundation and Global Business Network. (2010, May). *Scenarios for the future of technology and international development*. https://archive.org/details/scenarios-for-the-future-of-technology-and-international-development-rockefeller-foundation-2010.

Salai, S. (2023, April 28). Covid report finds suicide calls, overdose deaths and mental illness soared in D.C. *Washington Times*. https://www.washingtontimes.com/news/2023/apr/28/covid-report-finds-suicide-calls-overdose-deaths-a/.

Sargant, W. W. (1997). *Battle for the mind*. Malor.

Schlesinger, Jr., A.M. (1965). *A thousand days: John F. Kennedy in the White House*. Houghton Mifflin Company.

Schwab, K., & Malleret, T. (2020). *Covid 19: The Great Reset*. World Economic Forum.

Scott, B. (2020, October 23). The cult of the brave new normal. *OffGuardian*. https://off-guardian.org/2020/10/23/the-cult-of-the-brave-new-normal/.

Scott, P. D. (2003). *Drugs, oil, and war: The United States in Afghanistan, Colombia, and Indochina*. Rowman and Littlefield.

Scott, P. D., & Marshall, J. (1991). *Cocaine politics: Drugs, armies, and the CIA in Central America*. University of California Press.

Shapiro, A. (2021, January 14). America's biggest owner of farmland is now Bill Gates. *Forbes*. https://www.forbes.com/sites/arielshapiro/2021/01/14/americas-biggest-owner-of-farmland-is-now-bill-gates-bezos-turner/.

Stewart, H., & Busby, M. (2020, March 13). Coronavirus: Science chief defends UK plan from criticism. *The Guardian*. https://www.theguardian.com/world/2020/mar/13/coronavirus-science-chief-defends-uk-measures-criticism-herd-immunity.

Strange, S. (1997). *Casino capitalism*. Manchester University Press.

Tapscott, M. (2020, December 2). Americans are suffering "delusional psychosis" about CCP virus, psychiatrist claims. *The Epoch Times*. https://www.theepochtimes.com/california-psychiatrist-claims-americans-are-suffering-a-delusional-psychosis-about-ccp-virus_3601044.html.

Toffler, A. (1970). *Future shock*. Bantam Books.

Trist, E. (1997). The environment and system response capability: A futures perspective. In E. Trist, F. Emery, & H. Murray (Eds.) *The social engagement of social science. A Tavistock anthology* (pp. 517–535). University of Pennsylvania Press.

Tunander, O. (2016). Dual state: The case of Sweden. In E. Wilson (Ed.), *The dual state: Parapolitics, Carl Schmitt, and the national security Complex* (pp. 171–192). Routledge.

Ullman, H., Wade Jr. J., Edney, L.A., Franks Jr., F., Horner, C., Howe, J., & Brendley, K. (1996). *Shock and awe: Achieving rapid dominance*. The National Defence University.

Valentine, D. (2017). *The CIA as organized crime*. Clarity Press.

Versluis, A. (2006). *The new inquisitions: Heretic-hunting and the intellectual origins of modern totalitarianism*. Oxford University Press.

What the New Normal looks like after Covid-19. (2020, July 28). *Bloomberg*. https://www.bloomberg.com/news/videos/2020-07-28/what-the-new-normal-looks-like-after-covid-19-video.

Whitaker, R. (1969). *Drugs and the law: The Canadian scene*. Methuen.

Wolfe, L. (1996a). The Tavistock roots of the "Aquarian conspiracy." *EIR, 23*(3), 23–27.

Wolfe, L. (1996b). Tavistock's imperial brainwashing project. *EIR, 23*(22), 24–29.

Wolin, S. S. (2008). *Democracy incorporated*. Princeton University Press.

Wood, P. (2018). *Technocracy: The hard road to world order*. Coherent Publishing.

World Health Organisation. (2019). *Non-pharmaceutical public health measures for mitigating the risk and impact of epidemic and pandemic influenza*. https://apps.who.int/iris/bitstream/handle/10665/329438/9789241516839-eng.pdf?ua=1.

Zimbardo, P. (2005). Mind control in Orwell's *Nineteen eighty-four*: Fictional concepts become operational realities in Jim Jones's jungle experiment. In A. Gleason, J. Goldsmith, & M. C. Nussbaum (Eds.), *On Nineteen eighty-four: Orwell and our future* (pp. 127–154). Princeton University Press.

CHAPTER 3

Trauma-based Mind Control

Increasing evidence has come to light of trauma-based mind control exercises performed on children in ritual abuse settings. Those exercises involve torture, near death experiences, and making victims feel responsible for the death of others. The traumatised child is made to feel completely powerless and dependent on the abuser for their survival. Highly disturbingly, similar techniques—involving psychological torture, intentional traumatisation, and false rescue—were carried out against the public during "Covid-19." Psychological torture techniques include the inculcation of chronic stress and the mandatory wearing of face masks (originally deployed against inmates at Guantánamo Bay). The public was traumatised by fear of death from the "virus" and was made to feel responsible for the deaths of others. A trauma bonding was instigated, intended to last decades and to bind an infantilised population in loyalty and obedience to its "omnipotent" masters. Predatory transnational power came to the false rescue in exchange for the surrendering of liberties.

The Franklin Scandal, Project Monarch, The Finders, and Satanic Ritual Abuse

The 1988 Franklin Scandal centred on a suspected child-trafficking ring in Omaha, Nebraska, which was accused of providing children to politicians in Washington, D.C. At the heart of the scandal was Lawrence E.

D. A. Hughes, *"Covid-19," Psychological Operations, and the War for Technocracy*, https://doi.org/10.1007/978-3-031-41850-1_3

King Jr., who appears to have had ties to the CIA through his arms and money transfers to Nicaragua during Iran-Contra (Vos, 2019). No one was prosecuted, however, apart from alleged victims. Alisha Owens, for example, was held in solitary confinement longer than any other person in Nebraskan history after telling her story. Paul Bonacci was prosecuted for perjury after claiming that King had sexually abused him as a minor, but in 1999 was awarded $1 million in damages.

In February 1993, Bonacci referenced Project Monarch in a video interview with Ted Gunderson, the former head of the Los Angeles FBI (Alexander, 1997). Project Monarch is an alleged spin-off from MKULTRA involving the torture, sexual abuse, and ritual murder of children for mind control purposes. When Anton Chaitkin asked former CIA Director William Colby in December 1993 "What about Monarch?" Colby is said to have replied angrily: "We stopped that between the late 1960s and the early 1970s" (cited in Alexander, 1997).

In no publicly available official document is there any mention of Project Monarch, meaning either that it never existed or that it is top secret. The U.S. Senate Select Committee on Intelligence report on MKULTRA (1977), for example, which only came about thanks to the investigative work of John Marks in exposing the existence of MKULTRA, makes no mention of Project Monarch. For critics such as Barkun (2003, p. 76), this is evidence of "the extension of the mind-control literature into areas for which there is no substantiation," giving rise to a genre of evidence-free "self-described victims," from alleged Monarch victims to victims of UFO abductions (which also feature claims of sexual abuse). Thomas (2007, p. 22), on the other hand, claims that the Senate Committee "focused on only the tip of the iceberg and the victims have been intimidated into silence and still suffer in the shadows even today." The CIA supposedly destroyed its files on MKULTRA and similar programmes following the Senate Committee report, yet it is widely suspected that these or similar classified programmes "continued on, quietly" (Phelan, 2020). This is probable given that the CIA has always operated beyond any meaningful scrutiny or oversight (Valentine, 2017). Thus, Monarch could have been a classified successor of MKULTRA, but the evidence is inconclusive.

The Finders is an organisation suspected of child sex trafficking, brain-washing, and blood rituals in Washington D.C., raising further suspicions of intelligence operations involving the sexual blackmail of politicians, as well as gruesome mind control experiments carried out on children

(Broze, 2019; Vos, 2019, 2021). Gunderson (cited in Alexander, 1997) describes The Finders as a CIA front set up in the 1960s to kidnap and torture-programme young children through "satanic sex orgies and bloody rituals as well as the murders of other children and slaughter of animals." The Finders' leader, Marion Pettie, was obsessed with the CIA, for whom his wife worked between 1957 and 1961 (Broze, 2019).

In 1993, the FBI, having dropped an initial investigation in 1987, launched an investigation into allegations of CIA involvement in The Finders. No one was ever prosecuted, and nothing came of the 1993 investigation apart from 324 heavily redacted pages (FBI, n.d.) released a few months after Jeffrey Epstein's death in October 2019, apparently intended to assuage public suspicion regarding intelligence agencies' use of children in sexual blackmail operations.

Though the details are sketchy, the above evidence offers some reason to suspect that horrific crimes against children, including torture, rape, and murder, may have been committed for purposes of political blackmail and pushing the limits of mind control experiments. Linked to this possibility are widespread claims of satanic ritual abuse (SRA) arising from the 1980s on. Thomas (2007, p. 52) describes SRA victims as "victims of MKULTRA experiments in childhood," noting that thousands of unrelated people from across the United States had all come forward with "essentially the same story [...] that as very young children these people were forced to participate in SRA, including child rape and ritual sacrifice." Lacter (2007) regretfully concludes, based on her professional experience of dealing with child abuse survivors, that "sophisticated abuser groups within the United States of America are using torture to install complex mind control programming in our children in order to further their own political or religious agendas."

As evidence of ritual abuse began to emerge in the late 1980s and 1990s, those alleging it were fiercely closed down. For example, the False Memory Syndrome Foundation, staffed with psychiatrists linked to CIA mind control projects, was created in 1992 "to deny the existence of cult mind control and child abuse" (Thomas, 2007, p. 52). The "satanic panic" was coined to make allegations of satanic ritual abuse appear attributable to mass hysteria on the part of evangelical Christians. The nonprofit Cult Awareness Network (CAN) was financially ruined by $5.2 million of lawsuits filed against it, and in 1996, "Scientology lawyers took possession of 20 years' worth of CAN's highly sensitive case files containing information on thousands of people who had turned to CAN for help in rescuing their friends and relatives"—Scientology being known for its litigious nature (Thomas, 2007, p. 51). The ferocity of the response to SRA claims only lends credence to them, however, ties between SRA and the CIA remain unexplored (Vos, 2021).

We should be cognisant of the "vast uptick in diagnoses" of Dissociative Identity Disorder (previously known as Multiple Personality Disorder) from 1980 on (Tracy, 2022). As per the American Psychiatric Association's *DSM-IV* (1994, p. 230), these involve "two or more distinct identities or personality states [...] recurrently tak[ing] control of the person's behavior", involving an "inability to recall important personal information that is too extensive to be explained by ordinary forgetfulness" or intoxication. According to one child psychiatrist,

> These distinct personalities or "alters" can have different characteristics, ages, genders, and names. Often at least one of them tends to encourage the individual to do "bad things" to themselves or others. DID is generally thought to develop among people who have been exposed to high levels of trauma and abuse where the dissociation and formation of other personalities forms as a defense against experiences that are too emotionally volatile to process directly. Many individuals with DID are known to be fairly susceptible to being hypnotized. (Rettew, 2022)

This clinical description is consistent with the alleged effects of mind control experiments in which perpetrators "systematically torture their victims for the intended purpose of coercing their victims' psyches into forming new dissociated self-states that they then work to exploit" via "hypnosis and behavioral conditioning" (Lacter, 2007). Did the sudden unexplained rise of DID create fertile ground for such claims, or were covert CIA "experiments," conducted on a mass scale, in particular through cults, a driver of the disorder?

Though the evidence is tentative, understanding the potential involvement of the CIA in the Franklin Scandal, Project Monarch, The Finders, and SRA claims is important when it comes to making sense of some of the darkest aspects of the "Covid-19" operation, which have to do with perceived near death experiences, making people feel responsible for the death of others, and false rescue of an infantilised population by seemingly "omnipotent" authorities. Even if some of the above material is, by design, hard to prove, a plausible pattern of abuse emerges, and is disturbingly consistent with the abuse meted out against the populations of many countries since 2020.

Torture

Psychological Torture

The "Covid-19" operation was in part based on techniques learned through CIA experimentation in torture, though the link is "at first sight far from from self-evident" (van der Pijl, 2022, p. 27). This is because torture has, for most of human history, been associated with *physical* means of coercion, e.g. to make the victim divulge information, confess to a heresy or crime, recant one's views, etc. Yet, as the ancient Roman jurist Ulpian understood, this form of torture proves remarkably ineffective for extracting reliable information: the strong will resist, while the weak will say anything to make it stop (McCoy, 2007, p. 207).

According to Kleinman (2006, p. 130), writing in a National Defence Intelligence College publication, "the scientific community has never established that coercive interrogation methods are an effective means of obtaining reliable intelligence information." In the "War on Terror," the purpose of physical torture seems, rather, to have been to extract *unreliable* information (Corbett, 2022). The footnotes to the *9/11 Commission Report*, for instance, contain no fewer than 211 references to "interrogation of KSM [Khalid Sheikh Mohammed]."

CIA torture techniques codified in manuals used to train authoritarian regimes in "interrogation" techniques largely dispense with the need for physical/pharmacological methods and favour psychological means instead, not least because they leave no physical traces (CIA, 1983). Psychological torture, according to Meerloo (1956, p. 27), "can often be more painful and mentally more paralyzing than the rack," even though it is deemed "more acceptable."

"From Chile to China to Iraq," writes Klein (2007, pp. 15–16), "torture has been a silent partner in the global free-market crusade. But torture is more than a tool used to enforce unwanted policies on rebellious peoples; it is also a metaphor of the shock doctrine's underlying logic." This is because the shock doctrine "attempt[s] to achieve on a mass scale what torture does one on one in the interrogation cell," i.e. break victims' will to resist. The shock doctrine can thus be understood as a form of psychological torture inflicted across entire societies.

Once it is understood that a psychological warfare operation was deployed in 2020 to shock the world's population into submitting to tyrannical measures which it would otherwise not accept, drawing in the process on CIA torture techniques specifically developed to break the human will, and that "torture implies *a systemic activity with a rational purpose*" (Amnesty International, 1973, p. 30), the true horror of what has taken place begins to fall into sharper relief.

Chronic Stress

The 1973 Amnesty International report on torture identifies three types of stress induced by "successful" torture: acute, sub-acute, and chronic. Acute stress is characterised by "shock response, sudden reflex, fight or flight" and corresponds to "capture in war" (Amnesty International, 1973, p. 35). Acute stress is not necessarily a bad thing: it represents a short-term adaptive reaction to challenges and forms "part of the survival mechanism," potentially enhancing the immune response (Rancourt et al., 2021, p. 133). In the "Covid-19" context, acute stress was triggered by the shock of the "lockdowns," a form of capture that necessitated dramatic adaptations to most people's way of life. It is revealing that Schwab and Malleret, writing in June 2020, refer to the "lockdowns" as "the period of acute stress" (2020, p. 159).

The sub-acute phase sets in when acute stress dies down and a new "medium term" phase begins, characterised by an "anxiety response while maintaining morale and personal integrity; a 'fighting posture' is retained" (Amnesty International, 1973, pp. 35–40). Ominously, however, "the aim of the torturer/interrogator" is to "erode that morale by destroying whatever props the individual has for his mental integrity." The aim is to induce what Meerloo (1956, p. 75) calls "the moment of sudden surrender," "when the victim, psychologically worn out, involuntarily surrenders to the captor: 'All right, all right, you can have anything you want.'" Or to quote Huxley (1958, p. 59): "If the stress to which he is subjected is sufficiently intense or sufficiently prolonged, he will end by breaking down as abjectly and as completely as the weakest of his kind."

Chronic or long-term stress is maladaptive and has detrimental effects on both physical and mental health; it "harms immune response" (Rancourt et al., 2021, p. 13). It can induce physical disease, from "illnesses like bronchopneumonia, to psychosomatic diseases such as duodenal ulcers, asthma and bronchitis, to coronary disease, T.B., and even to cancer" (Amnesty International, 1973, pp. 35–45). Psychologically, it can lead to a "continuous state of anxiety, depression, suicidal ideation, dissociation, derealization, and regression" and is ultimately what "the torturer seeks to orchestrate." Taken too far, "thought processes, bodily desires and functions become retarded" and a "fugue" state can set in, whereby the prisoner "appears to 'switch off' all awareness, looks bland and untroubled, exhibits no response to pain." This is consistent with the CIA "interrogation" manuals: "If the debility-dependency-dread state is unduly prolonged, the subject may sink into a defensive apathy from which it is hard to arouse him" (CIA, 1983, § K-3). The challenge, therefore, is to use chronic stress to induce states that allow for maximum psychological manipulation, but without going so far that the victim "switches off."

Rancourt et al. (2021, pp. 134–137) find that all-cause mortality data from the United States for 2020/21 is inconsistent with a viral "pandemic" (because of jurisdictional heterogeneity; see Chap. 6), yet wholly consistent with the chronic stress generated by the enormous socio-economic disruptions brought about through Covid policy, which disproportionately impacted those at the bottom of the "societal dominance hierarchy" with the fewest means to adapt, suppressing their immune systems. In effect, the state had "recreated the conditions that produced the horrendous bacterial pneumonia epidemic of 1918"—in other words, wartime conditions: the scale of socio-economic disruption seen under "Covid-19" has only ever been witnessed in times of war. It was known *before* the "lockdowns" that quarantining individuals leads to "post-traumatic stress symptoms, confusion, and anger" (Brooks et al., 2020), and so it proved with the catastrophic impact of the "lockdowns" on the public's mental health (see Chap. 5).

Rancourt et al., (2021, pp. 121, 135–7) go further by claiming that there was, in fact, a bacterial pneumonia epidemic in the United States in 2020/21, as there was in 1918–1920, to which most "Covid-19" deaths were misattributed. They note that antibiotic prescriptions which might have treated bacterial pneumonia fell by half in March/April 2020. This is particularly suspicious given the remarkable "similarity in state-wise distributions of life expectancy at birth [...] and antibiotic prescriptions" that would automatically point towards the wisdom of maintaining antibiotic availability, regardless of "Covid-19" (Rancourt et al., 2021, p. 131). Safe and effective therapeutic agents such as hydroxychloroquine and ivermectin were deliberately suppressed, creating comparable conditions to

1918–20, when antibiotics had not yet been discovered (Rancourt et al., 2021, pp. 136–7).

These facts lead to troubling questions about intent and possible democide, and Rancourt et al. (2021, p. 132) are clear that "aggressive government and medical response to the WHO 11 March 2020 declaration of a pandemic"—and not the virus—was responsible for most of the deaths during the so-called "first wave." Moreover, further unexpected upsurges in all-cause mortality in the United States—during the summer of 2020, winter 2020/21, and the summer of 2021—also reflect "deaths induced by the government measures, via the combined poverty, obesity and climatic factors, made potent by sustained chronic psychological stress" (Rancourt et al. 2021, p. 115).

On this evidence, chronic stress, a deliberate aim of psychological torture, was intentionally induced through "Covid-19" menticide, and large numbers of people have lost their lives or become seriously ill as a result.

Simple Techniques to Disturb Mental Equilibrium

In 1954, McGill's Donald O. Hebb and Woodburn Heron paid male college students twice the daily average wage to lie on a soft bed in a sensory deprivation cubicle, with light diffused by translucent goggles, auditory stimulation limited by soundproofing, and tactical perception impeded by thick gloves and a U-shaped foam pillow. A *Time* article on the experiment notes of the participants: "little by little their brains go dead or slip out of control," leading to intense hallucinations ("Science: Twilight of the Brain," 1954) and, in Hebb's words, "the breakdown of the organized activity of complex central processes" in the brain (cited in McCoy, 2007, p. 41). The experiment revealed "a human mental equilibrium so delicate that just a few simple tools—goggles, gloves, and a foam pillow—could induce a state akin to acute psychosis in many subjects within just forty-eight hours" (McCoy, 2007, p. 37).

Seizing on the McGill findings, Morse Allen, who headed the CIA's Project ARTICHOKE, oversaw an experiment in March 1955, in which an army volunteer was put inside a sensory deprivation box. After 40 hours, the volunteer began "an hour of crying loudly and sobbing in a most heartrending fashion" in Allen's words, before kicking his way out. When Allen told brain surgeon Maitland Baldwin about this, Baldwin was persuaded that "the isolation technique could break any man, no matter how intelligent" (cited in McCoy, 2007, p. 38). Harvard psychiatrists conducting similar experiments in 1957 using a water tank and a hood instead of a box concluded that "sensory deprivation can produce major mental and behavioral changes in man" (cited in McCoy, 2007, p. 40).

These experimental findings were appropriated by the CIA for "interrogation" purposes. The *KUBARK Manual* summarises them as follows:

> (1) the deprivation of sensory stimuli induces stress; (2) the stress becomes unbearable for most subjects; (3) the subject has a growing need for physical and social stimuli; and (4) some subjects progressively lose touch with reality, focus inwardly, and produce delusions, hallucinations, and other pathological effects (CIA, 1963, p. 89).

A hand-edited version of this passage in the *Human Resource Exploitation Training Manual*, includes the line "Extreme deprivation of sensory stimuli induces unbearable stress and anxiety and is a form of torture" (CIA, 1983, § K-7).

In addition to sensory deprivation, self-inflicted pain proved crucial to CIA torture techniques. Self-inflicted pain "causes victims to feel responsible for their suffering and thus capitulate more readily to their torturers" (McCoy, 2007, p. 8). Such techniques are evident in the infamous 2003 photograph from Abu Ghraib prison in which a hooded Iraqi on a box stands with arms outstretched, wires attached: lowering the arms results in electro-shock (self-inflicted pain) while the hood induces sensory deprivation (McCoy, 2007, p. 8). At the same prison, U.S. military police paraded Iraqi prisoners naked with plastic sandbags over their heads, thus "combining psychological humiliation with the pain of restricted breathing" (McCoy, 2007, p. 59)—two additional elements of effective torture.

In January 2002, images emerged from Guantánamo Bay of caged prisoners wearing blackout goggles, gloves, thick caps, and industrial earmuffs, kneeling with hands and feet bound, heads bowed in a stress position, facing outwards towards the edge of the cage (Dyer, 2002; cf. "Open letter from former Guantánamo prisoners," 2013). As the *Guardian* notes, "Early photographs [from the McGill experiment] show volunteers, goggled and muffled, looking eerily similar to prisoners arriving at Guantánamo" ("Nobody is talking," 2005). The goggles, gloves, caps, and earmuffs at Guantánamo Bay, a torture facility, were obviously intended as means of torture. Duncan Forrest of the International Committee of the Red Cross claimed that the sensory deprivation was "bordering on torture" and "could cause immediate and lasting psychological symptoms akin to post-traumatic stress disorder if it lasted more than about 20 hours" (cited in Dyer, 2002). Being made to kneel in a stress position also fits the CIA's concept of "self-inflicted" pain: presumably, the inmates fear being beaten if they move.

Face Masks as Instruments of Psychological Torture

Extremely disturbing about the images from Guantánamo Bay, for our purposes, is that the inmates are all wearing blue surgical face masks. In one image from Amnesty International (2020), goggles, gloves, caps, and earmuffs are not being worn but face masks are. It seems difficult to escape the conclusion that the mandatory wearing of such masks has something to do with psychological torture. Certainly, face masks restrict breathing, and they are psychologically humiliating, insofar as they make the wearer look ridiculous/grotesque (Potts, 2020), serve no useful purpose (Jefferson et al., 2023; Children's Health Defence, n.d.), resemble muzzles (Hitchens, 2020), and are associated with slavery (Stephens Nuwer, 2016, p. 145; Strongman, 2021), servitude (Greenwald, 2021), and sadomasochism (Needham, 2014). The face masks at Guantánamo Bay may also be another form of self-inflicted pain, with inmates too frightened to pull them down for fear of punishment.

According to the *KUBARK Manual*, "whereas pain inflicted on a person from outside himself may actually focus or intensify his will to resist, his resistance is likelier to be sapped by pain which he seems to inflict upon himself" (CIA, 1963, p. 94). For example, ordering a prisoner to stand to attention or sit on a stool for a prolonged period may be more effective than a beating, because if the prisoner complies with the order,

> His conflict is then an internal struggle. As long as he maintains this position, he is attributing to the [captor] the ability to do something worse, but there is never a showdown where the [captor] demonstrates this ability. After a period of time, the subject may exhaust his internal motivational strength. (CIA, 1983, § K-10)

Wearing a face mask on command is a seemingly innocuous act, like being told to stand or sit for an extended period of time. Seldom does it come to a "showdown" where a person is physically compelled to wear a mask; most people *consent* to wearing one.

When worn for long periods of time in non-sterile conditions, however, face masks cause the wearer to re-inhale their own exhaled air, including bacteria that gather in the stale zone between the mouth and the mask. This can lead to "psychological and physical deterioration as well as multiple symptoms described [as] Mask-Induced Exhaustion Syndrome" (Kisielinski et al., 2021). These include increase in breathing resistance, increase in blood carbon dioxide, decrease in blood oxygen saturation, increase in heart rate, increase in blood pressure, decrease in cardiopulmonary capacity, increase in respiratory rate, shortness of breath and difficulty breathing, headache, dizziness, feeling hot and clammy, decreased ability to concentrate, decreased ability to think, drowsiness, decrease in empathy perception, impaired skin barrier function with itching, acne, skin lesions and irritation, and general fatigue and exhaustion.

Mask wearers, therefore, face an internal struggle arising from their consent to an absurd, medically senseless practice (Jefferson et al., 2023) which they must instinctively know to be harmful. Mask wearing is a filthy habit (because of the recycled bacteria) and a form of self-harm (physically and psychologically). The sight of people with the mask below their nose or chin was all too common and is evidence that mask wearing is widely experienced as unpleasant and oppressive. Consenting to wearing a face mask under these circumstances is perverse and masochistic.

"It's just a piece of cloth," mask proponents claim, yet, "millions of people are considerably more tormented by facemasks than what we would expect is reasonable or even possible for something that is indeed merely an 'inconvenience.'" Even so, Hertzberg (2021) continues, "few people are able to work out for themselves what about [face masks] is so abusive or terrible." This is because of the hidden psychological warfare functions that face masks serve. In Johnson's (2020, § 5.2) view, they constitute a "form of psychological torture—a form of domestic terrorism, as it has been carried out on the general population, not in a few isolated cases." A diabolical poster by Hull University Teaching Hospitals NHS Trust shows a "kissing" couple, hooded and masked, with the strap line "We really need to see less of each other" (Rix, 2021), consistent with CIA methods. Face masks additionally serve to inculcate fear, train obedience, signal conformity, create an absurd/alien reality, dehumanise and deindividuate the wearer, and are a marker of cult allegiance (see Volume 2 of this book). Because they work on so many different levels at once, they represent an extremely potent, and evil, instrument of psychological warfare. The fact that virtually all states mandated their use for no sound scientific reason (Eugyppius, 2023) is one of numerous indicators that a transnational deep state (Hughes, 2022) is now at war with humanity.

Trauma

"Covid-19" as Mass Trauma Event

The "Covid-19 pandemic" was a mass trauma event. According to the British Psychological Society (2020), "There is global acknowledgment that society has suffered a collective trauma, experienced mass confusion, heightened anxiety, and increased depression both physical and financial." NHS England's clinical director for mental health told a Parliamentary committee in May 2020 that the "demand for mental healthcare would increase 'significantly' once the lockdown ended and would see people needing treatment for trauma for years to come" (cited in Schwab & Malleret, 2020, p. 92).

As with any traumatic event, a profound sense of unreality set in for many people after March 2020, expressible in the sentiment "this cannot be happening." For example, Stephanie Seneff, co-author of an important peer-reviewed journal article warning of the potential dangers of the "Covid-19 vaccines" (Seneff & Nigh, 2021), opines: "I still feel like I'm in a surreal time. I just can't quite understand that this is actually taking place. It doesn't make sense to me" (Mercola & Seneff, 2021).

A key theme of ritual abuse is that the human mind is most susceptible to programming when traumatised by the fear of imminent death: "Torture involving states of extreme pain and terror, to the point of near-death, is required to install mind control programming" (Lacter, 2007). In the "Covid-19" context, military-grade propaganda about a "deadly virus" (see Chap. 4) was enough to make many people fear for their lives, with some believing they could die if they passed within six feet of another person.

For traumatised people, the world no longer feels like a safe place. In 2020, "very banal decisions," such as whether to go out in public, became "tainted with a sense of dread" (Schwab & Malleret, 2020, p. 159). This was true, not only for those traumatised by the propaganda about death and disease, but also for nonconformists who risked encountering fear-driven hysteria on the part of mask wearers (see Chap. 6). Kidd and Ratcliffe (2020) observe that the world is "no longer homely in the way it once was" and is instead "suffused with an air of dread," the physical public sphere becoming "a place where many fear to tread."

Killing Granny

In ritual abuse, it is not only fear for one's own life that is effective in inducing trauma, but also the victim's conviction that they have harmed or killed someone else, especially a loved one: "States of despair, self-hatred, paranoia, and global distrust of humanity are also effective. These are induced through [*inter alia*] forcing the child to hurt or kill others" (Lacter, 2007). Victims may find that their memories return "in layers," from being made to believe that they were guilty for a child's punishment/suffering, to "seeing people hurt or even killed," to "realizing that they [themselves] participated in the sacrifices" (Thomas, 2007, pp. 21, 50). Actual murder/sacrifice, however, is not necessarily required. In some instances, Lacter (2011) notes, "victims are tricked into believing that the murders are actual to terrorize them."

As part of the "Covid-19" operation, Britons were traumatised into believing that they could be responsible for killing other people if they did not do as they were told. On March 22, 2020, for example, London mayor Sadiq Khan announced: "more will die unless people stay at home" (Williams, 2020). A terrifying propaganda campaign was launched. New Government/NHS "advertisements" appeared in the British media with messages such as "IF YOU GO OUT, YOU CAN SPREAD IT. PEOPLE WILL DIE" and "DON'T MEET UP WITH MATES. HANGING OUT IN PARKS COULD KILL."

The "ANYONE CAN GET IT. ANYONE CAN SPREAD IT" posters from late March/early April 2020 utilise a range of different backgrounds and target young people in particular, e.g. young men socialising, or a girl hugging her grandmother. They all include an arrow pointing to one of the figures and the phrase "HAS MILD CORONAVIRUS. HASN'T NOTICED." The implication is that a young person with no symptoms of disease might be responsible for killing their elderly relatives—an effective means of traumatising young people.

On May 5, 2020, the Department of Health and Social Care put out a short video showing four young people socialising. Sinister text and an arrow point to the person on the left: "HAS MILD CORONAVIRUS, HASN'T NOTICED." The camera then pans to the next person and more sinister text appears: "LIVES WITH HIS LITTLE SISTER," "PASSES IT TO HIS LITTLE SISTER," "SISTER ENDS UP IN HOSPITAL." The clip ends with a shot of the sister in hospital wearing an oxygen mask. The subtext is that absolute obedience to authority—to the point of renouncing one's in-person friendships—is required to avoid the trauma of doing harm to children/relatives.

Health Secretary Hancock on September 8, 2020, told university students not to "kill your gran" by helping to spread coronavirus (Smyth & Bennett, 2020). On September 22, 2020, the Prime Minister told the nation in a televised address, "The tragic reality of having Covid is that your mild cough can be someone else's death knell" (Prime Minister's Office, 2020). On November 26, 2020, the Chief Medical Officer claimed: "Would I say people should hug and kiss their elderly relatives? No I would not. They want to survive to get hugged again" (cited in Davidson, 2020). Independent SAGE's Gabriel Scally told *Good Morning Britain* on November 19, 2020, "There is no point in having a very merry Christmas and then burying friends and relations in January and February" (cited in Walker, 2020).

On December 15, 2020, BBC Newsbeat (aimed at young people) warned students not to return home for Christmas, reminding them, "Don't hug your Nan at Christmas and then bury her in January" (Pandey, 2020). The same day, Margaret Greenwood, MP, wrote,

> We cannot underestimate the profound psychological impact that it would have on a child to go to school, come home with Covid-19 and infect a family member and for that family member to then die. Loss in childhood is devastating; for a child to feel that it was their fault would be traumatic in the extreme. (Greenwood, 2020)

On New Year's Eve, UCL Professor Hugh Montgomery, who directs two companies (Turbinate Technologies Ltd. and Panthair Ltd.) that supply PPE including face masks, told the BBC: "People who do not follow social distancing rules or wear masks [...] have blood on their hands [...] They are spreading this virus [...] They won't know they have killed people but they have" ("Covid rule-breakers 'have blood on their hands,'" 2020).

In January 2021, the UK Government and NHS unleashed a new volley of sinister posters using the same reddish yellow filter as the ones from March 2020. They all made the demonstrably false (Fenton et al., 2021) claim that "around 1 in 3 people with coronavirus don't have any symptoms." Their headline claims were: "A STEP TOO CLOSE COULD BE A STEP TOO FAR," "CORONAVIRUS TAKES THE TRAIN TOO," "EXERCISE SAFELY DON'T RUN THE RISK," "DON'T LET A COFFEE COST LIVES," "DON'T HELP THE VIRUS SPREAD," and "CATCH-UPS COST LIVES." As with the March 2020 propaganda, the idea is that everyday activities such as going to the supermarket, travelling by train, exercising in the park, going to a coffee shop, and meeting up with friends can kill other people. A 30-second government radio advertisement from January 2021, contained the line "If you bend the rules, people will die." The Cabinet Office agreed not to repeat that claim after being reprimanded by the Advertising Standards Authority (Rumsby, 2021), but the damage had already been done.

Trauma Bonding

Trauma bonding can arise in situations where victims come to identify viscerally with their abusers and will go to great lengths to defend them. "Bettelheim syndrome," for instance, describes "those [Nazi] concentration camp inmates who coped psychologically with their traumatic environment by identifying with their guards in hopes of survival" (Mega et al., 2000, p. 262). Even under less extreme conditions, trauma bonding is a "recognised psychosocial process whereby forced isolation, anxiety, physical threat, and other forms of stressful conditions can lead to social bonding between jailers and prisoners or captors and hostages" (Adler, 2010, p. 227).

It is not difficult to recognise such conditions in the "Covid-19" operation (see Chaps. 2 and 4). The result has been trauma bonding on a society-wide scale, with many people refusing to countenance the idea that they are the victims of serious psychological abuse carried out by the very authorities who are meant to protect them.

There has been a tendency among commentators on "Covid-19" to *defend* governments, typically attributing the catastrophic harm caused by government policies to incompetence rather than malice (Hanlon's razor). According to Ponsonby (2020), for instance, "The sheer number of U-turns of late suggest a government constantly at the mercy of events where changes take place because the initial stances have not been thought through." According to Canadian pathologist Roger Hodkinson, "There's no big conspiracy here; it's like the Americans say: never let a good crisis go to waste"; "SARS-CoV-2" was probably released accidentally from the Wuhan lab, whereupon bad people tried to capitalise on the situation (in Allen, 2021). Alting von Geusau (2021) refers to "mostly well-meant yet often ill-advised government-imposed Corona measures."

In reality, the "Covid-19" operation represents a premeditated, meticulously, and maliciously orchestrated attack on the minds and bodies of the public that was enacted in coordinated fashion by governments around the world. "Millions of lives have been lost," Kingston (2022) notes, "not due to a virus, but due to COVID-19 government policies and medical countermeasures." The diabolical actions taken were not mere accidents or mistakes. They were crimes, including preventing young children from reaching crucial developmental milestones, forcing hospital patients to die alone without saying goodbye to their families, and pushing millions of people into poverty and starvation (Gutentag, 2021). As Gerrish (2021) understands, nothing was accidental: "What we are facing is calculated, and it's a mistake to call it 'madness,' because it's very precise; it's very calculated. We need to understand that in order to be able to deal with what we're facing." Scott (2022) realises that "there are real perpetrators from within our own government and external parties wishing to do us harm."

This is not merely a matter of opinion. On July 15, 2020, a 188-page report was published by the Department of Health and Social Care, the Office for National Statistics, the Government Actuary's Department, and the Home Office (2020). "When morbidity is taken into account," the report states on p. 2, "the estimates for the health impacts from a lockdown and lockdown induced recession are greater in terms of QALYs (quality-adjusted life years) than the direct COVID-19 deaths," as is shown in Fig. 1 of the report. In other words, the UK Government *knew* that "lockdowns" would prove more harmful than "Covid-19," yet it kept the population under near-continual "lockdown" until July 19, 2021.

The flimsy excuse given in the report is that, without mitigations, "up to 1.5 m direct COVID-19 deaths" would occur (p. 2). As evidence of this, the report cites the "'Unmitigated RWC [reasonable worst case]'

(31st March) scenario," described in its Annex G as "a scenario provided to SAGE," however, no reference is provided. Documents for SAGE's March 31, 2020, meeting include a "Reasonable worst-case planning scenario, 29 March 2020" (the "31st March" designation is inaccurate and sloppy). That document places the "number of direct Covid-19 deaths in a first wave" (March 30–September 2020) at 50,000, and the "number of cases requiring hospitalisation" at 260,000 (Cabinet Office, 2020, p. 2). This is for a six-month period, rather than the 12-month period used in the DHSC/ONS/GAD/HO report, whose Annex G shows 504,000 (not 1.5 million) deaths arising from the unmitigated "direct impact from Covid" and 1.1 million deaths attributable to "insufficient critical care beds." The numbers in the two documents cannot be reconciled, meaning that the 1.5 million figure appears to have been plucked out of thin air. The 504,000 unmitigated direct "Covid-19" deaths figure, meanwhile, comes close to the widely ridiculed 510,000 deaths in Ferguson et al. (2020, p. 7), and the tactic of abusing modelling to create a hyperbolic threat to push through unjustifiable policies (see Chap. 4) is the same.

Doctors for COVID Ethics (2023, pp. 183–184) concludes with respect to the "vaccine" rollout:

> It is no longer possible to construe the actions of the authorities as "honest mistakes." [..,] The rushed approval without necessity, the outright threats and the coercion, the systematic censorship of honest science, and the suppression of the truth about the numerous killed or severely injured vaccine victims have all gone on for far too long to permit any doubts as to intent and purpose. Our governments and the national and international administrative bodies are waging an undeclared war on all of us.

This is in keeping with the Omniwar concept explicated in Chap. 1. Margaret Anna Alice's "Anthem for Justice" (2023) makes crystal clear that "mistakes were *not* made."

Perpetrators in Parliament

Not only governments, but legislatures, too, were responsible for implementing the attack on the general population. The UK Parliament, for instance, did nothing to hold the Government to account over its harmful and deadly "Covid-19" policies. It repeatedly voted—or did not even bother to vote (Steerpike, 2021)—in favour of renewing the Coronavirus Act, which enables "coercive power over citizens on a scale never previously attempted" (Sumption, 2020, p. 1). It voted in favour of "vaccine" mandates for care home workers in July 2021, when no impact assessment had been published and most of the public was against the mandate (Rennie, 2021). It voted in favour of "vaccine" mandates for NHS workers in December 2021 (Mitchell, 2021), even though a House of Lords committee two weeks earlier found that there was insufficient evidence to support such mandates (Kmietowicz, 2021). On the same day (December 14, 2021), it voted in favour of "vaccine passports" to enter nightclubs and other large venues (Stewart & Allegretti, 2021).

Petitions which attract over 100,000 signatures trigger a "debate" in Parliament. Such petitions to "Prevent any restrictions on those who refuse a Covid-19 vaccination" (September 2020), "Repeal the Coronavirus Act 2020" (October 2020), "Ban the use of face masks in schools" (April 2021), "End all requirements to wear face coverings immediately" (May 2021), "Open a public inquiry into Covid-19 vaccine safety" (June 2022), "not sign any WHO Pandemic Treaty unless it is approved via public referendum" (April 2023), and "Hold a parliamentary vote on whether to reject amendments to the IHR 2005" (July 2023) led nowhere. On each occasion, the Government simply reasserted its position, and a 1–2 hour charade involving half a dozen or so MPs took place (the "debate").

In December 2022, when Andrew Bridgen MP told Prime Minister Sunak that the "Covid-19 vaccines" had caused more deaths and serious adverse reactions than all conventional vaccines worldwide in the past 50 years, Sunak replied "Let me first say that I believe that Covid vaccines are safe and effective," and the House of Commons cheered (Allen, 2022). In March 2023, when Bridgen rose to address the House regarding the dubious efficacy of "booster shots," MPs were seen talking to one another before scuttling out the chamber (Head, 2023). When Bridgen tabled an adjournment "debate" on excess deaths in the UK in October 2023, fewer than 20 of 650 MPs turned up, though the public gallery was packed (Harrity, 2023), and BBC coverage added a series of desperate overlays such as "Official NHS guidance states that government-administered vaccines are safe and often essential for public health" (Wilson, 2023). The Government has so far refused to order an inquiry into either excess deaths or "vaccine" damage, and the so-called

"Covid-19 Inquiry" predictably turned out to be a whitewash aimed at covering up criminal malfeasance (Shaw, 2023).

This level of betrayal of the public arguably amounts to treason. At every stage, the entire political class (including Bridgen, who voted for the "measures" and was pushing "booster shots" as late as December 2021) has sold out the British people and helped to implement a systematic programme of abuse orchestrated by the transnational deep state (Hughes, 2022). "We've watched all our freedoms being whittled away and our money being squandered and our lives ruined and our country destroyed, to no obviously effective purpose," Delingpole (2021) records, "and our MPs have largely surrendered to all this without a fight." It is unclear in what measure MPs have been bribed, brainwashed, and bullied into submission, but it is hard to disagree with Davis' (2021c) conclusion that they "are almost entirely complicit and have offered virtually no resistance to the removal of representative democracy." It takes trauma-bonding not to see this.

Permanent Scars and Intergenerational Trauma

John Rawlings Rees oversaw a group of psychiatrists working for the U.S. Strategic Bombing Survey, affiliated with the OSS Special Operations Command. That group, which included U.S.-based Tavistock operatives Kurt Lewin, Rensis Likert, and Margaret Mead, was responsible for the Anglo-American plan to firebomb Dresden, a cultural landmark of little strategic value, in February 1945. The rationale was that the terror thereby inflicted on Germans—who were already facing certain defeat—would leave them "permanently psychologically scarred" by the realisation that "'all that is German' could be wiped out in an instant" by the United States and its allies (Digital Citizen, 2003).

The destruction of Hiroshima and Nagasaki in August 1945, for which there was no military necessity (Alperovitz, 1995, pp. 329–331), was intended to make what Secretary of State James Byrnes in May 1945 called "a profound psychological impression on as many inhabitants as possible," preferably targeting "a vital war plant employing a large number of workers and closely surrounded by workers' houses" (cited in Kort, 2007, p. 184). The war crimes perpetrated against Germany and Japan within six months of one another, with both nations already effectively defeated, were shock and awe operations intended to traumatise entire populations, and particularly the working class, into submission in the postwar period, with the aftermath of World War I having already warned of the surge of labour unrest and revolutionary activity that would follow the war's end (van der Pijl, 2022, p. 269).

The idea of lifelong scarring following a traumatic event is consistent with ritual abuse and trauma-based mind control, in which "abuser groups seek life-time control of their victims. Submission is not rewarded with freedom in a year or in a decade. To submit is to begin a life-sentence. The longer one submits, the longer one is abused" (Lacter, 2007). Typically, there is "no conscious awareness of the programming"; survivors only begin to recover memories of the abuse between the ages of 30 and 50, and it "generally takes many more years for the survivor to become aware of the mind control programming and its ongoing effects on her or him" (Lacter, 2007). Thus, given knowledge of the techniques for how to do so, trauma can be used to manipulate people unconsciously for most, if not all, of their lives.

WEF director Klaus Schwab seems obsessed with metaphors of cutting and scarring—of trauma injuries that never fully heal. There will be no going back to how things were before the "pandemic," he claims, because "the cut which we have now is much too strong in order not to leave traces" (in Roscoe, 2022). "For many people," Schwab and Malleret write, "traversing the COVID-19 pandemic will be defined as living a personal trauma. The scars inflicted may last for years" (2020, p. 91). And again: "The societal upheaval unleashed by COVID-19 will last for years, and possibly generations," and "the longer lockdowns last, the greater the structural damage they inflict by leaving permanent scars in the economy [...]" (2020, pp. 34, 24).

One of the ways in which trauma-based mind control works is by threatening or enacting a repeat of the original torture/trauma should the victim refuse to obey programmed commands (Lacter, 2007). In that respect, consider Bill Gates' words from January 2021:

> The world now understands how seriously we should take pandemics. No one needs to be convinced that an infectious disease could kill millions of people or shut down the global economy. The pain of this past year will be seared into people's thinking for a generation. I am hopeful that we'll see broad support for efforts that make sure we never have to experience this hardship again. (Gates & Gates, 2021)

Note the similarity here between "pain […] seared into people's thinking for a generation" and Schwab and Malleret's claim that "The scars inflicted may last for years," "possibly generations" (2020, pp. 34, 24). Seen through the lens of trauma-based mind control, Gates' words constitute a subliminal threat: unless popular support is secured for global technocratic agendas, the trauma of 2020 could be revisited, perhaps through what Gates (2020, 2021; Gates & Gates, 2021) has repeatedly referred to as "the next pandemic."

False Rescue

Demonstrating "Omnipotence"

In a category called "Demonstrating 'omnipotence,'" Biderman's Chart of Coercion recommends getting the victim to believe in the absolute power of the abuser. This involves suggesting the futility of resistance/ confrontation, pretending that cooperation is taken for granted, and claiming to have complete control over the victim's fate (Amnesty International, 1973, p. 49). The CIA torture manuals operate on much the same principles: "Throughout his detention, subject must be convinced that his 'questioner' controls his ultimate destiny, and that his absolute cooperation is essential to survival" (CIA, 1983, § F-4).

Svali (2000, p. 2) notes that in certain cults, "the child will have seen people tortured or killed for disobedience, and so, literally, the perpetrator WILL have the perceived power of life and death over the child." For victims of ritual abuse, as recounted by a survivor, "the only reality they know is the reality created by the abusers, by their violent, punitive training and by their lies […] They have no sense of sovereignty over their own existence" (cited in Lacter, 2011). Under these circumstances, loyalty and attachment to the perpetrator become a survival mechanism as the victim reaches out to "the only available hand for relief"—at which point the perpetrator "WILL rescue and stop the abuse […], but for a price: their unrelenting loyalty and obedience" (Svali, 2000, p. 2). Lacter (2011) corroborates this claim based on her professional experience of dealing with ritual abuse survivors: "The abusers often torture their victims to near-death and stage fake rescues, to make victims believe that the abusers or their deities have complete control of their life." The victim typically does not realise that the abuser and the rescuer are one and the same: the tormentor is also the saviour.

Lacter (2011) adds an important caveat: "Memories of abusers' actions must also be carefully scrutinised for possible deception, faked and staged acts, 'smoke and mirrors,' and use of film combined with drugged states to make victims believe that the events in the film actually occurred." In other words, some of the abuse that the victim is forced to witness might be simulated. These words were published *before* the leaking of a GCHQ Joint Threat Research Intelligence Group presentation in 2014, which mentions both "false flag operation" and "false rescue operation" in a section titled "DISRUPTION" ("The Art of Deception," 2014, Slide 47). False flag operations are staged attacks blamed on an official enemy (cf. Hughes, 2020, pp. 56–57), often involving terrorism, while "false rescue operations" sound continuous with Lacter's (2011) "fake rescues." Given that the provenance of many twenty-first-century terrorist attacks remains ambiguous (Hughes, 2022), and that evidence-based questions posed by independent researchers since 2013 raise the possibility that elements of certain terrorist attacks may have been simulated, there is reason to suspect that the "fake rescue" technique deployed against victims in ritual abuse settings may also have been deployed against the public in the context of false flag terrorism. If so, then, in both cases, victims are rescued from a simulated existential threat in return for their obedience.

Agamben (2021, p. 13) observed early in the "Covid-19" crisis: "Limitations on freedom are thus being willingly accepted, in a perverse and vicious cycle, in the name of a desire for security—a desire that has been generated by the same governments that are now intervening to satisfy it." This tactic follows a playbook whereby dictators promise security in exchange for liberty (Zimbardo, 2007, pp. 274–5). Forgotten is Benjamin Franklin's adage that "those that would sacrifice essential liberty for a little temporary security deserve neither liberty nor security" (cited in Underwood, 2007, p. 103).

The "lockdowns" served as a demonstration of "omnipotence" by "elites now capable of arrogating to themselves powers that might once have been considered the preserve of malevolent gods," e.g. blocking out the sun, genetically modifying nature, and placing over half the world's people under a form of house arrest (Broudy & Hoop, 2021, p. 375; Sumption, 2020, p. 1). As Curtin (2021) observes, "to lockdown hundreds of millions of healthy people, to insist they wear useless masks, to tell them to avoid human contacts, to destroy the economic lives of regular people [...] have created vast suffering that was meant to teach people a lesson about who was in control […].” Broadberry (2022) reaches a similar conclusion: “They are telling you, in no uncertain terms, that you are without recourse, these events are beyond your control, as is your own destiny for that matter. Eventually a sense of apathy and abulia engulfs humanity,” demoralising the population.

During the “pandemic,” the same “global predators” (Breggin & Breggin, 2021) responsible for spreading existential fear stepped in with a raft of measures to keep the public “safe.” There is nothing new in this *modus operandi*: “From terrorism to WMD to Red Scares to COVID-19, a declared state of emergency serves to set the stage […] Whether the national security state, Big Tech or Big Pharma, it is predatory transnational power in a saviour’s disguise to the rescue, every time” (Kyrie & Broudy, 2022a). The only solution offered was the “vaccine” plus a range of authoritarian measures, and the public was expected to get behind the false benevolence of “trusted allies,” such as Big Pharma, the WHO (responsible for the “pandemic” declaration), Bill Gates, GAVI, government scientists, the Trusted News Initiative, and Big Tech. As artificially manufactured crises of varying kinds proliferate, global power elites “will protect the planet, defend the internet, restore goods and services, or fight pathogens, using (nano)technology, censorship, totalitarian control, and removal of citizens’ freedoms and rights, or what is left of them” (Kyrie & Broudy, 2022a).

Infantilisation

The flip side of demonstrating “omnipotence” is the infantilisation of the public, a known weapon of psychological warfare. Totalitarianism, Meerloo (1956, pp. 107, 36, 112) writes, “appeals to this confused infant in all of us,” who “long[s] for a way out of the responsibilities that democracy and maturity place on [citizens]” and instead finds refuge in “the ecstasy of being taken up and absorbed in wild, uncontrolled collective feelings, the safety of being anonymous, of being merely a cog in the wheel of the all-powerful state.”

Huxley (1958, p. 54) writes: “Children, as might be expected, are highly susceptible to propaganda. They are ignorant of the world and its ways, and therefore completely unsuspecting. Their critical faculties are undeveloped.” This describes most adults today, who are clueless about propaganda and psychological operations and are therefore easy to manipulate.

According to Minnicino (1974, p. 53), "infantilization—officially, the [Freudian] theory of anal sadism—is at the basis of the [Tavistock] psywar strategy." Minnicino cites Henry V. Dicks' "Anal Sadistic Basis of our Culture." Dicks, a Tavistock man and a psychological profiler for the RAND Corporation, was part of the United Nations Relief and Rehabilitation Administration in postwar Germany. There, he was responsible for propaganda by the Supreme Headquarters Allied Expeditionary Force, which accompanied the deliberate starvation of Germans: "Your body is disappearing. It is turning into shit. You are turning into shit" (Minnicino, 1974, p. 54). The aim was to regress victims psychologically to an infantile, pre-toilet training stage.

According to the *KUBARK Manual*, "The interrogatee's mature defenses crumble as he becomes more childlike" (CIA, 1963, p. 103). The aim is to drive the prisoner "deeper and deeper into himself, until he no longer is able to control his responses in an adult fashion" (CIA, 1983, § K-4). "A psychologically immature subject, or one who has been regressed" does not have to take responsibility for their actions and proves "incapable of resistance" (CIA, 1983, § K-13). At this point, the interrogator can assume the role of a "parental figure," resulting in a "strengthening of the subject's tendencies toward compliance" (CIA, 1963, p. 90).

In more recent times, the rise of applied behavioural psychology has seen the state assume an increasingly paternalistic role: "If we think the state is making decisions for us, we may absolve ourselves of the responsibility to take charge of our own behaviour" (Dolan et al., 2010, p. 70). The effect is to infantilise the population.

The media is also used to infantilise the population. In 2009, for instance, when six of the richest Americans (Bill Gates, Warren Buffett, Michael Bloomberg, Oprah Winfrey, Ted Turner, and Mark Zuckerberg) met behind closed doors for six hours in New York, potentially "raising the specter of eugenics" (Frank, 2009), ABC's John Berman produced a report that presented them as cartoon superheroes: "the new supermen and wonder woman. The superrich friends. Not fighting bad guys, but fighting for good, nonetheless" (cited in J. Corbett, 2020). The *Guardian* ran a similar piece titled "They're called the Good Club—and they want to save the world" (Harris, 2009).

During the "Covid-19 pandemic," strenuous efforts were made to infantilise the population. For example, the media-driven panic buying of toilet roll in the spring of 2020 may have been aimed at regressing the population along Tavistock lines (Minnicino, 1974, pp. 53–54). As Kluger (2020) notes, "Toilet paper has primal—even infantile—associations, connected with what is arguably the body's least agreeable function in a way we've been taught from toddlerhood."

In Britain, the public was encouraged to draw rainbows and put them up in front windows as a supposed show of solidarity with NHS workers—a primary/elementary school-type activity. Governments began telling citizens exactly how to behave, like children: stay indoors, await permission to come out, stand two metres apart, wear face masks, etc. Anthony Fauci told an infantilised U.S. public in November 2020: "Do what you're told" (cited in Farr, 2020). In the view of Royo-Bordonada et al. (2020), mask mandates represent "a paternalistic action by the authorities, which tend to treat citizens like children." Schwab and Malleret (2020, p. 87) characteristically give the game away when claiming that, during a pandemic, "our sense of vulnerability and fragility increases, as does our dependence on those around us, as for a baby or a frail person."

The Centres for Disease Control and Prevention (CDC, 2022) used infantilising cartoon imagery to tell the public how to wear face masks. Chicago Mayor Lori Lightfoot and Amy Eshleman dressed up in superhero costumes with masks on and a hand sanitiser billboard around their necks, calling themselves the "Rona Destroyers" ("Mayor Lightfoot, first lady Amy Eshleman don costumes," 2020). The BBC repeatedly used cartoon imagery in its "Covid-19" messaging, presenting face masks and injections in cheerful, child-friendly terms rather than as potentially harmful. In August 2021, New York City mayor Bill de Blasio offered a bribe for getting injected, in the form of a limited-edition Marvel comic, urging "Fight back against evil. In this case, evil is Covid" ("Transcript: Mayor de Blasio holds Media Availability," 2021).

For the most part, the infantilising propaganda was successful. Most grown adults behaved like children, doing whatever they were told without taking any personal responsibility for their actions, signalling their "virtue" while their behaviour fuelled the evil psychological operation. Those in the "Covidian cult," Hopkins (2021) writes, "have been reduced to a state approaching infancy." Their excessive trust in government and the mainstream media, Davis (2021b) notes, "means that they no longer recognise the need to think for themselves [as] they consider unquestioning obedience to authority to be the only rational position." In their mindless repetition of thought-terminating clichés such as "Covidiot!" and "conspiracy theorist!" they resemble "school-aged children bullying each other with name-calling in a playground setting" (McClurg, 2022). Their naive belief in absurd official narratives is like children's belief in fairy tales. While Omniwar is being waged against them, they believe that the government is there to protect them, that the media would never intentionally deceive them, and that the pharmaceutical industry, which profits from human sickness, wants to cure them. Davis (2021a) is correct: "We really must put aside this infantile notion that 'the authorities' care about us or our loved ones. We mean nothing to them." Worse, the public is the undeclared enemy in the war for technocracy.

Evil Comes to Light

Ritual abuse claims are hard to substantiate, because abusers go to great lengths to cover their tracks. A sensationalist literature has arisen around those claims. The alleged crimes involving the torture, traumatisation, and terrorisation of children fall so far outside what ordinary people believe to be possible that cognitive dissonance may interfere with the ability to give such claims the attention they deserve. Moral repulsion at those sickening acts creates an additional barrier to looking into them. A population that is itself under the spell of trauma-based mind control will struggle to challenge the programming.

Nevertheless, despite the many obstacles to investigating claims of ritual abuse and trauma-based mind control, mounting evidence is coming to light which indicates not only that those phenomena are real, but that psychological warfare techniques developed from them have also been deployed against populations worldwide. For those paying attention, the Franklin Scandal, Project Monarch, The Finders, and SRA all have probable links to the CIA, apparently for the dual purpose of creating mind-controlled "slaves" (cf. my remarks on Project BLUEBIRD [renamed ARTICHOKE] and MKULTRA Subproject 136 in Hughes, 2022) and the sexual blackmail of politicians and other influential figures. The revelations around Jeffrey Epstein and the transnational "elite" paedophile network around him only scratch the surface of the longstanding nexus between Anglo-American and Israeli intelligence and organised crime (Webb, 2022a, 2022b). State-sponsored crime networks—and not democratically elected governments—have been running the show for a very long time, using psychological operations to control the public.

With the "Covid-19" operation, new levels of viciousness were unleashed against populations. Psychological torture techniques were deployed to create acute stress. Mandatory face masks, trialled on inmates at Guantánamo Bay, were rolled out on entire populations. Members of the public were traumatised by relentless propaganda about death and disease and by messaging that they themselves could be the cause of loved ones' deaths. A trauma bonding was instigated, intended to last decades and to bind an infantilised population in loyalty and obedience to its "omnipotent" masters.

As populations come to understand the full extent of the abuse that has been perpetrated against them, resistance to the evil and psychopathic deep state that controls their governments seems certain to grow.

References

Adler, N. (2010). Enduring repression: Narratives of loyalty to the Party before, during and after the gulag. *Europe-Asia Studies, 62*(2), 211–234. https://doi.org/10.1080/09668130903506797.

Agamben, G. (2021). *Where are we now?* Rowman & Littlefield.

Alexander, A.B.H. (1997). Sex, drugs, the CIA, mind control, and your children. *Probe Magazine*. http://www.whale.to/b/alexander.html.

Alice, M. A. (2023). *Mistakes were not made: An anthem for justice*. https://margaretannaalice.substack.com/p/mistakes-were-not-made-an-anthem-57a.

Allen, R. (2021, June 22). *The Richie Allen Show, Tuesday June 22nd 2021*. https://podcasts.apple.com/us/podcast/the-richie-allen-show-tuesday-june-22nd-2021/id1090284266?i=1000526518391.

Allen, R. (2022, December 7). MP Tells Sunak mRNA jabs breaking records for deaths and adverse events. *Richie Allen*. https://richieallen.co.uk/mp-tells-sunak-mrna-jabs-breaking-records-for-deaths-adverse-events/.

Alperowitz, G. (1995). *The decision to use the atomic bomb and the architecture of an American myth*. Fontana.

Alting von Geusau, C. W. J. M. (2021, November 17). Totalitarianism and the five stages of dehumanization. *Brownstone Institute*. https://brownstone.org/articles/totalitarianism-and-the-five-stages-of-dehumanization/.

American Psychiatric Association. (1994). *Diagnostic and statistical manual of mental disorders* (4th ed.). American Psychiatric Publishing, Inc.

Amnesty International. (1973). *Report on torture*. Duckworth.

Amnesty International. (2020, May 18). Our final plea to Obama to close Guantánamo. *Amnesty International*. https://www.amnesty.org.uk/our-final-plea-obama-close-guantanamo.

Barkun, M. (2003). *A culture of conspiracy. Apocalyptic visions in contemporary America*. University of California Press.
Breggin, P. R., & Breggin, G. R. (2021). *Covid-19 and the global predators: We are the prey*. Lake Edge Press.
British Psychological Society. (2020, May 1). *Towards the new normal, and beyond….* https://www.bps.org.uk/news-and-policy/towards-new-normal-and-beyond.
Broadberry, D. (2022, May 7). Revelation of the method. *OffGuardian*. https://off-guardian.org/2022/05/07/revelation-of-the-method/.
Brooks, S. K., Webster, R. K., Smith, L. E., Woodland, L., Wessely, S., Greenberg, N., & Rubin, G. J. (2020). The psychological impact of quarantine and how to reduce it: Rapid review of the evidence. *The Lancet, 395*(10227), 912–920. https://doi.org/10.1016/S0140-6736(20)30460-8.
Broudy, D., & Hoop, D. K. (2021). Messianic mad men, medicine, and the media war on empirical reality: Discourse analysis of mainstream Covid-19 propaganda. *International Journal of Vaccine Theory, Research, and Practice, 2*(1), 365–388. https://doi.org/10.56098/ijvtpr.v2i1.22.
Broze, D. (2019, March 26). Who will find what the Finders hide? *The Conscious Resistance Network*. https://theconsciousresistance.com/TheFinders/.
Cabinet Office. (2020, March 29). *Reasonable worst-case planning scenario—29/03/2020*. https://www.gov.uk/government/publications/reasonable-worst-case-planning-scenario-29-march-2020.
Central Intelligence Agency. (1963). *KUBARK counterintelligence interrogation*. https://nsarchive2.gwu.edu/NSAEBB/NSAEBB27/docs/doc01.pdf.
Central Intelligence Agency. (1983). *Human resource exploitation training manual*. https://nsarchive2.gwu.edu/NSAEBB/NSAEBB122/#hre.
Centres for Disease Control and Prevention. (2022, February 25). *The use and care of face masks*. www.cdc.gov/coronavirus/2019-ncov/prevent-getting-sick/about-face-coverings.html.
Children's Health Defence. (n.d.). *The science of masks*. https://childrenshealthdefense.org/the-science-of-masks/.
Corbett, J. (2020). Who is Bill Gates? *The Corbett Report*. https://www.corbettreport.com/gates/.
Corbett, J. (2022, October 10). Torturing the truth. *The Corbett Report*. https://www.corbettreport.com/torture/.
Covid rule-breakers "have blood on their hands." (2020, December 31). *BBC News*. www.bbc.co.uk/news/uk-55479018.
Curtin, E. (2021, June 19). What I know and don't know about SARS-CoV-2 virus. *Behind the Curtain*. http://edwardcurtin.com/what-i-know-and-dont-know-about-sars-cov-2-virus/.
Davidson, T. (2020, November 26). Families warned not to hug elderly loved ones "if they want to survive to be hugged again." *The Daily*

Mirror. https://www.mirror.co.uk/news/politics/breaking-families-should-not-hug-23074712.

Davis, I. (2021a, January 3). What vaccine trials? *OffGuardian*. https://off-guardian.org/2021/01/03/what-vaccine-trials/.

Davis, I. (2021b, July 12). Covidiot or covid-idiot? Which one are you? *Iain Davis*. https://iaindavis.com/covidiot/.

Davis, I. (2021c, December 14). The UK new normal dictatorship. *UK Column*. https://www.ukcolumn.org/article/the-uk-new-normal-dictatorship.

Delingpole, J. (2021, December 14). Democracy is dead in the UK—and everywhere. *Breitbart*. https://www.breitbart.com/europe/2021/12/14/democracy-is-dead-in-the-uk-and-everywhere/.

Department of Health and Social Care, Office for National Statistics, Government Actuary's Department, & Home Office (2020). *Direct and indirect impacts of COVID-19 on excess deaths and morbidity: Executive summary*. https://www.gov.uk/government/publications/dhsconsgadho-direct-and-indirect-impacts-of-covid-19-on-excess-deaths-and-morbidity-15-july-2020.

Digital Citizen. (2003, September 25). 9/11 official theory. Are you brainwashed? *Phil Taylor's Papers*. https://universityofleeds.github.io/philtaylorpapers/vp01eff8.html.

Doctors for Covid Ethics. (2023a). *mRNA Vaccine Toxicity*. https://doctors4covidethics.org/mrna-vaccine-toxicity/.

Dolan, P., Hallsworth, M., Halpern, D., King, D., & Vlaev, I. (2010). *MINDSPACE: Influencing behaviour through public policy*. Cabinet Office and Institute for Government. https://www.instituteforgovernment.org.uk/sites/default/files/publications/MINDSPACE.pdf.

Dyer, O. (2002). Prisoners' treatment is "bordering on torture," charity says. *BMJ*, 324, Article 187. https://doi.org/10.1136/bmj.324.7331.187.

Eugyppius. (2023, May 3). German Government admits it has no evidence face masks work. *The Daily Sceptic*. https://dailysceptic.org/2023/05/03/german-government-admits-it-has-no-evidence-face-masks-work/.

Farr, C. (2020, November 12). Fauci says U.S. has "independent spirit," but now is the time to "do what you're told." *CNBC*. https://www.cnbc.com/2020/11/12/fauci-says-us-has-independent-spirit-but-now-is-the-time-to-do-what-youre-told.html.

Federal Bureau of Investigation. (n.d.). *The Finders*. https://vault.fbi.gov/the-finders.

Fenton, N., Neil, M., & McLachlan, S. (2021). *What proportion of people with Covid-19 do not get symptoms?* http://www.eecs.qmul.ac.uk/~norman/papers/asymptomatics.pdf.

Ferguson, N. M, Laydon, D., Nedjati-Gilani, G., Imai, N., Ainslie, K., Baguelin, M., Bhatia, S., Boonyasiri, A., Cucunubá, Z., Cuomo-Dannenburg, G., Dighe, A., Dorigatti, I., Fu, H., Gaythorpe, K., Green, W., Hamlet, A., Hinsley, W., Okell, L. C., van Elsland, S., Ghani, A. C., et al. (2020). *Report 9: Impact of non-pharmaceutical interventions (NPIs) to reduce Covid-19 mortality and healthcare demand*. https://www.imperial.ac.uk/media/imperial-college/medicine/sph/ide/gida-fellowships/Imperial-College-COVID19-NPI-modelling-16-03-2020.pdf.

Frank, R. (2009, May 26). Billionaires try to shrink world's population, report says. *Wall Street Journal*. https://www.wsj.com/articles/BL-WHB-1322.

Gates, B. (2020, December 22). These breakthroughs will make 2021 better than 2020. *GatesNotes*. https://www.gatesnotes.com/About-Bill-Gates/Year-in-Review-2020.

Gates, B. (2021, December 7). Reasons for optimism after a difficult year. *GatesNotes*. https://www.gatesnotes.com/About-Bill-Gates/Year-in-Review-2021.

Gates, B., & Gates, M. (2021, January 27). The year global health went local. *GatesNotes*. https://www.gatesnotes.com/2021-Annual-Letter.

Gerrish, B. (2021, May 29). Testimony to Reiner Füllmich: Our oppressors are very frightened people. *UK Column*. https://www.ukcolumn.org/index.php/article/brian-gerrishs-testimony-to-reiner-fullmich-our-oppressors-are-very-frightened-people.

Greenwald, G. (2021, September 14). The masking of the servant class: Ugly Covid images from the Met Gala are now commonplace. *Glenn Greenwald*. https://greenwald.substack.com/p/the-masking-of-the-servant-class.

Greenwood, M. (2020, December 15). Current guidance is failing clinically vulnerable families. *Schools Week*. https://schoolsweek.co.uk/current-guidance-is-failing-clinically-vulnerable-families/.

Gutentag, A. (2021, June 28). The war on reality. *Tablet*. https://www.tabletmag.com/sections/news/articles/the-war-on-reality-gutentag.

Harris, P. (2009, May 31). They're called the good club—and they want to save the world. *The Guardian*. https://www.theguardian.com/world/2009/may/31/new-york-billionaire-philanthropists.

Harrity, P. (2023, October 20). MP Andrew Bridgen debates excess deaths in Parliament, 20th October 2023. *The Exposé*. https://expose-news.com/2023/10/20/mp-andrew-bridgen-debates-excess-deaths-in-parliament-20th-october-2023/.

Head, T. (2023, March 19). WATCH: Andrew Bridgen empties Parliament with anti-vax tirade. *The London Economic*. https://www.thelondoneconomic.com/news/who-is-andrew-bridgen-anti-vax-mp-speech-vaccine-harms-345383/.

Hertzberg, A. (2021, December 27). Facemasks are not a mere "inconvenience." *The Brownstone Institute*. https://brownstone.org/articles/facemasks-are-not-a-mere-inconvenience/.

Hitchens, P. (2020, July 19). Face masks turn us into voiceless submissives—and it's not science forcing us to wear them, it's politics. *Mail on Sunday*.

https://hitchensblog.mailonsunday.co.uk/2020/07/peter-hitchens-face-masks-turn-us-into-voiceless-submissives-and-its-not-science-forcing-us-to-wear-.html.

Hopkins, C. J. (2021, April 21). The Covidian cult (part II). *Consent Factory, Inc.* https://consentfactory.org/2021/04/21/the-covidian-cult-part-ii/.

Hughes, D. A. (2022, July 29). Wall Street, the Nazis, and the crimes of the deep state. *Propaganda in Focus*. https://propagandainfocus.com/wall-street-the-nazis-and-the-crimes-of-the-deep-state/.

Hughes, D. A. (2020). 9/11 truth and the silence of the IR discipline. *Alternatives, 45*(2), 55–82. https://doi.org/10.1177/0304375419898334.

Huxley, A. (1958). *Brave new world revisited*. Harper and Row.

Jefferson, T., Dooley, L., Ferroni, E., Al-Ansary, L. A., van Driel, M.L., Bawazeer, G. A., Jones, M. A., Hoffmann, T. C., Clark, J., Beller, E. M., Glasziou, P. P., & Conly, J. M. (2023). Physical interventions to interrupt or reduce the spread of respiratory viruses. *Cochrane Database of Systematic Reviews, 1*, Article CD006207. https://doi.org/10.1002/14651858.CD006207.pub6.

Johnson, A. (2020, September 22). *COVID-19—Evidence of fraud, medical malpractice, acts of domestic terrorism and breaches of human rights*. https://cvpandemicinvestigation.com/2020/09/covid-19-evidence-of-fraud-medical-malpractice-acts-of-domestic-terrorism-and-breaches-of-human-rights/#_Toc56846505.

Kidd, I. J., & Ratcliffe, M. (2020, November). Welcome to Covidworld. *The Critics*. https://thecritic.co.uk/issues/november-2020/welcome-to-covidworld/.

Kingston, K. (2022, October 20). Part 6: Dismantling Covid-19 deceptions: Gain-of-function mRNA research is not what experts lead us to believe. *The Kingston Report*. https://karenkingston.substack.com/p/part-6-gain-of-function-mrna-research.

Kisielinski, K., Giboni, P., Prescher, A., Klosterhalfen, B., Graessel, D., Funken, S., Kempski, O., & Hirch, O. (2021). Is a mask that covers the mouth and nose free from undesirable side effects in everyday use and free of potential hazards? *International Journal of Environmental Research and Public Health, 18*(8), Article 4344. https://doi.org/10.3390/ijerph18084344.

Klein, N. (2007). *The shock doctrine*. Metropolitan Books.

Kleinman, S. M. (2006). KUBARK counterintelligence interrogation review: Observations of an interrogator—lessons learned and avenues for further research. In R. Swenson (Ed.), *Educing information* (pp. 95–140). National Defence Intelligence College.

Kluger, J. (2020, March 14). In the wake of the coronavirus, here's why Americans are hoarding toilet paper. *Time*. https://time.com/5803273/hoarding-toilet-paper/.

Kmietowicz, Z. (2021). Evidence is insufficient to back mandatory NHS staff vaccination, says House of Lords committee. *BMJ*, 375, 2957. https://doi.org/10.1136/bmj.n2957.

Kort, M. (2007). *The Columbia guide to Hiroshima and the bomb*. Columbia University Press.

Kyrie, V., & Broudy, D. (2022a, May 22). Hiding in plain sight: Technocratic tyranny behind a medical mask. *Propaganda in Focus*. https://www.propagandainfocus.com/hiding-in-plain-sight-technocratic-tyranny-behind-a-medical-mask/.

Lacter, E. P. (2007, June 29). Relationships between mind control programming and ritual abuse. *End Ritual Abuse*. http://www.whale.to/b/lacter2.html.

Lacter, E. P. (2011, May 11). Ritual abuse and torture-based mind control: Reducing and preventing re-contact with abusers. *End Ritual Abuse*. https://endritualabuse.org/ritual-abuse-and-torture-based-mind-control-reducing-and-preventing-re-contact-with-abusers/.

Mayor Lightfoot, first lady Amy Eshleman don costumes for video on how to have a safe halloween during Covid-19. (2020, October 25). *CBS News*. https://www.cbsnews.com/chicago/news/mayor-lightfoot-covid-19-halloween/.

McClurg, J.S. (2022, March 22). Epithets and the infantilized citizen. *Modern Montaigne's Newsletter*. https://modernmontaigne.substack.com/p/epithets-and-the-infantilized-citizen.

McCoy, A. (2007). *A question of torture: CIA interrogation, from the Cold War to the War on Terror*. Henry Holt and Company.

Meerloo, J.A. (1956). *The rape of the mind. The psychology of thought control, menticide, and brainwashing*. World Publishing Company.

Mega, L. T., Mega, J. L., Mega, B. T., & Harris, B. M. (2000). Brainwashing and battering fatigue. Psychological abuse in domestic violence. *North Carolina Medical Journal*, *61*(5), 260–265. https://pubmed.ncbi.nlm.nih.gov/11008456/.

Mercola, J., & Seneff, S. (2021). The rapid mass deployment of Covid-19 vaccinations and its possible biological effects on the population: A special interview with Stephanie Seneff, Ph.D. *Mercola*. https://mercola.fileburst.com/PDF/ExpertInterviewTranscripts/DrMercola-StephanieSeneff-TheRapidMassDeploymentofCOVID19Vaccinations.pdf.

Minnicino, M. (1974). Low intensity operations: The Reesian theory of war. *The Campaigner*, *7*(6), 37–55.

Mitchell, G. (2021, December 15). Mandatory vaccination for NHS staff in England voted through by MPs. *Nursing Times*. https://www.nursingtimes.net/news/coronavirus/mandatory-vaccination-for-nhs-staff-in-england-voted-through-by-mps-15-12-2021/.

Needham, G. (2014). Bringing out the Gimp: Fashioning the SM imaginary. *Fashion Theory, 18*(2), 149–168. https://doi.org/10.2752/175174114X13890223974506.

Nobody is talking. (2005, February 18). *The Guardian*, https://www.theguardian.com/world/2005/feb/18/usa.afghanistan.

Open letter from former Guantánamo prisoners. (2013, May 4). *The Observer*. https://www.theguardian.com/world/2013/may/04/open-letter-former-guantanamo-prisoners.

Pandey, M. (2020, December 15). Coronavirus and Christmas: Going home not "worth the risk." *BBC Newsbeat*. https://www.bbc.com/news/newsbeat-55173161.

Phelan, J. (2020, March 24). Media watch: Groundbreaking UN torture report shunned by mainstream. *Activist Post*. https://www.activistpost.com/2020/03/media-watch-groundbreaking-un-torture-report-shunned-by-mainstream.html.

Pijl, K. van der. (2022). *States of emergency. Keeping the global population in check*. Clarity Press.

Ponsonby, B. (2020, September 3). Boris Johnson's showman act is starting to wear thin. *STV News*. https://news.stv.tv/opinion/boris-johnson-uniquely-ill-equipped-to-be-prime-minister.

Potts, S. C. (2020, June 9). The cult of the mask. *The Remnant*. https://remnantnewspaper.com/web/index.php/articles/item/4927-the-cult-of-the-mask#_ftnref1.

Prime Minister's Office. (2020, September 22). *Prime Minister's statement on coronavirus (Covid-19): 22 September 2020*. https://www.gov.uk/government/speeches/prime-ministers-statement-on-coronavirus-covid-19-22-september-2020.

Rancourt, D., Baudin, M., & Mercier, J. (2021). *Nature of the Covid-era public health disaster in the USA, from all-cause mortality and socio-geo-economic and climatic data*. https://denisrancourt.ca/uploads_entries/1635189453861_USA%20ACM%20into%202021%20-%20article----12d.pdf.

Rennie, J. (2021, July 14). *MPs ignore public consultation and vote for compulsory vaccinations for care home staff*. https://www.carehome.co.uk/news/article.cfm/id/1653220/mps-vote-compulsory-vaccination-care-home-staff.

Rettew, D. (2022, March 17). The TikTok-inspired surge of dissociative identity disorder. *Psychology Today*. https://www.psychologytoday.com/gb/blog/abcs-child-psychiatry/202203/the-tiktok-inspired-surge-dissociative-identity-disorder.

Rix, D. (2021). *We really need to see less of each other*. https://davidrix.wordpress.com/2021/01/05/we-really-need-to-see-less-of-each-other/.

Roscoe, M. (2022, July 20). Podcaster and Hollywood actor spark mass Twitter debate over "the Great Reset." *EuroWeekly News*. https://euroweeklynews.com/2022/07/20/hollywood-actor-twitter-debate-the-great-reset/.

Royo-Bordonada, M. A., Garcia-Lopez, F. J., Cortés, F., & Zaragoza, G. A. (2020). Face masks in the general healthy population Scientific and ethical issues. *Gaceta Sanitaria, 35*(6), 580–584. https://doi.org/10.1016/j.gaceta.2020.08.003.

Rumsby, B. (2021, January 21). Government to discontinue Covid ad accusing joggers or those exercising of being "highly likely" to have the virus. *The Telegraph*. https://www.telegraph.co.uk/news/2021/01/21/government-discontinue-covid-ad-accusing-joggers-exercising/.

Schwab, K., & Malleret, T. (2020). *Covid 19: The Great Reset*. World Economic Forum.

Science: Twilight of the brain. (1954, October 4). *Time magazine*. https://content.time.com/time/subscriber/article/0,33009,857596,00.html.

Scott, B. (2022, November 21). Menticide 101 and the brainwashing of a world: Part III—new courage for old lies. *UK Column*. https://www.ukcolumn.org/article/menticide-101-and-the-brainwashing-of-a-world-part-iii-new-courage-for-old-lies.

Seneff, S., & Nigh, G. (2021). Worse than the disease? Reviewing some possible unintended consequences of the mRNA vaccines against Covid-19. *International Journal of Vaccine Theory, Practice, and Research, 2*(1), 38–79. https://doi.org/10.56098/ijvtpr.v2i1.23.

Shaw, M. (2023, June 27). Covering up crime—The real purpose of the Covid Inquiry. *TCW*. https://www.conservativewoman.co.uk/covering-up-crime-the-real-purpose-of-the-covid-inquiry/.

Smyth, C., & Bennett, R. (2020, September 8). Don't kill granny with coronavirus, warns Matt Hancock. *The Times*. https://www.thetimes.co.uk/article/affluent-youth-are-catching-coronavirus-most-says-matt-hancock-qvbpxw2nk.

Steerpike. (2021, October 20). MPs extend the Coronavirus Act without a vote. *The Spectator*. https://www.spectator.co.uk/article/watch-mps-extend-the-coronavirus-act-without-a-vote/.

Stephens Nuwer, D. (2016). "I'll be blamed ef I hanker after making my bowels a brick-yard": Dirt eating in the antebellum and early modern South. *The Southern Quarterly, 53*(3/4), 141–155.

Stewart, H., & Allegretti, A. (2021, December 14). MPs back Covid passes in England amid large Tory rebellion. *The Guardian*. https://www.theguardian.com/world/2021/dec/14/covid-plan-b-mps-back-tougher-rules-face-masks-england-omicron.

Strongman, R. (2021, November 4). The mask of your enslavement: The image, history, and meaning of Escrava Anastácia. *Brownstone Institute*. https://brownstone.org/articles/the-mask-of-your-enslavement-the-image-history-and-meaning-of-escrava-anastacia/.

Sumption, J. (2020, October 27). *Government by decree: Covid-19 and the constitution*. Cambridge Freshfields Annual Law Lecture. Retrieved June 13, 2020, from https://resources.law.cam.ac.uk/privatelaw/Freshfields_Lecture_2020_Government_by_Decree.pdf.

Svali. (2000, October 12). *Trauma bonding: The pull to the perpetrator*. https://www.dougriggs.org/Trauma_Bonding.pdf.

The art of deception: Training for a new generation of online covert operations. (2014, February 24). *The Intercept*. https://theintercept.com/document/art-deception-training-new-generation-online-covert-operations/.

Thomas, M. (2007). *Monarch: The new Phoenix program*. CreateSpace.

Tracy, N. (2022, January 4). The amazing history of dissociative identity disorder (DID). *Healthy Place*. https://www.healthyplace.com/abuse/dissociative-identity-disorder/the-amazing-history-of-dissociative-identity-disorder-did.

Transcript: Mayor de Blasio holds Media Availability. (2021, August 26). NYC. https://www.nyc.gov/office-of-the-mayor/news/589-21/transcript-mayor-de-blasio-holds-media-availability#/0.

U.S. Senate Select Committee on Intelligence. (1977). *Project MKULTRA, the CIA's program of research in behavioural modification*. https://www.intelligence.senate.gov/sites/default/files/hearings/95mkultra.pdf.

Underwood, L. J. (2007). Terror by consent: The modern state and the breach of the social contract. Peter Lang.

Valentine, D. (2017). *The CIA as organized crime*. Clarity Press.

Vos, E. (2019, August 23). Long before Epstein: Sex traffickers and spy agencies. *Consortium News*. https://consortiumnews.com/2019/08/23/long-before-epstein-sex-traffickers-spy-agencies/.

Vos, E. (2021, June 3). The Finders: CIA ties to child sex cult obscured as coverage goes from sensationalism to silence. *Mintpress News*. https://www.mintpressnews.com/the-finders-cia-ties-child-sex-cult-obscured-media-coverage/277543/.

Walker, P. (2020, November 19). Christmas gatherings could wipe out Covid gains, UK experts warn. *The Guardian*. https://www.theguardian.com/politics/2020/nov/19/uk-family-christmas-covid-gordon-brown.

Webb, W. (2022a). *One nation under blackmail, volume 1*. Trine Day.

Webb, W. (2022b). *One nation under blackmail, volume 2*. Trine Day.

Williams, T. -A. (2020, March 22). More will die unless people stay at home: Mayor Sadiq Khan hits out at Londoners and tells them to stop socialising as he launches furious rant at the government for "not letting him attend Cobra meetings". *Daily Mail*. https://www.dailymail.co.uk/news/article-8139577/Mayor-Sadiq-Khan-hits-Londoners-tells-stop-socialising.html.

Wilson, R. (2023, November 8). BBC issues apologetic statement for using biased on-screen captions during Andrew Bridgen's speech in Parliament on

Excess Deaths. *The Exposé*. https://expose-news.com/2023/11/08/bbc-issues-apologetic-statement-for-using/.
Zimbardo, P. (2007). *The Lucifer effect: Why good people turn evil*. Random House.

CHAPTER 4

Fear and Threat

Western governments have long used manufactured fear as a means of keeping the population susceptible to propaganda. A "pandemic" is a powerful fear concept, yet there is no credible evidence of a viral pandemic in 2020. "Covid-19" does not meet any credible (pre-2009) definition of a "pandemic," and attempts to present "Covid-19" as a new "Spanish flu" are bogus. The exaggerated threat of "Covid-19" was a function of military-grade propaganda, emanating from governments and the media, involving a barrage of terrifying images, messages, and "alert levels." The BBC played a particularly culpable role in spreading fear. Death statistics were manipulated. Propaganda about hospitals being overwhelmed by "Covid-19" admissions camouflaged a sinister attack on public health. The primary purpose of face masks and PCR tests was to spread fear. Waves of fear/terror were sent by "new variants," "immunity escape," and the open letter by Geert Vanden Bossche. The spurious concept of "long Covid" projects the danger out into the future.

Existential Threat and Social Control

Totalitarian regimes have historically ruled through terror in the form of direct threat of physical violence, viz. the GPU, the Gestapo, and Orwell's (1984, p. 390) image of "a boot stamping on a human face—for ever." Under totalitarianism, Meerloo (1956, p. 28) writes, "The terrorized victims finally find themselves compelled to express complete conformity

D. A. Hughes, *"Covid-19," Psychological Operations, and the War for Technocracy*, https://doi.org/10.1007/978-3-031-41850-1_4

to the tyrant's wishes." Western governments, in contrast, have not ruled through terror in the same way, because more effective means have been found. As Huxley (1958, p. 5) writes, "government through terror works on the whole less well than government through the non-violent manipulation of the environment and of the thoughts and feelings of individual men, women and children."

That "non-violent manipulation" (absence of direct physical threat) has much in common with Pavlovian conditioning. Pavlov, Huxley (1958, p. 30) comments, found that "the deliberate induction of fear, rage or anxiety markedly heightens the dog's suggestibility"; and if kept in that state for long enough, "the brain goes 'on strike,'" allowing new behaviour patterns to be installed with ease. Similar is true of humans: "threat, tension, and anxiety, in general, may accelerate the establishment of conditioned responses, particularly when those responses tend to diminish fear and panic," and those responses "can develop even when the victim is completely unaware that he is being influenced" (Meerloo, 1956, p. 50). Even as CIA mind control programmes in the 1950s and 1960s explored these premises through experiments on individuals, similar techniques were already being rolled out against the entirety of U.S. society.

For example, Senator Arthur Vandenberg's 1947 recommendation to "scare hell out of the American people" (his nephew, Hoyt Vandenberg, was CIA Director at the time) was officially justified by the alleged threat posed by the USSR. Mechanisms for keeping the population and policymakers in fear, not least of imminent death, included the "Doomsday clock" (1947), the apocalyptic rhetoric of NSC-68 (1950), the contagion metaphor for communism, the "Second Red Scare" based on alleged fifth column communism, the 1952 *Duck and Cover* film used to terrorise school children, graphic accounts of the potential effects of a nuclear attack on the United States in the *Wall Street Journal* and *Reader's Digest*, and Kissinger's (1957, Chapter 3) description of the effects of a 10 megaton nuclear weapon detonated in New York. All of these threats were hyperbole. As Talbott (1990, p. 36) retrospectively admits, "For more than four decades, Western policy has been based on a grotesque exaggeration of what the U.S.S.R. could do if it wanted." Kennedy's alleged "missile gap," for instance, was massively in favour of the United States in the 1960s.

With the end of the "Cold War," a new existential threat had to be found. In 1991, the Club of Rome proposed a new "common enemy against whom we can unite," i.e. "humanity itself" for its disastrous inference in natural processes (King & Schneider, 1991, p. 115). But when the green agenda failed to gain traction, multiple premonitions of a "new Pearl Harbour" appeared between 1997 and 2001 (Hughes, 2020, pp. 76–77). According to Cyrulik (1999, p. 6), of CIA partner think tank CSIS, "A threat that causes Americans to live in fear, to trade liberty for security, and to change our way of life would make for a powerful tool." "9/11" duly took place and the "War on Terror" made "transnational terrorism" the new existential threat. "Entrapment terror" ensued, i.e. "the mental effect of routine exposure to a 24/7 corporate news cycle of psychological operations against the masses, weaponizing the language of terror and trapping news consumers in a near-blinding state of fear" (Broudy & Hoop, 2021, p. 371). Rational dialogue and critical questioning of the official 9/11 narrative were crippled as society became divided into propagandised true believers and heretical "conspiracy theorists," to use a term weaponised by the CIA as long ago as the 1960s (deHaven Smith, 2013, p. 25), yet still deployed uncritically by far too many academics in their servile defence of authority.

The same principle of finding an "existential threat" with which to terrorise the public was again operationalised during the "Covid-19" operation, only this time, the "invisible enemy" was neither "fifth column" communists, nor "terrorists," nor "humanity itself," but, rather, a "deadly virus."

The "Covid-19 Pandemic"

"Pandemic" as a Fear Concept

A "pandemic" is a very powerful term when it comes to creating fear, because it suggests ubiquitous disease and death (*pan demos*—across all people). Epidemics, according to England's Chief Medical Officer, Chris Whitty (2018), "cause substantial panic, and have substantial social and economic impacts, very often way out of proportion to their actual medical importance." Schwab and Malleret (2020, p. 14) know that "The spread of infectious diseases has a unique ability to fuel fear, anxiety and mass hysteria." Much rides, therefore, on the responsible usage of terms such as "epidemic" and "pandemic." When the WHO formally declared pandemic status for "Covid-19" on March 11, 2020, its Director-General noted: "Pandemic is not a word to use lightly or carelessly. It is a word that, if misused, can cause unreasonable fear [...]" (WHO, 2020a).

When that same WHO Director-General claimed on February 25, 2020, that the world should do more to prepare for a possible coronavirus pandemic ("Coronavirus: World must prepare for pandemic, says WHO," 2020), the Dow Jones index went into a tailspin and lost 36% of its value in a single month (to March 23, 2020). On March 12, 2020, the day after the WHO "pandemic" declaration, U.S. stock markets experienced their largest single-day percentage fall since Black Monday (1987). Yet, when the "pandemic" declaration was made, there were only 4291 "Covid-19" deaths worldwide, only 1440 of which were outside China, only 29 of which were in the United States (Chossudovsky, 2021, p. 22). For perspective, the 4291 deaths represented 0.000055% of a global population of 7.8 billion in 2020. There was no sound scientific reason to invoke the fear-generating language of a "pandemic."

No sooner was the "pandemic" declared than "Covid-19" cases and deaths began to surge worldwide at an unnaturally fast rate that cannot plausibly be accounted for by viral spread and the "extraordinary forecasting ability of the global health-monitoring system" (Rancourt, 2020a, 2020b, 2020c, p. 3). As Engler (2022) writes of Lombardy: "A virus doesn't spread across thousands of kilometres within days [generating] peaks [of deaths] at the same time"; rather, like a 2003 heatwave in France that was blamed on neglect, the cause was probably attributable to the state. In Britain, the surge in care home deaths "everywhere all at once" in early April 2020 was "more likely the result of synchronous policy panic than a deadly virus" (Kenyon, 2022). The surge in deaths in the United States, Rancourt (2020a, p. 1) argues, owed not to a "novel virus," but was, rather, a "likely signature of mass homicide by government response," a contention fleshed out in a later paper (Rancourt et al., 2021) and supported by Senger's (2022b) argument that "over 30,000 Americans appear to have been killed by mechanical ventilators or other forms of medical iatrogenesis throughout April 2020, primarily in the area around New York." If, as some critics claim, SARS-CoV-2 was already circulating in 2019—in Brazil (Fongaro et al., 2021), France (Deslandes et al., 2020), Spain (Allen & Landauro, 2020), the United States (Rice, 2022), and Italy (Apolone et al., 2021), specifically Lombardy (Amendola et al., 2022)—and if "fatal infections were in decline before full UK lockdown" (Wood, 2021), then the sudden worldwide spike in deaths in the spring of 2020 makes even less sense from an epidemiological perspective.

What Counts as a "Pandemic"?

The WHO published a document on "pandemic preparedness" in 1999, which was revised in 2005 and 2009. The 1999 version defines a pandemic in terms of "unparalleled tolls of illness and death" (cited in Cohen & Carter, 2010, p. 1275). The 2005 version requires "several, simultaneous epidemics worldwide with enormous numbers of deaths and illness" (WHO, 2005). The May 2009 version, in contrast, which was released one month before the "swine flu pandemic" was declared, states that "Pandemics can be either mild or severe in the illness and death they cause, and the severity of a pandemic can change over the course of that pandemic" (cited in Flynn, 2010). Thus, since May 2009, according to the WHO, a "pandemic" has technically been possible without anyone getting seriously ill or dying.

Under the 2009 criteria, a pandemic goes through six stages and is only declarable once it reaches phase 6 (sustained community-level outbreaks in two or more WHO regions). Germán Velásquez, Director of the WHO Secretariat on Public Health, Innovation, and Intellectual Property until 2010, was asked in 2018, "Could they have declared the pandemic level 6 also with the old [pre-2009] definition?" Velásquez replied, "No, because the severity, the number of deaths, would have been a factor. Since that was no longer one of the criteria, it made it easier to declare a pandemic" (cited in Day, 2020).

When WHO Director-General Margaret Chan declared a pandemic on June 11, 2009, only 144 people worldwide had died from swine flu. Chan described the disease as "unstoppable" but also as "moderate." According to the WHO in August 2010, well past the peak of the "pandemic," swine flu had claimed 18,449 lives in laboratory-confirmed cases (WHO, 2010). The risk of swine flu causing serious illness was shown to be no higher than that of the seasonal flu (DeNoon, 2010). In Germany, where around 10,000 people die each year from seasonal influenza, only 189 people died of swine flu between 2009 and 2010 (Keil, 2010, p. 2).

The WHO declaration of a swine flu "pandemic" triggered an estimated £14 billion worth of pre-arranged contracts obligating governments to purchase swine flu vaccinations from pharmaceutical companies in the event of a level 6 pandemic (Day, 2020). By the same logic, had the WHO declared sneezing to be a pandemic, that, too, would have been sufficient to trigger a vaccination campaign (Keil, 2010, p. 2).

In the wake of this scandal, a *British Medical Journal* investigation uncovered multiple conflicts of interest involving the WHO and big pharma (Cohen & Carter, 2010, p. 1279). The Parliamentary Assembly of the Council of Europe's Subcommittee on Health, called on the Council to investigate the WHO's ties to pharmaceutical companies, noting in a formal motion that "the definition of an alarming pandemic must not be under the influence of drug-sellers" (Wodarg et al., 2009).

Calling "Covid-19" a "pandemic" served to inculcate fear in a public not wise to the scam. Scientifically speaking, however, the WHO's "pandemic" concept is close to worthless, because it tells us nothing about serious illness and death. For reasons that follow, it is far more accurate to use Davis' (2021a) term and to call "Covid-19" a "pseudopandemic."

The Bogus "Spanish Flu" Analogy

"Covid-19" was misleadingly compared to the "Spanish flu," which Wikipedia (as of June 2023) calls "one of the deadliest pandemics in history." For example, Ferguson et al. (2020, p. 3) claim: "The last time the world responded to a global emerging disease epidemic of the scale of the current COVID-19 pandemic with no access to vaccines was the 1918–19 H1N1 influenza pandemic." According to Mike Davis, "COVID-19's currently guesstimated 2% mortality rate is comparable to the Spanish flu, and like that monster it probably has the ability to infect a majority of the human race unless antiviral and vaccine development quickly come to the rescue" (cited in Fuchs, 2021, p. 3). Schwab and Malleret (2020, p. 13) ask, "Is the pandemic like the Spanish flu of 1918 (estimated to have killed more than 50 million people worldwide in three successive waves)?" There was a massive surge of interest in "Spanish flu" on Google Trends in spring 2020.

Black (2020) observes that the Wikipedia page on the "Spanish" flu was heavily edited in the months preceding the WHO "pandemic" declaration (from December 2019). Given that Wikipedia is a "micro-managed propaganda organ" and that most edits served to downgrade the severity of the "Spanish flu," this is worthy of note. The case fatality rate for the "Spanish flu" on Wikipedia was reduced from "an estimated 10–20%" to "2–3%," even though the latter figure, implying 12–18 million deaths, cannot be reconciled with the generally accepted death toll of over 50 million (Johnson & Mueller, 2002). Wikipedia's downgraded 2–3% CFR, Black (2020) proposes, can be cited by the media and others as "evidence that COVID-19 is as dangerous as, or more dangerous than, the Spanish Flu."

In March 2020, the WHO provided a "meaningless" (because based predominantly on bad outcomes) estimate of the CFR for "Covid-19" at 3.4% (Ioannidis, 2020). As more "cases" were identified, this figure fell to just above 2%, where it stabilised in 2021. According to data collected by Johns Hopkins University (n.d.), the mean CFR average across all countries (as of February 2021) was 2.15%. Based on data retrieved from the WHO (n.d.-a) Coronavirus dashboard in February 2021, the CFR was 2.2%; by November 2021 it was 2.0%. Thus, the official CFR for "Covid-19" fell precisely in the 2–3% range of Wikipedia's downgraded CFR for the "Spanish flu," enabling a false comparison of "Covid-19" to the "Spanish flu" in line with Black's (2020) prediction. Once "Covid-19" was replaced by the Russia-Ukraine conflict as the primary focus of the 24/7 news cycle in February 2022, Wikipedia put "Spanish flu" deaths back up to "17 million to 50 million, and possibly as high as 100 million," implying a CFR of 3–8% to 16%, though CFR was no longer mentioned.

According to the CDC (2018), the "Spanish flu" killed "at least 50 million" people out of a global population of ca. 1.5 billion. Today, the world's population stands at just over 8 billion, over five times higher. This means that a "Spanish flu" equivalent today would kill well over 250 million people, although this number would need to be revised downwards to account for developments in modern medicine including the advent of antibiotics to treat secondary infections, as well as differential access to such medicine in different parts of the world. A 2006 study factoring in such considerations estimates, based on the 2004 world population of 6.46 billion that a "Spanish flu" equivalent would claim 51–81 million lives (Murray et al., 2006). Given that the global population has increased by 22% since 2004, it seems reasonable to extrapolate that range to 66–99 million lives today. A ballpark figure, therefore, would be 82 million lives. Yet, according to the WHO (n.d.-a) Coronavirus Dashboard in March 2022 (24 months into the "pandemic," a time frame comparable to the "Spanish flu"), "Covid-19" had killed ca. 6 million people, barely one-fourteenth of this figure. Furthermore, given that the average age of death for "Spanish" flu victims was 28, compared to a median age of death of 83 for "Covid-19" in England and Wales (ONS, 2021a), the former was far more deadly in terms of life-years lost.

Exaggerating the Danger

The Role of the UK Government

Under the pretext that the public had to be terrified into compliance for its own good, the UK Government unleashed a campaign of fear against its own citizens. As former Q.C. Lord Sumption observes,

> Fear was deliberately stoked up by the government: the language of impending doom; the daily press conferences; the alarmist projections of the mathematical modellers; the manipulative use of selected statistics; the presentation of exceptional tragedies as if they were the normal effects of Covid-19; above all the attempt to suggest that that Covid-19 was an indiscriminate killer, when the truth was that it killed identifiable groups, notably those with serious underlying conditions and the old, who could and arguably should have been sheltered without coercing the entire population. These exaggerations followed naturally from the logic of the measures themselves. They were necessary in order to justify the extreme steps which the government had taken, and to promote compliance. (Sumption, 2020, p. 10)

The methods used by the UK Government, as well as their terrible impact on members of the public, are documented in Dodsworth's book, *A State of Fear: How the UK Government Weaponised Fear During the Covid-19 Pandemic* (2021). The term "weaponised" here indicates psychological warfare against the public.

The Independent Scientific Pandemic Insights Group on Behaviours (SPI-B), which is a behavioural science subgroup of SAGE, bears significant culpability for helping to wreck the mental health of the nation. Yeadon (2020) blames SAGE for psychologically "torturing the population." On March 22, 2020, SPI-B advised the Government that "The perceived level of personal threat needs to be increased among those who are complacent, using hard-hitting emotional messaging" (2020, pp. 1–2). Cue the sickening propaganda campaign described in Chapter 3 that aimed to instil the fear of death in people and make them believe that they could unwittingly kill others if they did not follow the "rules." These methods, in Scott's (2022) view, made the population "psychologically and physically unwell," their aim being "to harm people." SPI-B's Gavin Morgan admitted that "using fear as a means of control is not ethical. Using fear smacks of totalitarianism" (cited in Rayner, 2021). Steve Baker MP remarked on the issue: "If we're being really honest, do I fear that

Government policy today is playing into the roots of totalitarianism? Yes, of course it is" (cited in Rayner, 2021).

Who sits on SPI-B and SAGE? Publicly available names can be found on the UK Government website (Government Office for Science, n.d.), and include an array of academics, members of the Behavioural Insights Team, the Cabinet Office, etc. More interesting, however, is that, for SPI-B, "4 participants have not given permission to be named." SAGE minutes from March 13 and 16, 2020, end: "Names of junior officials and the secretariat are redacted. Participants who were Observers and Government Officials were not consistently recorded therefore this may not be the complete list" (SAGE, 2020a, 2020c). Who are the mystery attendees? How many of them are there? What is their role? Why is the public not allowed to know their identities? The SAGE minutes themselves would not be publicly available were it not for a legal challenge by Simon Dolan in 2020 to get them released. The secrecy and lack of transparency are red flags; one suspects the influence of British intelligence.

In May 2020, Boris Johnson announced "five alert levels" for "Covid-19" (Prime Minister's Office, 2020b). Those alert levels were modelled on the same colour-coded system that operated during the "War on Terror," allowing fear levels to be dialled up and down. Layered onto this was the tier system of "lockdown" imposed in autumn 2020, with the four tiers (as of December 2020) being classified, respectively, as "medium alert," "high alert," "very high alert," and "stay at home." There was no "low alert" or "zero alert." In May 2021, the UK Government (n.d.-b) announced an Emergency Alerts system that "will warn you if there's a danger to life nearby. In an emergency, your phone or tablet will receive an alert with advice about how to stay safe." The system continues to be developed, but it essentially trains the population to be fearful upon command. Given that the public gets its news from diffuse sources, an Emergency Alert to everyone's smartphone at a moment of acute tension could cause mass panic and hysteria, which social engineers have decades of experience in exploiting. The model is Orson Welles' 1938 radio adaptation of H.G Wells' *War of the Worlds* (1898), which caused panic in the United States when people were unable to distinguish fiction from reality, not least because the radio served as an accepted vehicle for important announcements at a time when millions were worried about war in Europe (Cantril, 2005, p. 68).

The Role of the Media

One means of "maximizing the psychological effects of a terror campaign," Digital Citizen (2003) notes, is "repetition of terrifying images, the kind that would make a person recoil, and then compelling that person to continue viewing them. Such terrifying images weaken the ability of the mind to reason, making it more susceptible to suggestion and manipulation." Much like the endlessly replayed videos of the planes striking the Twin Towers, or of the final moments of those buildings (including their occupants), the media in 2020/21 was awash with imagery of mass death, disease, ICUs, patients on ventilators, people wearing face masks, frightening-looking graphs and forecasts, and the ubiquitous computer-generated image of the "SARS-CoV-2" virion.

In the "shock and awe" early stages of the "Covid-19" operation, the threat from "SARS-CoV-2" was wildly exaggerated by the media. As Yoram Lass, the former Director-General of the Israeli Health Ministry, put it in March 2020, "SARS-CoV-2" is a "virus with public relations" (cited in Magen, 2020). For example, ludicrous staged footage emerged from China of people falling dead on the street (some putting their arms out to break their fall) and being surrounded by figures in hazmat suits (cf. Agence France-Press, 2020). Similar images of forensic experts in hazmat suits removing bodies from the streets came out of Ecuador (Ibbetsen, 2020). On April 10, 2020, the BBC published an article titled, "New York ramps up mass burials amid outbreak," again featuring workers in hazmat suits. In fact, many news outlets ran with aerial footage of the mass burial site in New York, as though to suggest that people were dying too fast to be given ordinary burials. However, Hart Island has been used for mass burials of unclaimed and unidentified bodies since 1869, with some 69,000 people having been buried there since 1980 (Nolan Brown, 2020). Footage of patients gasping for air in ICUs in Lombardy was broadcast without providing the context that Lombardy is one of the most air polluted regions in the world, and, as Lass points out, "Italy is known for its enormous morbidity in respiratory problems, more than three times any other European country" (cited in Magen, 2020). Other footage from an Italian hospital was presented by CBS as from a hospital in New York and by 7 News as from a hospital in Melbourne. None of this deception would have been necessary if "Covid-19" were as deadly as claimed.

"Mortality-salience increases ideological conformity," Kyrie & Broudy (2022) write: it therefore pays for the authorities to "issue frequent mortality-reminders to keep thoughts of harm and death salient (e.g. frequent TV terror alerts or daily COVID cases and death counts)." In 2020/21, it was impossible to escape such messaging in state and corporate media. In 2022/23, in contrast, with excess mortality (consisting mostly of "deaths not involving Covid-19") consistently running well above the five-year average in England and Wales in the wake of the "lockdowns" and the "vaccine" rollout (ONS, 2023, Fig. 1), the frequent mortality-reminders were quietly dropped.

To see the despicable lengths to which the media would go in order to amplify fear of "Covid-19," consider the following *Mail* headline from March 2021: "Grandmother, 66, who was terrified of infecting her family with Covid killed herself by stepping in front of a train when she felt 'a little under the weather' with a cold, inquest hears" (Saunt, 2021). The article goes on to reveal that the woman had reported anxiety issues to her GP since 2007 and that she had admitted visiting a train track with suicidal thoughts in 2013. Her suicide probably had little, if anything, to do with "Covid-19," yet the depraved *Mail* headline spun it that way to spread fear.

The Role of the BBC

An Office of Communications report from 2018 finds that 27% of UK adults "nominate BBC One as their single most important news source"; 62% watch it (Ofcom, 2018). Across social media platforms, the BBC is the "most commonly followed news platform" (37% of UK adults). Of those who get their news not through social media, 63% use the BBC website/app. The BBC News website reaches 74% of the total digital audience of UK adults one way or another. These are astonishing statistics. They suggest that somewhere in the region of two-thirds of UK adults get their news from the BBC, with over a quarter rating the BBC as their most trusted source. In terms of the top current affairs programmes across all channels, 72–78% believe that the BBC, ITV, Channel 4, Sky, Channel 5, BBC Radio, and LDC are "impartial." This shows how easy it is for a handful of broadcast corporations to manipulate a gullible public.

The BBC was a lead culprit when it came to instilling fear of "Covid-19." For example, consider how often the phrase "record number" (or equivalent) featured in BBC headlines: "NI [Northern Ireland] hits another record number of cases" (16/10/20), "Record numbers in hospital in Wales" (12/11/20), "UK announces daily record number of Covid cases" (29/12/20), "The UK has recorded its highest number of Coronavirus deaths in a single day" (8/1/21), "Uruguay registers record number of new Covid cases" (11/1/21), "Record number of daily deaths reported in UK" (13/1/21), "UK records daily high of 1820 deaths" (20/1/21), "UK counts record number of COVID deaths" (21/1/21), "'Record number' of Covid intensive care patients transferred" (22/1/21), etc. Throughout the state and corporate media, in fact, "record numbers" and "new highs" were stressed wherever possible; "cases," hospitalisations and death rates seemed constantly to be "surging," "sharply up," "rising alarmingly," etc., without any necessary context or sense of perspective being provided.

A search on the BBC News website for "how worried should" reveals that the BBC likes to use that phrase to scaremonger wherever possible, e.g. "How worried should we be about melting ice caps?," "Nuclear N. Korea: How worried should we be?," "North Korea-U.S. tensions: How worried should you be?," "How worried should NATO be about Russia's military ZAPAD exercises?," "How worried should we be for our health service?," "The falling FTSE: How worried should we be?," "Global debt: How worried should we be?," "China's economic slowdown: How worried should we be?," "How worried should the West be about China?," "Obesity: How worried should we be?" "How worried should be you be about knife crime?," "How worried should we be about deadly cyber attacks?," "How worried should we be about 'Big Brother' technology?," "How worried should we be about deepfakes?," "Swine flu: How worried should we be?," "Covid: How worried should we be?," and "New Covid strain: How worried should we be?." It is clear that a primary function of the BBC is to keep the population in a perpetual state of anxiety.

Exaggerated Death Statistics

It has been known since 2005 that official death figures are "more PR than science" when it comes to selling vaccines (Doshi, 2005; cf. Hammond, 2018). But in order to sustain the illusion of a "pandemic," the manipulation of official mortality data since 2020 was unprecedented (Davis, 2021a, Chap. 12). For example, until August 2020, anyone in England who died following a positive test result for "Covid-19" was labelled a "Covid-19" death on the death certificate, even if they died of other causes (Davis, 2021c). When Loke and Heneghan (2020) drew attention to this problem, Public Health England ruled that "Covid-19" could still appear as the underlying cause of death provided there had been a positive "Covid-19" test within 28 days of death or the death occurred within 60 days of a first positive test (Newton, 2020). This is as arbitrary as claiming that someone died within 28 or 60 days of getting a haircut: there is no proof of causation.

Any medical doctor could certify the cause of death, even having only met the patient "via video/visual consultation," or indeed having never "seen the deceased before death," based purely on the "best of their knowledge and belief" (ONS & HM Passport Office, 2020, p. 2). Section 19 of the Coronavirus Act withdrew Form 5 of the cremation medical certificate (requiring the opinion of a second medical practitioner), meaning that there was no way for relatives to challenge "Covid-19" on the death certificate, the evidence quickly being incinerated (Beeley, 2020).

Despite all these artifices to inflate the number of official "Covid-19" deaths, the all-cause age-standardised mortality rate in England and Wales in 2020 was lower than during any year between 1970 and 2008, and only the tenth highest year of the twenty-first century (ONS, 2021b)—inconsistent with an extraordinary "pandemic" year. According to the ONS on January 11, 2021, the median age of death "due to COVID-19" in England and Wales was 83; the mean was 80, vs. an average life expectancy in 2018–2020 of 79 for men and 83 for women (ONS, 2021c). Thus, "Covid-19" did not affect life expectancy, other than to help men who contracted it live *longer*. Yet, as late as August 2021, the Department of Health and Social Care (2021) still maintained that "COVID-19 is the biggest threat this country has faced in peacetime history."

Once the "vaccines" were rolled out, the Scientific Pandemic Influenza Group on Modelling, Operational subgroup (SPI-M–O, 2021) worried that, with a "large proportion of the adult population [...] vaccinated, the current definition of death (i.e. death within 28 days of a positive COVID-19 test) will become increasingly inaccurate [...] It will also potentially distort estimates of vaccine efficacy." An unnamed senior SAGE source reportedly claimed: "If the definition remains the same, these people would be counted as 'vaccine failures,' whereas the vaccine prevented death from Covid, but they really died from something else"

(Merrick, 2021). Thus, whereas "died within 28 days of a positive test result" was enough to classify a "Covid-19" death, regardless of the true cause of death, the same criterion was not allowed to apply after "vaccination." On the contrary, being "unvaccinated" was classed as either "having no record of receiving any vaccination or having had a first dose administered within 14 days of receiving a positive covid test" (Christie, 2022). In other words, a person could test positive for "Covid-19" up to two weeks after their first "Covid-19 vaccine" and still be classed as "unvaccinated"—conveniently enough, given that most reported serious adverse reactions to the "vaccine" occur within the first few days of it being administered (OpenVAERS, n.d.). The statistics were clearly massaged to exaggerate deaths from the "virus" and to minimise deaths from the "vaccine."

Hospital Propaganda

An important device for elevating fear levels in the United Kingdom was propaganda that hospitals were on the brink of being overwhelmed by "Covid-19" admissions. On March 23, 2020, the Prime Minister announced that Covid-19 restrictions were necessary to "protect our NHS and to save many many thousands of lives" (Prime Minister's Office, 2020a). The slogan, drilled into the public at every available opportunity, was "STAY HOME. PROTECT THE NHS. SAVE LIVES."

Yet, by April 13, 2020, around 40% of NHS beds lay unoccupied, "about four times the normal number" (West, 2020). An additional 8000 private hospital beds and 20,000 staff, including 700 doctors, were commissioned by the NHS, yet those beds remained empty and staff were left "bored" and "twiddling their thumbs" (Adams, 2020). According to leaked documents, "Two-thirds of the private sector capacity that was block-purchased by the NHS—costing hundreds of millions of pounds—went unused by the service over the summer [of 2020], despite rocketing long waits for operations" (Thomas, 2020). Videos emerged online of alleged hospital workers performing complex choreographed dance routines (which must presumably have taken time to learn and rehearse) without a patient in sight. John Wright of Bradford Royal Infirmary wrote in March 2021 that "the Covid pandemic has transformed our hospitals. Car parks are empty, once-bustling corridors are quiet…" ("Coronavirus doctor's diary: Has Covid changed hospitals for the better?," 2021).

SAGE's "reasonable worst-case planning assumptions" in spring 2020 projected "up to 90,000 beds with ventilators to care for COVID-19 patients" (National Audit Office [NAO], 2020, p. 6). Anticipated ventilator shortages did not occur, however, with only 2150 new ventilators of the 30,000 ordered being dispatched to the NHS based on demand; and even at the peak of the "first wave," 43% of ventilator beds remained unoccupied (NAO, 2020, p. 23).

Seven Nightingale hospitals were erected by the military as a supposed emergency overflow to deal with the imminent inundation of regular hospitals with "Covid-19" patients. Yet, by October 2020, most had "never had a patient" (Quinn, 2020). By the end of 2020, only 28 patients were being treated across all Nightingale hospitals (an average of four patients per hospital), only 249 patients had been admitted all year, and the London Nightingale had reportedly been "stripped of most of its 4000 beds, ventilators and even signs" (Andrews, 2020). Why, given the greatly increased waiting times for treatment for diseases other than "Covid-19" (Triggle & Jeavans, 2021), were the Nightingales not made dedicated "Covid-19" treatment centres, to alleviate the burden on the rest of the NHS? Instead, in March 2021, it was announced that four of the Nightingale hospitals would close permanently (Blanchard, 2021).

It is the NHS's responsibility to protect the taxpayers who fund it. Yet, the government's "Protect the NHS" message led to a precipitous drop in hospital admissions, (Matthews, 2020). In September 2020, the number of hospital operations carried out was "25% lower than in previous years" (Butcher, 2021). According to the ONS (2021d, Fig. 6), excess deaths in hospitals in England and Wales remained below the five-year-average between mid-May and mid-October 2020. Ambulance callouts in England in 2020 remained at or below normal levels (Public Health England, 2021c, Fig. 1). According to NHS England (2020), "Hospital treatment and intensive care has been available to any individual who clinicians determined would benefit from it throughout the pandemic as it normally would be." Public Health England data (2021a, Fig. 1) show that emergency department admissions in 2020 at no point rose above pre- "pandemic" levels and *fell* from mid-September 2020 into 2021 as "Covid-19 cases" officially rose. None of this is consistent with a healthcare system on the brink of being overwhelmed by a "pandemic."

Those with WEF webpages acted as primary propagandists. NHS England Chief Executive Simon Stevens (https://www.weforum.org/people/simon-stevens) claimed in November 2020 that "the equivalent of 22 of our hospitals" were "full of [11,000] coronavirus patients" (cited in Iacobucci, 2020b). Spread across 875 hospitals in England (Interweave Healthcare, 2021), this averages out at only 13 per hospital—hardly overwhelming. According to Daniel Sokol (https://www.weforum.org/agenda/authors/daniel-sokol), "The government is petrified at the prospect of the NHS being overwhelmed. Yet, it already is. Elective operations have all but stopped in many hospitals and resources reallocated towards the covid-19 effort" (Sokol, 2021). Elective operations did not stop because of "Covid-19," however; they stopped because the NHS cancelled "non-urgent" procedures based on a grotesque exaggeration of the "Covid-19" threat. Trish Greenhalgh (https://www.weforum.org/agenda/authors/trish-greenhalgh) claimed on January 18, 2021, that "the NHS is truly overwhelmed for the first time in its 70-year history because of the rise in COVID hospital admissions" (Greenhalgh, 2021).

Greenhalgh's claims regarding "Covid-19" need to be treated with caution. The Oxford professor was, after all, an early promoter of face masks (Greenhalgh et al., 2020), an advocate of joggers and cyclists wearing masks (Greenhalgh, 2021), a perpetual source of unreliable information about masks (Citizen Journalists, 2023), and a champion of "lockdowns" until high "vaccine" uptake is achieved among adolescents (Gurdasani et al., 2021). Face masks (Jefferson et al., 2023; Kisielinski et al., 2021; Children's Health Defence, n.d.), "lockdowns" (Bhattacharya & Packalen, 2020; Stringham, 2020; Rancourt et al., 2021; Dettmann et al., 2022; Bardosh, 2023; Harrison, 2023), and "vaccinating" young people (Dowd, 2022; Hughes, 2022a) were all unnecessary and dangerous.

Greenhalgh's claim about the NHS being overwhelmed by "Covid-19" hospital admissions is easily disproved. For example, Craig et al. (2021) show that the number of Accident and Emergency patients presenting with an acute respiratory infection in early January 2021 was "well below normal levels," and the total number of hospital patients "remains the same or even lower than in previous years." Even the BBC admits that "hospitals were at about 87% occupancy in December [2020] and early January [2021]," i.e. "noticeably lower than a usual year [of] between 93 and 95%" (Butcher, 2021). By February 2021, NHS hospital bed use in England still had not surpassed 2019 levels (NHS England, 2021). Greenhalgh's false claim is, then, not dissimilar from contemporaneous propaganda about temporary morgues being set up in parts of Britain because hospitals were running out of space (Reuters,

2021). A year later, the playbook was the same, viz. headlines such as "NHS England makes plans for field hospitals in preparation for wave of Omicron Covid cases" (Parsley, 2021).

Pressures on the NHS in late 2020 and early 2021, such as they were, owed not to an unmanageable flood of "Covid-19" patients, but, rather, to the "enhanced Infection Prevention Control measures" (NHS England, n.d.-b) put in place to deal with such patients. There were around 10,000 fewer NHS beds in 2020 than in 2019 owing to the alleged need to maintain distance between patients (Johnston, 2021). NHS staff were expected to change PPE between treating patients (Craig et al., 2021). Staff testing positive for "Covid-19" were told to "self-isolate," leading to a reduction in workforce capacity.

It is unclear how many "Covid-19" hospital admissions should have been labelled as such in the first place. Dee (2021), for instance, analyses a large data set of electronic admissions records for an unnamed NHS Trust between January 1 and June 13, 2021, and finds that "Only 9.7% (204 of 2102) of declared COVID cases actually exhibited the fundamental basis for symptomatic disease." The rest, presumably, were misdiagnosed using the PCR test. At any rate, the figures are unreliable.

Ostensibly to prevent hospitals from being overwhelmed by a tsunami of "Covid-19" cases that never came, NHS clinical services and scheduled operations designated "non-urgent" were postponed or cancelled (Stevens & Pritchard, 2020). This meant that large numbers of people could not get screened for illness, or get an operation, creating a "ticking time bomb of health problems" (Shayler, 2022, p. 23). Britons could not see their GP in person or obtain necessary dental care because of government orders that had no statutory basis, yet which left many people in pain or discomfort (Sumption, 2020, pp. 6–7). Five million patients were waiting for surgery in England in March 2021, the highest figure since records began (Pym, 2021). By May 2021, 10% of NHS patients had to wait over a year for treatment, while disruption to cancer services had produced 45,000 "missing cancer patients" following drops in GP referrals and screening services (Triggle & Jeavans, 2021). Heart attacks in England, up 9% on the previous year, reached record levels in 2021/22, owing to difficulties in getting GP appointments and prescriptions for vital medication (Donnelly, 2023). Four in ten patients surveyed in England in November 2022 claimed that their health had worsened while waiting to be admitted to hospital (Care Quality Commission, 2023). Meanwhile, the number of deaths registered in private homes in England has (as of December 30, 2023) remained above the five-year average *every single week* since March 2020 (Office for Health Improvement and Disparities, n.d. [search by place of death]). This all fits the model of clandestine Omniwar, with deprivation of necessary healthcare being used to weaponise public health, causing widespread illness and death by stealth.

The *Spectator* (n.d.) shows some disturbing graphs highlighting the devastating impact of Government/NHS "Covid-19" policies on public health in England. Takeaway points include:

- Hospital waiting lists increased from just over 4 million pre-Covid to 7.75 million in September 2023—nearly double.
- The number of patients spending 12 hours or more from decision to admit to admission each month in A&E departments rose from a previous high of 2800 in 2020 to 54,500 in December 2022 (42,850 as November 2023).
- The average wait time for an ambulance increased from 20 to 30 minutes pre-Covid to around 50–60 minutes in 2022 (90 minutes in December 2022), falling back to below 40 minutes in 2023.
- Patients waiting more than 18 weeks on a hospital waiting list increased from 745,000 in February 2020 to 3 million in April 2023. Patients waiting longer than 52 weeks increased from 1600 in February 2020 to 436,000 in March 2021 and have held steady at around 350,000 to 400,000 per month.
- The number of hip and knee replacements halved between 2019 and 2020, comparing unfavourably to other countries.
- GP appointments have gone from being 80% face-to-face and 14% by phone to 64% face-to-face and 32% by phone.
- There have been 8 million fewer monthly referrals for non-emergency, consultant-led treatment than before the "pandemic."

Taken together, we are looking here at the perfect cocktail for a sicker population. This damage to the NHS, inflicted not by a virus but by government policy, looks very much like an attack on the health of the population, duplicitously delivered under the guise of "public health."

The government's attack on the NHS ramped up in autumn 2021, when Health Secretary, Sajid Javid, announced that "Covid-19 vaccination" would be made mandatory for NHS workers (Baker, 2021), despite risking an exodus of healthcare workers from the profession. In the United States, for instance, vaccine mandates for hospital workers meant that thousands of hospital workers resigned or were fired, resulting in critical staff shortages and "dangerous reductions" in ICU beds (Blaylock, 2022). There was already a shortage of 35,000 nurses in England in June 2021, with NHS Trusts resorting to hiring people unqualified for nursing roles, potentially jeopardising patient safety (Campbell, 2021). The abortive attempt to mandate "Covid-19 vaccination" for NHS workers revealed a flagrant disregard for public health, not only because of concerns surrounding the safety of the "vaccines" (Seneff & Nigh, 2021), but also because of the detrimental impact on the NHS.

The dismantling of the NHS took another leap forwards with the passage of the Health and Care Act in April 2022, which removes the statutory requirement for the NHS to offer treatment to all citizens and for emergency services to be provided for everybody in a given area (Pollock & Roderick, 2021). Instead, the principle of universal free healthcare is replaced with "the limited concept of 'core responsibility' for specified groups of people and the conferring of 'discretions' on providers, enabl[ing] further reductions in and closures of services, pushing those who can afford to do so into paying or their health care" (Pollock & Roderick, 2021). In other words, it is a major move towards privatising the NHS. The birth of the NHS in 1948, like the first welfare state under Bismarck, did not happen by accident. Both were major concessions by the ruling class at a time of social instability and revolutionary potential. The attempt to privatise the NHS reflects an attack on the lower classes who will struggle to afford healthcare and will consequently be made sicker.

The attack on the NHS long predates "Covid-19." For example, between 2000 and 2021 the number of NHS hospital beds fell from 240,000 to 158,000, a cut of just over a third (Statista, 2020). Meanwhile, the UK population rose from 58.9 million in 2000 to 67 million in 2021, a 13.8% increase (ONS, n.d.). This means that the number of NHS hospital beds per 1000 people fell from 4.1 in 2000 to 2.4 in 2020, a significant 41% reduction. The United Kingdom now has one of the lowest rates of hospital beds per capita of any OECD country (Organisation for Economic Co-operation and Development, n.d.). The Royal College of Surgeons and the British Medical Association both complained of chronic bed shortages in 2016, and the Faculty of Intensive Care Medicine in 2018 reported that 80% of ICUs were sending patients to other hospitals because of bed and staff shortages (Kayser, 2020). Pressures on the NHS have arisen, not from disease within the population, but, rather, from a longstanding agenda to undermine the NHS in the interests of the ruling class.

"Non-Pharmaceutical Interventions" as Instruments of Fear

Face Masks as Instruments of Fear

Reflecting on her experience of living in East Asia during the SARS epidemic, Laurie Garret of the Council on Foreign Relations told an audience at the National Academy of Medicine in 2018:

> The major efficacy of a mask is that it causes alarm in the other person, and so you stay away from each other [...] It is alarming. When you walk down the street and everyone coming towards you has a mask on, you definitely do social distancing. It is just a gut thing. But did the mask help them? Did the mask keep the virus out? Almost certainly not. (cited in Senger, 2022a)

The lessons of East Asians' willingness to wear masks and "social distance," believing they were doing the right thing in the absence of any hard scientific evidence, were weaponised against Western populations in 2020, when Garrett suddenly became adamantly pro-mask.

As official "cases," hospitalisations, and deaths involving "Covid-19" tailed off in England in summer 2020 (daily deaths approached zero in August [UK Government, n.d.-a]), face masks were mandated to maintain fear levels and the performance of the "pandemic." Psychologically, face masks act as a "crude, highly visible indicator that danger is all around," even when it is not (Sidley, 2020). Without the masks (and the signage and the plexiglass and the performance of danger through "social distancing"), there would have been no visible indication of a "pandemic."

The mask mandates were never about public health. In the spring of 2020, senior public officials around the world explicitly recommended *against* such mandates. On March 4, 2020, England's chief medical officer, Chris Whitty, stated: "our advice is clear, that wearing a mask if you don't have an infection really reduces the risk almost not at all" (cited in Davis, 2020a). On March 12, 2020, England's deputy chief medical officer, Jenny Harries, claimed that masks can "actually trap the virus" and that, "for the average member of the public walking down a street, it is not a good idea" to wear one (cited in Baynes, 2020). On April 23, 2020, the government's chief scientific adviser, Patrick Vallance, claimed: "The evidence on face masks has always been quite variable, quite weak. It's quite difficult to know exactly, there's no real trials on it" (cited in Davis, 2020a). According to Health Secretary Matt Hancock on April 24, 2020, "The evidence around the use of masks by the general public, especially outdoors, is extremely weak" (cited in Davis, 2020a). On April 28, 2020, England's deputy chief scientific adviser, Angela McLean (previously chief scientific adviser to the MoD) asserted that "there is weak evidence of a small effect in which a face mask can prevent a source of infection going from somebody who is infected to the people around them" (Reuters, 2020). Yet, despite this high-level medical establishment consensus by late April 2020, mask mandates on UK public transport were announced on June 4, 2020 (to begin on June 15); for shops it was July 24.

The WHO (2020c, p. 1) followed a similar pattern. On January 29, 2020, it advised: "a medical mask is not required [in the community setting], as no evidence is available on its usefulness to protect non-sick persons." On February 7, 2020, the WHO's Christine Francis explained, "If you do not have these symptoms [cough, fever, difficulty breathing], you do not have to wear masks because there is no evidence that they protect people who are not sick" (cited in Langton, 2020). On March 30, 2020, Mike Ryan, the executive director of the WHO health emergencies programme, claimed, "there is no specific evidence to suggest that the wearing of masks by the mass population has any particular benefit. In fact, there's some evidence to suggest the opposite [...]" (cited in Howard, 2020). On April 6, 2020, the WHO (2020e, p. 1) reiterated its position that "there is currently no evidence that wearing a mask (whether medical or other types) by healthy persons in the wider community setting, including universal community masking, can prevent them from infection with respiratory viruses, including COVID-19." Yet, on June 5, 2020, the WHO's Maria Van Kerkhove unexpectedly claimed: "We have new research findings. We have evidence now that if [masking] is done properly it can provide a barrier [against] potentially infectious droplets" (Kelland, 2020).

As with the UK "lockdown" decision of March 23, 2020 (see Chapter 2), it is worth asking who exactly was responsible for the mask mandates, given that senior public health officials, both in the United

Kingdom and at the WHO, saw no reason for them in April 2020. Clearly, we are not actually dealing here with public health. Rather, we are looking at a transnational deep state (Hughes, 2022b) capable of intervening at the highest levels of governments and international organisations at a moment's notice, exercising veto power over decisions previously taken and issuing new policies on a whim. Face masks were never about public health; rather, they are an extremely potent instrument of psychological warfare.

According to WHO interim guidance of June 5, 2020, "At present, there is no direct evidence (from studies on COVID-19 and in healthy people in the community) on the effectiveness of universal masking of healthy people in the community to prevent infection with respiratory viruses, including COVID-19" (WHO, 2020f, p. 6). Nine studies plus one meta-analysis are cited that "could be considered to be *indirect* evidence for the use of masks (medical or other) by healthy individuals in the wider community" (my emphasis). The meta-analysis was commissioned by the WHO itself and is seriously flawed (Swiss Policy Research, 2020). On this pathetic evidence base, the WHO (2020f, p. 6) recommends that "governments should encourage the general public to wear masks in specific situations and settings." To be clear, the worldwide mask mandates, based on WHO guidance, were instituted based on no direct evidence of their efficacy.

To make matters worse, the WHO's recommendation that the public be masked was accompanied by a list of potential harms caused by face masks. These include: self-contamination either through hand practice or reusing masks that are wet, soiled, or damaged; facial skin lesions, irritant dermatitis, or worsening acne through prolonged usage; droplet transmission to the eyes; and discomfort (WHO, 2020f, p. 4). To these harmful effects, the WHO interim guidance of December 1, 2020, which again concedes the "limited evidence of protective efficacy of mask wearing in community settings," adds "headache and/or breathing difficulties," "facial temperature changes," "difficulty with communicating clearly, especially for persons who are deaf or have poor hearing or use lip reading," and "improper mask disposal leading to increased litter in public places and environmental hazards" (WHO, 2020g, pp. 6, 10). Thus, not only was there no direct evidence of the efficacy of mask mandates, but there was also no evidence of their safety.

A mere six days after the WHO's anti-scientific recommendation that governments encourage the practice of public mask wearing, Rancourt (2020b) found that "No RCT [randomised controlled trial] study with verified outcome shows a benefit for HCW [healthcare workers] or community members in households to wearing a mask or respirator. There is no such study. There are no exceptions"; moreover, "no study exists that shows a benefit from a broad policy to wear masks in public." A literature review published in April 2020 had reached a similar conclusion: "The evidence is not sufficiently strong to support widespread use of facemasks as a protective measure against COVID-19" (Brainard et al., 2020). Royo-Bordonada et al. (2020) note: "At present, there is no evidence on the effectiveness of universal masking of healthy people in the community to prevent infection with respiratory viruses, including SARS-CoV-2." According to Heneghan and Jefferson (2020), "there is no available good quality evidence on whether, for example, masks prevent transmission of Covid-19 in the community and (if so) which types."

Although post hoc studies emerged seeking to justify mask mandates, so did studies finding against face mask usage (Children's Health Defence, n.d.; LifeSite News, 2021). The key point is that there was no scientific basis for mask mandates *when they were introduced*. The belated pro-mask studies amount to little more than a rationalisation of arbitrary power. The fact that "case" rates surged in country after country *after* masks were mandated confirms that masks were never effective in "stopping the spread."

The WHO, Rancourt (2020c, p. 4) observes, violated the Golden Rule of medical ethics: "You don't recommend an intervention without policy-grade evidence for both harms and benefits." In Britain, no risk assessment was carried out by the government before mask mandates were introduced, and my MP was unable to provide one when I asked for it in July 2020. Rancourt (2020c, p. 5) is correct that mask mandates represent "the worst decisional model that can be applied in a rational and democratic society," i.e. "forced preventative measures without a scientific basis, while recklessly ignoring consequences." Indeed, the failure of public policy to heed the potential *harms* of face mask wearing was stark. As Cayley (2020) observes, "most of the studies touting good effects like reduced viral load have paid no attention to potential ill effects." According to Kisielinski et al. (2021), "Up until now, there has been no comprehensive investigation as to the adverse health effects masks can cause."

James Meehan, MD, writes: "In February and March [2020] we were told not to wear masks. What changed? The science didn't change. The politics did. This is about compliance. It's not about science" (cited in Manley, 2020). Compelling behaviour change was fundamental. Independent SAGE's Gabriel Scally claimed in August 2020 that the face mask "acts as a reminder that these aren't normal times and that we've all got to change our behaviour" ("'Re-think Face Masks in Shops,' Says Scientist," 2020). A government "Covid-19" taskforce advisor was even more explicit: "Masks are a behavioural psychology policy. We need to stop pretending that it's about public health. Nudge is a big thing in government" (cited in Dodsworth, 2021b). However, face masks were not mere "nudges" to encourage the public to adopt supposedly beneficial behaviours for the good of society. Rather, face masks are instruments of menticidal attack, designed to break the public down psychologically. One obvious function (among many) is to trigger visceral fear of disease and a sense that the environment has become strange and threatening. The increased stress and anxiety make the public more susceptible to propaganda and psychological manipulation.

There are physiological, as well as psychological, reasons why mask wearing increases fear levels. Covering the mouth and nose with a mask can lead to hypercapnia, i.e. abnormally high CO_2 levels in the blood (Kisielinski et al., 2021). In mice, "rising CO_2 concentrations elicit intense fear" and it has been shown that "the amygdala [acts] as an important chemosensor that detects hypercarbia [hypercapnia] and acidosis and initiates behavioral responses" (Ziemann et al., 2009). In humans, "the amygdala has a central role in anxiety responses to stressful and arousing situations" and can activate the "fight-or-flight" response (Linsambarth et al., 2017; Moyer, 2019). Therefore, by increasing CO_2 levels, face masks can physiologically trigger fear and anxiety in the wearer.

PCR Tests as Instruments of Fear

Another instrument for spreading fear was the PCR test, which was wrongly used to diagnose "cases" of "Covid-19" (hence the misleading phrase "tested positive for Covid-19"). The inventor of the PCR test, Kary Mullis (1993) never intended it to be used for diagnostic purposes, calling it "a process used to make a whole lot of something out of something. [...] It doesn't tell you that you're sick." In Mullis' words, "PCR detects a very small segment of the nucleic acid which is part of a virus itself" and doubles the amount of it in successive cycles of the RT-PCR process (cited in Farber, 2020a). Thus, David Crowe explains, "PCR is really a manufacturing technique [...] If you double 30 times, you get approximately a billion times more material than you started with" (cited in Farber, 2020a). This can be useful for experimental purposes, but it cannot distinguish whether the genetic material detected implies active infection or mere "dead particles" following recovery from infection (Heneghan & Jefferson, 2020). Canadian microbiologist Jared Bullard testified under oath that PCR tests can detect non-viable viral fragments for up to 100 days, even though a person with "Covid-19" is infectious only for one to two weeks (Justice Centre for Constitutional Freedoms [JCCF], 2021).

The "Covid-19" PCR test manufacturers themselves clearly indicate that their product cannot diagnose disease:

> The instruction manual of "RealStar" by Altona Diagnostics: "For research use only! Not for use in diagnostic procedures." "Multiplex RT-qPCR Kit" of Creative Diagnostics: "This product is for research use only and is not intended for diagnostic use." The product announcement of the "LightMix Modular Assays" by Roche: "These assays are not intended for use as an aid in the diagnosis of coronavirus infection. For research use only. Not for use in diagnostic procedures." (Steinhagen, 2020)

It is, therefore, curious that Public Health England (2021b) claims that "COVID-19 cases are identified [diagnosed] by taking specimens from people and testing them for the presence of the SARS-CoV-2 virus. If the test is positive, this is referred to as a case. If a person has had more than one positive test they are only counted as one case."

The idea that a positive test for the "SARS-CoV-2" virus—whether using PCR, lateral flow, or any other form of test—implies the presence of the disease known as "Covid-19" is ludicrous, because it ignores the role of the human immune system. It is commonplace for viruses to be carried asymptomatically, with the virus remaining present in harmlessly low levels, because the immune system prevents it from replicating. Harrit (2021) makes this point succinctly:

> To be sick is to have symptoms. If you are not sick, you are not contagious. It used to be common sense that you are healthy unless you are not. Sense is not common anymore during the alleged Covid-19 pandemic. Now you are sick until proven healthy – and contagious by default. The vehicle for this scam is the RT-PCR test run at >35 cycles and beyond.

According to biochemist David Rasnick, "You don't start with testing; you start with listening to the lungs," i.e. clinical symptoms first (cited in Farber, 2020a). Yet, against such elementary principles, the ONS and Oxford University partnered on a well-remunerated study in 2020 to "find out how many people have Covid-19, either with or without symptoms across the UK" (Slater, 2020). The aim seems to have been to normalise the concept of symptomless disease.

The number of cycles the RT-PCR test involves is known as the cycle threshold, with each cycle doubling the amount of genetic material under examination. The more cycles that are run, the higher the chance of a positive test result, because there is more material to detect. At a certain cycle threshold, the test becomes too sensitive and may yield false positive results, detecting material that was not originally present in sufficient quantity to be infectious. There is no absolute value to that cycle threshold, and different laboratories use different cycle thresholds (itself problematic in terms of consistency of standards). Nevertheless, according to the authoritative MIQE (Minimum Information for Publication of Quantitative Real-Time PCR Experiments) guidelines of 2009, "Cq values > 40 are suspect because of the implied low efficiency and generally should not be reported [...]" (Bustin et al., 2009, p. 618). One of the authors of those guidelines, Stephen Bustin, claims in an April 2020 interview, "I would be very unhappy about a 40-cycle PCR [...] Above a cycle of about 35, then you start to worry about the reliability of your results [...] Try to be sure that the results you get are in the twenties to thirties" (The Infectious Myth, 2020, 30:00).

Yet, NHS England worked to a cycle threshold of 45 when testing for "SARS-CoV-2" (Science & Technology Committee, 2020). A WHO summary table of protocols being used around the world shows France using 50 cycles, Germany, Thailand, and the United States using 45 cycles, and Hong Kong, and Japan using 40 cycles (WHO, 2020b). The Canadian province of Manitoba used between 40 and 45 cycles (JCCF, 2021). Kim et al. (2020), in the early "isolation" of "SARS-CoV-2," perform PCR amplification with 40 cycles. This implies the likelihood of high false positive rates in PCR testing across the world.

Did the PCR tests test exclusively for "SARS-CoV-2," as any reliable test must? For the "Covid-19" PCR test to be valid, Bustin claims, "the SARS-CoV-2-specific primers and probes [...] must be 100% specific for the virus and so amplify only viral sequences" (Bustin & Nolan, 2020).

However, research published by the Spanish medical journal *D-Salud-Discovery* (Blanca, 2020), whose findings are independently verified by Davis (2020b), casts doubt on whether this is the case. It finds, for instance, that the PCR test protocol of the Pasteur Institute tests for genetic sequences present in "dozens of sequences of the human genome itself and in those of about a hundred microbes." The Japanese PCR protocol yields similar results: 93 human genome sequences and 100 microbe sequences with 94–100% similarity (Blanca, 2020). These findings are achieved by entering key genetic sequences from WHO-approved PCR protocols into the Basic Local Alignment Search Tool (BLAST), which enables a given sequence to be compared to all sequences stored in the U.S. National Institutes of Health.

Although the PCR test was unfit for purpose, the authorities were eager to use it everywhere. On March 16, 2020, the WHO Director-General pleaded, "We have a simple message for all countries: test, test, test" (WHO, 2020d). The UK Department of Health and Social Care (2020a) published a document on April 4, 2020 titled, *Coronavirus (COVID-19) Scaling Up Our Testing Programmes*, and NHS Test and Trace was established on May 28. Operation Moonshot aimed to administer 10 million tests a day by 2021 at the astronomical cost to the taxpayer of £100 billion, but the scheme was abandoned after the Good Law Project threatened legal action over misuse of public funds (Iacobucci, 2020a). In July 2020, the Rockefeller Foundation (2020) called on everyone to get tested at least twice a month—a new mass industry involving "perhaps as many as 300,000" people (ca. 0.1% of the population) to administer 30 million tests per week and run contact tracing in the United States.

Why the urgency to "test, test, test" using an obviously flawed testing protocol? One reason is that tests create "cases" and "cases" create fear. The more tests that are carried out using a test liable to produce false positive results, the more "cases" there will be (the so-called "casedemic"). "Cases" here, however, are not the same as active infections that cause illness. They are, rather, an artifice to inflate fear levels, e.g., via media reports of "surging case numbers" and "deaths within 28 days of a positive test for coronavirus." When the United Kingdom ended free testing in April 2022, the "Covid-19 case rate" plummeted by 38% in a single week (Matthews, 2022).

There is nothing new in this scam. Reflecting on HIV testing between 1984 and 1996, Mullis remarks: "The number of cases went up epidemically, you know, exponentially, because the number of tests that was done went up exponentially" ("PCR inventor Kary Mullis talks about Anthony Fauci," 2020). Yet, the number of active HIV infections in North America, Mullis adds, remained steady during the same period, at around a million. The reported "cases" nevertheless generated huge public fear around the virus, driving demand for pharmaceutical products and, thus, profit for Big Pharma.

In 2007, nearly 1000 healthcare workers at a medical centre in New Hampshire were furloughed following an apparent whooping cough outbreak. However, it proved to be a false alarm: "Not a single case of whooping cough was confirmed with the definitive test, growing the bacterium, *Bordetella pertussis*, in the laboratory. Instead, it appears the health care workers probably were afflicted with ordinary respiratory diseases like the common cold" (Kolata, 2007). The reason for the false alarm was PCR testing and the fact that epidemiologists and infectious disease specialists "placed too much faith in a quick and highly sensitive molecular test that led them astray." The sensitivity of the PCR test "makes false positives likely, and when hundreds or thousands of people are tested [...] false positives can make it seem like there is an epidemic."

The strategy for dealing with the 2009 "swine flu pandemic" (neither endemic in pigs nor a pandemic in any pre-2009 sense of the term) can be summarised as: "Publicise all cases where the virus has been detected. That is, set up surveillance stations everywhere and notify the community of every case of the virus found in the population—even if the infection does not cause any disease [...]" (Wilyman, 2020). This chimes with Marc van Ranst's cynical media strategy for spreading fear of H1N1 (EvidenceNotFear, 2020).

During "Covid-19," the mass testing regime became self-sustaining, as those found to have been in contact with a positive "case" were themselves asked to take a test, even if neither party was symptomatic. On and on it went: healthy people producing false positive test results, drawing in even more people for testing. To encourage more and more people to get tested, some 700 test centres were set up under NHS Test and Trace, the average distance to one being just 2.4 miles (Department of Health and Social Care, 2020b). However, if amateur video footage of empty testing centres is anything to go by, this was largely just propaganda.

Viral Terror

Waves of Fear

Totalitarian menticide involves creating successive waves of fear and terror. As Meerloo (1956, p. 147) notes, "Each wave of terrorizing [...] creates its effects more easily—after a breathing spell—than the one that preceded it because people are still disturbed by their previous experience." Linked to these "waves of terrorizing" is the totalitarian "strategy of fractionalized fear," whereby victims' minds are more easily conditioned "in a quiet period between acute tensions," when their guard may be down (Meerloo, 1956, p. 168).

The threat of new "waves" of "SARS-Cov-2" served a similar function, i.e. to terrify and demoralise the public and wear it down psychologically. The alleged virus need not be especially virulent for the mere threat of its resurgence (with attendant implications associated with "lockdown") to be used to keep the population fearful and apprehensive. Schwab and Malleret (2020, p. 91) appear to explain the desired effect: "On a planetary scale, our collective sense of mental wellbeing has taken a very severe knock. Having dealt with the first wave, we are now anticipating another that may or may not come, and this toxic emotional mix risks producing a collective state of anguish." That "very severe knock," however, was caused by government policies, not by a virus which, by the authors' admission, had killed only "0.006%" of the global population at that point (2020, p. 99). It is the anticipation (created by propaganda) that causes the anguish, not anything in nature.

Invoking "waves" of the virus means that the threat of some future dread can be used to keep the population anxious and uncertain. The idea of a "second epidemic peak" was seeded by SAGE (2020b, p. 4) as early as March 13, 2020: "it is a near certainty that countries such as China, where heavy suppression is underway, will experience a second peak once measures are relaxed." This chimes with "Report 9" three days later: "Once interventions are relaxed (in the example in Fig. 3, from September onwards), infections begin to rise, resulting in a predicted peak epidemic later in the year" (Ferguson et al., 2020, p. 10). During the summer of 2020, when "Covid-19" case, hospitalisation, and mortality rates all plummeted in England (UK Government, n.d.-a), the propaganda was that "Hospitals will need as much capacity as they can get if there is a second wave" (Chalmers, 2020a). In one possible scenario envisaged by Schwab and Malleret (2020, p. 21), "the first wave is followed by a larger wave that takes place in the third or fourth quarter of 2020, and one or several smaller subsequent waves in 2021 (like during the 1918–1919 Spanish flu pandemic)." This is essentially what happened in England (only with the "second wave" peak coming in mid-January 2021, rather than Q4 of 2020), forming a supposed three-peak distribution over a two-year period much like the "Spanish flu" a century earlier (UK Government, n.d.-a; Taubenberger & Morens, 2006, Fig. 1).

The three "waves" of "Covid-19," like those of the "Spanish flu," are a form of pseudoscience: "Viruses do not do waves. That's just a myth based on poor understanding of influenza at the end of WW1, a century ago" (Yeadon, 2020). It makes no sense, other than to spread fear, to treat "Covid-19" as a single ongoing event with multiple "waves." "Modern human mortality in mid-latitude temperate-climate regions," Rancourt (2020a, p. 4) notes, "is robustly seasonal," and this is why, for instance, we speak of the "flu season" rather than amalgamating the last several flu seasons' data (as the WHO [n.d.-a] Covid-19 Dashboard does for "Covid-19"). In the Czech Republic, "the three individual waves (autumn 2020 to spring 2021) […] lacked direct genomic relationship between each other," and the Omicron variant "did not reveal direct evolutionary connection to any of the previous SARS-CoV-2 variants" (Kämmerer et al., 2023; cf. Tanaka & Miyazawa, 2023), rendering it doubtful that "new variants" were responsible for new "waves" of the virus.

Once "Covid-19″ had apparently formed the classic Gompertz curve in the spring of 2020, there was no reason, based on the principle of viral entropy, to expect a "second wave" larger than the first in the winter. Prior and naturally acquired immunity meant that "endemic equilibrium" should have been imminent" by the autumn of 2020 (Yeadon, 2020). According to Oxford-AstraZeneca's Sarah Gilbert, "viruses tend to become less virulent over time as they spread through a population becoming more immune" (cited in Knapton, 2021). An open letter to the Prime Minister, dated November 8, 2020, and signed by 469 medics, states: "It is notable that [the] UK death rate is currently sitting around average for this time of year. The use of the term 'second wave' is therefore misleading" and the government response to the virus is "disproportionate" (Davies, 2020). The so-called "second wave" that purportedly followed in winter 2020 is, therefore, not scientifically credible.

In 2021, fear of a future virological threat was linked to the potential return of influenza, which, in a historically unprecedented turn of events, had supposedly vanished in 2020 (see Chapter 6). In February 2021, SAGE's John Edmunds predicted "an out-of-season [influenza] epidemic perhaps in the autumn, rather than winter" (Patel, 2021). Susan Hopkins, in charge of Public Health England's "Covid-19" strategy, claimed in March 2021 that the United Kingdom must prepare for a "hard winter" of "flu and other similar illnesses" (cited in Topping, 2021). Boris Johnson claimed in June 2021: "You can never exclude the possibility that there will be some new disease, some new horror we haven't budgeted for or accounted for [...] Things like flu may come back this winter, we may have a rough winter for all sorts of reasons" (Jones, 2021). A July 2021 report by the Academy of Medical Sciences (2021), commissioned by Patrick Vallance, predicts the perfect storm: a "third peak of COVID-19 infections over the summer of 2021," followed by a possible "new variant," while "outbreaks of RSV in the autumn and influenza in the winter could be around twice the magnitude of a 'normal' year, and might overlap (at least partially) with a peak in COVID-19 infections." Mike Tildesley, a modeller from the University of Warwick, claimed in August 2021: "If [flu and other respiratory infections] return on the scale we expect we could see really major pressures build on the NHS that could raise some very difficult questions" (Triggle, 2021b). Actual influenza rates for the winter of 2021/22 were lower than for any of the six winters preceding "Covid-19" (WHO, n.d.-b), thus confirming the well-established pattern of using public health forecasts to spread fear during the "Covid-19 pandemic."

Since the "Covid-19" operation was wound down in early 2022, artificially manufactured waves of fear have continued to roll across Western societies, viz. the Marburg and monkeypox scares, the "climate emergency" (Plimer, 2021), the threat of food and fuel shortages, fear-mongering rhetoric of nuclear war attached to the Ukraine conflict, runaway inflation and the cost-of-living crisis, "disinformation" (the pretext for online censorship), concerns about immigration (see Chapter 8), threats of cyber-attacks/outages (Cyber Polygon, n.d.), etc. This goes beyond Mencken's (2009, p. 24) contention that "The whole aim of practical politics is to keep the populace alarmed, and hence clamorous to be led to safety, by menacing it with an endless series of hobgoblins, all of them imaginary." Rather, we are looking here at psychological warfare: "These fear-waves and threats (negative stimuli;

conditioning à la Pavlov) are designed deliberately to grind people down, to make them submit, to induce breakdown, to coerce them to give up [...]" (Scott, 2022).

"New Variants" and "Immunity Escape"

In order to maintain fear levels among the population, the concept of "new variants" was introduced in Britain in December 2020, based on Public Health England data (2020a, pp. 5, 48) regarding unusually high "case" rates in Kent. Matt Hancock wrote in a WhatsApp conversation on December 13, 2020: "When do we deploy [a military term] the new variant" in order to "frighten the pants off everyone with the new strain"? To which his special adviser, Damon Poole, replied: "Yep that's [sic.] will get proper behaviour change" (Haigh, 2023). Hancock announced the new variant and Tier 3 restrictions the next day.

The term "new variant" is interesting in and of itself, since influenza routinely develops new strains, yet there is no comparable level of fear-mongering attached. The underlying idea, propagated by the media, is that "SARS-CoV-2 consistently evolves into an ever more dangerous iteration of itself" (Davis, 2021b)—the opposite of viral entropy. The idea was thus seeded that the virus mutates in such a way as to evade all forms of acquired immunity, be they cross-reactive T-cell immunity, naturally acquired immunity to the virus, or vaccine-derived immunity.

The first "Variants of Concern" originated in the United Kingdom, Brazil, and South Africa (Golemi-Kotra, 2021), the same three countries used in AstraZeneca's phase 3 trials (Voysey et al., 2021). The odds of this precise combination of countries appearing randomly together are 7 million to one against (1/193 * 1/192 * 1/191), suggesting either that the AstraZeneca "vaccines" cause immune escape or that this incredible coincidence was scripted in order to promote the idea of immune escape.

Official sources did not portray the "Kent variant" as especially virulent. Public Health England (2020b) on December 20, 2020, for instance, offered "no evidence that this variant causes more severe disease or higher mortality." Gates (2020) claimed on December 22, 2020, that the new variant "seems to spread faster but not to be more deadly." Johns Hopkins Medical Centre saw "[no] indication that the new strain is more virulent or dangerous in terms of causing more severe COVID–19 disease" (Bollinger & Ray, 2020). Analysis of relevant UK data by Davis (2021b) reveals that up to early December 2020, "the new variants had accounted for an increased rate of transmission—but significantly lower rates of hospitalisation and mortality."

Yet, SAGE (2020d) treated the "new variant" as a pretext for authoritarianism: "Given the increase in risk associated with the new variant," it claimed, "a commensurate strengthening in the measures taken [...] may be needed." This was despite inherent scientific uncertainty, reflected in SAGE's use of hedging phrases such as "not yet known whether [...]," "not yet any evidence which suggests [...]," "not yet clear whether [...]," and "currently no evidence of [...]." Neil Ferguson likewise claimed: "the new variant without doubt will make the relaxation of restrictions more difficult" (cited in Glaze, 2021). "New variant" thus became synonymous with scientifically baseless restrictions on liberty, providing a "psychological justification for actions the government may wish to take anyway" (Dodsworth, 2021a, p. 116).

Notwithstanding the dubiousness of the "new variant" concept, the idea was propagated that "new variants" might somehow evade all forms of acquired immunity. The "specter of vaccine escape mutants" was mooted as early as June 2020 (Branch, 2020). Once the "vaccines" were rolled out in December 2020, an early concern was that too long a gap between "vaccine" doses could create "more potential for viral evolution" (Saad-Roy et al., 2021). In early January 2021, the New and Emerging Respiratory Virus Threats Advisory Group (2021) warned that "SARS-CoV-2 variants may arise which evade monoclonal antibody therapies, convalescent plasma therapy, vaccine derived immunity, or naturally acquired immunity." The BBC warned in February 2021: "Growing levels of immunity from further rollout of the vaccine will favour variants that can sneak past the vaccine" (Triggle, 2021a). Whitty expressed confidence that a vaccine-resistant variant would emerge (cited in Boyd, 2021). Ferguson warned of "the worst case scenario [that] we have a new variant pop up which does manage to evade the vaccines [...]" (cited in Walsh, 2021). An *Express* headline pointed to a "vaccine-resistant variant" about to "smash" the United Kingdom (Falvey, 2021). This is all scripted and intended to maintain fear of the "virus" even as the "vaccines" intended to deal with that virus were being rolled out.

The WHO's Maria Van Kerkhove warned in August 2021 that "new variants could emerge which evade vaccines," claiming that so many new variants had emerged that the Greek letter scheme introduced to label them a few months earlier would soon be exhausted and that the WHO might have to name them after star constellations ("COVID-19

Variants could be named after constellations," 2021). The *Sun* warned with respect to the Lambda variant that "'unusual' mutations can 'dodge vaccines'" (Zorzut, 2021). According to the *New York Post*, the Epsilon variant, despite being removed from the WHO's "variants of interest" in July 2021, "could evade vaccines" (O'Neill, 2021). In September, the WHO claimed it was monitoring the new "Mu" variant, which has "the potential to evade immunity provided by a previous Covid-19 infection or vaccination" (Lovelace Jr., 2021). The propaganda strategy is clear, i.e. to maintain constant fear of immune escape via a proliferation of "new variants."

Geert Vanden Bossche

The issue of immune escape received special attention following publication of an open letter by Geert Vanden Bossche (2021). Vanden Bossche, a virologist with experience of working for Big Pharma, GAVI, and the Bill & Melinda Gates Foundation, claims that mass vaccination with leaky vaccines could lead to more virulent strains of "Covid-19" developing in vaccinated people, which in turn could kill the unvaccinated, leading to a never-ending need to vaccinate against ever more dangerous strains. It was first theorised in 2001 that vaccines could in principle select for the evolution of increased virulence (Gandon et al., 2001). Empirical confirmation was provided in 2015: immunisation of chickens against Marek's disease "enhances the fitness of more virulent strains, making it possible for hyperpathogenic strains to transmit"; this is because leaky vaccination "prolongs host survival but does not prevent infection, viral replication or transmission" (Read et al., 2015). If similar were to occur in humans, then "the normal 'life cycle' of a virus, from highly virulent and dangerous, to more infectious but less dangerous ('virus entropy') may be fundamentally affected or even reversed" (van der Pijl, 2022, p. 247). This contravention of Virology 101 seems *prima facie* unlikely, however.

The Vanden Bossche open letter reads more as fear propaganda than as science. For example, it refers to "killer vaccines" and claims that mass vaccination threatens to "wipe out large parts of our human population" by "turning a relatively harmless virus into a bioweapon of mass destruction." If so, how might those behind the "bioweapon" expect to survive? Do they have the antidote? Vanden Bossche (2021) dramatically appeals to professional reputation rather than carefully supported scientific argumentation: "In this agonizing letter, I put all of my reputation and credibility at stake." Yet, an unreferenced, five-page letter is not the place to do this; rather, a peer-reviewed journal article, or at the very least a preprint would have been more appropriate, notwithstanding the urgency of the subject matter.

Like a tabloid newspaper, Vanden Bossche's open letter places multiple, sometimes sensationalist, phrases in capital letters to grab attention, e.g. "THE SINGLE MOST IMPORTANT PUBLIC HEALTH EMERGENCY OF INTERNATIONAL CONCERN." Phrases such as "racing against the clock" and "there is not one second left for gears to be switched" add to the drama but detract from scientific credibility. The virus itself is anthropomorphised as a kind of master criminal that will "take on another coat" as part of its "strategy" to replicate and increase its "return on selection investment." The open letter also makes emotive reference to the vulnerability of children to "Covid-19," even though there is little to no credible scientific evidence to support this assertion (Hughes, 2022a).

Vanden Bossche's scientific claims are spurious. For example, he presents a jaundiced view of the human immune system (Frei, 2021), focusing on initial "passive immunity" but not subsequent "adaptive immunity" in which T-cells are produced. He tries to downplay cross-reactive T-cell immunity as "short-lived," only mentioning T-cells twice, even though it is known that "CD4+ T cells, CD8+ T cells, and neutralizing antibodies all contribute to control of SARS-CoV-2 in both non-hospitalized and hospitalized cases of COVID-19" (Sette & Crotty, 2021). Because "SARS-CoV-2" is a coronavirus, there is already a certain degree of cross-reactive T-cell memory (found in ca. 28–50% of people) and therefore "some degree of pre-existing immunity in the population" (Sette & Crotty, 2021). The "Variants of Concern" do not change this, for they "do not significantly disrupt the total SARS-CoV-2 T cell reactivity" (Tarke et al., 2021).

Despite criticising leaky "Covid-19" vaccines for endangering all human life, Vanden Bossche (2021) reaches a surprising conclusion: "Paradoxically, the only intervention that could offer a perspective to end this pandemic (other than to let it run its disastrous course) is …VACCINATION." Thus, he does nothing to challenge the "Covid-19" vaccination agenda. Instead, he proposes "large vaccination campaigns" that will prime NK (natural killer) cells so that they "acquire immunological memory" and thereby become able to "recognize and kill Coronaviruses at large (include all their variants) at an early stage of infection"—even though there is still no cure for the common cold.

If Vanden Bossche were right, deaths among the "unvaccinated" would have spiralled out of control. Instead, not only did Omicron fit the viral entropy model of more transmissible but less deadly (it was likened to the common cold), but health outcomes among "unvaccinated" people proved better than for the "vaccinated" (see Chapter 7). It is therefore hard to escape the conclusion that Vanden Bossche is yet another medical establishment figure responsible for propagating a pseudoscientific fear narrative. Almost no one had heard of him before he entered the scene, and he disappeared just as quickly, having played his part.

"Long Covid"

The threat severity of "Covid-19" was hyped via the new concept of "long Covid," which NHS England (n.d.-a) vaguely defines in terms of "symptoms that develop during or following an infection consistent with COVID-19 which continue for more than 12 weeks and are not explained by an alternative diagnosis." Those symptoms are said by NHS England to be "wide-ranging and fluctuating, and can include breathlessness, chronic fatigue, 'brain fog,' anxiety and stress," as well as "generalised pain, fatigue, persisting high temperature and psychiatric problems."

All of those symptoms, however, can be explained by alternative diagnoses. According to one GP, "most [of those] symptoms are so common that we see them in general practice all the time" (cited in Cox, 2021). Without a control group, it is impossible, in the words of NIAID's Michael Sneller, to "attribute any abnormality to the viral infection"; for example, "about 12% of our COVID group complains of tinnitus, and about 14% of the control group has tinnitus" (cited in Couzin-Frankel, 2021). Blankenburg et al. (2022) find "no statistically significant difference (Fisher's exact test) in the occurrence of any neurocognitive or pain symptoms" among 1560 school children with "long Covid" symptoms, regardless of whether they tested seropositive or seronegative.

The term "long Covid" was coined by a patient advocacy organisation called Body Politic in a May 2020 report based on online surveys of people self-reporting persistent symptoms. However, of those surveyed, "nearly half (47.8%) never had testing and 27.5% tested *negative* for Covid-19," meaning that less than a quarter had tested positive (Devine, 2021). In a December 2020 report by the same organisation, only 15.9%

of respondents "had tested positive for the virus at any time" (Devine, 2021). To be clear, only 16–25% of those self-reporting "long Covid" in these early surveys had tested positive for "SARS-CoV-2." Proponents of "long Covid" sometimes attribute such low rates to the initial scarcity of testing kits, as though more testing would undoubtedly have revealed many more "cases" (Re'em, 2021). Yet, in the May 2020 report above, more people tested negative than positive, suggesting that less than half of tests overall would have come back positive.

A later scientific study corroborates this hypothesis: in 467 12–25-year-olds, "long Covid" symptoms after six months (based on the WHO definition of "Post-COVID-19 Condition") were found in 49% of those who had previously tested positive for "SARS-CoV-2," but also 47% of those had tested *negative* (Selvakumar et al., 2023)—offering no convincing evidence that "long Covid," if it exists, has anything to do with "Covid-19." Rather, Selvakumar et al. (2023) conclude, "initial symptom severity and psychosocial factors" are the key predictors of "long Covid," there being no hard evidence what caused those symptoms, while the "psychosocial factors" mean that it could all be in the mind. An even larger study of 5086 11–17-year-olds delivers a similar verdict: "these symptoms may be causally related to multiple factors and not just the original SARS-COV-2 infection" (Pereira et al., 2023).

The existence of "long Covid," which has no equivalent in, say, "long rhinovirus" or "long influenza," was not established through scientific investigation; rather, it was promoted by patient advocacy groups like Body Politic bringing together people convinced they have the illness. To a sceptic, this looks "a lot like amalgam poisoning, electricity allergy, and chronic Lyme disease—i.e. conditions that some people diagnose themselves with (doctors rarely diagnose them), but for which there are no diagnostic tests, and for which there is no scientific evidence" (Rushworth, 2020). Devine (2021), too, compares "long Covid" to chronic Lyme disease, "a term whose usage is discouraged because it describes a range of symptoms without requiring evidence of prior infection with the bacterium that causes Lyme disease; some see it as quackery [...]." One "long Covid" advocacy group, Patient-led Research, ran a study in which "the majority [73%] of participants did not report receiving a positive SARS-CoV-2 diagnostic or antibody test result," nevertheless claiming that this "should not be used as an indicator to rule out Long COVID in patients who otherwise have *suggestive symptoms*" (Davis et al., 2021, my emphasis). There is no plausible connection here between the virus and the alleged long-term symptoms. Rather, "long Covid" turns out to be "basically whatever the person who thinks they have it says it is. Anything and everything can be attributed to long covid" (Rushworth, 2020).

Despite the lack of science, "long Covid" patient advocacy organisations rapidly gained disproportionate influence. For example, take Lisa McCorkell of Body Politic and Patient-Led Research, whose highest academic qualification is a Master of Public Policy in 2020. In April 2021, McCorkell gave evidence to Congress as one of seven "expert witnesses" alongside the heads of the NIH and CDC, as well as two professors from Stanford and Yale. In her testimony, McCorkell (2021) notes that Body Politic formed part of the WHO's "long Covid" working group and held "ongoing meetings" with the CDC's Post-COVID Conditions Unit, producing research that has been cited in "over 70 scientific publications, guidance for clinicians, and policy documents." Thus, a patient advocacy group run by five young people without prior academic publications, whose work on "long Covid" contains obvious methodological flaws, supposedly informed scientific debate and policymaking at the highest levels of public health, including the WHO, CDC, and NIH. This is not credible. A more plausible explanation is that there is a high-level agenda to promote "long Covid," and patient advocacy groups are either being exploited or were astroturfed to push the agenda.

To see why many people *believe* they have a condition called "long Covid," consider why so many people believe they may have had "Covid-19" in the first place. Not only is it "hard to tell the difference" between "Covid-19" and influenza "based on symptoms alone" (CDC, 2021; see Chapter 6), but the media also encouraged the public to identify any and every symptom with "Covid-19," including hives (Haglage, 2020), chilblains (Young, 2020), parosmia (Brewer, 2021), insomnia (McCann, 2022), hiccups, tinnitus, and stammering (Hagan, 2021), mouth disease, hearing loss, blood clots, conjunctivitis, and diarrhoea (Mullin & Chalmers, 2021), erectile dysfunction (Ruiz, 2020), "green poop" (Sweeney, 2022), eye swelling (Hockaday, 2022), and brain fog (Parsons, 2022). Some of these symptoms were crudely renamed "Covid toes," "Covid eye," "Covid brain," etc.

The media was relentless in promoting the existence of "long Covid." According to the *Manchester Evening News*, there are "more than 200 symptoms associated with long Covid" (Cox, 2021). The *Guardian* published a series of articles on "long Covid," relating "harrowing tales of people who never fully recovered from a Covid infection, experiencing pain, 'brain fog,' irritable bowel syndrome, and a huge range of other disorders with no end in sight" (see Ritchie, 2021). The *Mail* insists "'Long Covid' IS real" and that three quarters of patients admitted to hospital with "Covid-19" symptoms were still showing symptoms three months later (Chalmers, 2020b). According to *National Geographic*, "people who only suffered mild infections can be plagued with life-altering and sometimes debilitating cognitive deficits" (Mullin, 2021).

A population saturated in propaganda of this kind (in particular, the majority that has no idea it is being propagandised) will naturally include many people who believe they have had "Covid-19" and "long Covid," regardless of whether or not they tested positive using an unreliable test. It is significant that some of the alleged symptoms of "long Covid," such as brain fog, fatigue, and body aches, are also found in chronic fatigue syndrome, a condition which for years was not taken seriously. Similarly, a common complaint among the "long Covid" community is that the condition was at first not taken seriously by medical professionals owing to lack of a positive test result (Guenot, 2021). To what extent, then, is "long Covid" embraced and promoted by communities legitimately seeking due recognition of their suffering from other causes?

It must also be acknowledged that "Covid-19" and "long Covid" are likely to be embraced by hypochondriacs and those with Munchhausen syndrome, i.e. people morbidly anxious about their own health or who feign disease in order to gain attention. This consideration is particularly important in view of Pentagon neuroscience adviser James Giordano's (2017) plans for psychological warfare:

> What I put over the internet is: this is a virus, bacteria, an agent that I have infiltrated into your fill-in-the-blank. I say it's a weapon of mass destruction, and what I tell you it's going to do is, it's going to produce paranoia, anxiety, and sleeplessness. What I've just done is I've recruited every paranoid hypochondriac to think that they have whatever that is [...] I create a legion of essentially what's known as the worried well.

Sneller et al. (2022) find that patients with a history of anxiety disorder (as well as women) are more likely to report PASC ("long Covid") and that there is "no evidence of persistent viral infection, autoimmunity, or abnormal immune activation in participants with PASC," casting doubt on any connection to the virus. In the absence of hard scientific evidence, "long Covid" could be psychogenic and based on "pseudoscience" that will "perpetuate patient denial of mental illness and psychosomatic symptoms" (Devine, 2021).

There is, in any case, something suspect about the vast array of symptoms attributed to "Covid-19" and "long Covid." On the one hand, Schwab and Malleret (2020, p. 21) seek to convince us that

> COVID-19 is a master of disguise that manifests itself with protean symptoms that are confounding the medical community. It is first and foremost a respiratory disease but, for a small but sizeable number of patients, symptoms range from cardiac inflammation and digestive problems to kidney infection, blood clots and meningitis. In addition, many people who recover are left with chronic kidney and heart problems, as well as lasting neurological effects.

According to the DHS Science and Technology Directorate (2021, p. 7), "COVID-19 also causes pneumonia, cardiac injury, secondary infection, kidney damage, pancreatitis, arrhythmia, sepsis, stroke, respiratory complications, and shock."

Yet, how can a respiratory disease produce such far-reaching effects across multiple failing organs? As Rushworth (2020) writes, "covid is not some magical entity, it's a coronavirus, and it behaves like other coronaviruses, and other respiratory viruses more generally. It would be strange for covid to cause symptoms that other respiratory viruses don't." Since when have coronaviruses caused coagulopathies, blood clots, and crossed the blood brain barrier to produce neurological disease? The danger of the virus in terms of clinical symptoms appears to have been greatly exaggerated.

A *Scientific American* headline from July 2021 reads: "A tsunami of disability is coming as a result of 'long Covid.' We need to plan for a future where millions of survivors are chronically ill" (Pomeroy, 2021). The idea of "long Covid" as "mass disabling event" (Lin II & Money, 2022) was, thus, propagated at a stage in the "vaccine" rollout where most U.S. adults had taken at least one shot—as opposed to, say, in December 2020, when "long Covid" had supposedly been around for at least seven months without "vaccines." Some of the most distressing videos of "vaccine"-injured people show them convulsing uncontrollably, indicating a neurological disorder unlikely to have been caused by a coronavirus. According to *Scientific American*, "Long Covid now looks like a neurological disease" (Sutherland, 2023). Readers must draw their own conclusions.

If "long Covid" were as serious as is made out, one might have expected that, after three years, the more than $1 billion poured into "long Covid" research by the NIH would have yielded some tangible results. Instead, Cohrs and Ladyzhets (2023) observe, "There's basically nothing to show for it [...] The National Institutes of Health hasn't signed up a single patient to test any potential treatments." This bears the hallmarks of a scam.

Societies in Distress

The "Covid-19" operation represents "a well-organized, very sophisticated propaganda campaign that has drawn on the human fear of death and disease" (Curtin, 2021). Building on fear tactics deployed during the "Cold War" and the "War on Terror," the pseudopandemic (Davis, 2021a) sought, in the most literal way, to put the fear of death into everyone, and would not have been possible without the media to amplify fear levels. Manipulated death statistics, propaganda about "overwhelmed" hospitals, face masks, PCR tests, viral "waves," "new variants," "immune escape," "long Covid"—all of it was about keeping populations in a state of heightened fear and anxiety so that they might be psychologically weakened and manipulated in various ways and ultimately rendered powerless to resist the transition to technocracy.

The real-life effects of this fear-mongering were evident in, for instance, "people body swerving in a supermarket to maintain distance from one another; hugging each other through plastic; washing one's shopping and leaving for three days before touching again; [and] shop owners washing physical cash in a fish tank" (Scott, 2021). Demand for underground bunkers and "prepping" products exploded ("The plague of fear breeds paranoia," 2020). People wore face masks when out walking without another human being in sight and while driving in their car alone (Sardi, 2021).

The Health Advisory & Recovery Team (HART, 2021) makes the indisputable point that "it is unacceptable for a civilised society to strategically inflict heightened emotional distress on its citizens as a means of inducing the behaviours that the government has, paternalistically, decided are the 'right' ones." The point is, however, that we no longer live in civilised societies. We live in wartime conditions, with the rule of law breaking down, in societies that can increasingly only be ruled by force, until a new settlement is reached (cf. Hughes et al., 2022).

References

Academy of Medical Sciences. (2021, July 15). *Covid-19: Preparing for the future*. https://acmedsci.ac.uk/file-download/4747802.

Adams, S. (2020, April 19). Private hospitals that have been taken over by the NHS in fight against coronavirus at the cost of hundreds of millions of pounds are "sinfully empty"—leaving hundreds of the country's top doctors "bored" and "twiddling their thumbs." *Daily Mail*. https://www.dailymail.co.uk/news/article-8233207/Private-hospitals-taken-NHS-fight-against-coronavirus-left-sinfully-empty.html.

Agence France-Press. (2020, January 31). A man lies dead in the street: The image that captures the Wuhan coronavirus crisis. *The Guardian*. https://www.theguardian.com/world/2020/jan/31/a-man-lies-dead-in-the-street-the-image-that-captures-the-wuhan-coronavirus-crisis.

Allen, N., & Landauro, I. (2020, June 26). Coronavirus traces found in March 2019 sewage sample, Spanish study shows. *Reuters*. https://www.reuters.com/article/us-health-coronavirus-spain-science/coronavirus-traces-found-in-march-2019-sewage-samplespanish-study-shows-idUSKBN23X2HQ.

Amendola, A., Canuti, M., Bianchi, S., Kumar, S., Fappani, C., Gori, M., Colzani, D., Kosakovsky Pond, S.L., Miura, S., Baggieri, M., Marchi, A., Borghi, E., Zuccotti, G., Raviglione, M.C., Magurano, F., Tanzi, E. (2022). Molecular evidence for SARS-CoV-2 in samples collected from patients with morbilliform eruptions since late 2019 in Lombardy, northern Italy. *Environmental Research, 215*(1), Article 113979. https://doi.org/10.1016/j.envres.2022.113979.

Andrews, L. (2020, December 29). Only 28 Covid patients are currently being treated in No10's £220million Nightingale hospitals while top doctor begs ministers to use ALL of the mothballed facilities—as make-shift units get dismantled "because there aren't enough staff to run them." *Daily Mail*. https://www.dailymail.co.uk/news/article-9095087/Londons-Nightingale-hospital-quietly-broken-arent-medics.html.

Apolone, G., Montomoli, E., Manenti, A., Boeri, M., Sabia, F., Hyseni, I., Mazzini, L., Martinuzzi, D., Cantone, L., Milanese, G., Sestini, S., Suatoni, P., Marchianò, A., Bollati, V., Sozzi, G., & Pastorino, U. (2021). Unexpected detection of SARS-CoV-2 antibodies in the prepandemic period in Italy. *Tumori Journal, 107*(5), 370–474. https://doi.org/10.1177/0300891620974755.

Baker, S. (2021, September 5). Health Secretary Sajid Javid plans to make vaccines a condition of employment for all NHS workers. *Daily Mail*. https://www.dailymail.co.uk/news/article-9958909/Health-Secretary-Sajid-Javid-plans-make-vaccines-condition-employment-NHS-workers.html.

Bardosh, K. (2023). How did the Covid pandemic response harm society? A global evaluation and state of knowledge review (2020-21). Preprint retrieved from https://doi.org/10.2139/ssrn.4447806.

Baynes, C. (2020, March 12). Coronavirus: Face masks could increase risk of infection, medical chief warns. *The Independent*. https://www.independent.co.uk/news/health/coronavirus-news-face-masks-increase-risk-infection-doctor-jenny-harries-a9396811.html.

Beeley, V. (2020, October 5). Removal of form 5 cremation certificate for deaths relating to covid-19 under the Coronavirus Act. *The Wall Will Fall*. https://thewallwillfall.org/2020/10/05/removal-of-form-5-cremation-certificate-for-deaths-relating-to-covid-19-under-the-coronavirus-act/.

Bhattacharya, J., & Packalen, M. (2020, May 16). Lives vs lives—the global cost of lockdown. *The Spectator*. https://www.spectator.co.uk/article/lives-vs-lives-the-global-cost-of-lockdown.

Black, C. (2020, March 9). Wikipedia slashes Spanish Flu death rate. *OffGuardian*. https://off-guardian.org/2020/03/09/wikipedia-slashes-spanish-flu-death-rate/.

Blanca, J.G. (2020, November). La estafa se constata: La PCR no detecta el SARS-CoV-2. *DSalud*. https://www.dsalud.com/reportaje/la-estafa-se-constata-la-pcr-no-detecta-el-sars-cov-2/.

Blanchard, S. (2021, March 8). Four out of England's seven Nightingale hospitals will close permanently next month while others will be used for vaccinations or NHS clinics in "transition" back to normal. *Daily Mail*. https://www.dailymail.co.uk/news/article-9339429/Coronavirus-Four-Englands-seven-Nightingale-Hospitals-CLOSE-permanently-month.html.

Blankenburg, J., Wekenborg, M. K., Reichert, J., Kirsten, C., Kahre, E., Haag, L., Schumm, L., Czyborra, P., Berner, R., & Armann, J. P. (2022). Comparison of mental health outcomes in seropositive and seronegative adolescents during the Covid-19 pandemic. *Scientific Reports*, *12*, Article 2246. https://doi.org/10.1038/s41598-022-06166-y.

Blaylock, R. L. (2022). Covid update: What is the truth? *Surgical Neurology International*, *13*, Article 167. https://doi.org/10.25259/SNI_150_2022.

Bollinger, R., & Ray, S. (2020, December 28). A new strain of coronavirus: What you should know. *Johns Hopkins Medicine*. www.hopkinsmedicine.org/health/conditions-and-diseases/coronavirus/a-new-strain-of-coronavirus-what-you-should-know.

Boyd, C. (2021, April 1). Chris Whitty says Britain will treat covid "like the flu" in future but warns we will be vulnerable to the disease for another two years and says a vaccine-resistant variant will emerge. *Daily Mail*. https://www.dailymail.co.uk/news/article-9427169/Chris-Whitty-warns-Britain-vulnerable-Covid-two-years.html.

Brainard, J., Jones, N., Lake, I., Hooper, L., & Hunter, P. R. (2020). Facemasks and similar barriers to prevent respiratory illness such as Covid-19: A rapid systematic review. Preprint retrieved from https://doi.org/10.1101/2020.04.01.20049528v1.

Branch, A. D. (2020). How to survive Covid-19 even if the vaccine fails. *Hepatology Communications, 4*(12), 1864–1879. https://doi.org/10.1002/hep4.1588.

Brewer, K. (2021, January 28). Parosmia: "Since I had Covid, food makes me want to vomit." *BBC News*. https://www.bbc.co.uk/news/stories-55824567.

Broudy, D., & Hoop, D. K. (2021). Messianic mad men, medicine, and the media war on empirical reality: Discourse analysis of mainstream Covid-19 propaganda. *International Journal of Vaccine Theory, Research, and Practice, 2*(1), 365–388. https://doi.org/10.56098/ijvtpr.v2i1.22.

Bustin, S. A., & Nolan, T. (2020). RT-qPCR testing of SARS-CoV-2: A primer. *International Journal of Molecular Sciences, 21*(8), Article 3004. https://doi.org/10.3390/ijms21083004.

Bustin, S. A., Benes, V., Garson, J. A., Hellemans, J., Huggett, J., Kubista, M., Mueller, R., Nolan, T., Pfaffl, M. W., Shipley, G. L., Vandesompele, J., & Wittwer, C. T. (2009). The MIQE guidelines: Minimum information for publication of quantitative real-time PCR experiments. *Clinical Chemistry, 55*(4), 611–622. https://doi.org/10.1373/clinchem.2008.112797.

Butcher, B. (2021, January 7). Covid: How busy are hospitals in England? *BBC News*. https://www.bbc.co.uk/news/55536762.

Campbell, D. (2021, June 9). NHS trusts hiring non-nurses for nursing roles, union warns. *The Guardian*. https://www.theguardian.com/society/2021/jun/09/nhs-trusts-hiring-non-nurses-for-nursing-roles-union-warns.

Cantril, H. (2005). *The invasion from Mars* (3rd ed.). Transaction Publishers.

Care Quality Commission. (2023, September 12). *Adult inpatient survey 2022*. https://www.cqc.org.uk/publications/surveys/adult-inpatient-survey.

Cayley, D. (2020). Pandemic revelations. *International Journal of Illich Studies, 7*(1), 22–69.

Centres for Disease Control and Prevention. (2018, May 11). *1918 Pandemic influenza: Three waves*. https://www.cdc.gov/flu/pandemic-resources/1918-commemoration/three-waves.htm.

Centres for Disease Control and Prevention. (2021, January 27). *Similarities and differences between flu and Covid-19*. https://www.cdc.gov/flu/symptoms/flu-vs-covid19.htm#table.

Chalmers, V. (2020b, August 8). "Long covid" is real: Three-quarters of coronavirus patients who were admitted to hospital still suffer symptoms three months later, study reveals. *Daily Mail*. https://www.dailymail.co.uk/news/article-8643457/Almost-75-hospital-Covid-19-patients-suffer-symptoms-three-months-later-study-claims.html.

Chalmers, V. (2020a, June 15). UK could offer everyone a flu jab this winter to cut serious cases and free up hospital beds for a second wave of covid-19—but vaccines are already in global short supply. *Daily Mail*. https://www.dailymail.co.uk/news/article-8421311/Flu-jabs-protect-NHS-second-wave-Covid-19.html.

Children's Health Defence. (n.d.). *The science of masks*. https://childrenshealthdefense.org/the-science-of-masks/.

Chossudovsky, M. (2021). *The 2020 worldwide corona crisis: Destroying civil society, engineered economic depression, global coup d'état, and the "Great Reset."* Centre for Research on Globalization.

Christie, B. (2022). Covid-19: Fact check—how many patients in hospital are unvaccinated? *BMJ, 376*, o5. https://doi.org/10.1136/bmj.o5.

Digital Citizen. (2003, September 25). 9/11 official theory. Are you brainwashed? *Phil Taylor's Papers*. https://universityofleeds.github.io/philtaylorpapers/vp01eff8.html.

Citizen Journalists. (2023, January 15). *Trish Greenhalgh caught out telling more lies on face masks*. https://citizenjournos.com/2023/01/15/trish-greenhalgh-caught-out-telling-more-lies-on-face-masks/.

Cohen, D., & Carter, P. (2010). WHO and the pandemic flu "conspiracies." *BMJ, 340*, 1274–1279. https://doi.org/10.1136/bmj.c2912.

Cohrs, R., & Ladyzhets, B. (2023, April 20). The NIH has poured $1 billion into long Covid research—with little to show for it. *STAT*. https://www.statnews.com/2023/04/20/long-covid-nih-billion/.

Coronavirus doctor's diary: Has Covid changed hospitals for the better? (2021, March 15). *BBC News*. https://www.bbc.co.uk/news/health-56379088.

Coronavirus: World must prepare for pandemic, says WHO. (2020, February 25). *BBC News*. https://www.bbc.co.uk/news/world-51611422.

Couzin-Frankel, J. (2021, April 13). How scientists are teasing apart the biology of long Covid. *Science*. https://www.sciencemag.org/news/2021/04/how-scientists-are-teasing-apart-biology-long-covid.

COVID-19 variants could be named after constellations once Greek alphabet is used up, WHO official says. (2021, August 8). *Sky News*. https://news.sky.com/story/amp/covid-19-variants-could-be-named-after-constellations-once-greek-alphabet-is-used-up-who-official-says-12376314.

Cox, C. (2021, August 18). Long covid—"200 symptoms, 1000 referrals" and the future for patients. *Manchester Evening News*. https://www.manchestereveningnews.co.uk/news/greater-manchester-news/200-long-covid-symptoms-treatment-20540582.

Craig, C., Engler, J., & Smalley, J. (2021, January 7). What does endemic Covid look like? *The Daily Sceptic*. https://dailysceptic.org/2021/01/07/what-does-endemic-covid-look-like/.

Curtin, E. (2021, June 19). What I know and don't know about SARS-CoV-2 virus. *Behind the Curtain*. http://edwardcurtin.com/what-i-know-and-dont-know-about-sars-cov-2-virus/.

Cyber Polygon. (n.d.). *What is Cyber Polygon?* https://cyberpolygon.com/about/.

Cyrulik, J. C. (1999). Asymmetric Warfare and the threat to the American homeland. *Association of the United States Army Landpower Essay Series* 99(8),1–12. https://www.ausa.org/sites/default/files/LPE-99-8-Asymmetric-Warfare-and-the-Threat-to-the-American-Homeland.pdf.

Davies, J. (2020, November 8). Official data is "exaggerating" the risk of Covid and talk of a second wave is "misleading," 500 academics tell Boris Johnson in open letter attacking lockdown. *Daily Mail*. https://www.dailymail.co.uk/news/article-8925427/Official-data-exaggerating-risk-Covid-500-academics-tell-Boris-Johnson.html.

Davis, I. (2020a, June 22). Face masks have put us in a state. *Iain Davis*. https://iaindavis.com/face-masks/.

Davis, I. (2020b, November 16). Covid-19: Evidence of global fraud. *Iain Davis*. https://in-this-together.com/covid-19-evidence-of-global-fraud/.

Davis, I. (2021a). *Pseudopandemic. New normal technocracy*. Independently published.

Davis, I. (2021b, February 2). Why is there a correlation between the vaccine rollout and increased Covid–19 mortality? *UK Column*. https://www.ukcolumn.org/article/why-there-correlation-between-vaccine-rollout-and-increased-covid%E2%80%9319-mortality.

Davis, I. (2021c, March 28). A deceptive construction—why we must question the Covid-19 mortality statistics. *UK Column*. https://www.ukcolumn.org/article/deceptive-construction-why-we-must-question-covid-19-mortality-statistics.

Davis, H. E., Assaf, G. S., McCorkell, L., Wei, H., Low, R. J., Re'em, Y., Redfield, S., Austin, J. P. & Akrami, A. (2021). Characterizing long covid in an international cohort: 7 months of symptoms and their impact. *EClinicalMedicine*. https://doi.org/10.1016/j.eclinm.2021.101019.

Day, J. (2020, May 12). WHO exposed: How health body changed pandemic criteria to push agenda. *The Express*. https://www.express.co.uk/news/world/1281081/who-world-health-organisation-coronavirus-latest-swine-flu-covid-19-europe-politics-spt.

Dee, J. (2021). *Report 11 audit of ED covid-19 coding*. https://iaindavis.com/ukc/DrJD-Analysis.pdf.

deHaven-Smith, L. (2013). *Conspiracy theory in America*. University of Texas Press.

Denoon, D. J. (2010, September 7). Study shows H1N1 swine flu symptoms, risk of serious illness no worse than seasonal flu. *Web MD*. https://www.webmd.com/cold-and-flu/news/20100907/h1n1-swine-flu-no-worse-than-seasonal-flu.

Department of Health and Social Care. (2020a). *Coronavirus (Covid-19) scaling up our testing programmes*. https://assets.publishing.service.gov.uk/government/uploads/system/uploads/attachment_data/file/878121/coronavirus-covid-19-testing-strategy.pdf.

Department of Health and Social Care. (2020b). *Business as usual for NHS test and trace over Christmas*. https://www.gov.uk/government/news/business-as-usual-for-nhs-test-and-trace-over-christmas.

Department of Health and Social Care. (2021). *Consultation document: Changes to human medicine regulations to support the rollout of covid-19 vaccines*. https://www.gov.uk/government/consultations/distributing-vaccines-and-treatments-for-covid-19-and-flu/consultation-document-changes-to-human-medicine-regulations-to-support-the-rollout-of-covid-19-vaccines.

Deslandes, A. Berti, V., Tandjaoui-Lambotte, Y., Alloui, C., Carbonnelle, E., Zahar, J. R., Brichler, S., & Cohen, Y. (2020). SARS-CoV-2 was already spreading in France in late December 2019. *International Journal of Antimicrobial Agents*, *55*(6), Article 106006. https://doi.org/10.1016/j.ijantimicag.2020.106006.

Dettmann, L. M., Adams, S., & Taylor, G. (2022, February 9). Investigating the prevalence of anxiety and depression during the first COVID-19 lockdown in the United Kingdom: Systematic review and meta-analyses. *British Journal of Clinical Psychology*, *61*(3), 757–780. https://doi.org/10.1111/bjc.12360.

Devine, J. (2021, March 22). The dubious origins of long Covid. *The Wall Street Journal*. https://www.wsj.com/articles/the-dubious-origins-of-long-covid-11616452583.

DHS Science and Technology Directorate. (2021). *Master question list for covid-19 (caused by SARS-CoV-2) weekly report, 23 February 2021*. https://www.dhs.gov/sites/default/files/publications/mql_sars-cov-2_-_cleared_for_public_release_20210223.pdf.

Dodsworth, L. (2021a, December 18). *A week of life under the ministry of fear*. https://lauradodsworth.substack.com/p/a-week-of-life-under-the-ministry.

Dodsworth, L. (2021b, December 18). A week of life under the ministry of fear. *Laura Dodsworth*. https://lauradodsworth.substack.com/p/a-week-of-life-under-the-ministry.

Donnelly, L. (2023, August 15). Heart attacks at record level after pandemic. *The Telegraph*. https://www.telegraph.co.uk/news/2023/08/15/heart-attack-hospitalisations-record-level-since-pandemic/.

Doshi, P. (2005). Are U.S. flu death figures more PR than science? *BMJ*, *331*, 1412. https://doi.org/10.1136/bmj.331.7529.1412.

Dowd, E. (2022). *"Cause Unknown": The epidemic of sudden deaths in 2021 and 2022*. Skyhorse.

Engler, J. (2022, August 22). The Lombardy analysis. *PANDA Uncut*. https://pandauncut.substack.com/p/the-lombardy-analysis.

EvidenceNotFear. (2020, April 20). *Communication and public engagement—Marc Van Ranst, Belgian Flu Commissioner*. https://evidencenotfear.com/communication-and-public-engagement-marc-van-ranst-belgian-flu-commissioner/.

Falvey, D. (2021, July 29). New lockdown warning as scientists fear "worrying" vaccine-resistant variant to smash UK. *The Express*. https://www.express.co.uk/news/politics/1469307/lockdown-warning-update-international-travel-rules-new-coronavirus-variant-import.

Farber, C. (2020a, April 7). Was the Covid-19 test meant to detect a virus? *UncoverDC*. https://uncoverdc.com/2020/04/07/was-the-covid-19-test-meant-to-detect-a-virus/.

Farber, C. (2020b, December 3). Ten fatal errors: Scientists attack paper that established global PCR driven lockdown. *uncoverdc.com*. https://www.uncoverdc.com/2020/12/03/ten-fatal-errors-scientists-attack-paper-that-established-global-pcr-driven-lockdown/.

Ferguson, N. M, Laydon, D., Nedjati-Gilani, G., Imai, N., Ainslie, K., Baguelin, M., Bhatia, S., Boonyasiri, A., Cucunubá, Z., Cuomo-Dannenburg, G., Dighe, A., Dorigatti, I., Fu, H., Gaythorpe, K., Green, W., Hamlet, A., Hinsley, W., Okell, L. C., van Elsland, S., Ghani, A. C., et al. (2020). *Report 9: Impact of non-pharmaceutical interventions (NPIs) to reduce Covid-19 mortality and healthcare demand*. https://www.imperial.ac.uk/media/imperial-college/medicine/sph/ide/gida-fellowships/Imperial-College-COVID19-NPI-modelling-16-03-2020.pdf.

Flynn, P. (2010, June 7). *The handling of the H1N1 pandemic: More transparency needed*. Council of Europe Parliamentary Assembly. Retrieved June 17, 2023, from https://pace.coe.int/en/files/12463/html.

Fongaro, G., Stoco, P. H., Souza, D. S. M., Grisard, E. C., Magri, M. E., Rogovski, P., Schörner, M. A., Barazzetti, F. H., Christoff, A. P., de Oliveira, L. F. V., Bazzo, M. L., Wagner, G., Hernández, M., & Rodríguez-Lázaro, D. (2021). The presence of SARS-CoV-2 RNA in human sewage in Santa Catarina, Brazil, November 2019. *Science of The Total Environment*, *778*(15), Article 146198. https://doi.org/10.1016/j.scitotenv.2021.146198.

Frei, R. (2021, March 16). The curious case of Geert Vanden Bossche. *Rosemary Frei*. https://www.rosemaryfrei.ca/the-curious-case-of-geert-vanden-bossche/.

Fuchs, C. (2021). *Communicating Covid-19. Everyday life, digital capitalism, and conspiracy theories in pandemic times*. Emerald Publishing.

Gandon, S., Mackinnon, M. J., Nee, S., & Read, A. (2001). Imperfect vaccines and the evolution of pathogen virulence. *Nature, 414*, 751–756. https://doi.org/10.1038/414751a.

Gates, B. (2020, December 22). These breakthroughs will make 2021 better than 2020. *GatesNotes*. https://www.gatesnotes.com/About-Bill-Gates/Year-in-Review-2020.

Giordano, J. (2017, August 29). *Brain science from bench to battlefield: The realities—and risks—of neuroweapons*. Centre for Global Security Research seminar, Lawrence Livermore National Laboratory. https://cgsr.llnl.gov/event-calendar/2017/2017-06-12.

Glaze, B. (2021, January 14). Covid lockdown rules "could be needed until Autumn" despite signs cases are "plateauing." *Daily Mirror*. https://www.mirror.co.uk/news/politics/covid-difficult-until-easter-least-23317176.

Golemi-Kotra, D. (2021, April 16). Covid-19 variants FAQ: How did the U.K., South Africa and Brazil variants emerge? Are they more contagious? How does a virus mutate? Could there be a super-variant that evades vaccines? *The Conversation*. https://theconversation.com/covid-19-variants-faq-how-did-the-u-k-south-africa-and-brazil-variants-emerge-are-they-more-contagious-how-does-a-virus-mutate-could-there-be-a-super-variant-that-evades-vaccines-159032.

Government Office for Science. (n.d.). *List of participants of SAGE and related sub-groups*. Retrieved June 17, 2023, from https://www.gov.uk/government/publications/scientific-advisory-group-for-emergencies-sage-coronavirus-covid-19-response-membership/list-of-participants-of-sage-and-related-sub-groups#scientific-pandemic-influenza-group-on-behaviours-spi-b.

Greenhalgh, T., Schmid, M. B., Czypionka, T., Bassler, D., & Gruer, L. (2020). Face masks for the public during the Covid-19 Crisis. *BMJ*, *369*, Article m1435. https://doi.org/10.1136/bmj.m1435.

Greenhalgh, T. (2021, January 18). Joggers and cyclists should wear masks if they can't maintain a physical distance from pedestrians. *The Conversation*. https://theconversation.com/joggers-and-cyclists-should-wear-masks-if-they-cant-maintain-a-physical-distance-from-pedestrians-153110.

Guenot, M. (2021, June 24). Long Covid patients say they feel gaslit by doctors that still don't believe them. *Business Insider*. https://www.msn.com/en-us/health/medical/long-covid-patients-say-they-feel-gaslit-by-doctors-that-still-dont-believe-them/ar-AALnXXM.

Gurdasani, D., Drury, J., Greenhalgh, T., Griffin, S., Haque, Z., Hyde, Z., Katzourakis, A., McKee, M., Michie, S., Pagel, C., Reicher, S., Roberts, A., West, R., Yates, C., & Ziauddeen, H. (2021). Mass infection is not an option: We must do more to protect our young. *The Lancet*, *398*, Article 10297, 297–298. https://doi.org/10.1016/S0140-6736(21)01589-0.

Hagan, P. (2021, January 16). Hiccups, tinnitus and stammering are bizarre signs of Covid too, say doctors—as it becomes clear the virus can affect the body from head to toe. *Mail on Sunday*. https://www.dailymail.co.uk/health/article-9154783/Hiccups-tinnitus-stammering-bizarre-signs-Covid-say-doctors.html.

Haglage, A. (2020, April 21). Coronavirus is causing hives and 4 other skin reactions—Here's what dermatologists warn you to look for." https://www.yahoo.com/lifestyle/coronavirus-hives-skin-reactions-dermatologist-152002908.html.

Haigh, E. (2023, March 5). Matt Hancock discussed "deploying" new virus variant to "frighten the pants off everyone" as former Health Secretary demands immunity on care home deaths during the pandemic. *Daily Mail*. https://www.dailymail.co.uk/news/article-11821671/Matt-Hancock-discussed-deploying-new-virus-variant-frighten-pants-everyone.html.

Hammond, J. R. (2018, June 19). How the CDC uses fear marketing to increase demand for flu vaccines. *Foreign Policy Journal*. https://www.foreignpolicyjournal.com/2018/06/19/how-the-cdc-uses-fear-marketing-to-increase-demand-for-flu-vaccines/.

Harrison, N. (2023, December 7). Lockdowns: A study of the harms. *UK Column*. https://www.ukcolumn.org/article/lockdowns-a-study-of-the-harms.

Harrit, N. (2021, March 27). "Making something out of nothing": PCR tests, CT values and false positives. A comment on the efficacy of the RT-PCR test in view of the Jaafar paper. *OffGuardian*. https://off-guardian.org/2021/03/27/making-something-out-of-nothing-pcr-tests-ct-values-and-false-positives/.

Health Advisory and Recovery Team. (2021, June 24). *The dubious ethics of covert psychological "nudges."* https://www.hartgroup.org/covert-psychological-nudges/.

Heneghan, C., & Jefferson, T. (2020, November 10). The nine worst Covid-19 biases. *The Spectator*. https://www.spectator.co.uk/article/the-nine-worst-covid-19-biases.

Hockaday, J. (2022, January 4). Boy, 9, almost blinded after suffering rare "Covid eye.'" *Metro*. https://metro.co.uk/2022/01/04/boy-9-almost-blinded-after-suffering-rare-covid-eye-15862249/.

Howard, J. (2020, May 14). Masks help stop the spread of coronavirus—the science is simple and I'm one of 100 experts urging governors to require public mask-wearing. *The Conversation*. https://theconversation.com/masks-help-stop-the-spread-of-coronavirus-the-science-is-simple-and-im-one-of-100-experts-urging-governors-to-require-public-mask-wearing-138507.

Hughes, D. A. (2020). 9/11 truth and the silence of the IR discipline. *Alternatives, 45*(2), 55–82. https://doi.org/10.1177/0304375419898334.

Hughes, D. A. (2022b, July 29). Wall Street, the Nazis, and the crimes of the deep state. *Propaganda in Focus*. https://propagandainfocus.com/wall-street-the-nazis-and-the-crimes-of-the-deep-state/.

Hughes, D. A. (2022a). "Covid-19 vaccines" for children in the UK: A tale of establishment corruption. *International Journal of Vaccine Theory, Practice, and Research, 2*(1), 209–247. https://doi.org/10.56098/ijvtpr.v2i1.35.

Hughes, D. A., Kyrie, V., & Broudy, D. (2022, November 29). Covid-19: Mass formation or mass atrocity? *Unlimited Hangout*. https://unlimitedhangout.com/2022/11/investigative-reports/covid-19-mass-formation-or-mass-atrocity/.

Huxley, A. (1958). *Brave new world revisited*. Harper and Row.

Iacobucci, G. (2020a, October 23). Covid-19: Government shelves plans to invest £100bn in mass testing. *BMJ*, *371*, Article m4112. https://doi.org/10.1136/bmj.m4112.

Iacobucci, G. (2020b, November 5). Covid-19: NHS is placed on highest alert level as intensive care beds fill up. *BMJ*, *371*, Article m4296. https://doi.org/10.1136/bmj.m4296.

Ibbetson, R. (2020, May 6). Bodies of Covid-19 victims lie in the streets of Ecuador as virus death toll across Latin America passes 15,000 with the pandemic yet to peak in the region. *Daily Mail*. https://www.dailymail.co.uk/news/article-8292391/Bodies-Covid-19-victims-lie-streets-Ecuadorian-city.html.

Interweave Healthcare (2021, October 27). *How many hospitals in the UK?* https://www.interweavetextiles.com/how-many-hospitals-uk/.

Ioannidis, J. P. A. (2020, March 17). A fiasco in the making? As the coronavirus pandemic takes hold, we are making decisions without reliable data. *STAT*. https://www.statnews.com/2020/03/17/a-fiasco-in-the-making-as-the-coronavirus-pandemic-takes-hold-we-are-making-decisions-without-reliable-data/.

Jefferson, T., Dooley, L., Ferroni, E., Al-Ansary, L. A., van Driel, M. L., Bawazeer, G. A., Jones, M. A., Hoffmann, T. C., Clark, J., Beller, E. M., Glasziou, P. P., & Conly, J. M. (2023). Physical interventions to interrupt or reduce the spread of respiratory viruses. *Cochrane Database of Systematic Reviews*, *1*, Article CD006207. https://doi.org/10.1002/14651858.CD006207.pub6.

Johns Hopkins University (n.d.). *Mortality analyses*. Retrieved June 17, 2023, from https://coronavirus.jhu.edu/data/mortality.

Johnson, N. P. A. S., & Mueller, J. (2002). Updating the accounts: Global mortality of the 1918–1920 "Spanish" influenza pandemic. *Bulletin of the History of Medicine*, *76*, 105–115. https://doi.org/10.1353/bhm.2002.0022.

Johnston, L. (2021, January 3). Hospitals have 13k fewer patients taking up beds—so why are millions more in Tier 4? *The Express*. https://www.express.co.uk/news/uk/1379012/covid-cases-uk-tier-4-areas-hospital-beds-NHS.

Jones, W. (2021, June 21). "You can never exclude the possibility that there will be some new disease," says Boris Johnson as he warns of "rough winter" ahead. *The Daily Sceptic*. https://dailysceptic.org/2021/06/21/you-can-never-exclude-the-possibility-that-there-will-be-some-new-disease-says-boris-johnson-as-he-warns-of-rough-winter-ahead/.

Justice Centre for Constitutional Freedoms. (2021, May 11). *Manitoba chief microbiologist and laboratory specialist: 56% of positive "cases" are not infectious*. https://www.jccf.ca/manitoba-chief-microbiologist-and-laboratory-specialist-56-of-positive-cases-are-not-infectious/.

Kämmerer, U., Pekova, S., Klement, R., Louwen, R., Borger, P., & Steger, K. (2023). RT-PCR test targeting the conserved 5'-UTR of SARS-CoV-2 overcomes shortcomings of the first WHO-recommended RT-PCR Test. *International Journal of Vaccine Theory, Practice, and Research*, *3*(1):818–846. https://doi.org/10.56098/ijvtpr.v3i1.71.

Kayser, R. (2020, April 23). Exercise Cygnus: UK government exercise justifies Covid-19 lockdown. *UK Column*. https://www.ukcolumn.org/article/exercise-cygnus-uk-government-exercise-justifies-covid-19-lockdown.

Keil, U. (2010, January 26). Introductory statement to Social, Health and Family Affairs Committee of the Parliamentary Assembly of the Council of Europe hearing: The handling of the H1N1 pandemic: More transparency needed? http://assembly.coe.int/CommitteeDocs/2010/20100126_ContributionKeil.pdf.

Kelland, K. (2020, June 5). Wear masks in public, says WHO, in update of Covid-19 advice. *Reuters*. https://www.reuters.com/article/us-health-coronavirus-who-masks-idUSKBN23C27Y.

Kenyon, T. (2022, August 23). It's everywhere all at once. *PANDA Uncut*. https://pandauncut.substack.com/p/its-everywhere-all-at-once.

Kim, J., Chung, Y., Jo, H. J., Lee, N., Kim, M. S., Woo, S. H., Park, S., Kim, J. W., Kim, H. M., & Han, M. (2020). Identification of coronavirus isolated from a patient in Korea with Covid-19. *Osang Public Health and Research Perspectives*, *11*(1), 3–7. https://doi.org/10.24171/j.phrp.2020.11.1.02.

King, A., & Schneider, B. (1991). *The first global revolution: A report by the Council of the Club of Rome*. Pantheon Books.

Kisielinski, K., Giboni, P., Prescher, A., Klosterhalfen, B., Graessel, D., Funken, S., Kempski, O., & Hirch, O. (2021). Is a mask that covers the mouth and nose free from undesirable side effects in everyday use and free of potential hazards? *International Journal of Environmental Research and Public Health*, *18*(8), Article 4344. https://doi.org/10.3390/ijerph18084344.

Kissinger, H. (1957). *Nuclear weapons and foreign policy*. Council on Foreign Relations.

Knapton, S. (2021, September 22). Nowhere left for Covid to go to mutate into a deadly variant, says Oxford vaccine creator. *The Telegraph*. https://www.telegraph.co.uk/news/2021/09/22/nowhere-left-covid-go-mutate-deadly-variant-says-oxford-vaccine/.

Kolata, G. (2007, January 22). Faith in quick test leads to epidemic that wasn't. *New York Times*. https://www.nytimes.com/2007/01/22/health/22whoop.html.

Kyrie, V., & Broudy, D. (2022, September 22). The Covid-19 concoction: A recipe for successful psychological operations. *Propaganda in Focus*. https://propagandainfocus.com/the-covid-19-concoction-a-recipe-for-successful-psychological-operations/.

Langton, K. (2020, April 17). Face masks: Should I be wearing a face mask? Will it help? *The Express*. https://www.express.co.uk/life-style/health/1270292/face-masks-should-I-wear-a-face-mask-do-face-masks-help-n95-ffp2-coronavirus.

LifeSite News. (2021, July 23). *47 studies confirm ineffectiveness of masks for Covid and 32 more confirm their negative health effects*. https://www.lifesitenews.com/news/47-studies-confirm-inefectiveness-of-masks-for-covid-and-32-more-confirm-their-negative-health-effects/.

Lin II, R. J., & Money, L. (2022, July 26). Fears of more long Covid, a "mass disabling event" as variants rip through California. *Los Angeles Times*. https://www.latimes.com/california/story/2022-07-26/covid-19-reinfection-worsens-long-term-risk-for-death-fatigue-heart-disorders.

Linsambarth, S., Moraga-Amaro, R., Quintana-Donoso, D., Rojas, S., & Stehberg, J. (2017). The Amygdala and Anxiety. In: B. Ferry (Ed.), *The amygdala: Where emotions shape perception, learning, and memories*. IntechOpen. https://doi.org/10.5772/intechopen.68618.

Loke, Y. K., & Heneghan, C. (2020, July 16). Why no-one can ever recover from Covid-19 in England—a statistical anomaly. *Centre for Evidence-based Medicine*. https://www.cebm.net/covid-19/why-no-one-can-ever-recover-from-covid-19-in-england-a-statistical-anomaly/.

Lovelace Jr., B. (2021, September 2). WHO says it is monitoring a new Covid variant called "mu." *NBC Bay Area*. https://www.nbcbayarea.com/news/business/money-report/who-says-it-is-monitoring-a-new-covid-variant-called-mu/2645890/.

Magen, H. (2020, March 22). Lockdown lunacy. *Globes*. https://en.globes.co.il/en/article-lockdown-lunacy-1001322696.

Manley, J. C. A. (2020, October 6). Medical doctor warns that "bacterial pneumonias are on the rise" from mask wearing. *Global Research*. https://www.globalresearch.ca/medical-doctor-warns-bacterial-pneumonias-rise-mask-wearing/5725848.

Matthews, A. (2020, October 18). Hidden toll. "Protect the NHS" message in lockdown led to 90% drop in hospital admissions which may have caused thousands of deaths. *The Sun*. https://www.thesun.co.uk/news/12961699/90-per-cent-drop-hospital-lockdown/.

Matthews, S. (2022, April 5). UK's "completely irrelevant" daily Covid cases plunge by 38% in a week to lowest level in a month following No. 10's decision to end free testing. *Daily Mail*. https://www.dailymail.co.uk/health/article-10687457/UKs-daily-Covid-cases-plunge-38-week-lowest-level-MONTH.html.

McCann, J. (2022, April 10). Is insomnia a Covid symptom? *i*. https://inews.co.uk/news/health/insomnia-covid-symptom-connection-lack-sleep-coronavirus-explained-1562765.

McCorkell, L. (2021). The long Covid experience: Evidence from patient-led research and the patient community. https://docs.house.gov/meetings/IF/IF14/20210428/112514/HHRG-117-IF14-Wstate-McCorkellL-20210428.pdf.

Meerloo, J. A. (1956). *The rape of the mind. The psychology of thought control, menticide, and brainwashing*. World Publishing Company.

Mencken, H. L. (2009). *In defence of women*. General Books.

Merrick, J. (2021, April 26). Current definition of Covid deaths could distort vaccine success data, scientists warn. *i*. https://inews.co.uk/news/politics/28-day-definition-covid-deaths-could-distort-vaccine-success-data-warn-scientists-973655.

Moyer, N. (2019, April 22). Amygdala hijack: When emotion takes over. *Healthline*. https://www.healthline.com/health/stress/amygdala-hijack.

Mullin, E. (2021, August 23). How does Covid-19 affect the brain? A troubling picture emerges. *National Geographic*. https://www.nationalgeographic.co.uk/science-and-technology/2021/08/how-does-covid-19-affect-the-brain-a-troubling-picture-emerges.

Mullin, G., & Chalmers, V. (2022, Jan 22). Tongue and approve: NHS urged to add "Covid tongue" to official symptoms list as experts fear 1 in 5 cases are missed. *The Sun*. https://www.thesun.co.uk/news/13822440/nhs-urged-add-covid-tongue-official-symptoms-list/.

Mullis, K. (1993). *Kary Mullis speaks to misuse of PCR* [Video]. Internet Archive. https://archive.org/details/kary-mullis-speaks-to-misuse-of-pcr-1993.

Murray, C., Lopez, A. D., Chin, B., Feehan, D., & Hill, K. H. (2006). Estimation of potential global pandemic influenza mortality on the basis of vital registry data from the 1918-20 pandemic: A quantitative analysis. *Lancet*, *368*, Article 9554, 2211–2218. https://doi.org/10.1016/S0140-6736(06)69895-4.

National Audit Office. (2020, September 30). *Investigation into how government increased the number of ventilators available to the NHS in response to COVID-19*. https://www.nao.org.uk/wp-content/uploads/2020/09/Investigation-into-how-the-Government-increased-the-number-of-ventilators.pdf.

New and Emerging Respiratory Virus Threats Advisory Group. (2021, January 7). *SARS-CoV-2 Immunity-escape Variants*. https://www.gov.uk/government/publications/sars-cov-2-immunity-escape-variants-7-january-2021.

Newton, J. (2020, August 12). Behind the headlines: Counting Covid-19 deaths. *Public Health Matters*. https://publichealthmatters.blog.gov.uk/2020/08/12/behind-the-headlines-counting-covid-19-deaths/#:~:text=88%25%20of%20deaths%20occurred%20within,the%20death%20certificate%20for%2064%25.

NHS England. (n.d.-a). Post-Covid syndrome (long Covid). Retrieved June 17, 2023, from https://www.england.nhs.uk/coronavirus/post-covid-syndrome-long-covid/.

NHS England. (n.d.-b). *Bed availability and occupancy data—overnight*. Retrieved June 22, 2023, from https://www.england.nhs.uk/statistics/statistical-work-areas/bed-availability-and-occupancy/bed-data-overnight/.

NHS England. (2020, October 25). *NHS and other professional bodies' response to the* Sunday Times, *25 October 2020*. https://www.england.nhs.uk/2020/10/nhs-and-other-professional-bodies-response-to-sunday-times/.

NHS England. (2021). *COVID-19 hospital activity* . https://adapnation.io/covid-insights/#h-nhs-england-insights.

Nolan Brown, E. (2020, April 10). No, NYC is not running out of burial space due to Covid-19. *Reason*. https://reason.com/2020/04/10/no-nyc-is-not-running-out-of-burial-space-due-to-covid-19/.

Office for Health Improvements and Disparities. (n.d.). *Excess mortality in England*. Retrieved December 30, 2023, from https://app.powerbi.com/view?r=eyJrIjoiYmUwNmFhMjYtNGZhYS00NDk2LWFlMTAtOTg0OGNhNmFiNGM0IiwidCI6ImVlNGUxNDk5LTRhMzUtNGIyZS1hZDQ3LTVmM2NmOWRlODY2NiIsImMiOjh9.

Office for National Statistics. (n.d.). *Populations estimates time series* . https://www.ons.gov.uk/peoplepopulationandcommunity/populationandmigration/populationestimates/timeseries/ukpop/pop.

Office for National Statistics. (2021a). *Average age of those who had died with Covid-19*. https://archive.ph/uFLe5#selection-713.1-713.48.

Office for National Statistics. (2021b). *Annual deaths and mortality rates, 1938–2020 (provisional)*. https://www.ons.gov.uk/peoplepopulationandcommunity/birthsdeathsandmarriages/deaths/adhocs/12735annualdeathsandmortalityrates1938to2020provisional.

Office for National Statistics. (2021c). *National life tables—life expectancy in the UK: 2018–2020*. https://www.ons.gov.uk/peoplepopulationandcommunity/birthsdeathsandmarriages/lifeexpectancies/bulletins/nationallifetablesunitedkingdom/2018to2020.

Office for National Statistics. (2021d). *Deaths registered weekly in England and Wales, provisional: week ending 15 January 2021*. https://www.ons.gov.uk/peoplepopulationandcommunity/birthsdeathsandmarriages/deaths/bulletins/deathsregisteredweeklyinenglandandwalesprovisional/weekending15january2021#deaths-registered-by-place-of-occurrence.

Office for National Statistics. (2023). *Deaths registered weekly in England and Wales, provisional*. https://www.ons.gov.uk/peoplepopulationandcommunity/birthsdeathsandmarriages/deaths/bulletins/deathsregisteredweeklyinenglandandwalesprovisional/latest.

Office for National Statistics & HM Passport Office. (2020). *Guidance for doctors completing medical certificates of cause of death in England and Wales*. https://assets.publishing.service.gov.uk/government/uploads/system/uploads/attachment_data/file/877302/guidance-for-doctors-completing-medical-certificates-of-cause-of-death-covid-19.pdf.

Office of Communications. (2018). *News consumption in the UK: 2018*. https://www.ofcom.org.uk/__data/assets/pdf_file/0024/116529/news-consumption-2018.pdf.

O'Neill, N. (2021, July 7). California "epsilon" strain of Covid-19 could evade vaccines, study says. *New York Post*. https://nypost.com/2021/07/07/california-epsilon-strain-of-covid-19-could-evade-vaccines-study/.

OpenVAERS. (n.d.). *VAERS Covid vaccine adverse event reports*. Retrieved June 17, 2023, from https://openvaers.com/covid-data.

Organisation for Economic Co-operation and Development. (n.d.). *Hospital beds*. Retrieved June 22, 2023, from https://data.oecd.org/healtheqt/hospital-beds.htm.

Orwell, G. (1984). *Nineteen eighty-four*. Oxford University Press.

Parsley, D. (2021, December 22). NHS England makes plans for field hospitals in preparation for wave of Omicron Covid cases. *i*. https://inews.co.uk/news/politics/nhs-england-makes-plans-for-field-hospitals-in-preparation-for-wave-of-omicron-covid-cases-1365680.

Parsons, J. (2022, March 9). Covid brain is real: Study shows virus shrinks regions of the brain. *Metro*. https://metro.co.uk/2022/03/09/covid-brain-is-real-study-shows-virus-shrinks-regions-of-the-brain-16242745/.

Patel, B. (2021, February 21). Falling immunity levels caused by social distancing could trigger 'more severe epidemic' of the flu this winter, experts warn. *Daily Mail*. https://www.dailymail.co.uk/news/article-9283433/Falling-immunity-levels-trigger-severe-epidemic-flu-winter-experts-warn.html.

PCR inventor Kary Mullis talks about Anthony Fauci—"he doesn't know anything really about anything." (2020, December 10). *Darachi.com*. https://darachi.com/kary-mullis-pcr-anthony-fauci.

Pereira, S. M. P., Shafra, R., Nugawela, M. D., Panagi, L., Hargreaves, D., Ladhani, S. N., Bennett, S. D., Chalder, T., Dalrymple, E., Ford,

T., Heyman, I., McOwat, K., Rojas, N. K., Sharma, K., Simmons, R., White, S. R., & Stephenson, T. (2023). Natural course of health and well-being in non-hospitalised children and young people after testing for SARS-CoV-2: A prospective follow-up study over 12 months. *The Lancet Regional Health—Europe*, *25*, Article 100554. https://doi.org/10.1016/j.lanepe.2022.100554.

Pijl, K. van der. (2022). *States of emergency. Keeping the global population in check*. Clarity Press.

Plimer, I. (2021). *Green murder*. Connor Court.

Pollock, A. & Roderick, P. (2021, December 7). If you believe in a public NHS, the new Health and Care bill should set off alarm bells. *The Guardian*. https://www.theguardian.com/commentisfree/2021/dec/07/public-nhs-the-new-health-and-care-bill-alarm-bells-privatisation.

Pomeroy, C. (2021, July 6). A tsunami of disability is coming as a result of 'long Covid.' *Scientific American*. https://www.scientificamerican.com/article/a-tsunami-of-disability-is-coming-as-a-result-of-lsquo-long-covid-rsquo/.

Prime Minister's Office. (2020a, March 23). *Prime Minister's statement on coronavirus (Covid-19): 23 March 2020*. https://www.gov.uk/government/speeches/pm-address-to-the-nation-on-coronavirus-23-march-2020.

Prime Minister's Office. (2020b, May 10). *Prime Minister's statement on coronavirus (Covid-19): 10 May 2020*. https://www.gov.uk/government/speeches/pm-address-to-the-nation-on-coronavirus-10-may-2020.

Public Health England. (2020a, November 26). *Coronavirus England briefing*. https://assets.publishing.service.gov.uk/government/uploads/system/uploads/attachment_data/file/938964/Coronavirus_England_briefing_26_November.pdf.

Public Health England. (2020b, December 20). *Covid-19 (SARS-CoV-2): Information about the new virus variant*. https://www.gov.uk/government/news/covid-19-sars-cov-2-information-about-the-new-virus-variant.

Public Health England. (2021a). *Emergency department syndromic surveillance system: England*. https://assets.publishing.service.gov.uk/government/uploads/system/uploads/attachment_data/file/950352/EDSSSBulletin2020wk53.pdf.

Public Health England. (2021b). *Re: Internal review of case ref: no. 2041—Explanation of supposed under-declaring of Covid-19 cases by PHE compared to the media*. https://www.whatdotheyknow.com/request/710144/response/1709463/attach/html/2/2231%20IR%20Linked%20to%202041%20Explanation%20of%20supposed%20under%20declaring%20of%20Covid%20cases%20by%20PHE.pdf.html.

Public Health England. (2021c). *National ambulance syndromic surveillance system: England*. https://assets.publishing.service.gov.uk/government/uploads/system/uploads/attachment_data/file/950350/NASS_Bulletin_2020_53.pdf.

Pym, H. (2021, May 28). Covid: Surgery waiting times could be cut with specialist hubs, say surgeons. *BBC News*. https://www.bbc.co.uk/news/health-57277793.

Quinn, B. (2020, October 8). What has happened to England's seven Nightingale hospitals? *The Guardian*. https://www.theguardian.com/society/2020/oct/08/what-has-happened-to-englands-seven-nightingale-hospitals.

Rancourt, D. (2020a). *All-cause mortality during Covid-19: No plague and a likely signature of mass homicide by government response*. https://denisrancourt.ca/entries.php?id=9&name=2020_06_02_all_cause_mortality_during_covid_19_no_plague_and_a_likely_signature_of_mass_homicide_by_government_response.

Rancourt, D. (2020b, June 11). *Masks don't work: A review of science relevant to Covid-19 social policy*. https://www.rcreader.com/commentary/masks-dont-work-covid-a-review-of-science-relevant-to-covide-19-social-policy.

Rancourt, D. (2020c, August 3). *Face masks, lies, damn lies, and public health officials: "A growing body of evidence."* https://denisrancourt.ca/uploads_entries/1626806985825_growing%20body%20of%20evidence%20mantra----5.pdf.

Rancourt, D., Baudin, M., & Mercier, J. (2021). *Nature of the Covid-era public health disaster in the USA, from all-cause mortality and socio-geo-economic and climatic data*. https://denisrancourt.ca/uploads_entries/1635189453861_USA%20ACM%20into%202021%20-%20article----12d.pdf.

Rayner, G. (2021, May 14). Use of fear to control behaviour in Covid crisis was "totalitarian," admit scientists. *The Telegraph*. https://www.telegraph.co.uk/news/2021/05/14/scientists-admit-totalitarian-use-fear-control-behaviour-covid/.

Read, A. F., Baigent, S. J., Powers, C., Kgosana, L. B., Blackwell, L., Smith, L. P., Kennedy, D. A., Walkden-Brown, S. W., & Nair, V. K. (2015). Imperfect vaccination can enhance the transmission of highly virulent pathogens. *PLoS Biology*, *13*(7), Article e1002198. https://doi.org/10.1371/journal.pbio.1002198.

Re'em, Y. (2021, March 30). The science behind "long Covid" and the desire to wish it away. *The Wall Street Journal*. https://www.wsj.com/articles/the-science-behind-long-covid-and-the-desire-to-wish-it-away-11617143543.

"Re-think face masks in shops," says scientist. (2020, August 7). *BBC News*. https://www.bbc.co.uk/news/uk-wales-53690540.

Reuters. (2020, April 28). *UK scientists say face masks have only small effect on coronavirus spread*. https://www.reuters.com/article/uk-health-coronavirus-britain-masks-idUKKCN22A2UU.

Reuters. (2021, January 12). *Temporary morgues set up as UK hospitals run out of space*. https://www.reuters.com/business/healthcare-pharmaceuticals/temporary-morgues-set-up-uk-hospitals-run-out-space-2021-01-12/.

Rice, B. (2022, August 31). Covid was spreading across the U.S. in 2019. *Brownstone Institute*. https://brownstone.org/articles/covid-was-spreading-across-the-u-s-in-2019/.

Ritchie, S. (2021, June 30). Does long Covid really exist? *UnHerd*. https://unherd.com/2021/06/does-long-covid-really-exist/.

Rockefeller Foundation. (2020, July 16). *National Covid-19 testing action plan: Pragmatic steps to reopen our workplaces and our communities*. https://www.rockefellerfoundation.org/national-covid-19-testing-action-plan/.

Royo-Bordonada, M. A., Garcia-Lopez, F. J., Cortés, F., & Zaragoza, G. A. (2020). Face masks in the general healthy population. Scientific and Ethical Issues. *Gaceta Sanitaria, 35*(6), 580–584. https://doi.org/10.1016/j.gaceta.2020.08.003.

Ruiz, K. (2020, December 6). Covid-19 could cause erectile dysfunction in patients who have recovered from the virus, doctor warns." *Daily Mail*. https://www.dailymail.co.uk/news/article-9022827/COVID-19-cause-erectile-dysfunction-doctor-says.html.

Rushworth, S. (2020, November 17). What is long Covid? *Sebastian Rushworth M.D.* https://sebastianrushworth.com/2020/11/17/what-is-long-covid/.

Saad-Roy, C. M., Morris, S. E., Metcalf, C. J. E., Mina, M. J., Baker, R. E., Farrar, J., Holmes, E. C., Pybus, O. G., Graham, A. L., Levin, S. A., Grenfell, B. T., & Wagner, C. E. (2021). Epidemiological and evolutionary considerations of SARS-CoV-2 vaccine dosing regimes. *Science, 372*(6540), 363–370. https://doi.org/10.1126/science.abg8663.

Sardi, B. (2021, March 26). The coming witch hunt against anti-vaxxers. *LewRockwell.com*. https://www.lewrockwell.com/2021/03/bill-sardi/the-coming-witch-hunt-against-anti-vaxxers/.

Saunt, R. (2021, March 4). Grandmother, 66, who was terrified of infecting her family with Covid killed herself by stepping in front of a train when she felt 'a little under the weather' with a cold, inquest hears. *Daily Mail*. https://www.dailymail.co.uk/news/article-9326755/Grandmother-terrified-giving-family-Covid-killed-stepping-train.html.

Schwab, K., & Malleret, T. (2020). *Covid 19: The Great Reset*. World Economic Forum.

Science and Technology Committee. (2020). *Oral evidence: UK science, research and technology capability and influence in global disease outbreaks, HC 136*. https://committees.parliament.uk/oralevidence/885/html/.
Scientific Advisory Group for Emergencies. (2020a). *Fifteenth SAGE meeting on Wuhan coronavirus (Covid-19), 13th March 2020*. https://assets.publishing.service.gov.uk/government/uploads/system/uploads/attachment_data/file/888783/S0383_Fifteenth_SAGE_meeting_on_Wuhan_Coronavirus__Covid-19__.pdf.
Scientific Advisory Group for Emergencies. (2020b). *Addendum to fifteenth SAGE meeting on Covid-19, 13th March 2020 held in 1 Victoria St, London, SW1H 0NN*. https://assets.publishing.service.gov.uk/government/uploads/system/uploads/attachment_data/file/888783/S0383_Fifteenth_SAGE_meeting_on_Wuhan_Coronavirus__Covid-19__.pdf.
Scientific Advisory Group for Emergencies. (2020c). *Sixteenth SAGE meeting on Wuhan coronavirus (Covid-19)*. https://assets.publishing.service.gov.uk/government/uploads/system/uploads/attachment_data/file/888784/S0384_Sixteenth_SAGE_meeting_on_Wuhan_Coronavirus__Covid-19__.pdf.
Scientific Advisory Group for Emergencies. (2020d). *Seventy-fourth SAGE meeting on Covid-19, 22nd December 2020*. https://assets.publishing.service.gov.uk/government/uploads/system/uploads/attachment_data/file/948606/s0991-sage-meeting-74-covid-19.pdf.
Scientific Pandemic Influenza Group on Modelling, Operational sub-group. (2021). *SPI-M-O: Consensus statement on Covid-19*. https://assets.publishing.service.gov.uk/government/uploads/system/uploads/attachment_data/file/979625/S1180_SPI-M-O_Consensus_Statement.pdf.
Scientific Pandemic Insights Group on Behaviours. (2020). *Options for increasing adherence to social distancing measures*. https://assets.publishing.service.gov.uk/government/uploads/system/uploads/attachment_data/file/882722/25-options-for-increasing-adherence-to-social-distancing-measures-22032020.pdf.
Scott, B. (2021, May 2). We are all Pavlov's dogs now. *UK Column*. https://www.ukcolumn.org/article/we-are-all-pavlovs-dogs-now.
Scott, B. (2022, September 19). Menticide 101 and the brainwashing of a world: Part II—beyond the fear. *UK Column*. https://www.ukcolumn.org/article/menticide-101-and-the-brainwashing-of-a-world-part-ii-beyond-the-fear.
Selvakumar, J., Havdal, L. B., Drevvatne, M., Brodwall, E. M., Berven, L. L., Stiansen-Sonerud, T., Einvik, G., Leegaard, T. M., Tjade, T., Michelsen, A. E., Mollnes, T. E., Lund-Johansen, F., Holmøy, T., Zetterberg, H., Blennow, K., Sandler, C. X., Cvejic, E., Lloyd, A. R., & Wyller, V. B. B. (2023). Prevalence

and characteristics associated with post-Covid-19 condition among nonhospitalized adolescents and young adults. *JAMA Network Open*, *6*(3), Article e235763. https://doi.org/10.1001/jamanetworkopen.2023.5763.

Seneff, S., & Nigh, G. (2021). Worse than the disease? Reviewing some possible unintended consequences of the mRNA vaccines against Covid-19. *International Journal of Vaccine Theory, Practice, and Research*, *2*(1), 38–79. https://doi.org/10.56098/ijvtpr.v2i1.23.

Senger, M.P. (2022a, May 9). The point of masks: To cause alarm. *Brownstone Institute*. https://brownstone.org/articles/the-point-of-masks-to-cause-alarm/.

Senger, M.P. (2022b, October 5). An estimated 30,000 Americans were killed by ventilators and iatrogenesis in April 2020. *The New Normal*. https://michaelpsenger.substack.com/p/an-estimated-30000-americans-were.

Sette, A., & Crotty, S. (2021). Adaptive immunity to SARS-CoV-2 and Covid-19. *Cell, 184*(4), 861–880. https://doi.org/10.1016/j.cell.2021.01.00.

Shayler, D. (2022). *From 9/11 to 'Covid-19': Fakery and the war waged on mankind*. https://www.bookofthelaw.org/downloads/911_to_covid19_fakery_and_the_war_waged_on_mankind.pdf.

Sidley, G. (2020, October 24). How the mean psychologists got us to comply with Coronavirus restrictions. *Coronababble*. https://www.coronababble.com/post/how-the-mean-psychologists-induced-us-to-comply-with-coronavirus-restrictions.

Slater, J. (2020, September 26). Covid survey: How to take part in the ONS survey and where can you spend the vouchers? *The Metro*. https://metro.co.uk/2020/09/26/covid-survey-how-to-take-part-in-ons-survey-where-spend-vouchers-13330472/.

Sneller, M. C. (2022). A longitudinal study of Covid-19 sequelae and immunity: Baseline findings. *Annals of Internal Medicine, 175*(7), 969–979. https://doi.org/10.7326/M21-4905.

Sokol, D. (2021, January 12). The NHS is not at risk of being overwhelmed—it already is. *BMJ*, 372, n62. https://www.bmj.com/content/372/bmj.n62.

Spectator (n.d.). *Data tracker—NHS*. Retrieved July 15, 2023, from https://data.spectator.co.uk/nhs.

Statista. (2020). *Annual number of hospital beds in the United Kingdom (UK) from 2000 to 2021*. https://www.statista.com/statistics/473264/number-of-hospital-beds-in-the-united-kingdom-uk/.

Steinhagen, H-J. (2020, October 7). The Covid crisis: A brief history of the pandemics of the 21st century (2000–2020). *Global Research*. https://www.globalresearch.ca/brief-history-2000s-pandemics/5723487.

Stevens, S. & Pritchard, A. (2020, March 17). Important and Urgent—next steps on NHS response to Covid-19. Letter to: Chief executives of all NHS trusts and foundation trusts, CCG accountable officers, GP practices and primary care networks, and providers of community health services. https://www.england.nhs.uk/coronavirus/wp-content/uploads/sites/52/2020/03/urgent-next-steps-on-nhs-response-to-covid-19-letter-simon-stevens.pdf.

Stringham, E.P. (2020, April 26). Open up society now, say Dr. Dan Erickson and Dr. Artin Massihi. *American Institute for Economic Research*. https://www.aier.org/article/open-up-society-now-say-dr-dan-erickson-and-dr-artin-massihi/.

Sumption, J. (2020, October 27). *Government by decree: Covid-19 and the constitution*. Cambridge Freshfields Annual Law Lecture. https://resources.law.cam.ac.uk/privatelaw/Freshfields_Lecture_2020_Government_by_Decree.pdf.

Sutherland, S. (2023, March 1). Long Covid now looks like a neurological disease, helping doctors to focus treatments. *Scientific American*. https://www.scientificamerican.com/article/long-covid-now-looks-like-a-neurological-disease-helping-doctors-to-focus-treatments1/.

Sweeney, E. (2022, April 12), Can Covid cause green poop? *Parade*. https://parade.com/1362991/ericasweeney/can-covid-cause-green-poop/.

Swiss Policy Research. (2020, September 9). *WHO mask study seriously flawed*. https://swprs.org/who-mask-study-seriously-flawed/.

Talbott, S, (1990, January 1). Rethinking the red menace. *Time*, *135*, 36–38. https://content.time.com/time/subscriber/article/0,33009,969092,00.html.

Tanaka, A., & Miyazawa, T. (2023). Raw data for "Unnatural evolutionary processes of SARS-CoV-2 variants and possibility of deliberate natural selection" (Raw data) [Data set]. Zenodo. https://doi.org/10.5281/zenodo.8254894.

Tarke, A., Sidney, J., Methot, N., Zhang, Y., Dan, J. M., Goodwin, B., Rubiro, P., Sutherland, A., da Silva Antunes, R., Frazier, A., Rawlings, S. A., Smith, D. M., Peters, B., Scheuermann, R. H., Weiskopf, D., Crotty, S., Grifoni, A., & Sette, A. (2021). Impact of SARS-CoV-2 variants on the total CD4+ and CD8+ T cell reactivity in infected or vaccinated individuals. *Cell Reports Medicine*, *2*(7), Article 100355. https://doi.org/10.1016/j.xcrm.2021.100355.

Taubenberger, J. K., & Morens, D. M. (2006). 1918 influenza: The mother of all pandemics. *Emerging Infectious Diseases*, *12*(1), 15–22. https://doi.org/10.3201/eid1201.050979.

The Infectious Myth. (2020). *Stephen Bustin on challenges with RT-PCR*. https://infectiousmyth.podbean.com/e/the-infectious-myth-stephen-bustin-on-challenges-with-rt-pcr/.

The plague of fear breeds paranoia and stupidity as demand for underground bunkers surges due to fear of covid-19. (2020, December 13). *The Exposé*. https://dailyexpose.co.uk/2020/12/13/the-plague-of-fear-breeds-paranoia-and-stupidity-as-demand-for-underground-bunkers-surges-due-to-fear-of-covid-19/.

Thomas, R. (2020, December 1). Leaks reveal two-thirds of private hospital capacity went unused by NHS. *HSJ*. https://www.hsj.co.uk/finance-and-efficiency/leaks-reveal-two-thirds-of-private-hospital-capacity-went-unused-by-nhs/7029000.article.

Topping, A. (2021, March 7). UK needs to prepare for "hard winter" of flu and respiratory viruses, says top medic. *The Guardian*, https://www.theguardian.com/society/2021/mar/07/uk-hard-winter-flu-respiratory-viruses-top-medic-population-immunity-covid.

Triggle, N. (2021a, February 22). Covid: Why can't we unlock more quickly? *BBC News*. https://www.bbc.co.uk/news/health-56153618.

Triggle, N. (2021b, August 4). Covid cases and hospital admissions down—is it over? *BBC News*. https://www.bbc.co.uk/news/health-58078900.

Triggle, N., & Jeavans, C. (2021, May 13). The NHS Covid legacy—long waits and lives at risk. *BBC News*. https://www.bbc.co.uk/news/health-57092797.

UK Government. (n.d.-a) *Coronavirus (Covid-19) in the UK*. Retrieved June 17, 2023, from https://coronavirus.data.gov.uk/.

UK Government. (n.d.-b). *About emergency alerts*. Retrieved June 17, 2023, from https://www.gov.uk/alerts.

Vanden Bossche, G. (2021, March 6). *To all authorities, scientists and experts around the world, to whom this concerns: The entire world population*. https://mcusercontent.com/92561d6dedb66a43fe9a6548f/files/bead7203-0798-4ac8-abe2-076208015556/Public_health_emergency_of_international_concert_Geert_Vanden_Bossche.01.pdf.

Voysey, M., Clemens, S. A. C., Madhi, S. A., Weckx, Folegatti, P. M., Aley, P. K., Angus, B., Baillie, V. L., Barnabas, S. L., Bhorat, Q. E., Bibi, S., Briner, C., Cicconi, P., Collins, A. M., Colin-Jones, R., Cutland, C. L., Darton, T. C., Dheda, K., Duncan, C. J. A., Pollard, A. J. (2021). Safety and efficacy of the ChAdOx1 nCoV-19 vaccine (AZD1222) against SARS-CoV-2: An interim analysis of four randomised controlled trials in Brazil, South Africa, and the UK. *The Lancet*, *397*, 99–111. https://doi.org/10.1016/S0140-6736(20)32661-1.

Walsh, F. (2021, May 5). Analysis. *BBC News*. https://www.bbc.co.uk/news/health-56984984.

West, D. (2020, April 13). NHS hospitals have four times more empty beds than normal. *HSJ*. https://www.hsj.co.uk/acute-care/nhs-hospitals-have-four-times-more-empty-beds-than-normal/7027392.article.

Whitty, C. (2018, October 10). *How to control an epidemic*. Gresham College. https://www.gresham.ac.uk/lectures-and-events/epidemics-pandemics-control.

Wilyman, J. (2020, March 9). How the World Health Organisation (WHO) created a 'pandemic' of a disease. *Vaccination Decisions*. https://www.vaccinationdecisions.net/how-the-world-health-organisation-who-created-a-pandemic-of-a-disease/.

Wodarg, W., Baselga, F. A., Ayva, L., Bajen, A. C., Czinege, I., Flynn, P., Grozdanova, D., Hancock, M., Huss, J. A., Marquet, B., McCafferty, C. A., Ohlsson, C., Ünal, M., & Volonte, L. (2009, December 18). *Faked pandemics—a threat for health. Motion for a recommendation*. Council of Europe Parliamentary Assembly. http://whale.to/vaccine/EDOC12110.pdf.

Wood, S. (2021). Inferring UK Covid-19 fatal infection trajectories from daily mortality data: Were infections already in decline before the UK lockdowns? *Biometrics, 78*(3), 1127–1140. https://doi.org/10.1111/biom.13462.

World Health Organisation. (2005). *Pandemic preparedness*. www.who.int/csr/disease/influenza/pandemic/en/.

World Health Organisation. (2010). *Pandemic (H1N1) 2009—update 112*. https://www.who.int/csr/don/2010_08_06/en/.

World Health Organisation. (n.d.-a). *Coronavirus (COVID-19) Dashboard*. Retrieved June 17, 2023, from https://covid19.who.int/.

World Health Organisation. (n.d.-b). *Influenza laboratory surveillance information*. Retrieved June 17, 2023, from https://app.powerbi.com/view?r=eyJrIjoiZTkyODcyOTEtZjA5YS00ZmI0LWFkZGUtODIxNGI5OTE3YjM0IiwidCI6ImY2MTBjMGI3LWJkMjQtNGIzOS04MTBiLTNkYzI4MGFmYjU5MCIsImMiOjh9.

World Health Organisation. (2020a, March 11). *WHO director-general's opening remarks at the media briefing on Covid-19—11 March 2020*. https://www.who.int/director-general/speeches/detail/who-director-general-s-opening-remarks-at-the-media-briefing-on-covid-19---11-march-2020.

World Health Organisation. (2020b, January 24). *Molecular assays to diagnose Covid-19: Summary table of available protocols*. https://www.who.int/docs/default-source/coronaviruse/whoinhouseassays.pdf.

World Health Organisation. (2020c, January 29). *Advice on the use of masks in the community, during home care and in health care settings in the context of the novel coronavirus (2019-nCoV) outbreak*. www.who.int/docs/default-source/coronaviruse/advice-on-the-use-of-masks-2019-ncov.pdf.

World Health Organisation. (2020d, March 16). *WHO director-general's opening remarks at the media briefing on Covid-19—16 March 2020*. https://www.who.int/director-general/speeches/detail/who-director-general-s-opening-remarks-at-the-media-briefing-on-covid-19---16-march-2020.

World Health Organisation. (2020e, April 6). *Advice on the use of masks in the context of Covid-19*. https://apps.who.int/iris/bitstream/handle/10665/331693/WHO-2019-nCov-IPC_Masks-2020.3-eng.pdf.

World Health Organisation. (2020f, June 5). *Advice on the use of masks in the context of Covid-19*. https://apps.who.int/iris/handle/10665/332293.

World Health Organisation. (2020g, December 1). *Advice on the use of masks in the context of Covid-19*. https://apps.who.int/iris/handle/10665/337199.

Yeadon, M. (2020, October 16). What SAGE has got wrong. *Lockdown Sceptics*. https://lockdownsceptics.org/what-sage-got-wrong/.

Young, S. J. (2020, October 29). Covid toes: The possible coronavirus symptom that can cause chilblain-like inflammation. *The Independent*. https://www.independent.co.uk/life-style/health-and-families/covid-toes-coronavirus-symptoms-feet-purple-swollen-rash-b1420702.html.

Ziemann, A. E., Allen, J. E., Dahdaleh, N. S., Drebot, I. I., Coryell, M., Wunsch, A. M., Lynch, C. M., Faraci, F. M., Howard, M. A., III., Welsh, M. J., & Wemmie, J. A. (2009). The amygdala is a chemosensor that detects carbon dioxide and acidosis to elicit fear behaviour. *Cell, 139*(5), 1012–1021. https://doi.org/10.1016/j.cell.2009.10.029.

Zorzut, A. (2021, July 2). Covid alert: Fears over the "Lambda" Covid variant that's hit UK as "unusual" mutations can "dodge vaccines." *The Sun*. https://www.thesun.co.uk/news/15469863/fears-over-the-lambda-covid-variant-in-uk/amp/.

CHAPTER 5

Cognitive Attack

Menticide attacks the cognitive faculties of victims to break down their mental integrity and render them susceptible to indoctrination. During "Covid-19," confusion was weaponised in various ways, including a proliferation of nonsensical and ever-changing "rules," last-minute U-turns on key Government decisions, unpredictability of restrictions easing or tightening, and a fundamental irrationality in Government behaviour. Verbal confusion was deployed against the public through constant mixed messaging. A strategy of continuous questioning by the media caused bewilderment. Words and phrases were twisted to mean their opposites, or were used in an esoteric fashion. The public was made to question its own sanity via means used to make social reality seem surreal. The past was rewritten to deny events that actually took place. The public was gaslighted to think that *anything but* the "vaccines" were to blame for injuries/deaths to young people. A Soviet-style abuse of psychiatry was used to pathologise dissent.

Weaponised Confusion

In order to break down the minds of men," Meerloo writes, totalitarianism "first needs widespread mental chaos and verbal confusion, because both paralyze [...] opposition and cause the morale of the enemy to deteriorate" (1956, pp. 28–29). Once broken down, the victim can no longer

D. A. Hughes, *"Covid-19," Psychological Operations, and the War for Technocracy*, https://doi.org/10.1007/978-3-031-41850-1_5

believe in anything apart from "the dictated and indoctrinated logic of those who are more powerful than he.

In cults, the deliberate use of confusion serves to "induce a trance state" in which members are more easily hypnotised; this confusion "usually results whenever contradictory information is communicated congruently" (Hassan, 1990, p. 68). So, "if a person is kept in a controlled environment long enough, hearing such disorienting language and confusing information, he will usually suspend his critical judgement and adapt to what he perceives everyone else is doing." Confusion and disorientation cause individuals to doubt themselves and defer to the group.

Experimental psychology shows that people are generally motivated to avoid addressing social issues that they deem too complex, or which they feel they lack any control over, and instead tend to defer to the government to deal with such issues (Shepherd & Kay, 2012, pp. 275–6). It follows that the intentional creation of confusion over major issues is an excellent means of keeping the public in a state of subjugation. The "bewildered herd" (Lippmann, 1922), as over a century of PR and media manipulation has shown, can be led by an "invisible government" (Bernays, 1928, p. 1) capable of "manufacturing consent" (Herman & Chomsky, 1988).

In the "War on Terror" context, the U.S. National Defence Intelligence College produced an edited volume euphemistically titled ***Educing Information***. "According to the research," one contributor notes, "confusion reduces resistance, and can be a particularly effective tool of influence when combined with a follow-up persuasive message (reframe)" (Borum, 2006, p. 29).

The same principle of using confusion to lower resistance and create subservience to authority was weaponised against the public through the "Covid-19" operation. Fagan (2020), for instance, was quick to observe: "Through a bombardment of lies, contradictions, and confusion, the state overwhelms your ability to reason clearly." The Academy of Ideas (2021) makes a similar observation: "Government officials, and their lackeys in the media, can use contradictory reports, nonsensical information and even blatant lies, as the more they confuse, the less capable will a population be to cope with the crisis [...]." People who are confused and unable to think straight in the face of a crisis tend to turn to authority for security.

In the context of an alleged "pandemic," the general public, with no grounding in virology, epidemiology, or other relevant scientific disciplines, has no way of independently assessing the "scientific" claims made. Rather, the highly specialised subject-matter made it easy for "the deployment of confusion" to serve as "a particularly powerful and central feature of the Covid-19 propaganda campaign" (Kyrie & Broudy, 2022). A bewildered public had little choice but to defer to government "experts" on perceived life and death matters—and even then, in the United Kingdom, the similarity between "SAGE" and "Independent SAGE" (iSAGE) "created significant public confusion" (Klarenberg, 2023).

Mental Chaos

Changing "Rules" That Make No Sense

UK citizens were expected to follow a proliferation of "rules" (Walker, 2020) that made little sense and were practically impossible to keep up with. For example, as the first "lockdown" restrictions were relaxed, radio phone-ins tried in vain to establish who, if anyone, understood how many people were "allowed" in one's back garden, based on different permutations of the "rules" (Perraudin, 2020). If guests were "allowed" in the back garden, were they "allowed" to use the downstairs toilet? Such was the mundane, and frankly insane, level of public discussion, all premised on invasive government overreach regarding what citizens can and cannot do on their own property.

The "rules" never made sense, nor were they intended to. In the United Kingdom, for instance, people were not "allowed" to meet in groups of more than six outdoors, yet in June 2020 police permitted thousands of protestors to march for BLM (Pyper & Brown, 2020). In pubs and restaurants, a mask was required when standing up but not when sitting down (Wardle, 2020), as though the virus only moved at a certain height. Bars and restaurants were pointlessly forced to close early (Takuku et al., 2022), as though the virus became more aggressive at certain times. The *Mail*'s Richard Littlejohn expressed a palpable sense of frustration:

> We're not going to take it anymore. You can sleep with your wife but can't play tennis with her. You can shoot ducks, but can't feed them. Boffins scare us with graphs, then change them. You can buy a pint to take away using an app on your mobile phone, but can't drink it inside or immediately outside a pub. Marks & Sparks can sell you a prawn sandwich,

> but not a pair of socks. Knickers are 'non-essential' on the High Street, but freely available on the internet. (Littlejohn, 2020)

"Impose too many illogical rules," Damien Green warned on November 29, 2020, "and soon we won't stick to smart ones [assuming there were any]" (D. Green, 2020).

The extensive number of "rules" that the public was expected to follow (e.g., around what kinds of behaviour were "expected" at different venue types) not only varied between the Home Nations (Chao-Fong, 2021), but they also changed (Cabinet Office, 2020) so often that it became hard, if not impossible to keep track of them (cf. Institute for Government, 2021). By the time that different "tier systems" were introduced in England, Wales, Scotland, and Northern Ireland in Q4 of 2020 (Department of Health and Social Care, 2020b), each with its own complex set of rules, restrictions, and exemptions, an almost Byzantine level of complexity had been introduced. No ordinary citizen could reasonably be expected to stay abreast of these "rules," especially when regions were moved between tiers (Department of Health and Social Care, 2020c). By July 2021, when the Government left it up to public transport and other companies to implement their own policies around mask wearing, there was not even an attempt at a consistent set of "rules." Gerrish (2021) plausibly infers: "the uncertainty and the change in the rules: that is part of the psychological attack," because they put people "in a position of stress and anxiety and confusion," making them "very susceptible to further messages and instructions."

Last-minute Government U-Turns

According to Kleinman (2006, p. 129) in a National Defence Intelligence College publication, "psychologists have identified the inability to effectively forecast near-term events as a major stressor in the detention environment." This, too, was a feature of the "Covid-19" operation.

"Like the abuser," Scott (2021a) writes, "the UK and Scottish Governments keep changing the story and goalposts [...]." A prime example of this was the UK Government's repeated last-minute U-turns on key decisions. On July 12, 2020, for example, the Minister for the Cabinet Office, Michael Gove, claimed that face masks should not be made mandatory in shops in England; two days later, the government announced they would be. Having vowed not to institute a second national "lockdown" in July

2020, the Prime Minister gave just five days' notice of the second "lock-down" on October 31 (Silver & Yang, 2020). On December 14, 2020, Matt Hancock announced that 11 million people in London, most of Essex and part of Hertfordshire would be plunged into Tier 3 restrictions with only 30 hours' notice (Tapsfield & Wilcock, 2020). Having promised the public at least five days' loosening of restrictions over Christmas, new Tier 4 restrictions were announced as late as December 20 that reduced that figure to zero for London and surrounding areas, while the rest of Britain saw five days reduced to just Christmas Day ("Christmas Rules Tightened," 2020). In late December 2020 and early January 2021, the government maintained that schools would remain open, yet at 8 pm on January 4, the day before most schools were due to go back, a new national "lockdown" was announced.

"Just as normality appears to beckon, the goalposts have been moved again," Lee (2021) writes of the Government's announcement of twice-weekly testing for everybody who wanted it in April 2021. In June 2021, there was a sudden exodus of thousands of British holidaymakers when Portugal was unexpectedly put on the government's "amber list" as part of a "traffic light" system classifying countries by risk of "Covid-19"; the system created stress and uncertainty for travellers. The goalposts continued to move as the British public was told "'we will be unlocking on June 21st,' then 'we should not unlock,' that 'we will not have vaccine passports,' then 'we should have vaccine passports,' that 'children will not be vaccinated,' then 'children should be vaccinated'" (Scott, 2021d).

On September 3, 2021, the JCVI announced that it did not recommend injections for healthy 12–15-year-olds; the following day, *The Times* ran a front-page headline: "Children set to be jabbed from early next week" (Smyth & Swinford, 2021). On September 12, 2021, the *Sunday Times* claimed that the Prime Minister was poised to abandon "the proposed compulsory certification scheme" (Shipman & Wheeler, 2021); the next day, the *Times* ran a piece titled, "Covid Vaccine Passports Can Still Help Defeat Winter Wave, No 10 Insists" (Wright, 2021); Oliver Wright was involved in both pieces. In August 2021 it was officially safe to attend UK nightclubs "unvaccinated"; in September it was not; and then it was again when the rule was rescinded.

The ultimate shifting of the goalposts came in February 2022, when the entire "Covid-19" narrative, having dominated the news channels for almost two years, was abandoned almost overnight in favour of the new narrative: Russia/Ukraine. It was as though its centrality to public consciousness had been nothing more than a function of propaganda in the first place. Those who had spent two years cheering on the suppression of individual rights and freedoms in the "Covid-19" context suddenly "stood with Ukraine," because they were told to. Having supported the most draconian of measures "to save just one life," many of those same people emerged strongly in favour of a no-fly zone over Ukraine that would risk major conflict. Having refused to have their own family over for Christmas if they were "unvaccinated," they opened their doors to Ukrainian refugees. After two years of attempting to make everyone wear masks and take the injections, in May 2022, they chanted "my body, my choice" as *Roe vs. Wade* was overturned.

Calculated Unpredictability of Treatment

Cognitive confusion and incapacitation are enhanced by calculated unpredictability of treatment, such that the victim never knows what to expect next. In a 1941 essay, Kurt Lewin of the Tavistock Clinic writes:

> One of the main techniques for breaking morale through a "strategy of terror" consists in exactly this tactic – keep the person hazy as to where he stands and just what he may expect. If, in addition, frequent vacillations between severe disciplinary measures and promises of good treatment, together with the spreading of contradictory news, make the cognitive structure of this situation utterly unclear, then the individual may cease to know when a particular plan would lead toward or away from his goal. Under these conditions, even those individuals who have definite goals and are ready to take risks will be paralyzed with severe inner conflicts in regard to what to do. (Lewin, 1948, p. 111)

One of the items on Biderman's "Chart of Coercion" is "occasional indulgences," which are intended to provide "positive motivation for compliance." The occasional indulgence arises from "fluctuations of interrogators' attitudes," i.e., is granted on a whim. It "hinders adjustment to deprivation" and offers the "tantalising" prospect of an improvement in conditions (Amnesty International, 1973, p. 49). According to the *KUBARK Manual*, the prisoner "is told that the changed treatment is a reward for truthfulness and an evidence that friendly handling will continue as long as he cooperates" (CIA, 1963, p. 84).

According to Amnesty International (1973, pp. 46–47), "occasional unpredictable brief respites" can make the victim feel obligated towards the torturer. The critical factor is that the treatment is constantly varied: "There is no time when a prisoner can be sure that he is through with a particular ordeal [...] Alleviation of the stress, whether due to spontaneous factors or deliberate manipulations, is intermittent, temporary, and unpredictable." Thus, to break a victim's will most effectively, it is not advisable to subject them to relentless suffering and deprivation: they may get used to it and become resilient. Rather, it is best to intersperse their suffering with occasional periods of respite. This encourages compliance in the hope of better treatment, prevents resistance from hardening, and creates a misguided sense of obligation towards the abuser.

We find a similar logic of unpredictable rewards and punishment, cloaked in pseudoscientific terminology, in the "Covid-19 countermeasures." As early as March 13, 2020, SAGE (2020) noted "evidence that people find quarantining harder to comply with the longer it goes on." Three days later, Neil Ferguson's infamous "Report 9" claimed that countermeasures may be "relaxed temporarily in relative [sic.] short time windows, but measures will need to be reintroduced if or when case numbers rebound" (Ferguson et al., 2020, pp. 1–2). When declaring the first "lockdown," the British Prime Minister claimed: "I can assure you that we will keep these restrictions under constant review. We will look again in three weeks, and relax them if the evidence shows we are able to" (Prime Minister's Office, 2020b). In keeping with technocracy, the power of granting respite was thus placed in the hands of unelected "scientific experts."

A pattern of abuse based on calculated unpredictability of treatment was established. When the tier system of "lockdowns" was introduced in the United Kingdom in autumn 2020, it was no longer a case of whether "lockdowns" are justifiable in the first place. Rather, a differential scale of abuse was put in place, involving constant fear of being moved into a worse tier. Relief at being in a lower tier was akin to the relief a victim feels for not getting a black eye from their abuser: they are not free, and there is always the threat of worse. As Anthony observes regarding whether the government would "allow" Christmas in 2020: "You forget that they are giving you something that was actually your right to have in the first place" (Anthony & Cullen, 2021).

As inalienable rights were attacked, occasional freedoms were "granted," but never commensurate with the plundering of fundamental rights and liberties. For example, the British Prime Minister outrageously claimed in April 2021: "It's only because of months of sacrifice and effort that we can take this small step towards freedom today," i.e. the "chance to see friends and family outdoors" (cited in Wilcock, 2021). To be clear, three separate "lockdowns" had been in effect almost continuously since March 2020, causing untold levels of harm and suffering (Bardosh, 2023; Dettmann et al., 2022; Harrison, 2023; Hughes et al., 2022). Yet, for acquiescing to this, the public was "granted" the most pathetic of supposed "rewards," when lawful freedom of association was always its right in the first place.

The simulated prison environment conjured up by "lockdowns" (a prison term) goes hand in hand with the idea of parole. In the Stanford Prison experiment, prisoners were invited to submit formal requests for parole based on their behaviour. This brought one rebellious prisoner to recant that he was "unworthy of better treatment. Since then he did his best to cooperate and no longer cause problems" (Perlstadt, 2018, p. 53). Thus, in prison conditions, the mere possibility of better treatment can be enough to induce behavioural change and compliance. As "lockdown" conditions eased, some commentators noticed the parallel with parole. According to Curtin (2021), "If you felt like a prisoner for the past year plus, now you will be paroled for a while." "Rather than being liberated from the Covid restrictions," Myers (2021) writes, "it is as if we are being put on parole. We can exercise some more freedoms, sure. But we do so in the knowledge that we could be hauled back under house arrest at any moment. This is no way to live."

Fundamental Irrationality in the System

Totalitarian menticide involves barraging the enemy with wave after wave of lies and illogicality:

> [Hitler] was never logical, because he knew that that was what he was expected to be. Logic can be met with logic, while illogic cannot – it confuses those who think straight. The Big Lie and monotonously repeated nonsense have more emotional appeal [...] than logic and reason. While the enemy is still searching for a reasonable counterargument to the first lie, the totalitarians can assault him with another. (Meerloo, 1956, p. 101)

The Science™ performed a similar function during the "Covid-19" operation. With the Gompertz curve having formed in the spring of 2020, for example, the worst of the alleged viral "pandemic" should have been over, yet UK mask mandates were illogically introduced *afterwards*, in the summer, when rates of respiratory illness are seasonally at their lowest. When Yeadon (2020) sought to introduce some rationality into proceedings by pointing to errors in SAGE methodology and the fact that "viruses do not do waves," the "second wave" duly appeared by dint of a "new variant." When the virulence of the "new variants" was called into question, the fear-mongering moved onto "immune escape" (see Chap. 4). Every attempt at reason and genuine science was met with a barrage of propaganda.

"One's sense of stability and trust in the world," Hertzberg (2021) notes, is rooted in "the belief that rationality is a limiting principle at some point upon what government and people/institutions with power in society are able and willing to do"; it is highly stressful to many people to see their governments behaving so irrationally. In that respect, it is significant that serious questions have been raised about the apparent cognitive impairment of Joe Biden, Kamala Harris, and Nancy Pelosi (plus John Fetterman following a stroke in 2022) (Hanson, 2022). The U.S. population, during the "Covid-19" era, was presented with a President, Vice-President, and Speaker of the House who at times behaved most peculiarly and appeared *non compos mentis*. The message tacitly conveyed to the public—most likely deliberately, given the timing and otherwise implausibility of allowing all three figures simultaneously to occupy top positions—was that irrationality lies at the heart of the political system, and, therefore, that reason offers no protection against tyranny and the arbitrary exercise of power.

Verbal Confusion

Mixed Messaging

As real science was junked in 2020, "Covid-19" messaging proved schizoid from the outset. For example: asymptomatic transmission does not drive epidemics (Fauci in January 2020, cited in Ballan, 2021); "anyone can spread it." There is "no obvious rationale" for "home quarantine" (WHO, 2019, p. 16); "lock down." Stay home; it is safer to be outdoors. "Three weeks to flatten the curve"; "the new normal." The public should not wear face masks; mask mandates (see Chap. 4). Never use contact tracing in a pandemic (WHO, 2019, p. 3); biosurveillance/contact tracing is essential. Scott (2021d), noting R.D. Laing's claim that contradictory messaging from a child's mother can drive a child into psychosis or schizophrenic breakdown, argues that "Covid-19" mixed messaging represents "a pernicious schizogenic tactic common to psychological abuse."

There was mixed messaging regarding the deadliness of "Covid-19." Health Secretary Hancock told parliament on March 23, 2020: "Coronavirus is the most serious public health emergency that has faced the world in a century" (Hansard, 2020)—only four days after the Advisory Committee on Dangerous Pathogens removed "Covid-19" from its list of high consequence infectious diseases (UK Health Security Agency, n.d.), and only 20 days after his department had published the following:

> Among those who become infected, some will exhibit no symptoms. Early data suggests that of those who develop an illness, the great majority will have a mild-to-moderate, but self-limiting illness – similar to seasonal flu. It is, however, also clear that a minority of people who get COVID-19 will develop complications severe enough to require hospital care, most often pneumonia. In a small proportion of these, the illness may be severe enough to lead to death. (Department of Health and Social Care, 2020a)

What happened in March 2020 to change this seasonal flu equivalent (see Chap. 6) into an alleged new "Spanish flu" (see Chap. 4)? Schwab and Malleret (2020, p. 8) note that past disease outbreaks have "forced empires to change course" and ask: "could the COVID-19 pandemic mark the onset of a similar turning point with long-lasting and dramatic consequences for our world today?" Yet, in the same book, they concede Schwab and Malleret (2020, p. 99) that "the consequences of COVID-19 in terms of health and mortality will be mild compared to previous pandemics."

There was substantial mixed messaging around the "vaccines." For example: the "vaccine" is the way out; NPIs remain necessary after injection. "Vaccinated" people become dead ends for the virus and cannot spread it (Choi, 2021); efficacy wanes and the "vaccine" prevents neither transmission nor infection (Loffredo, 2021). For most of 2021, "fully vaccinated" meant having had two injections; then it changed to include a third injection or "booster shot" (Wright & Tapsfield, 2021).

Contrast the following *Mail* headlines from August 15 and 27, 2023: "Here comes the "real deal"! Scientists raise alarm over new Covid variant and call for return of face masks" (Stearn, 2023) vs. "Mask study published by NIH suggests N95 Covid masks may expose wearers to dangerous level of toxic compounds linked to seizures and cancer" (Joshu, 2023). The messaging is schizoid by design and is intended to cause confusion.

Continuous Questioning

In prisoner interrogations in totalitarian regimes, "the victim is bombarded with questions day and night" (Meerloo, 1956, p. 28). CIA Director Allen Dulles (1953, p. 21) recounts the tale of a man who had been "subjected for 75 days to the monotony of interrogation." For POWs in the Korean War, "Under the daily signal of dulling routine questions [...] their minds went into a state of inhibition and diminished alertness" (Meerloo, 1956, p. 45). Biderman's chart of coercion includes "threats of endless interrogation" (Amnesty, 1973, p. 49). The *Human Resource Exploitation Training Manual* recommends "nonsense questioning" in which "two or more 'questioners' ask the subject questions which seem straightforward but which are illogical and have no pattern"; finding this "mentally intolerable," even "very orderly and logical subjects [...] begin to doubt their sanity" (CIA, 1983).

From the beginning of "Covid-19," the BBC News website, accessed by roughly three quarters of British online news users (Ofcom, 2018), featured a "Coronavirus" bar containing five lead articles whose titles were almost always framed as questions. This means that a very large number of people in Britain and around the world who turn to the BBC for their news were subliminally barraged with questions for ca. two years, until the bar was finally retired.

Consider the following BBC article titles, all from 2020 (date/month in brackets): "Coronavirus: What are viruses?" (20/1), "How do I protect myself from coronavirus?" (4/3), "Can AI help to fight coronavirus?" (12/3), "Coronavirus: What are the facts? (13/3), "Coronavirus: Do masks work?" (16/3), "Coronavirus: What does 'delay' mean for you?" (16/3), "How do I know if I have coronavirus?" (18/3), "Coronavirus: What is social distancing?" (23/3), "Should I wear a mask to stop coronavirus?" (17/4), "How can you tell if it's hay fever or coronavirus?" (20/4), "What are the EU coronavirus schemes?" (22/4), "How close are we to a coronavirus vaccine?" (23/4), "Coronavirus: how to wear a face covering?" (14/5), "What does a Covid-secure office look like?" (15/5), "Does contact tracing stop coronavirus?" (2/6), "Coronavirus: What's the risk for ethnic minorities?" (10/6), "Covid in Scotland: What are the latest lockdown rules?" (24/6), "Has Covid testing gone wrong?" (29/6), "Can you get coronavirus twice?" (9/7), "Coronavirus vaccine: how close are we? (29/7), "Coronavirus and lockdowns: what is the latest?" (13/9), "Covid: how worried should we be?" (17/10), "Has Covid stolen my future?" (18/10), "Long Covid: Who is more likely to get it?" (21/10), "Coronavirus vaccine: How close are you to getting one?" (16/11), "When will the Covid-19 vaccine be ready?" (17/11), "Will there be more than one coronavirus vaccine?" (17/11), "Will you take the vaccine?" (17/11), "When will you be eligible for the Covid vaccine?" (24/11), "What can you do in a Covid Christmas?" (25/11), "Covid: What are the new tiers and lockdown rules in England, Scotland, Wales and Northern Ireland?" (27/11), "How will I get a vaccine?" (2/12), "What's in the vaccine?" (12/2), "A Covid Vaccine: The End of the Pandemic?" (12/12), "Covid vaccine: How does a vaccine get approved?" (14/12), "New Covid strain: how worried should we be?" (15/12), "What has Covid done for climate crisis?" (27/12), "Covid: What is happening with schools in January?" (29/12), and "Covid-19 in the UK: How many coronavirus cases are there in your area?" (ongoing).

Although this may look like the BBC performing a public service by trying to answer questions readers may have, in the context of psychological warfare the constant questioning exacerbates public confusion and uncertainty. It also wears people down by inculcating them with a sense that they never really know what is happening and, implicitly, that they should trust the authorities to tell them what to do.

Damage to the Meaning of Words

Propaganda has always done damage to the meaning of words. As Fromm wrote in 1942,

> Never have words been more misused in order to conceal the truth than today. Betrayal of allies is called appeasement, military aggression is camouflaged as defence against attack, the conquest of small nations goes by the name of a pact of friendship, and the brutal suppression of the whole population is perpetrated in the name of National Socialism. (Fromm, 1960, p. 236)

How little times change. §5 of the 2002 U.S. National Security Strategy proposes pre-emptive warfare as a means of camouflaging the U.S. invasion of Iraq the following year (recalling Hitler's invasion of Norway). The mass atrocities of the "Covid-19" era (Hughes et al., 2022) were perpetrated in the name of keeping people "safe," "the greater good," etc. War is Peace, Freedom is Slavery, Ignorance is Strength.

Consider the damage done to language and the meaning of words by the "Covid-19" operation. Staying apart from other people, a profoundly antisocial act, is called "social distancing." "Staying apart," Australians were told, "keeps us together" (R. Green, 2020). "Stay home. Protect the NHS. Save Lives" can be reinterpreted as "House arrest (Sumption, 2020). Nazification of the NHS (Corbett, 2021). Lockdown deaths (Rancourt et al., 2021)." "Freedom passports," as they were originally branded in the United Kingdom, require people to show their (digital ID) papers as in any totalitarian society. Peaceful protestors have been branded "right-wing extremists." Truth has been labelled "misinformation" by "fact checkers" paid to promote Establishment narratives, while pseudoscience has been propagated by pro-Establishment so-called "scientists" (see Chaps. 4 & 6).

The Science™ is a form of anti-scientific cult thinking that insists on consensus (a political category) instead of scepticism (the essence of real science). Under The Science™, the meanings of scientific terms can be altered at will to fit political agendas. A "pandemic" since the WHO's redefinition of the term in 2009 does not imply serious illness or death (Keil, 2010, p. 2). The WHO redefined "herd immunity" in 2020 as exclusively a function of "vaccination" (removing reference to natural immunity)—compare the June 9 and November 13 definitions (WHO, 2020a, 2020b). The CDC in 2021 redefined "vaccination" to exclude all reference to immunity: "protection" or alleviation of symptoms, rather than preventing infection or transmission, became sufficient, rendering the "Covid-19 vaccines" no different from drugs or treatments (Hughes, 2022, p. 210).

With the U.S. economy entering recession in mid-2022, the definition of recession was changed so that it no longer meant two consecutive quarters of negative GDP growth (Billot, 2022). The *Cambridge English Dictionary* changed its definition of a woman from "an adult female human being" to include also "an adult who lives and identifies as female though they may have been said to have a different sex at birth" (Cambridge University Press, n.d.). In keeping with totalitarianism, words just mean whatever the authorities want them to mean, no matter how unscientific. "They can change the rules of reason or truth at the drop of a hat," Scott (2021c) claims, and "whatever they suggest, it will be couched via an abuse of language, science and reason, to confuse us and lead us further into menticide and breakdown."

Davis (2021) observes of the ruling class: "They consistently use deceptive language to conceal their intentions [...] We must unpick their language to fully comprehend their intentions, in the hope that we can resist and deny them." In that spirit, I propose the following glossary of deceptive terms since 2020:

Table 5.1 Glossary of deceptive terms

Deceptive Term	True Meaning
"Anti-vaxxers"	Those who insist on bodily autonomy and the right not to be penetrated against their will
"Build back better"	Destroy everything of public value
"Civil society"	Illusion of democratic accountability
"Critical"	Pretending to speak truth to power while turning a blind eye to deep state power structures
"Fourth Industrial Revolution"	Twenty-first-century political counterrevolution
"Global health architecture"	Scaffold for one world government/ global dictatorship
"Human augmentation"	Biodigital enslavement
"Independent"	Beset by conflicts of interest
"Lockdown"	Pretext for attack on civil liberties
"Misinformation"	Free speech
"Online safety"	Pretext for censorship
"Open and inclusive" / "no one left behind"	Intended to ensnare/enslave everyone (Wood, 2018, p. 39)
"Pandemic preparedness"	Military readiness, planning for martial law
"Pharmacovigilance"	Bio surveillance of the population
"Protect others" and "the common good"	Erasure of individual rights and freedoms
"Public health"	Death by stealth (deprivation of necessary healthcare services, long-waiting lists, injecting dangerous experimental products, etc.)
"Regulator"	Enabler of Big Pharma (Gyngell, 2022)
"Resilience"	Maladaptation
"Safe and effective"	Dangerous and ineffective
"Security"	Social control
"Slavery"	Associated with colonial legacies, not the biodigital future

(continued)

(continued)

Deceptive Term	True Meaning
"Smart"	Mindless consent to the technocratic control grid
"Stay safe"	Take measures that are harmful to health, e.g. face masks, "self-isolation," "social distancing," staying indoors, not seeing relatives
"Stewardship"	Theft of the global commons (Davis, 2021)
"Sustainable"	Prolonging the rule of the ruling class
"The Science"™	Pseudoscientific dogma
"Transhumanism"	Eugenics
"Trusted sources"	Co-opted liars
"Trust"	Manipulating public opinion
"Vaccine"	Injectable military technology
"Zero" ("zero Covid," "carbon zero")	Pretext for total social control

Once one learns to decode the deliberately deceptive language, the agendas become more visible.

The Production of Insanity

Gaslighting

The term "gaslighting," Merriam-Webster's word of the year in 2022, derives from Patrick Hamilton's 1938 stage play *Gas Light*, in which an abusive husband tries to drive his wife insane (in order to steal from her) by clandestinely dimming the gas lights in the house and denying his wife's perception that the lights are dimmer. Gaslighting, in contemporary parlance, is a form psychological manipulation intended to make the victim "question the validity of their own thoughts, perception of reality, or memories," typically leading to "confusion, loss of confidence and self-esteem, uncertainty of one's emotional or mental stability, and a dependency on the perpetrator" (Merriam-Webster, 2021).

An obvious example of gaslighting in the "Covid-19" context was NHS/UK Government "look them in the eyes" propaganda (Duffy, 2021), evidently intended to guilt-trip anyone resisting the official narrative and to make them question their own judgement. The scientific literature, nevertheless, indicates that looking someone in the eye is a "bad predictor" of whether or not they are lying (Gray, 2011, p. 31).

The public was made to question its own sanity through the creation of a nonsensical and harmful medicalised environment that was ostensibly to keep people "safe." As van der Pijl (2022, p. 29) observes: "Making face masks compulsory, social distancing and similar, medically senseless or even counterproductive measures evoke an absurd, unreal atmosphere that deeply affects people's state of mind."

Gaslighting can involve pretending things happened when they did not (or vice versa), to interfere with the victim's memory and undermine their sense of perception. As a matter of historical record, Boris Johnson told the British public on March 18, 2020: "we think now that we must apply further downward pressure on that upward curve by closing the schools. So I can announce [...] that after schools shut their gates from Friday afternoon, they will remain closed for [...] the vast majority of pupils until further notice" (Prime Minister's Office, 2020a). Yet, when a High Court challenge was made to the decision to close schools, the defence successfully argued that

> the government had not exercised any power to close schools. Rather, they had requested schools not to provide education on school premises save for the children of key workers and vulnerable children, and to comply with their continuing duties to provide education by other means. (Dolan & Ors v. Secretary of State for Health and Social Care & Anor, 2020)

With the help of Justice Lewis and some legalese, history was rewritten and the Government was exonerated of the enormous educational and psychological damage caused by its actions.

Or consider the catastrophic damage to mental health caused by the lockdowns, which is consistent with a campaign of psychological warfare. Critics pointed to "heightened levels of depression, anxiety, substance abuse, and complicated bereavement" (Marmarosh et al., 2020, p. 122). One meta-analysis of different studies finds that "individuals may experience symptoms of psychosis, anxiety, trauma, suicidal thoughts, and panic attacks" as a result of the "pandemic" (Salari et al., 2020). According to the ONS (2020), the rate of depression among UK adults rose from 10% (July 2019–March 2020) to 19% (June–November 2020); 60% of adults reported feeling stressed or anxious; and 34% reported a deterioration in their mental health (in keeping with a report by the Royal

College of Psychiatrists [2022]). A 2022 meta-analysis finds that the first UK "lockdown" increased the rate of depression to 32% (Dettmann et al., 2022). Yet, the BBC in 2023 gaslights the public that "people's general mental health and anxiety symptoms hardly deteriorated at all during the pandemic" (Roxby, 2023), while according to Sky News, "Covid did not affect happiness around the world" (Franks, 2023). The *Times* even expressed "lockdown nostalgia" (Walker, 2023).

Justin Trudeau, having prevented people from entering or exiting Canada without proof of "Covid-19 vaccination," having stifled media opposition to the "Covid-19" official narrative, having forced countless people to choose between their job/education and getting the shot, and having sought to freeze the bank accounts of supporters of the Truckers' Convoy, claimed in April 2023: "there are people who've probably gotten very sick from [Covid-19] vaccinations," but "individuals are allowed to make their own choices" (see Armstrong, 2023). Similarly, New Zealand Prime Minister Chris Hipkins, who as Covid Response Minister introduced "vaccine" mandates in 2021, claimed in September 2023: "I acknowledge that it was a challenging time for people, but they ultimately made their own choices. There was no compulsory vaccination, people made their own choices" (cited in Southwell, 2023).

Gaslighting Around "Covid-19 Vaccine" Damage

Perhaps the cruellest form of gaslighting has been the military-grade propaganda campaign to convince the public that "Covid-19 vaccine" damage was caused by ***anything but*** the dangerous experimental technologies that were shot into billions of people in the absence of adequate safety data. From the beginning, the "safe and effective" mantra could not be reconciled with "the expected high volume of Covid-19 vaccine Adverse Drug Reaction[s]," to quote the MHRA on the eve of the UK "vaccine" rollout (Tenders Electronic Daily, 2020).

From September 2021 on—once the "Covid-19 vaccine" had been offered to the entire adult population and was moving down the age ranges to target children—the media went into overdrive to provide any justification whatsoever for heart attacks, strokes, and sudden deaths that did not involve the "vaccines." Those symptoms were instead linked to: "young adult cannabis consumers" (CNN), "physical activity" (*Irish Times*), "pandemic stress and poor diet" (*Sunday Times*), "skipping breakfast" (*Express*), "lonely older women" (*Times*), "shovelling snow"

(*Mail*), energy drinks (*Express*), a "popular fizzy drink" (*Sun*), living under a flight path (*Mail*), moderate consumption of alcohol (*Mail*), "hotter nights" (*Guardian*), "traffic noise" (*CTV News*), an "entirely new kind of 'highly reactive' chemical [...] found in Earth's atmosphere" (*Mail*), "clocks changing" (Express), "cold weather" (*News Punch*), "hot weather" (*Express*), "humid weather" (*Express*), "solar storms" (*New Scientist*), "flight delays" (*Sun*), "falling asleep with the TV on" (*New York Post*), "certain sleeping positions" (*News Punch*), a "shower habit" (*Express*), "loneliness" (CTV News), "car fumes from exhaust and heavy braking" (*Mail*), "mild Covid" (*Times*), "long Covid" (*Sun*), "no symptoms at all" (*Mail*), "tiny particles in the air" (*Science Alert*), "soil" (*Sun*), "artificial sweeteners" (*SLAY*), patients missing out on statins (*Times*), "Broken Heart Syndrome" (NBC, *Mirror*), a "cold snap" (*Sky News*), "lack of masking" (*SLAY*), women having children in their early 20s (*Mail*), not smiling enough (*Mail*), and vaping (*Insider*). Blood clots, meanwhile, were linked to "binge-watching TV" (WebMD), "nutrients in eggs" (*Express*), "alcohol, tea, and coffee" (Express), "women under 40" (*Sun*), "the common cold" (*Sun*), and "extreme heat" (*Telegraph*).

Thus, having terrorised the public into believing that ordinary coughs and sneezes, and even "asymptomatic transmission" by healthy people, posed a potentially lethal threat (see Chap. 4), the media strove relentlessly to normalise blood clots, heart attacks, strokes, neurological disorders, "died suddenly," and the novel "Sudden Adult Death Syndrome" (SADS) from the time of the "vaccine" rollout.

In an apparent attempt to normalise "Covid-19 vaccine" damage in October 2022, the BBC soap opera *EastEnders* included a scene of a young woman suffering tremors, the left side of her face dropping, followed by a collapse and convulsions—reminiscent of the proliferation of real-life videos of that nature circulating online since the "vaccine" rollout. The ITV soap opera Coronation Street, in a December 2022 episode, included the "died suddenly" motif, helping to normalise the idea of sudden death at a time when people all over the world were publicly collapsing and convulsing (Dowd, 2022; Broudy et al., 2022).

The media feigned ignorance of what exactly was killing young people and causing the excess mortality that could not be ignored (Cuffe & Shraer, 2023). For example, consider the following headlines from between June and September 2022: "Healthy young people are dying suddenly and unexpectedly from a mysterious syndrome—as doctors seek answers through a new national register" (*Daily Mail Australia*), "Fit and healthy Kiwis dying unexpectedly from mysterious adult condition" (*NZ Herald*), "There are thousands more UK deaths than usual and we don't know why" (*New Scientist*), "Heart attacks are becoming increasingly more common in women under 50 and medical experts can't figure out why" (*Daily Record*). And from 2023: "Why are Americans dying so young?" (*Financial Times*, no mention of "vaccines"); "Brits are dying in their tens of thousands—and we don't really have any idea why" (*Mirror*); and "excess deaths are on the rise—but not because of Covid" (*Telegraph*, no mention of "vaccines").

The media sought to cover up "vaccine" damage to children and young people. Further to the evidence provided in Hughes (2022, § 10), consider the following headlines: "Video games could trigger heart attacks in children" (*Times*), "Air pollution may spur irregular heart rhythms in healthy teens" (*Newsroom*), "Air pollution causing heart failure and sudden death in healthy teenagers" (*SLAY*), "Wonder why youngsters are getting heart attacks after hitting the gym?" (*Hindustan Times*), and "University student 'dies of joy' after hearing he'd passed his exams with flying colours" (*Mirror*). The point with such headlines is not that each and every one definitively masks a "vaccine"-induced injury/death, but that their transnational proliferation works to normalise the abnormal, i.e. heart attacks in children and young people—coinciding with the "Covid-19 vaccine" rollout.

This is all additional to the media's constant churning out of duplicitous pro-vaccine headlines, e.g.: "Why vaccinated people dying from Covid-19 doesn't mean the vaccines are ineffective" (CNN), "JABULOUS: No deaths linked to Pfizer and Moderna Covid jabs, major new study finds" (*Sun*), "Revealed, just SEVENTY-FIVE Brits have been killed by Covid vaccines as experts hail data as proof jabs are incredibly safe and NOT behind surging excess deaths" (*Mail*). The media even promoted the idea that "vaccines" could be used to help cure known effects of "Covid-19 vaccine" damage, viz. "Scientists discover world's first cure for heart attacks using the same mRNA technology as Covid vaccines" (*Mail*).

A *Lancet Infectious Diseases* study sponsored by the Rhodes Trust, the WHO, the UK Medical Research Council, GAVI, the Bill & Melinda Gates Foundation, the National Institute for Health Research, and Community Jameel finds—predictably, given its backers—that "Covid-19 vaccination" saved "tens of millions of lives globally" (Watson et al.,

2022, p. 1293). But as Rancourt and Hickey (2023) demonstrate, the modelling in the study is flawed. In country after country, it shows a huge surge in all-cause mortality (ACM) and excess mortality for 12 months in 2021, assuming the "vaccines" had not been rolled out. Epidemiologically, this is implausible "following several presumed waves of infection, and past one year of declared pandemic" (Rancourt & Hickey, 2023, p. 8). In many countries, such as the United States, the actual ACM in 2021 shows no decrease that could be associated with the "vaccines"; on the contrary, there are additional peaks. The modelling appears even more ridiculous in the case of countries such as Finland, Norway, and Australia, where there was no noticeable increase in all-cause mortality in 2020 despite a supposed "pandemic" raging. Watson et al. (2022) expect us to believe that, having made no discernible impact for a year, "Covid-19" would suddenly have let rip in 2021 were it not for the "vaccines." In countries such as Qatar and Singapore, the modelled ACM is, at its peak, approximately ten times (!) higher than the actual ACM, which, however, remained broadly unchanged between 2018 and 2022—obvious nonsense.

Although the Watson et al. (2022) paper looks more like "vaccine" propaganda than genuine science, it had been cited in scientific sources over 900 times by December 2023. Published in a supposed leading journal, it confers intellectual respectability on claims such as that made in the 2023 announcement of the Nobel Prize in Physiology or Medicine (awarded for work facilitating the development of "Covid-19 mRNA vaccines"), i.e. "The vaccines have saved millions of lives and prevented severe disease in many more, allowing societies to open and return to normal conditions." On the day of the announcement, the mainstream media gushed that the "vaccines" had saved "millions" and "tens of millions" of lives (see Rancourt & Hickey, 2023, pp. 2–3). As usual, the opposite appears to be true: Rancourt et al. (2023, p. 3) deduce 17 million "vaccine"-induced deaths up to September 2022. And so the gaslighting around the "vaccines" continues.

The Political Abuse of Psychiatry

In the Soviet Union, the political abuse of psychiatry was systematic and widespread (British Medical Association, 1992, pp. 63–84). Political opposition was classified as a psychiatric problem, allowing for medical incarceration and the removal of dissidents from society (Bonnie, 2002).

This was particularly useful as "a tool in the struggle against dissidents who cannot be punished by legal means" (Podrabinek, 1980, p. 63). Soviet dissident, Viktor Feinberg, was told by a psychiatrist after 25 years in prison: "Your illness consists of dissenting opinions. As soon as you renounce them and adopt a correct point of view, we will let you go" (cited in Zimbardo, 2005, p. 142). Solzhenitsyn (1970) describes "the incarceration of free-thinking healthy people in madhouses" as "spiritual murder," a psychological "variation of the gas chamber."

In the West, dissent has been increasingly pathologised since 9/11 (Corbett, 2023). In the "Covid-19" era, however, the monstrous Soviet practice of weaponising psychiatry to discipline dissidents has made an unwelcome return—in the West. The abuse began when German medical lawyer Beate Bahner issued a press release on April 3, 2020, condemning the lockdown measures as "flagrantly unconstitutional, infringing to an unprecedented extent many of the fundamental rights of citizens" and calling on the public to take to the streets in protest (Thomson, 2020). For this, she was arrested and placed in a psychiatric ward, where she claims to have been "treated like a terrorist" and violently abused by authorities.

Swiss cardiologist Thomas Binder was arrested by an anti-terrorist squad in mid-April 2020 after speaking out against unscientific restrictions, the flawed PCR test, etc. (Hudak, 2022). He was then involuntarily committed to a psychiatric institution and forced to take psychiatric medication as a condition of his release. As with Bahner, the anti-terrorist pretext indicates that the anti-terrorism architecture put in place under the "War on Terror" is now being deployed against political dissidents.

On December 10, 2020, the retired French professor of pharmacology and toxicology, Jean-Bernard Fourtillan, was forcibly placed in solitary confinement at the Uzès psychiatric hospital, the order having been given by the local *préfet*, "the official representative of the French executive" (Smits, 2020). Fourtillan had become well-known for his view, expressed in the independent film *Hold-Up* (released on November 11, 2020), that the manufactured "Covid-19" crisis was being used to impose a dangerous "vaccine" on the world.

The British press assisted in weaponising psychiatry against dissidents. Seizing on an academic paper asking whether "antisocial traits matter" when it comes to "compliance with containment measures to the COVID-19 pandemic" (Miguel et al., 2020), the *Mail* headline was: "People who won't wear face masks are more likely to be sociopaths and feel 'socially detached,' study claims" (Chalmers, 2020). The *Mirror* went with "People refusing to wear face masks are 'likely to be sociopaths' says study" (Holland, 2020). The *Times* ran with, "Refusal to wear a facemask linked to sociopathy" (Blakely, 2020).

Kuhn et al. (2021) link "coronavirus conspiracy beliefs" (assumed without question to be invalid) to "delusion-related reasoning biases" and "paranoia." Going even further, Miller (2020) argues that "neuropsychological impairments" involving "faulty prefrontal systems" in the brain are to blame for questioning the official "Covid-19" narrative, implicitly opening the door to neurosurgery/lobotomy as effective treatment for political dissent, recalling Ken Kasey's *One Flew Over the Cuckoo's Nest* (1962). In an article that uses a still from the film version of Kasey's book as its main image, Elmer (2021) comments on Forsberg et al. (2020): "In summary and effect, these Oxford doctors of medical law and ethics have advised the UK Government to equate anyone who refuses to take the COVID-19 vaccine voluntarily with someone with a mental health disorder." Demonstrating the gravity of this error, Elmer notes that under the UK Mental Health Act, medical treatment can be administered without the recipient's informed consent, and thus the Oxford Uehiro Centre for Practical Ethics was ultimately "advocating sectioning the UK public to enforce compulsory vaccination."

The pathologisation of dissent impacted ordinary citizens. Some employers, for example, made their employees attend counselling sessions following their decision to refuse "vaccination." When pub landlord Rod Humphris threw Labour leader Keir Starmer out of his establishment for failing to challenge "lockdown" policy in April 2021, Labour replied that Humphris was "deluded"—an example of Soviet-style "psychopathologisation of dissidents" in Scott's (2021b) view. In May 2021, an Irishman who had filmed police disrupting Mass in the name of "Covid-19 countermeasures" was arrested in his house at 3:30am a week later under mental health legislation, based on an allegation supposedly made by his long-deceased mother (UK Column, 2021, 45:00).

Meryl Nass, a leading voice against Covid medicalised tyranny, had her licence suspended in January 2022 and was ordered to undergo a psychiatric evaluation for prescribing Ivermectin, reminiscent of "the Soviet KGB during the period when dissidents were incarcerated in psychiatric gulags to silence their dissent" (Blaylock, 2022, p. 2).

In April 2022, independent journalist Ramola D was arrested and was detained against her will for six days in a psychiatric facility (D, 2022).

She believes she was targeted for reporting on a collaboration between the U.S. Department of Defence and the Department of Justice to roll out a programme of mass surveillance and targeting of the population using electromagnetic weaponry.

The College of Physicians and Surgeons of Ontario in October 2022 mooted the idea of "prescription medications and/or referral to psychotherapy" for patients refusing to take a "Covid-19 vaccine" (Zwicker, 2022). In the same month, the increasingly politicised direction of travel was also evident in the Canadian Psychiatric Association's (2022) claim that "certain political movements have challenged the diagnosis of delusions."

Driving the Public Mad

The "Covid-19" operation involved an orchestrated, multi-pronged attack on the cognitive function of the minds of the public. Confusion was weaponised via the mental chaos arising from nonsensical "rules," last-minute government U-turns, deliberately unpredictable treatment of the public, and a barrage of lies designed to convey that the system itself is fundamentally irrational (even though it follows a very clear class logic). Constant mixed messaging, continuous questioning, damage to the meaning of words, and an esoteric ruling class vocabulary all contributed to verbal confusion. The public was gaslighted in various ways, from the implementation of a seemingly absurd/surreal social environment, to denial of past events, to cover-up of "vaccine" injury, to a Soviet-style political abuse of psychiatry.

"Covid-19" was, in Scott's (2021d) assessment, "an anti-human and psychotic narrative; a schizogenic and menticidal narrative; [intended] to drive us mad and destroy our reason, beliefs and values." Based on the evidence provided in this chapter, this seems like an accurate assessment. We are dealing here with a psychological warfare operation designed to cripple the cognitive capabilities of targeted populations. Troublingly, that operation was implemented by the very governments and media whose role it supposedly is to *protect* the public and expose abuses of power. This provides further evidence that all institutions aligned with the transnational ruling class are now arrayed against the public, to force through the transition to technocracy. The fact that Soviet-style methods have been openly adopted is yet another warning sign that liberal democracy is on the brink of giving way to totalitarianism unless a revolutionary alternative can be found.

References

Academy of Ideas. (2021, April 24). The manufacturing of a mass psychosis—can sanity return to an insane world? *Academy of Ideas*. https://academyofideas.com/2021/04/manufacturing-of-a-mass-psychosis-can-sanity-return-to-an-insane-world/.

Amnesty International. (1973). *Report on torture*. Duckworth.

Anthony, J., & Cullen, D. (2021, January 6). Breaking the Covid trance: How the Irish people were psychologically manipulated [Speech transcript]. *UK Column*. https://www.ukcolumn.org/article/breaking-covid-trance-how-irish-people-were-psychologically-manipulated.

Armstrong, M. (2023, April 28). Trudeau claims he never forced vaccinations. *Armstrong Economics*. https://www.armstrongeconomics.com/international-news/politics/trudeau-claims-he-never-forced-covid-vaccinations/.

Ballan, A. (2021, July 15). Covid—start at the beginning and question everything. *TCW*. https://www.conservativewoman.co.uk/covid-start-at-the-beginning-and-question-everything/.

Bardosh, K. (2023). How did the Covid pandemic response harm society? A global evaluation and state of knowledge review (2020–21). Preprint retrieved from https://doi.org/10.2139/ssrn.4447806.

Bernays, E. (1928). *Propaganda*. Horace Liveright.

Billot, J. (2022, July 29). Wikipedia takes cue from White House and redefines "recession." *Unherd*. https://unherd.com/thepost/wikipedia-takes-cue-from-white-house-and-re-defines-recession/.

Blakely, R. (2020, August 31). Refusal to wear a facemask linked to sociopathy. *The Times*. https://www.thetimes.co.uk/article/refusal-to-wear-a-facemask-linked-to-sociopathy-69zr7hcqh.

Blaylock, R.L. (2022). Covid update: What is the truth? *Surgical Neurology International*, 13, Article 167. https://doi.org/10.25259/SNI_150_2022.

Bonnie, R. (2002). Political abuse of psychiatry in the Soviet Union and in China: Complexities and controversies. *The Journal of the American Academy of Psychiatry and the Law, 30*(1), 136–144. https://doi.org/10.2139/ssrn.1760001.

Borum, R. (2006). Approaching truth: Behavioral science lessons on educing information from human sources. In R. Swenson (Ed.), *Educing information* (pp. 17–44). National Defence Intelligence College.

British Medical Association. (1992). *Medicine betrayed: The participation of doctors in human rights abuses*. Zed Books.

Broudy, D., Hughes, D. A., & Kyrie, V. (2022, December 10). The Psychology of Covid-19 Atrocities. *Doctors For Covid Ethics*. https://doctors4covidethics.org/session-iv-understanding-tactics-of-oppression-2/.

Cabinet Office. (2020, September 22). *Coronavirus (Covid-19): What has changed—22 September*. https://www.gov.uk/government/news/coronavirus-covid-19-what-has-changed-22-september.

Cambridge University Press. (n.d.). Woman. In *Cambridge English Dictionary*. Retrieved June 22, 2023, from https://dictionary.cambridge.org/dictionary/english/woman.

Canadian Psychiatric Association. (2022). *W38 – Delusions, unusual beliefs, and conspiracy theories: Has the boundary shifted*? https://www.cpa-apc.org/w38-delusions-unusual-beliefs-and-conspiracy-theories-has-the-boundary-shifted/.

Central Intelligence Agency. (1963). *KUBARK Counterintelligence Interrogation*. https://nsarchive2.gwu.edu/NSAEBB/NSAEBB27/docs/doc01.pdf.

Central Intelligence Agency. (1983). *Human resource exploitation training manual*. https://nsarchive2.gwu.edu/NSAEBB/NSAEBB122/#hre.

Chalmers, V. (2020, August 31). People who won't wear face masks are more likely to be sociopaths and feel "socially detached," study claims. *Daily Mail*. https://www.dailymail.co.uk/news/article-8681001/People-wont-wear-face-masks-likely-sociopaths-study-claims.html.

Chao-Fong, L. (2021, December 27). What are Covid rules in England, Wales, Scotland and Northern Ireland? *The Guardian*. https://www.theguardian.com/world/2021/dec/27/what-are-covid-rules-in-england-wales-scotland-and-northern-ireland.

Choi, J. (2021, May 16). Fauci: Vaccinated people become "dead ends" for the coronavirus. *The Hill*. https://thehill.com/homenews/sunday-talk-shows/553773-fauci-vaccinated-people-become-dead-ends-for-the-coronavirus/.

Christmas rules tightened for England, Scotland and Wales. (2020, December 20). *BBC News*. https://www.bbc.co.uk/news/uk-55379220.

Corbett, K. P. (2021, August 7). The "Nazification" of the NHS. *The Light Paper*. https://thelightpaper.co.uk/assets/pdf/Light-12h.pdf.

Corbett, J. (2023, March 20). Dissent into madness: Crazy conspiracy theorists. *The Corbett Report*. https://corbettreport.substack.com/p/dissent-into-madness-crazy-conspiracy.

Cuffe, R., & Schraer, R. (2023, January 10). Excess deaths in 2022 among worst in 50 years. *BBC News*. https://www.bbc.co.uk/news/health-64209221.

Curtin, E. (2021, May 11). Second stage terror wars. *Behind the Curtain*. https://edwardcurtin.com/second-stage-terror-wars/.

D, R. (2022, April 20). Ramola D: released from political persecution of wrongful psych hold in Carney hospital, Dorchester. *The Everyday Concerned Citizen*. https://everydayconcerned.net/2022/04/20/ramola-d-released-from-political-persecution-of-wrongful-psych-hold-in-carney-hospital-dorchester-after-6-days-of-illegal-unconstitutional-arrest-detainment-kidnapping-by-quincy-police-departme/.

Davis, I. (2021, October 12). Seizing everything: The theft of the global commons—part 1. *Iain Davis*. https://in-this-together.com/global-commons-part-1/.

Department of Health and Social Care. (2020a, March 3): *Coronavirus action plan: a guide to what you can expect across the UK*. https://www.gov.uk/government/publications/coronavirus-action-plan/coronavirus-action-plan-a-guide-to-what-you-can-expect-across-the-uk.

Department of Health and Social Care. (2020b). *Business as usual for NHS test and trace over Christmas*. https://www.gov.uk/government/news/business-as-usual-for-nhs-test-and-trace-over-christmas.

Department of Health and Social Care. (2020c). *Review of local restriction tiers: 17 December 2020*. https://www.gov.uk/government/speeches/review-of-local-restriction-tiers-17-december-2020.

Dettmann, L. M., Adams, S., & Taylor, G. (2022, February 9). Investigating the prevalence of anxiety and depression during the first COVID-19 lockdown in the United Kingdom: Systematic review and meta-analyses. *British Journal of Clinical Psychology*, *61*(3), 757–780. https://doi.org/10.1111/bjc.12360.

Dolan & Ors v. Secretary of State for Health and Social Care and Anor, EWHC 1786. (2020). https://www.bailii.org/ew/cases/EWHC/Admin/2020/1786.html.

Dowd, E. (2022). *"Cause Unknown": The epidemic of sudden deaths in 2021 and 2022*. Skyhorse.

Duffy, N. (2021, January 22). New Government ad campaign targets rule-breakers with messages from Covid patients and staff. *i*. https://inews.co.uk/news/uk/new-government-ad-campaign-targets-rule-breakers-covid-19-patients-staff-842022.

Dulles, A. (1953). How the communists "wash brains." *United States Army Combat Forces Journal*, July: 20–21.

Elmer, S. (2021, January 8). Our default state: Compulsory vaccination for covid-19 and human rights law. *Architects For Social Housing*. https://architectsforsocialhousing.co.uk/2021/01/08/our-default-state-compulsory-vaccination-for-covid-19-and-human-rights-law/.

Fagan, P. (2020, July 28). Face masks make you stupid. *The Critic*. https://thecritic.co.uk/face-masks-make-you-stupid/.

Ferguson, N.M, Laydon, D., Nedjati-Gilani, G., Imai, N., Ainslie, K., Baguelin, M., Bhatia, S., Boonyasiri, A., Cucunubá, Z., Cuomo-Dannenburg, G., Dighe, A., Dorigatti, I., Fu, H., Gaythorpe, K., Green, W., Hamlet, A., Hinsley, W., Okell, L. C., van Elsland, S., Ghani, A. C. (2020). *Report 9: Impact of non-pharmaceutical interventions (NPIs) to reduce Covid-19 mortality and healthcare demand*. https://www.imperial.ac.uk/media/imperial-college/medicine/sph/ide/gida-fellowships/Imperial-College-COVID19-NPI-modelling-16-03-2020.pdf.

Forsberg, L., Black, I., Douglas, T., & Pugh, J. (2020, July 22). *Compulsory vaccination for Covid-19 and human rights law*. https://committees.parliament.uk/writtenevidence/9253/pdf/.

Franks, J. (2023, March 20). Covid did not affect happiness around the world, study reveals. *Sky News*. https://news.sky.com/story/covid-did-not-affect-happiness-around-the-world-study-reveals-12838836.

Fromm, E. (1960). *Fear of freedom*. Routledge and Kegan Paul.

Gerrish, B. (2021, May 29). Testimony to Reiner Füllmich: Our oppressors are very frightened people. *UK Column*. https://www.ukcolumn.org/index.php/article/brian-gerrishs-testimony-to-reiner-fullmich-our-oppressors-are-very-frightened-people.

Gray, R. (2011). Lies, liars, and lie detection. *Federal Probation, 75*(3), 31–36.

Green, D. (2020, November 29). Impose too many illogical rules and soon we won't stick to smart ones. *The Times*. https://www.thetimes.co.uk/article/impose-too-many-illogical-rules-and-soon-we-wont-stick-to-smart-ones-lhdhm0p2f.

Green, R. (2020, May 4). Victorian government launches "staying apart keeps us together" campaign via M&C Saatchi. *Campaign Brief*. https://campaignbrief.com/victorian-government-launches-staying-apart-keeps-us-together-campaign-via-mc-saatchi/.

Gyngell, K. (2022, July 6). The doctor who turned her health watchdog into a Covid vaccine lapdog. *TCW*. https://www.conservativewoman.co.uk/the-doctor-who-turned-her-health-watchdog-into-a-covid-vaccine-lapdog/.

Hansard. (2020, March 23). *Coronavirus Bill. Volume 674: debated on Monday 23 March 2020*. https://hansard.parliament.uk/Commons/2020-03-23/debates/F4D06B4F-56CD-4B60-8306-BAB6D78AC7CF/CoronavirusBill.

Harrison, N. (2023, December 7). Lockdowns: A study of the harms. *UK Column*. https://www.ukcolumn.org/article/lockdowns-a-study-of-the-harms.

Hassan, S. (1990). *Combatting cult mind control* (2nd ed.). Park Street Press.

Herman, E., & Chomsky, N. (1988). *Manufacturing consent: The political economy of the mass media*. Pantheon.

Hertzberg, A. (2021, December 27). Facemasks are not a mere "inconvenience." *The Brownstone Institute*. https://brownstone.org/articles/facemasks-are-not-a-mere-inconvenience/.

Holland, P. (2020, September 1). People refusing to wear face masks are "likely to be sociopaths" says study. *Daily Mirror*. https://www.mirror.co.uk/news/weird-news/people-refusing-wear-face-masks-22610789.

Hudak, T. (2022, September 19). Dr. Thomas Binder interview—how psychology was weaponized to suppress truth in the age of Covid. *Children's Health Defence*. https://childrenshealthdefense.eu/eu-affairs/dr-thomas-binder-interview-how-psychology-was-weaponized-to-suppress-truth-in-the-age-of-covid/.

Hughes, D. A. (2022). "Covid-19 vaccines" for children in the UK: A tale of establishment corruption. *International Journal of Vaccine Theory, Practice, and Research*, *2*(1), 209–247. https://doi.org/10.56098/ijvtpr.v2i1.35.

Hughes, D.A., Kyrie, V., & Broudy, D. (2022, November 29). Covid-19: Mass formation or mass atrocity? *Unlimited Hangout*. https://unlimitedhangout.com/2022/11/investigative-reports/covid-19-mass-formation-or-mass-atrocity/.

Institute for Government. (2021, December). *Timeline of UK Government coronavirus lockdowns and measures, March 2020 to December 2021.* https://www.instituteforgovernment.org.uk/sites/default/files/2022-12/timeline-coronavirus-lockdown-december-2021.pdf.

Joshu, E. (2023, August 27). Mask study published by NIH suggests N95 Covid masks may expose wearers to dangerous level of toxic compounds linked to seizures and cancer. *Daily Mail*. https://www.dailymail.co.uk/health/article-12443319/Mask-study-published-NIH-suggests-N95-Covid-masks-expose-wearers-dangerous-level-toxic-compounds-linked-seizures-cancer.html.

Kasey, K. (1962). *One flew over the cuckoo's nest*. Viking Press.

Keil, U. (2010, January 26). Introductory statement to social, health and family affairs committee of the parliamentary assembly of the council of Europe hearing: The handling of the H1N1 pandemic: More transparency needed? http://assembly.coe.int/CommitteeDocs/2010/20100126_ContributionKeil.pdf.

Klarenberg, K. (2023, March 30). Leaked emails: "Independent" SAGE crushed dissent over Covid restrictions. *Propaganda in Focus*. https://propagandainfocus.com/leaked-emails-independent-sage-crushed-dissent-over-covid-restrictions/.

Kleinman, S. M. (2006). KUBARK counterintelligence interrogation review: Observations of an interrogator—lessons learned and avenues for further research. In R. Swenson (Ed.), *Educing information* (pp. 95–140). National Defence Intelligence College.

Kuhn, S. A. K., Lieb, R., Freeman, D., Andreou, C., & Zander-Schellenberg, T. (2021). Coronavirus conspiracy beliefs in the German-speaking general population: Endorsement rates and links to reasoning biases and paranoia. *Psychological Medicine, 52*(16), 4162–4176. https://doi.org/10.1017/S0033291721001124.

Kyrie, V., & Broudy, D. (2022, September 22). The Covid-19 concoction: A recipe for successful psychological operations. *Propaganda in Focus*. https://propagandainfocus.com/the-covid-19-concoction-a-recipe-for-successful-psychological-operations/.

Lee, J. (2021, April 5). This perverse plan for twice-weekly Covid tests will spark fear-mongering and anxiety. *Daily Mail*. https://www.dailymail.co.uk/debate/article-9438575/twice-weekly-Covid-tests-spark-fear-mongering-anxiety-writes-DR-JOHN-LEE.html.

Lewin, K. (1948). *Resolving social conflicts*. Harper.

Lippmann, W. (1922). *Public opinion*. Harcourt, Brace, and Company.

Littlejohn, R. (2020, November 6). We're not going to take it any more. You can sleep with your wife but can't play tennis with her. You can shoot ducks, but can't feed them. Boffins scare us with graphs, then change them... *Daily Mail*. https://www.dailymail.co.uk/debate/article-8922907/Britain-isnt-going-writes-RICHARD-LITTLEJOHN.html.

Loffredo, J. (2021, November 15). Fauci, Gates admit Covid vaccines don't work as advertised. *The Defender*. https://childrenshealthdefense.org/defender/jeremy-hunt-fauci-gates-covid-vaccines-boosters/.

Marmarosh, C. L., Forsyth, D. R., Strauss, B., & Burlingame, G. M. (2020). The psychology of the Covid-19 pandemic: A group-level perspective. *Group Dynamics: Theory, Research, and Practice, 24*(3), 122–139. https://doi.org/10.1037/gdn0000142.

Meerloo, J. A. (1956). *The rape of the mind. The psychology of thought control, menticide, and brainwashing*. World Publishing Company.

Merriam Webster. (2021). Gaslighting. *Merriam-Webster.com Dictionary*. https://www.merriam-webster.com/dictionary/gaslighting.

Miguel, F. K., Machadob, G. M., Pianowskib, G., & de Francisco Carvalho, L. (2020). Compliance with containment measures to the COVID-19 pandemic over time: Do antisocial traits matter?". *Personality and Individual Differences, 168*(2021), 110346. https://doi.org/10.1016/j.paid.2020.110346.

Miller, B. L. (2020). Science denial and Covid conspiracy theories: Potential neurological mechanisms and possible responses. *Journal of the American Medical Association, 324*(22), 2255–2256. https://doi.org/10.1001/jama.2020.21332.

Myers, F. (2021, July 13). Are we heading for a Winter lockdown? *Spiked*. https://www.spiked-online.com/2021/07/13/are-we-heading-for-a-winter-lockdown/.

Office for National Statistics. (2020). *Coronavirus and depression or anxiety in Great Britain*. https://www.ons.gov.uk/peoplepopulationandcommunity/healthandsocialcare/healthandwellbeing/datasets/coronavirusanddepressionoranxietyingreatbritain.

Office of Communications. (2018). *News consumption in the UK: 2018*. https://www.ofcom.org.uk/__data/assets/pdf_file/0024/116529/news-consumption-2018.pdf.

Perlstadt, H. (2018). How to get out of the Stanford prison experiment: Revisiting social science research ethics. *Current Research Journal of Social Sciences, 1*(2), 45–59. https://doi.org/10.12944/CRJSSH.1.2.01.

Perraudin, F. (2020, June 1). UK lockdown rules: What you are allowed to do from Monday. *The Guardian*. https://www.theguardian.com/world/2020/may/29/uk-lockdown-rules-what-are-the-key-changes.

Pijl, K. van der. (2022). *States of emergency. Keeping the global population in check*. Clarity Press.

Podrabinek, A. (1980). *Punitive medicine*. Karoma Publishers.

Prime Minister's Office. (2020a, March 18). *Prime Minister's statement on coronavirus (Covid-19): 18 March 2020*. https://www.gov.uk/government/speeches/pm-statement-on-coronavirus-18-march-2020.

Prime Minister's Office. (2020b, March 23). *Prime Minister's statement on coronavirus (Covid-19): 23 March 2020*. https://www.gov.uk/government/speeches/pm-address-to-the-nation-on-coronavirus-23-march-2020.

Pyper, D., & Brown, J. (2020, June 4). Black Lives Matter protests: UK reaction to the killing of George Floyd. *House of Commons Library*. https://commonslibrary.parliament.uk/black-lives-matter-protests-uk-reaction/.

Rancourt, D., Baudin, M., & Mercier, J. (2021). *Nature of the Covid-era public health disaster in the USA, from all-cause mortality and socio-geo-economic and climatic data*. https://denisrancourt.ca/uploads_entries/1635189453861_USA%20ACM%20into%202021%20-%20article----12d.pdf.

Rancourt, D., & Hickey, J. (2023). Quantitative evaluation of whether the Nobel-Prize-winning COVID-19 vaccine actually saved millions of lives. *CORRELATION*. https://correlation-canada.org/nobel-vaccine-and-all-cause-mortality/.

Roxby, P. (2023, March 9). Mental-health crisis from Covid pandemic was minimal—study. *BBC News*. https://www.bbc.co.uk/news/health-64890952.

Royal College of Psychiatrists. (2022, March 22). One third of UK public says their mental health has deteriorated as a result of the pandemic. https://www.rcpsych.ac.uk/news-and-features/latest-news/detail/2022/03/22/one-third-of-uk-public-says-their-mental-health-has-deteriorated-as-a-result-of-the-pandemic.

Salari, N., Hosseinian-Far, A., Jalali, R., Vaisi-Raygani, A., Rasoulpoor, S., Mohammadi, M., Rasoulpoor, S., & Khaledi-Paveh, B. (2020). Prevalence of stress, anxiety, depression among the general population during the Covid-19 pandemic: a systematic review and meta-analysis. *Globalization of Health*, *16*(57). https://doi.org/10.1186/s12992-020-00589-w.

Schwab, K., & Malleret, T. (2020). *Covid 19: The Great Reset*. World Economic Forum.

Scientific Advisory Group for Emergencies. (2020). *Addendum to fifteenth SAGE meeting on Covid-19, 13th March 2020 held in 1 Victoria St, London, SW1H 0NN*. https://assets.publishing.service.gov.uk/government/uploads/system/uploads/attachment_data/file/888783/S0383_Fifteenth_SAGE_meeting_on_Wuhan_Coronavirus__Covid-19__.pdf.

Scott, B. (2021a, January 3). Psychological attack on the UK. *UK Column*. https://www.ukcolumn.org/article/psychological-attack-uk.

Scott, B. (2021b, May 2). We are all Pavlov's dogs now. *UK Column*. https://www.ukcolumn.org/article/we-are-all-pavlovs-dogs-now.

Scott, B. (2021c, September 18). Escape from menticide: Possible futures/parallel social structures. *Borderline*. https://dr-bruce-scott.com/2021/09/18/escape-from-menticide-possible-futures-parallel-social-structures/.

Scott, B. (2021d, October 13). Beyond a state of fear: Menticide and schizogenesis. *Borderline*. https://dr-bruce-scott.com/2021/10/13/beyond-a-state-of-fear-menticide-and-schizogenesis/.

Shepherd, S., & Kay, A. C. (2012). On the perpetuation of ignorance: System dependence, system justification, and the motivated avoidance of sociopolitical information. *Journal of Personality and Social Psychology, 102*(2), 264–280. https://doi.org/10.1037/a0026272.

Shipman, T., & Wheeler, C. (2021, September 12). Covid vaccine passports scrapped for winter by Boris Johnson. *The Sunday Times*. https://www.thetimes.co.uk/article/covid-vaccine-passports-scrapped-for-winter-by-boris-johnson-5g2fdb2zn.

Silver, J., & Yang, Y. (2020, July 19). Johnson vows no second lockdown, asks cabinet back to work. *Bloomberg*. https://www.bloombergquint.com/onweb/u-k-s-johnson-tells-cabinet-to-return-to-office-next-week-mail.

Smits, J. (2020, December 11). Accomplished pharma prof thrown in psych hospital after questioning official Covid narrative. *LifeSite News*. https://www.lifesitenews.com/news/accomplished-pharma-prof-thrown-in-psych-hospital-after-questioning-official-covid-narrative.

Smyth, C., & Swinford, S. (2021, September 4). Children set to be jabbed from early next week. *The Times*.

Solzhenitsyn, A. (1970, June 17). Solzhenitsyn's statement. *The New York Times*. https://archive.is/loBB7#selection-261.0-261.24.

Southwell, D. (2023, September 4). New Zealand Prime Minister Chris Hipkins claims no one was forced to take Covid vaccines despite bringing in mandates when he was minister. *Daily Mail Australia*. https://www.dailymail.co.uk/news/article-12477405/New-Zealand-Prime-Minister-Chris-Hipkins-claims-no-one-forced-Covid-vaccines-despite-bringing-mandates-minister.html.

Stearn, E. (2023, August 15). Here comes the "real deal"! Scientists raise alarm over new Covid variant and call for return of face masks. *Daily Mail*. https://www.dailymail.co.uk/health/article-12408505/Here-comes-real-deal-Scientists-raise-alarm-new-Covid-variant-call-return-face-masks.html.

Sumption, J. (2020, October 27). *Government by decree: Covid-19 and the constitution*. Cambridge Freshfields Annual Law Lecture. https://resources.law.cam.ac.uk/privatelaw/Freshfields_Lecture_2020_Government_by_Decree.pdf.

Takuku, R., Yokoyama, I., Tabuchi, T., Oguni, M., & Fujiware, T. (2022). SARS-CoV-2 suppression and early closure of bars and restaurants: A longitudinal

natural experiment. *Scientific Reports*, *12*, Article 12623. https://doi.org/10.1038/s41598-022-16428-4.
Tapsfield, J., & Wilcock, D. (2020, December 14). London, parts of Essex and Hertfordshire go into tier 3 at a day's notice: Lockdown from midnight tomorrow after Hancock says new "faster-spreading variant" of Covid is rampant in South East and daily cases rise by 37% to 20,263. *Daily Mail*. https://www.dailymail.co.uk/news/article-9051155/MPs-warned-coronavirus-cases-London-chart-ahead-Tier-3-decision.html.
Tenders Electronic Daily. (2020, November 11). *United Kingdom–London: Software package and information systems. 2020/S 207–506291 contract award notice*. https://archive.is/2JXqO#selection-763.0-775.21.
Thomson, A. (2020, April 14). Coronavirus lockdown: German lawyer detained for opposition. *UK Column*. https://www.ukcolumn.org/article/coronavirus-lockdown-german-lawyer-detained-opposition.
UK Column. (2021, May 3). *UK Column news—3 May 2021*. https://www.ukcolumn.org/ukcolumn-news/uk-column-news-3rd-may-2021.
UK Health Security Agency (n.d.). *High consequence infectious diseases (HCID)*. Retrieved June 17, 2023, from https://www.gov.uk/guidance/high-consequence-infectious-diseases-hcid#full-publication-update-history.
Walker, H. (2023, May 15). I have lockdown nostalgia, and I'm not alone. *The Times*. https://www.thetimes.co.uk/article/i-have-lockdown-nostalgia-and-im-not-alone-hm76h6hv9.
Walker, P. (2020, May 11). Coronavirus lockdown: What are the new rules announced by Boris Johnson? *The Guardian*. https://www.theguardian.com/world/2020/may/10/uk-coronavirus-lockdown-what-has-boris-johnson-announced.
Wardle, S. (2020, October 3). Is there really any point in wearing your mask to walk to a table in a pub or restaurant? Answer—almost none. Just like having your temperature checked when walking into a building is a total waste of time… *Daily Mail*. https://www.dailymail.co.uk/health/article-8801307/Coronavirus-UK-NO-reason-wear-mask-walk-table-pub.html.
Watson, O. J., Barnsley, G., Toor, J., Hogan, A. B., Winskill, P., & Ghani, A. C. (2022). Global impact of the first year of COVID-19 vaccination: A mathematical modelling study. *The Lancet Infectious Diseases, 22*(9), 1293–1302. https://doi.org/10.1016/S1473-3099(22)00320-6.
Wilcock, D. (2021, March 29). Out with the old and in with the red, white and new! Boris Johnson backed by the Union Jack as he hosts his first press conference in Downing Street's new £2.6 million press briefing room to welcome the latest stage of lockdown lifting. *Daily Mail*. https://www.dailymail.co.uk/news/article-9415203/Union-Jack-backed-Boris-Johnson-gives-press-conference-new-2-6million-briefing-room.html.
Wood, P. (2018). *Technocracy: The hard road to world order*. Coherent Publishing.

World Health Organisation (2019). *Non-pharmaceutical public health measures for mitigating the risk and impact of epidemic and pandemic influenza.* https://apps.who.int/iris/bitstream/handle/10665/329438/9789241516839-eng.pdf?ua=1.

World Health Organisation. (2020a, June 9). *Coronavirus disease (Covid-19): Serology.* https://web.archive.org/web/20201105013101/https://www.who.int/news-room/q-a-detail/coronavirus-disease-covid-19-serology.

World Health Organisation. (2020b, November 13). *Coronavirus disease (Covid-19): Serology, antibodies and immunity.* https://www.who.int/news-room/q-a-detail/coronavirus-disease-covid-19-serology.

Wright, J., & Tapsfield, J. (2021, December 13). Brits will need three jabs for a vaccine passport: Javid says booster shots will be needed for passes once Brits have had a "reasonable chance" to get them. *Daily Mail.* https://www.dailymail.co.uk/news/article-10305373/Javid-warns-change-fully-vaccinated-status-New-Year.html.

Wright, O. (2021, September 13). Covid vaccine passports can still help defeat winter wave, no. 10 insists. *The Times.* https://www.thetimes.co.uk/article/covid-vaccine-passports-can-still-help-defeat-winter-wave-no-10-insists-3zv90szj8.

Yeadon, M. (2020, October 16). What SAGE has got wrong. *Lockdown Sceptics.* https://lockdownsceptics.org/what-sage-got-wrong/.

Zimbardo, P. (2005). Mind control in Orwell's *Nineteen eighty-four*: Fictional concepts become operational realities in Jim Jones's jungle experiment. In A. Gleason, J. Goldsmith, & M. C. Nussbaum (Eds.), *On* Nineteen eighty-four*: Orwell and our future* (pp. 127–154). Princeton University Press.

Zwicker, M. (2022, October 6). Ontario College of Physicians recommends "medication" and "psychotherapy" to encourage Covid vaccination. *LifeSite News.* https://www.lifesitenews.com/news/ontario-college-of-physicians-recommends-medication-and-psychotherapy-to-encourage-covid-vaccination/.

CHAPTER 6

Weaponised Deception

Totalitarianism is facilitated by what Hannah Arendt calls "gigantic lies and monstrous falsehoods," which the masses are organised to believe. This tradition has a long history, even in the West. The "Covid-19 pandemic" was a Big Lie: there is no credible epidemiological evidence to support its existence. Rather, the "pandemic" was a media-driven social phenomenon that served to deflect attention from far-reaching technocratic agendas being advanced across every area of life. "Pandemic preparedness" provides cover for building the institutional architecture of global dictatorship under the pretext of public health. It is unclear whether "SARS-CoV-2" is real: problems exist regarding its alleged "isolation" (involving cytopathic effects, genome sequencing, and electron microscopy images). There is, however, evidence to suggest that "SARS-CoV-2" may, in part, have been influenza rebranded. The "vaccines," which instead of protecting people have caused catastrophic harm, are in fact military products aimed at controlling the population in multiple ways. Yet, despite the "Covid-19" narrative being saturated with deceit, most people cannot and will not see it, owing to cognitive dissonance.

D. A. Hughes, *"Covid-19," Psychological Operations, and the War for Technocracy*, https://doi.org/10.1007/978-3-031-41850-1_6

The Big Lie

Totalitarianism and Big Lies

Hitler in *Mein Kampf* coins the idea of the Big Lie, i.e. a lie so huge that ordinary people would not imagine it to be possible:

> [I]n the big lie there is always a certain force of credibility; because the broad masses of a nation are always more easily corrupted in the deeper strata of their emotional nature than consciously or voluntarily; and thus in the primitive simplicity of their minds they more readily fall victims to the big lie than the small lie, since they themselves often tell small lies in little matters but would be ashamed to resort to large-scale falsehoods. It would never come into their heads to fabricate colossal untruths, and they would not believe that others could have the impudence to distort the truth so infamously (Hitler, 1939, p. 183)

The idea is that if the lie is big enough, and driven by sufficiently powerful propaganda, the masses will not think to question it. "If you repeat a lie often enough," explains Klaus Schwab's protégé, Yuval Harari, "people will think it's the truth. And the bigger the lie, the better, because people won't even think about how something so big can be a lie" (cited in Hughes, 2022b). Note Hitler's targeting of the "primitive" mind, or what behavioural psychologists today call the "automatic brain" (Dolan et al., 2010, p. 73). The dynamics of mass psychology can be used to override the conscious mind. Individuals can be made to consent, freely in their own mind, to propositions based on Big Lies that they do not recognise as such.

Arendt (1962, p. 333) writes of totalitarianism that a "terrible, demoralizing fascination" is to be found in the "possibility that gigantic lies and monstrous falsehoods can eventually be established as unquestioned facts," provided the masses can be organised to believe them. This is true even if the lies are crude and obvious: "Simple forgeries from the viewpoint of scholarship appeared to receive the sanction of history itself when the whole marching reality of the movements stood behind them and pretended to draw from them the necessary inspiration for action." A gigantic lie propagated with sufficient force, guile, and repetition, particularly when motivating political behaviour, comes to be accepted as true.

"The individual is handicapped by coming face-to-face with a conspiracy so monstrous he cannot believe it exists," J. Edgar Hoover (1956, p. 48) said of communism. A favoured *modus operandi* of the intelligence agencies, however, is projective attack, i.e. accusing others of the very tactics and strategies which they themselves adopt. It is the intelligence agencies who sit at the heart of the monstrous lies and conspiracies that have facilitated Western imperialism, causing so much harm to the world (Hughes, 2022b; Valentine, 2017). Samuel Huntington, who had ties to the CIA, admitted in 1981 that the "Cold War" was a cover story used to legitimise U.S. imperialism: "You may have to sell [intervention in another country] in such a way as to create the misimpression that it is the Soviet Union that you are fighting. That is what the United States has been doing ever since the Truman Doctrine" (cited in Hoffmann et al., 1981, p. 14).

Manufacturing Global Consciousness

1968 marked a seminal moment in the history of global class relations. During the Prague Spring of that year, Dubček's call for "socialism with a human face" was made in April, and Soviet tanks finally rolled in to crush the resistance on August 21. On the other side of the "Iron Curtain," "May '68" in Paris saw a month of civil unrest that very nearly spilled over into revolution after President de Gaulle was forced to flee the country.

The lesson of 1968, from a ruling-class perspective, was that it was no longer enough for different political leaderships—including nominal enemies—to come together on an ad hoc basis to put down working-class revolts as and when they arose, as in East Germany in 1953 and Hungary in 1956 (Glaberman & Faber, 2002, pp. 171–2; Wilford, 2008, p. 49). Rather, the transnationalisation of resistance must be met with the coordination of ruling-class interests in permanent counterrevolution at the global level. Hence, organisations such as the World Economic Forum and the Trilateral Commission were founded in the early 1970s to improve coordination of capitalist interests transnationally. The ultimate direction of travel, already mooted after the destruction of Hiroshima and Nagasaki in the name of avoiding nuclear Armageddon, is a world state, controlled by a global ruling class (in which sense the WEF's logo, "improving the state of the world," has always been ambiguous).

In order to engineer a move from a world of nation-states to a world state, it is essential to create what Brzezinski (1970, p. 29) calls "a new global consciousness" (which, he recognises, does not have the support of "the majority of humanity") and a shared set of global problems that demand globally coordinated responses and a sense of common purpose. In this context, it is important to ask critical questions, not only about the alleged moon landings (1969–1972) but also about the environmental movement and the global population control agenda, which all came about soon after (and even during) the events of 1968.

As with the events of "9/11," academia has failed to conduct due diligence into the authenticity of the moon landings, despite a proliferation of evidence outside academia that has caused more and more people to conclude that the moon landings were faked. In rare instances where academics do touch on the subject, their typical point of departure, unsupported by evidence, is that the moon landings were real, and the move then tends to be to explain the supposed psychological "deficiency" in those who think they were not (Hattersley et al., 2022; Lewandowsky et al., 2013; Swami et al., 2013). In the absence of any serious investigation into the subject, however, academia is in no place to comment. Without getting into the details of the debate, it is sufficient for our purposes simply to note that, *if* the moon landings were faked, this would be consistent with an attempt to foster the "new global consciousness" called for by Brzezinski (1970, p. 29). As President Nixon claimed while purportedly on the phone to the moon in July 1969, "For one priceless moment in the whole history of man, all the people on this Earth are truly one." Fakery of the moon landings would also provide proof of concept that it is possible to deceive the entire world about something provided virtually every government and major news outlet runs with the same narrative.

The Club of Rome, founded by Aurelio Peccei, Alexander King, and David Rockefeller in April 1968, launched the global environmental movement. It was particularly influential with its *Limits to Growth* report (Meadows et al., 1972). The Rockefeller Commission Report (Centre for Research on Population & Security, 1972) and the Kissinger Report (National Security Council, 1974) promote global "population control." The misanthropic, antiquated Malthusian logic is always the same: human beings are a scourge on the face of the Earth and must learn to change their selfish ways if they are to live "sustainably" in harmony with their environment. Put differently, human beings must modify their behaviour in accordance with the centralisation of power at the global level, and wealth must never be equitably redistributed.

Would the transnational deep state (Hughes, 2022b) really have the audacity/depravity to attempt to deceive the entire world population? We know that the CIA was secretly steering the Congress for Cultural Freedom, the National Student Association, the International Commission of Jurists, the AFL-CIO, and Radio Free Europe. When this all became public knowledge in 1967/1968, it marked "the first occasion in the postwar period when Americans learned *en masse* that they were being systematically deceived by federal officials" (Wilford, 2008, p. 251). CIA director William Casey is reputed to have claimed in 1981: "We'll know our disinformation program is complete when everything the American public believes is false" (McLovincraft, 2020). Ex-CIA agent John Stockwell claimed in the 1980s: "It goes beyond your wildest imagination, the extent to which the CIA has gone to manipulate public opinion" (Lena, 2023).

We also know about the enormous influence of the Rockefeller family. In the nineteenth century, before the family fortune was made, William Avery Rockefeller, Sr. allegedly travelled from town to town selling "a cancer cure consisting of oil and laxative" (snake oil) and is reported to have bragged: "I cheat my boys every chance I get. I want to make 'em sharp" (Wood, 2018, p. 55). He and his great grandson, David Rockefeller, were both, in Wood's estimation, "lying deceivers, con men and hucksters. David only played his part with a lot more money at his disposal." Thus, with respect to Rockefeller influence through foundations, multinational corporations, NGOs, politicians, lobbyists, and the United Nations (not least the "sustainable development" agenda), it is "no mystery why deception and fraud run amok: as the ancient proverb states, 'The fish stinks from the head'" (Wood, 2018, p. 168). By the early 1970s, Rockefeller forces had built up a "repertoire of hoaxes," including the 1973 "oil hoax" (Minnicino, 1974, p. 53; cf. Engdahl, 2004, Chap. 9).

Meanwhile in the 1970s, NATO used deception to suppress leftist opposition in Europe by deploying false flag terrorism against populations and blaming it on "far left" organisations—Operation Gladio being the best-known example (Ganser, 2005). "Phony strikes" and infiltrated movements and trade unions also involved deception, leaving the working class "faced with the situation in which world events are designed for effect"; in such a world, "the criterion for insanity is to say that reality is what it appears to be" (Minnicino, 1974, p. 53).

9/11 and the Big Lie

According to the *9/11 Commission Report* (Kean & Hamilton, 2004), "Al Qaeda" attacked the United States on September 11, 2001. It only took a few months for Griffin (2005) to dismantle that report on the basis of its many "omissions and distortions." Other investigations have shown the official "9/11" narrative to be unsupportable on just about every level (Meyssan, 2002; Griffin & Scott, 2006; Zarembka, 2008; Wood, 2011; Gourley, 2012; Davidsson, 2013, 2020; Griffin & Woodworth, 2018). The 9/11 attacks and the ensuing "War on Terror" fit the classic pattern of deep state operations, including Big Lies, false flag attacks and a globalised Strategy of Tension (Hughes, 2022b).

Governments, international organisations, think tanks, the media, and academia have shamefully spent over two decades endorsing the official narrative of "9/11," on which all the horrors of the "War on Terror," now coming home to Western populations (see Chap. 8), are premised (Hughes, 2020, pp. 55–56). Notwithstanding a few honourable exceptions, the role of academia in refusing to scrutinise the events of 9/11 and challenge the obvious lies on which the official narrative is based—even when presented with evidence in peer-reviewed form in a mainstream journal (Hughes, 2020, cf. Hughes, 2021)—is chilling.

Outside academia, more astute commentators quickly realised what was happening: "The brainwashing methods are relatively simple and classic. First, use the terror itself to put people into a state of shock, making them more susceptible to suggestion. Then resort to the 'Big Lie' technique to repeatedly hammer home your psywar message" (Digital Citizen, 2003). Tony Blair's (2002) claim that Iraq was prepared to deploy WMD "within 45 minutes of an order to use them" was another Big Lie. Shayler (2022, p. 10) notes the similarities between "9/11" and the "Covid-19 pandemic": "In both cases, the official accounts are not just slightly wrong. They are the exact opposite of the truth: In both cases, the evidence simply never existed to support the official line." Meanwhile, evidence exposing the Big Lie was ignored or suppressed, "meaning millions of people have unnecessarily died or suffered other severe forms of harm, injury or loss."

The "Pandemic"

The "Covid-19 Pandemic" as a Big Lie

Under "Covid-19," Agamben observes, humanity is once again "entering a phase of its history where truth is being reduced to a moment within the march of falsity" (2021, p. 48). According to Knightly (2021), in keeping with the post-1968 context, "Covid has shown us [that] supposedly enemy nations suddenly come to an accord and demonstrate almost total unity of purpose to spread one big lie." "Hitler's notion of the 'grossly impudent lie,'" remark Broudy and Hoop (2021, p. 379), "is especially prescient today" given the power of organisations such as the Bill and Melinda Gates Foundation to shape global health narratives through direct influence on international organisations such as the WHO and the UN, the media, and the policies of many governments.

Would it be possible to fake a global pandemic given such a configuration of powerful actors? Indeed, it would, as the fake "swine flu pandemic" of 2009 illustrates (Fumento, 2010; cf. Keil, 2010; Wodarg et al., 2009). All that is needed is to fudge the meaning of the term "pandemic" (see Chap. 4) and to run a cynical PR campaign transnationally, such as the one orchestrated by Marc van Ranst (see EvidenceNotFear, 2020).

2009 served as a dry run for 2020, when again a "pandemic" was declared which, upon closer examination, turns out to be nothing of the kind (Davis, 2021). The "Covid-19 pandemic" was, in the view of Kyrie and Broudy (2022a), conjured out of "mass hysteria, malpractice, censorship and juggled data." In the view of distinguished pathologist Roger Hodkinson in his testimony to Alberta state officials in November 2020, the "Covid-19 pandemic" represents "the greatest hoax ever perpetrated on an unsuspecting public" (cited in Children's Health Defence, 2020).

There is no credible epidemiological sense in which "Covid-19" can be said to have been a viral "pandemic." In the United States, for example, New York City and certain North-East coastal states witnessed a large spike in mortality between March and June, 2020, yet 34 of 48 continental U.S. states did not see any such spike, a feature that is "impossible for a virulent and contagious respiratory disease virus acting in a society free from local aggression or local environmental disaster" (Rancourt et al., 2021, p. 138, Fig. 15). Meanwhile, all-cause mortality in Canada in 2020 remained normal in relation to the previous decade, begging the question of how an allegedly virulent and contagious pathogen failed to cross the world's longest international land border between two major trading partners (Rancourt et al., 2021, pp. 125, 128–9). Such jurisdictional heterogeneity runs "contrary to pandemic behaviour, and contrary to any (1945–2021) season of viral respiratory disease burden in the Northern hemisphere" (Rancourt et al., 2021, p. 62).

The spread of the "virus" across EU member states in Q2 and Q3 of 2020 was inconsistent with a viral pandemic. Engelbrecht and Köhnlein (2020), for example, observe that neighbouring European countries registered very different "Covid-19" excess mortality rates, e.g. no excess mortality in Germany and Portugal, but noticeable excess mortality in Belgium and Spain. Those differences were irrespective of the severity of "lockdown" measures, with most of the excess deaths occurring within a 2–3 week period around early April. Similarly, England has displayed excess mortality since March 2020, according to EuroMOMO data, whereas Scotland, Wales, and Northern Ireland have not (Kendrick, 2022).

Matters (2020), writing in September 2020, notes that "Covid-19" death rates are negligible for around three quarters of the world's countries, yet accrue predominantly in the USA, UK, and EU member states. New York City, for instance, had recorded 229,000 "Covid-19" deaths, compared to just 470 such deaths in Singapore. Why was the "virus" so much more lethal in the West—home to some of the world's best healthcare systems—than in other regions of the world?

Similar was true of "case" rates. Hover the cursor over the dark blue part of the scale bar along the bottom of the map for "cumulative confirmed Covid-19 cases per million people" (WHO, n.d.-c). Dark blue refers to 300,000 + such cases, the highest category. Highlighted on the map is essentially "the West," i.e. the United States, nearly all of Western Europe, Australia, and New Zealand, plus key allies including Israel and South Korea, as well as US-controlled Puerto Rico and French Guiana. Even though the USA, Europe, and Australia/New Zealand are oceans apart (and remember that air travel was heavily restricted), the "virus" was allegedly most concentrated in those regions, giving it a peculiarly Western-centric character, while the entire continent of Africa, where "vaccines" were least available, was virtually ignored.

It is hard to escape the impression that the "pandemic" was a social construct manufactured predominantly in the West, based on high death rates in particular cities coupled with the kinds of statistical manipulation and military-grade propaganda discussed in Chap. 4. This is consistent with a transnational deep state operation (Hughes, 2022b) aimed at replacing Western liberal democracy with technocracy. In that respect, it is telling that Secretary of State and former CIA Director, Mike Pompeo, at the start of the "pandemic," referred to being in a "live exercise" (a military term)—and that President Trump, standing right behind him, muttered "you should have let us know" ("Mike Pompeo we're in a live exercise here," 2020). This evidences the redundancy of the visible government when it comes to what Scott (2017, Chap. 9) calls "deep events," i.e. events which profoundly transform the trajectory of politics and society, yet whose provenance is deliberately concealed.

Covid Theatre: Performing the "Pandemic"

If the "pandemic" were real in any meaningful sense—e.g. "Covid-19" having a high infection fatality rate, as opposed to the 0.05% median IFR for the under-70s identified by Ioannidis (2021), dropping to 0.03% for the under-60s, 0.011% for the 30–39 age range, 0.002% for 20–29, and 0.0003% for 0–19 (Pezullo et al., 2023)—why was the propaganda so fierce? "In a genuine pandemic," Dymond (2020) observes, "this constant mental battering would be superfluous," for no one would need to be persuaded of the danger of a high fatality disease outbreak. As with the 2009 "swine flu pandemic" (EvidenceNotFear, 2020; Fumento, 2010), the "Covid-19 pandemic" was a heavily *mediated* event.

Because human cognition is, to a significant extent, unconsciously emotion-driven (we tend to feel rather than reason our way to opinions), "acting as if we are infectious agents by wearing masks fosters greater belief in the official narrative" (Kyrie & Broudy, 2022b). The British public was, accordingly, encouraged through government/NHS propaganda to "Act like you've got it." Outwardly healthy people *performed* the "pandemic" through "social distancing," "self-isolation," face masks, etc., making it a social, if not epidemiological, reality. Without the performance—"Covid theatre" in the words of Florida Governor Ron DeSantis (see Harsanyi, 2022)—there would have been no visible evidence that anything was wrong. The PCR tests also served as "crucial 'theatre props' in convincing [the public] that the *COVID-19 Story* was a real pandemic" (Kingston, 2022).

Much like ducking and covering in the context of nuclear war, or using duct tape to protect against biological, chemical, or radiological terrorism (Meserve, 2003), the idea that wearing a piece of cloth on one's face, or putting up plexiglass screens, or standing on stickers six feet apart could offer any meaningful protection to anyone against the "new Spanish flu" is preposterous. The "measures" were not about keeping people safe (even the UKHSA [2023, p. 5] retrospectively concedes "There is a lack of strong evidence on the effectiveness of NPIs to reduce COVID-19 transmission"). Rather, they were designed to convince the public of a new existential threat and to condition obedience and conformity (see Volume 2 of this book). Like the addict who finds endless rationalisations for their addictive behaviour, most people find that behaviour change compels a change in cognition rather than vice-versa (Festinger, 1957, 6). Enactment of the "measures" by the public, accordingly, makes the "pandemic" seem real to those taking part in the performance, no matter how absurd it is.

Politicians and their advisers played starring roles in the Covid theatre. The daily performances of government "scientists" at Downing Street press briefings, for example, intensified the drama of the "pandemic." Suspicions have been raised that Boris Johnson was merely playing a part when claiming that doctors were preparing to announce his death after he was allegedly hospitalised by "Covid-19" (McCrae, 2023). One month later Johnson was hosting lockdown-breaking parties at 10 Downing Street (Kottasová et al,. 2022), at which no one "followed the rules."

Politicians and royalty put masks on just before going on stage, sometimes removing the mask almost straight away, having modelled to the public the desired form of behaviour. At the G7 summit in June 2021, world leaders bumped elbows, wore masks, and "socially distanced"—but only for the cameras (Myers, 2021). At the COP 26 summit in Glasgow in November 2021, arriving leaders put on a mask after getting out of their car (in the fresh air), walked along the red carpet past a mask-wearing ceremonial guard, then removed the mask once inside the venue—all scientifically absurd, yet necessary for maintaining the charade of the "pandemic."

The "Pandemic" as Technocratic Smokescreen

Decoying, camouflage, strategic misdirection, magic tricks, etc., have historically been key to military and intelligence operations (Melton & Wallace, 2009, pp. 9–29; Kyrie & Broudy, 2022a). The "Covid-19 pandemic," correspondingly, acts as a smokescreen to deflect attention from far-reaching technocratic agendas being advanced across every area of life. As van der Pijl (2022, p. 31) recognises, those agendas have nothing to with health, and "everything to do with preserving the power of [a] transnational ruling class threatened by a restless population demanding rectification of the absurd inequalities produced by [twenty-first century capitalism]." Fundamentally, we are in a global class war (Hughes et al., 2023, § V), in which a proportionately tiny transnational ruling class is attempting to use its vast resources to subjugate the rest of humanity through technocratic control mechanisms such as central bank digital currency, social credit scoring (ESG scores for corporations), total surveillance, and the Internet of Bodies/Internet of Nano-Things (Kyrie & Broudy, 2022c, p. 363).

Even though war is being waged against the population, the ruling class decoys by claiming that we must "declare war on this virus" (United Nations, 2020). Bill Gates (2020) claims: "This is like a world war, except in this case, we're all on the same side." In reality, the battlelines have been drawn along global class lines, and the ruling class has taken advantage of the element of surprise to attack first. Just as the "War on Drugs" was cover for CIA drug-trafficking operations (Scott & Marshall, 1991), and just as the "War on Terror" served to spread terror and terrorism (Chomsky, 2003, p. 211), so the "war on the virus" provides cover for profoundly harmful measures taken in the name of public health.

Further evidence that the "pandemic" provides cover for authoritarian political agendas is provided by Schwab and Malleret (2020, p. 117) in their blueprint for the "Great Reset." Most people, they claim, fearing for their lives in a "pandemic," will be willing to allow state power to override individual rights, but then, "when the crisis is over, some may realize that their country has suddenly been transformed into a place where they no longer wish to live." By the time the lie is exposed, it is too late, "for the grossly impudent lie always leaves traces behind it, even after it has been nailed down, a fact which is known to all expert liars in this world and to all who conspire together in the art of lying" (Hitler, 1939, p. 183). Schwab seems familiar with this principle: there will be no going back to how things were, because "the cut which we have now is much too strong in order not to leave traces" (cited in Roscoe, 2022). Or consider Gates' (2021) view on how the "pandemic" has advanced technocracy: "Even after this pandemic ends, it's clear that much of the digitization it brought on is here to stay."

It is futile to couch resistance to technocratic tyranny in the pseudo-medical terminology intended to distract and deceive the masses. As

Hopkins (2021c) puts it, "This isn't an academic argument over the existence, severity, or the response to a virus. *This is a fight to determine the future of our societies.*" Squabbling over whether or not viruses exist, Fitts notes, "has zero effect on stopping the control grid. At this time in our history, if we don't stop the control grid, we're going to be slaves" (Fitts & Betts, 2022).

No amount of reason, common sense, and scientific pleading makes any difference to the pursuit of technocratic agendas: "Those in charge have long since signalled that they have no intention of returning to a liberal democracy founded on the recognition of inalienable individual rights and freedoms" (Ruechel, 2021). Therefore, trying to confront them with data is futile. Blaylock (2022) asks: "[Have] scientific evidence, carefully done studies, clinical experience and medical logic had any effect on stopping these ineffective and dangerous vaccines?" His answer: "Absolutely not! The draconian efforts to vaccinate everyone on the planet continues (except the elite [...])." Petitioning the government to change course or calling for an inquiry is futile, because "appealing to reason (e.g., we need our freedoms back because X, Y, Z) and logic (e.g., the facts show otherwise) will have no effect on the totalitarians pushing the COVID-19 menticide" (Scott, 2021b).

"Pandemic Preparedness"

So-called "pandemic preparedness" exercises have been carried out most years since 2005 and can be traced at least as far back as Operation Dark Winter in 2001 (O'Toole et al., 2002). Names such as Tara O' Toole, Tom Inglesby, and Robert Kadlec attach themselves repeatedly to such exercises, as does Johns Hopkins University. In recent years, such exercises have become more frequent, including Clade-X (2018), Crimson Contagion (2019), Event 201 (2019), SPARS (Brunson et al., 2020), and Catastrophic Contagion (2022). In England, 11 such exercises were carried out between 2015 and 2019 (Dyer, 2021).

How serious is the "pandemic" threat that demands all this "preparedness"? According to Rancourt et al. (2021, p. 137), "No [WHO-]declared pandemic (1957–58, 1968, 2009) has ever caused a detectable increase in yearly all-cause mortality in the USA, since 1900, except 1918, which has been incorrectly assigned as an influenza pandemic." Most deaths attributed to the "Spanish flu" were in fact the result of secondary bacterial pneumonia and would have been preventable had antibiotics been invented (National Institutes of Health, 2008). The 1957–58 and 1968 outbreaks killed ca. 1 million people each (mostly older adults), while "swine flu" killed between 123,000 and 203,000 people (WHO, 2019a, p. 7). To put these figures in context, 290,000 to 650,000 people die of seasonal influenza every year, and 1.6 million people die of tuberculosis (at a far younger average age), meaning that WHO-declared "pandemics" have "killed far fewer people and at an older age than most other major infectious diseases" (Bell, 2022). "Pandemic preparedness" therefore makes little sense from a global health perspective.

Common to "pandemic preparedness" simulations is a failure to consider how to preserve constitutional rights during a pandemic and the promotion instead of a military-style response:

> The simulations war-gamed how to use police powers to detain and quarantine citizens, how to impose martial law, how to control messaging by deploying propaganda, how to employ censorship to silence dissent, and how to mandate masks, lockdowns, and coercive vaccinations and conduct track-and-trace surveillance among potentially reluctant populations. (Kennedy Jr., 2021, p. 382)

"Pandemic preparedness" is a pretext for moving society in the direction of martial law. It is code for what used to be called "military readiness" (Watt, 2023), cloaked in the garb of public health, because the public is the target.

Despite the bogusness of "pandemic preparedness," the transnational ruling class now seeks to amend the 2005 International Health Regulations and introduce a WHO Pandemic Treaty that would legally cede national sovereignty to the WHO Director-General when it comes to "pandemic response." This opens the door to a global health dictatorship able to decree compulsory "lockdowns," "vaccinations," and the centralisation of health data surveillance tied to a global digital passport and ID system (Kheriaty, 2022). Countries will be financially incentivised to report disease outbreaks, but will lose out on international aid and face trade embargoes and sanctions if they do not toe the WHO line, making future PHEIC declarations more likely, not less, especially if such a declaration can be based on the precautionary principle rather than an actual crisis (Knightly, 2022).

This entire scam, which ultimately seeks to institute a world state via the intermediary mechanism of medical martial law, is premised on the need to prepare for what Gates has repeatedly referred to as "the next pandemic," involving "a different pathogen" and possible bioterrorism (Gates, 2020b, 2021; Gates & Gates, 2021; Gilchrist, 2022). GAVI ran a series of articles on its website between March and May 2021 on candidates for the next pandemic. Warren Buffett claimed in July 2021: "There will be another pandemic" ("Billionaire Warren Buffett predicts new pandemic," 2021). According to Fauci in April 2023, "if we really want to prevent the next pandemic – and there will be one – there will absolutely be an outbreak of another pandemic [...]" (cited in Fleetwood, 2023).

International organisations followed suit. On December 29, 2020, the head of the WHO emergencies programme, Mark Ryan, warned: "This [pandemic] is not necessarily the big one" (cited in Steinbuch, 2020). On March 1, 2021, EU Commission president Ursula von der Leyen warned that the EU must prepare for an "era of pandemics" (cited in Fleming, 2021). On April 20, 2021, the UK Government (2021) announced a "new global partnership launched to fight future pandemics" On May 24, 2021, the WHO Director-General noted the "evolutionary certainty that there will be another virus with the potential to be more transmittable and more deadly than this one" (International Schiller Institute, 2021).

These attempts to normalise the dubious "pandemic" concept, as though "pandemics" could occur every few years, getting progressively more severe, bear no relation to scientific reality. In truth, since the advent of antibiotics, there has never been a "pandemic" that poses significantly more risk to human health than other diseases. "Covid-19," with an average death age of over 80 in England and Wales (ONS, 2021), was anything but the existential threat the media made it out to be (see Chap. 4). The idea that we need to prepare for an "era of pandemics," given the difficulty of identifying *any* convincing "pandemic" in the last century, is risible.

The "Virus"

Does SARS-CoV-2 Exist?

The WHO (2020) announced that a novel coronavirus was "isolated on 7 January, 2020." Scientific research teams from around the world in 2020 claimed to have "isolated" the virus (Harcourt et al., 2020; Kim et al.,

2020; Matsuyama et al., 2020; Park et al., 2020; Zhou et al., 2020; Zhu et al., 2020).

However, "isolation" in Virology does not mean what the layman might expect, i.e. to separate an object from everything that is not that object. Rather, in the case of "SARS-CoV-2," "isolation" begins as follows:

> Oropharyngeal samples are diluted with viral transfer medium containing nasopharyngeal swabs and antibiotics (Nystadin, penicillin-streptomycin 1:1 dilution) at 1:4 ratio and incubated for 1 hour at 4°C, before being inoculated onto Vero cells. Inoculated Vero cells were cultured at 37°C, 5% CO2 in 1× Dulbecco's modified Eagle's medium (DMEM) supplemented with 2% fetal bovine serum and penicillin-streptomycin. (Kim et al., 2020)

In other words, to "isolate" "SARS-CoV-2," it is first necessary to ***add*** Nystatin and penicillin–streptomycin, then to ***add*** the resultant mixture to African green monkey kidney epithelial cells, which have themselves been cultured in DMEM, foetal bovine serum, and penicillin–streptomycin. This metaphorical "brew" of ingredients is then left to "simmer" (incubate). Is this science, or is it witchcraft?

The different genetic elements are given time to mix with one another, in ways that may be unanticipated or unknown—Mikovits, for instance, alleges that the U.S. blood supply became contaminated with XMRV through such processes (Mikovits & Heckenlively, 2020). Finally, "virus replication and isolation are confirmed through cytopathic effects, gene detection, and electron microscopy" (Kim et al., 2020). Each of these three methods is problematic, however, for the following reasons.

Cytopathic Effects

In the case of "SARS-CoV-2," a CDC study shows cytopathic effects in monkey kidney cells (Harcourt et al., 2020) following the addition of amphotericin B, which is known to be toxic to kidneys (Sabra & Branch, 1990). Is "SARS-CoV-2" causing the kidney cells to degenerate, or is amphotericin B? Or are any of the other elements of the Dulbecco minimal essential medium, including 10% foetal bovine serum, penicillin–streptomycin, and antibiotics/antimycotics (Harcourt et al., 2020)? Or, is a combination of these various ingredients causing the observed cytopathic effects? What controlled studies have been done to find out?

In the CDC study, no cytopathic effect was observed "in any of the cell lines except in Vero [monkey] cells"; moreover, "HUH7.0 [human liver cells] and 293 T [human embryonic kidney] cells showed only modest viral replication, and A549 [human lung cancer] cells were incompatible with SARS-CoV-2 infection" (Harcourt et al., 2020). Where, then, is the evidence of life-threatening disease in humans caused by "SARS-CoV-2" (Menage, 2020)?

Similar findings appear elsewhere. For example, Matsuyama et al. (2020) describe "the amount of SARS-CoV-2 RNAs in the culture supernatants of [...] A549 cells" as "low" and "measurably higher when VeroE6 cells were used." Zhou et al. (2020) claim "to have "successfully isolated the virus [...] from both Vero E6 and Huh7 [human liver] cells [...] Clear cytopathogenic effects were observed in cells after incubation for three days (Extended Data Fig. 6a, b)." However, only Vero E6 cells, and not human cells, feature in those figures.

Gene Detection

On January 10, 2020, the first "coronavirus genome from a case of a respiratory disease from the Wuhan outbreak" was published (Wuhan-Hu-1, GenBank accession number MN908947), and on January 12, five more sequences were added to the GISAID (Global Initiative on Sharing All Influenza Data) database (Corman et al., 2020b). Incredibly, on January 13—*one day* after those sequences being published—Corman et al. (2020a) published a "protocol and preliminary review" for "Diagnostic detection of Wuhan coronavirus 2019 by real-time RT-PCR." In only 24 hours, apparently, the authors managed to analyse the newly available sequences alongside 729 SARS-CoV sequences, conduct multiple tests of their own, design a new PCR protocol involving the first primers and probes targeting the virus, write up, and publish their findings! This 24-hour window is as implausible as the one on January 21–22 involving double-blind peer-review of the flawed *Eurosurveillance* paper based on this research (Corman et al., 2020b; cf. Borger et al., 2020). Nevertheless, the resultant "Drosten protocol" was accepted by the WHO without question.

Corman et al. (2020b) admit that their study proceeded "without having virus material available." In other words, the WHO-adopted Drosten PCR protocol was based on a computer sequence from a gene bank, not an actual viral isolate. As Kevin Corbett puts it, "They had a code, but no body for the code. No viral morphology [...] This is basically a computer virus" (cited in Farber, 2020). It is unclear whether anything in nature corresponds to that which is designated "SARS-CoV-2": no laboratory or institution provides certified pure (i.e. unadulterated with other sources of genetic material) samples of "SARS-CoV-2," as at least 211 FOIA requests made in 35 countries had confirmed by August 2022 (Massey, 2022). Public Health England's (2021c) boilerplate reply refers to the suspect *Eurosurveillance* paper above in circular fashion. In Massey's (2022) view, without "SARS-CoV-2" having been isolated/purified in any meaningful fashion, and in the absence of controlled experiments, there is no scientific proof that the virus—on which the entire "Covid-19" operation was premised—exists.

Fragments of a hoof, a tail hair, and a horn are not enough to deduce the existence of a unicorn, Cowan (2020) teases, yet the principle of using computerised genome sequencing to create a viral genome out of fragments of genetic material is very similar. As of April 1, 2022, Bailey (2022) notes, 9.6 million "SARS-CoV-2 genomes" had been uploaded to GISAID, yet "not one of these in silico-assembled genomic sequences has ever been shown to exist in nature, let alone come from inside a disease-causing particle."

Electron Microscopy

Everyone is familiar with the computer-generated images of the "SARS-CoV-2" virion. When Bill Gates appears in videos holding a model of that virion, the intention is to underscore the physical existence, appearance, and threat of the virus. Scientists staring down an electron microscope at a "SARS-CoV-2" virion should, presumably, see something similar, and electron microscopy images are indeed presented by Zhou et al., (2020, Fig. 6 g), Zhu et al., (2020, Fig. 3), and Park et al., (2020, Figs. 1C and 1D).

However, all is not as straightforward as it seems. In the 1970s, normal cellular components, such as phagocytic vacuoles, microvesicular bodies, and extracellular breakdown products, were often mistaken for viral particles in ultrastructural images (Cassol et al., 2020). Following the SARS outbreak of 2003, the CDC drew specific attention to the risk of mistaking *coronavirus* particles for normal cellular components, including "coated vesicles, multivesicular bodies, perichromatin granules, glycocalyceal bodies, and cellular projections" (Goldsmith et al., 2004, p. 325).

In the case of "SARS-CoV-2," scientists sounded "a note of caution for inferring viral tissue infection by morphology alone using electron microscopy images from tissues obtained from biopsies or autopsy material in patients with COVID-19" (Cassol et al., 2020). For example, an inclusion within a podocyte in a case of thrombotic microangiopathy in a native kidney biopsy specimen falls within the diameter range for "SARS-CoV-2" (60–140 nm) and displays "an electron-dense rim likely representing endocytic coated vesicles," resembling a viral corona (Cassol et al., 2020, Fig. 1A). Yet, it is not a viral particle.

No sharp distinction can be drawn between viruses and extracellular vesicles (EVs): "it is currently virtually impossible to specifically separate and identify EVs that carry viral proteins, host proteins, and viral genomic elements from enveloped viral particles that carry the same molecules" (Nolte-'t Hoen et al., 2016). Because nearly all cells produce EVs, it is likely that "every viral preparation is in fact a mixture of virions and EVs" (Nolte-'t Hoen et al., 2016). Different particle types exist along a spectrum, including "virus-like particles" which resemble an infectious virus particle yet contain no viral RNA (Nolte-'t Hoen et al., 2016, Fig. 1). This means that alleged images of "SARS-CoV-2" might not be showing an infectious virus particle after all.

Implications

The scientific evidence in support of the existence of "SARS-CoV-2" is not as strong as one might reasonably expect. It rests on cytopathic tests where the cause of cell degeneration is unproven, gene sequencing where it is unclear that the assembled genome corresponds to anything in nature, and electron microscope images that do not necessarily show infectious virus particles. The onus, therefore, is on virologists to *prove*, or at least demonstrate beyond reasonable doubt, the existence of "SARS-CoV-2" in ways that do not succumb to these methodological deficiencies, ideally via controlled studies. Given that world-transforming measures were enacted on the basis of "SARS-CoV-2" causing "Covid-19," providing such proof is scientifically and morally imperative.

All other evidence of the existence of "SARS-CoV-2" lies in the secondary realm of epidemiology and appeals to symptoms/sickness, diagnostic testing for the presence of the alleged virus, and antibodies supposedly developed in response to the "virus." Yet, there is no proof of what caused the symptoms/sickness, the testing is known to be bunk (see Chap. 4), and it is unclear how reliably antibodies can be tied back to "SARS-CoV-2" specifically, given that controlled experiments have not been done (Cowan, 2023).

In the absence of any compelling scientific evidence that "SARS-CoV-2" exists, the door is opened to possibly the biggest lie of all—namely, the existence of "SARS-CoV-2" itself. Seen through the lens of psychological operations, rather than virology/epidemiology, there are reasons to suspect foul play. Paraphrasing Yeadon (2023):

- The effects of a released bioweapon cannot be predicted with confidence, yet megalomaniac social engineers seek total control in everything they do.
- Molecular biology relies on computer sequencing, complex algorithms, and assumptions, all of which can be manipulated, making it easy to cheat.
- If "SARS-CoV-2" were real and as deadly as claimed, why the need to fudge case and mortality data (see Chap. 4)?
- The "lab leak" narrative, pushed by state and corporate media in 2022/23 following vigorous denial in 2020/21, begs the question: did the "virus" originate in nature, or was it engineered in a lab? Either way, the media wants us to think that it is real, yet the media has lied about everything when it comes to "Covid-19."

An important caveat should be added: *even if* "SARS-CoV-2" does exist, then its virulence in no way justifies the massively disproportionate measures that were taken to counter it.

Rebranding the Flu?

One of the most remarkable events of 2020/21 was the worldwide disappearance of influenza from the moment that "Covid-19" entered the scene (WHO, 2021; Public Health England, 2021a, Fig. 7, 2021b, Fig. 13). What explains this?

The most facile explanation is that non-pharmaceutical interventions intended to stop the spread of "Covid-19" also halted the spread of influenza. The following February 2021 headline from the *Independent* is representative: "Not a single case of flu detected by Public Health England this year as Covid restrictions suppress virus" (Lovett, 2021).

If such measures were so effective that they eliminated influenza, they would surely also have suppressed "Covid-19," but instead the latter was presented as an ever-present menace.

Hope-Simpson (1992, p. 119) identifies a "vanishing trick" performed by type A influenza virus in 1946–7, when a new strain of influenza, named "A prime" (written A'), replaced the original strain first discovered in 1932–33 across the world. Any analogy between 2020–21 and 1946–47, however, is forlorn. Hope-Simpson (1992) addresses new strains within the influenza virus, not the displacement of influenza itself by an alternative virus.

Studies of viral interference (the ability of one virus to reduce the effects of another) are in their infancy and interactions between viruses are "currently not well understood" (Sunde, 2021). Allowing Sunde the benefit of the doubt that viral interference nevertheless offers a plausible explanation for the disappearance of influenza in 2020/21, the implication is that "SARS-CoV-2" was already everywhere in March/April of 2020 for influenza to have vanished. If so, all efforts to "stop the spread" of "SARS-CoV-2," including "lockdowns," mask wearing, social distancing, hand sanitising, etc., were pointless.

Every explanation of influenza's alleged disappearance contradicts the "Covid-19" narrative in one way or another. Is the disappearance of the flu—something which has never happened before—another Big Lie? When the northern hemisphere entered the traditional flu season in 2020, both the U.S. CDC and Public Health England decided, almost simultaneously, to merge influenza and "Covid-19" death reporting. The CDC (2020) announced on October 6, 2020, that "Due to the ongoing COVID-19 pandemic, the system will suspend data collection for the 2020–21 influenza season," adding that "COVID-19 coded deaths were added to P&I to create the PIC (pneumonia, influenza, and/or COVID-19) classification." Public Health England (2020) announced that "as of 8 October 2020, the information in this report will be published in a combined Weekly flu and COVID-19 Surveillance Report on GOV.UK." This seemingly coordinated move, at exactly the time when flu cases normally start to surge, is suspicious, because it made it easy, in theory, to recategorise influenza deaths as "Covid-19" deaths.

Perhaps influenza deaths were already being miscategorised as "Covid-19" deaths. One possibility is that "Mandatory Covid-19 tests, run at high cycle thresholds and suffering from cross-reactivity with other pathogens […] resulted in false positives for Covid-19, when in fact the pathogen causing symptoms may have been flu" (Neil et al., 2023). This would explain, for instance, how "Covid-19" *appeared* to form reliable epidemiological data from country to country, something which otherwise would be difficult, though not impossible, to fake if there were no "SARS-CoV-2." Those testing positive for "SARS-CoV-2" were told to "self-isolate" for up to 14 days, well beyond the four days needed for an accurate flu test, so even if a flu test were later taken, it would be too late (Neil et al., 2023). Diagnosing influenza out of season also meets with "clinical and bureaucratic barriers" that "Covid-19" diagnosis does not, owing to "powerful incentives directed by a centralised bureaucracy."

Prior to "Covid-19," there were "290,000–650,000 influenza-related respiratory deaths" each year (WHO, 2019b). If influenza deaths were redesignated as "Covid-19" deaths in 2020/21, that would automatically add hundreds of thousands of deaths to the worldwide "Covid-19" annual death toll (which does not reset at the start of each year as for any other disease, but is rather kept cumulatively on the WHO Covid-19 dashboard to exaggerate the severity of the disease in the minds of the public). "Globally, the flu almost completely disappeared throughout 2020 and 2021," notes Knightly (2023), but "meanwhile, a new disease called 'Covid,' which has [near] identical symptoms and a similar mortality rate to influenza, was apparently affecting all the people normally affected by the flu." This seems quite the coincidence.

The CDC (2021) acknowledges that it is hard to tell the difference between "Covid-19" and influenza "based on symptoms alone"; the only clear difference in symptoms is that "Covid-19" may result in loss of taste or smell (but so can hay fever). Additional complications associated with the two diseases are again almost identical. The claimed rate of asymptomatic carriage is 77% for influenza (Hayward et al., 2014) and 78% for "Covid-19" (Schraer, 2020)—almost identical.

Whitty chose April Fool's Day in 2021 (with connotations of mockery) to announce that "Britain will treat Covid 'like the Flu' in future" (Boyd, 2021). Gates in May 2022 described "Covid-19" as "kind of like the flu although a bit different," disingenuously claiming that that it was not known in spring 2020 that "Covid-19" had a low fatality rate and killed mostly the elderly ("Bill Gates says COVID is 'kind of like the flu,'" 2022). Yet, this is precisely what was known, as when, for instance, Ioannidis (2020b) wrote: "Among people < 70 years old, infection fatality rates ranged from 0.00% to 0.26% with median of 0.05%." In March 2020, Ioannidis (2020a) wrote: "If we had not known about a new virus out there, and had not checked individuals with PCR tests, the number of total deaths due to "influenza-like illness" would not seem unusual this year." Had the public been reassured that "Covid-19" was similar to influenza, however, the fear campaign would have fallen flat and the resultant "measures" would been rejected outright (Chossudovsky, 2021).

"Whatever Covid actually is," Yeadon (2023) writes, "I don't believe that what was called influenza disappeared conveniently in early 2020. It's another lie. It's what they do. It's all they do." Based on the above evidence, it seems hard to disagree with that conclusion.

The "Vaccines"

"Covid-19 Vaccines" as Military (not Pharmaceutical) Products

In the United States, the "Covid-19" injectables are, legally speaking, military products that evade normal commercial and clinical rules and procedures under 10 U.S. Code § 4021 (Latypova, 2022a, 2022b; cf. Watt, 2023). Under the 2005 Public Readiness and Emergency Preparedness (PREP) Act, undisclosed military countermeasures can be deployed at the sole discretion of the Health and Human Services (HHS) Secretary in the event of a public health emergency (for which declaration no criteria exist). This is what happened in March 2020, when Emergency Use Authorization for medical countermeasures was granted under 21 USC 360bbb-3(k), such that those countermeasures "shall not be considered to constitute a clinical investigation." The Food and Drug Administration (2020, p. 7, n.6) was aware of that law, citing it in a document dated October 22, 2020, and thus of the legal status of the "Covid-19 vaccines" as non-medicines. The so-called "clinical trials" for the "vaccines" continued nevertheless, with the regulators providing "theatre" or "performance art" to deceive the public into believing that pharmaceutical products were being developed (Latypova, 2022a, 2022b).

Operation Warp Speed (OWS), the U.S. project to develop, produce, and distribute 300 million doses of a "coronavirus vaccine" by January 2021, was compared to the Manhattan Project by President Trump when he unveiled it on May 16, 2020 (Smith, 2020), a clear allusion to top-secret military technology. "Warp speed" is a science fiction concept associated with Star Trek, and the possibility that the "Covid-19 vaccines" contain black technology is discussed below.

OWS was led, not by scientists and healthcare specialists, but by the military. An organisational chart shows that 61 of the 90 leadership positions in OWS were occupied by DoD officials, including four generals (Florko, 2020). The military's role was not merely to assist with logistics; rather, the DoD was "in full control" of the "vaccination" programme from its inception, including "development, manufacturing, clinical trials, quality assurance, distribution and administration" (Altman et al., 2023). The White House Coronavirus Response Coordinator was Deborah Birx, whose colourful scarves created a civilian appearance while media reports touted her as the next head of the HHS, a civilian agency (Cancryn et al., 2020); Birx, however, holds the rank of Colonel. The "Covid-19 vaccine" rollout in the United States, as in Europe, was a camouflaged military operation from start to finish (Ponton, 2023a, 2023b).

Under Operation Warp Speed, contracts were clandestinely awarded to "vaccine" companies via Advanced Technology International, which has close ties to the CIA (Webb, 2020). The use of a non-governmental intermediary meant that regulatory oversight and transparency conferred by regular federal contracting mechanisms could be bypassed. HHS, for example, which was supposed to be overseeing OWS, claimed to have "no records" of a $1.6 billion contract awarded to Novavax (Lupkin, 2020). This is how deep state operations work, with public bodies left clueless about what is really going on.

How was it possible to manufacture billions of doses within such a short time frame? In Latypova's (2022a, 45:35) assessment, the pharmaceutical companies lacked the required capacity to achieve this, and it was only possible because of the "established defence contracting infrastructure" put in place by BARDA years earlier. A slide on "OWS/BARDA Vaccine Manufacturing" from a presentation by the HHS Administration for Strategic Preparedness and Response divides the manufacturing "portfolio" into two: "vaccines" on the left and "vaccine supporting efforts" on the right (Latypova, 2022a, 44:50). Under "vaccines" fall the various manufacturers, while on the right are Marathon Medical, Emergent Biosolutions, Smiths Medical, Cytiva, BD, Corning, Grand River, Ology, Retractable Technologel Inc., SiO2, The Texas A&M University System, and Snapdragon. All the "vaccine" manufacturers except for Moderna are marked as "Demo," whereas nearly all of the "vaccine supporting efforts" are marked as "manufacturing" and/or "capacity."

Latypova (2022b) proposes that "Demo" refers to Other Transaction Authority, a method of contracting favoured by the DoD, which allows vaguely defined "prototypes" or "demonstrations" to evade regulatory scrutiny. The real manufacturing/capacity-building, she proposes, has been done elsewhere, with Big Pharma content to make vast profits, with freedom from liability (Health & Human Services Department, 2020), in exchange for maintaining the charade that a "public health" crisis is being met with "pharmaceutical" products.

The "Covid-19 vaccines" in the United States do not meet any normal pharmaceutical distribution rules for flagging safety and quality issues in the supply chain (Latypova, 2022b). Unit doses are not barcoded and traceable, and alleged cold chain storage requirements mean that they are handled through a "black box" DoD distribution system. Most suspiciously, Latypova adds, "Independent testing of the vials for verification of the product conformity to label is prohibited"—unsurprisingly, given what they have been shown to contain (Hughes, 2022c).

I have explained previously why "Covid-19 vaccines" do not qualify as vaccines (Hughes, 2022a, p. 210). Kingston (2023) argues that they are, legally speaking, bioweapons, not pharmaceutical products. They "do not prevent infection or disease, were not conducted under *bona fide* research, and serve no peaceful purpose (meaning they cause harm)," thus meeting the definition of a biological weapon under 18 USC 175. Therefore, to call the "Covid-19 vaccines" "bioweapons" is not hyperbole; rather, "bioweapon" is "the only accurate legal term" to describe them. The plan to "disguise bioweapons intentionally deployed against the public," in Kingston's (2022) view, represents "one of the most evil deceptions in the history of humanity."

In a biopolitical era where control is exercised directly over human bodies (Agamben, 1998), the so-called "vaccines" in principle make ideal bioweapons, because their contents are injected straight into the blood, breaching the body's natural immune defences (skin, the gut, the nasopharyngeal cavity, etc.). If the people are the undeclared enemy in the war for technocracy, then those injections can penetrate behind enemy lines.

Ulterior Motives

What exactly is the purpose of the military injectables masquerading as "Covid-19 vaccines"? Evidently, it is not to safeguard "public health," as evidenced by the record number and variety of reported serious adverse reactions (OpenVAERS, n.d.; MHRA, n.d.; WHO, n.d.-a [search "COVID-19 vaccine"]). UK ONS data shows that the "vaccines" kill more people than they save (Kirsch, 2022a). There is a tight statistical correlation between the number of shots taken and the increased likelihood of death (Oller & Santiago, 2022; Santiago & Oller, 2023; Chudov, 2022a). Governments' failure to halt the "vaccine" rollout long ago in the face of such evidence is sinister, if not treasonous.

A damning 180-page study by Rancourt et al. (2023), based on analysis of all-cause mortality data (ACM) from 17 equatorial and Southern-Hemisphere countries, finds "no association in time between COVID-19 vaccination and any proportionate reduction in ACM" (p. 2), i.e. the "vaccines" do not save lives. On the contrary, nine of the 17 countries showed *no* excess mortality for ca. one year after the WHO "pandemic declaration" on March 11, 2020, yet excess mortality began to appear around the time of the "vaccine" rollout. In Chile and Peru, where the most detailed data is available, booster shots correlated with unprecedented peaks in ACM for the elderly in the summer. The all-ages vaccine-dose fatality rate, i.e. the ratio of inferred vaccine-induced deaths to vaccine doses delivered in a population, comes out as 0.126 (± 0.004)%, for a "virus" with a 0.05% IFR for the under-70s (Ioannidis, 2021), implying ca. 17 million deaths worldwide from the 13.5 billion injections delivered by September 2023—1000 times higher than has been reported in clinical trials, adverse effect monitoring, and cause-of-death statistics from death certificates (Rancourt et al., 2023, p. 3).

Consistent with a depopulation agenda (Chudov, 2022b), birth rates since the "Covid-19 vaccine" rollout dropped precipitously in 19 European countries (an average 7% decline) (Pfeiffer, 2022), including Germany and Sweden (by 14% and 10%, respectively) (Bujard & Andersson, 2022), Switzerland (by 10–15%) (Swiss Policy Research, 2022), and the United Kingdom (11.2%) (Naked Emperor, 2023). In New Zealand, birth rates between July 2022 and June 2023 were 28% lower than during the corresponding period in 2018/19 (Hatchard, 2023). Additional concerns have been raised about the potential gene drive application of the injections, "a highly controversial new genetic extinction technology" funded by the Defence Advanced Research Projects Agency (DARPA) and the Gates Foundation that renders offspring incapable of reproduction (Latham, 2017)—an effect that would remain hidden for a generation, but which would have radical effects in terms of global population reduction.

mRNA injections allegedly work by deceiving the immune system: the modification "makes the RNA look more like something that the cell would produce itself, because invaders such as bacteria cannot usually make these modifications to their own mRNA" (Dolgin, 2015). In the case of the "Covid-19" injections, "the modified nucleobase helps cloak mRNA vaccines from the immune system" (Nance & Meier, 2021, p. 753). On this basis, Santiago (2022b, p. 631) asks, "would it be an impossible leap of logic to suppose that serious deception is taking place on a worldwide scale?" He proposes that the "Covid-19" injections reverse transcribe XNA into the human genome to redirect human evolution (Santiago, 2022a, p. 588). Although his argument is somewhat speculative, it underscores the fact that we simply do not know what exactly has been shot into billions of people worldwide, or what the implications are for humanity.

There appears to be a concerted effort to use "vaccines" to "programme" human bodies. According to Moderna CEO, Stéphane Bancel, "mRNA is like software" (Garde, 2017). Moderna's Chief Medical Officer, Tal Zaks (n.d.), claimed in a TEDx talk that "we are actually hacking the software of life." This resembles Harari's (2017) claim that "we are learning [...] how to hack humans, how to engineer them, how to manufacture them." Moderna describes its "Covid-19 vaccine" as "an operating system on a computer." President Biden's Executive Order of September 12, 2022, calls for the development of "genetic engineering technologies and techniques to be able to write circuitry for cells and predictably program biology in the same way in which we write software and program computers [...]" (White House, 2022). All of which begs the question: is the transnational deep state (Hughes, 2022b) trying, under cover of "vaccination," to hack the human body for eugenics purposes, much as the NSA, in conjunction with Big Tech, managed to gain backdoor access to virtually all computers?

Or, is the goal to hook human bodies up to the technocratic control grid through convergent IT/Bio/Nano revolutions for purposes of human enslavement, i.e. infiltration of human bodies with covert military technologies? (see Chap. 8). The world was deceived about the contents of the "Covid-19" injectables (Hughes, 2022c), which "enjoy a largely positive public image as pharmaceutical, rather than technological, tools" (Kyrie & Broudy, 2022a). It is often overlooked, in this context, that the infamous "Lockstep" scenario by the Rockefeller Foundation and Global Business Network (2010), which eerily foreshadows the response to "Covid-19," appeared in a document whose title (*Scenarios for the Future of Technology and International Development*) foregrounds technology, not public health.

Doctors for COVID Ethics: A Critique

Despite abundant evidence that the "Covid-19 vaccines" are military, rather than pharmaceutical products, whose purpose can only be nefarious, prominent critics of the "vaccines" remain wedded to the pharmaceutical paradigm. Doctors for COVID Ethics, for instance, argues that "the risks and the manifest harm which we have seen with the COVID-19 mRNA vaccines were predictable from first principles of immunology" (D4CE, 2023, pp. 4–6). Three key mechanisms are identified to account for the toxicity of mRNA vaccines: "1. the chemical toxicity of lipid nanoparticles, 2. direct toxicity of the spike protein, whose expression is induced by the vaccines, and 3. the destructive effects of the immune response to the spike protein" (DC4E, 2023, p. 181). This resembles the five sources of harm identified by Parry et al. (2023), i.e. inflammatory properties of lipid-nanoparticles, toxicity of the spike protein produced by gene codes, N1-methylpseudouridine in the synthetic mRNA, widespread biodistribution of the mRNA and DNA codes, and human cells producing a foreign protein in ribosomes that can engender autoimmunity. Because of these mechanisms, all future mRNA "vaccines" can be expected to cause harm, with clinical trials already underway for such "vaccines" against cytomegalovirus, Epstein-Barr virus, and respiratory syncytial virus (D4CE, 2023, p. 181).

The value of the Doctors for COVID Ethics analysis is to show that, even if we accept that we are dealing with pharmaceutical products designed to trigger an immune response, "mRNA vaccines" are unsafe from first principles. Therefore, no case can be made for their clinical usage.

However, D4CE seems closed to the possibility that the "mRNA vaccines" might not be intended as pharmaceutical products. For example, it questions whether "mRNA vaccine" toxicity is caused by the "vaccines working as intended," i.e. by triggering an immune system response, or, rather, by "undeclared ingredients or contaminants," noting, "This question cannot be dismissed out of hand" (2023, p. 1). Alternatives to the "working as intended" hypothesis, however, are discarded by the end of the first page. Confirmation bias is, thus, strong in the book, and some important counterfactuals are not considered. For example, what if the "Covid-19 vaccines," as military products, are *not* primarily intended to trigger an immune response? Latypova (2022a, 20:40), for instance, claims that whatever is being produced in human bodies because of the "mRNA vaccines" is *not* the "SARS-CoV-2" spike protein, since the molecular weights of the two proteins (180 kDA vs. 141 kDA) do not match.

What proportion of people have been injured and/or killed by the "Covid-19 vaccines"? Rancourt et al. (2023, p. 3) place the all-ages vaccine-dose fatality rate at 0.126%. Though unacceptable, should it not be much higher if "mRNA vaccines" cause harm from first principles, following 21 months (to September 2022) of "the destructive effects of the immune response to the spike protein" (D4CE, 2023, p. 181)? Perhaps more time is needed for the full impact of the injections to become clear, but the evidence seems inconsistent with a systemic and predictable harming of the "vaccinated" population. On the other hand, if the "vaccines" are covert military technologies (cf. Chap. 8), then their covert deployment would depend on them doing *least* harm, notwithstanding "collateral damage" arising from injecting novel technologies into human bodies on such a massive scale.

By September 2022 (when the UK MHRA stopped publishing figures), there were 464,000 Yellow Card reports for "Covid-19 vaccines," accounting for 1.5 million reactions and 2272 deaths (MHRA, n.d.). Traditionally, such reports only account for 10% of the estimated total, although the MHRA (2019) maintains that publicity around "Covid-19 vaccines" renders the 10% figure unreliable. Generously assuming the 10% figure to be reliable, however, it implies up to 4.64 million "vaccine"-injured people in the UK, out of a "vaccinated" adult population of 54 million (UKHSA, 2022, Table 5), i.e. 8.6%, with a 0.042% mortality rate. If "mRNA vaccines" cause harm from first principles, and if "the adenovirus-based vaccines produced by AstraZeneca and Johnson & Johnson have fairly similar profiles of adverse events to the mRNA vaccines" (D4CE, 2023, p. 182), then why was at least 91.4% of the UK "vaccinated" population *not* injured after 21 months? And why did 99.96% survive?

There is reason to suspect that *some* "Covid-19 vaccine" vials contain *no* mRNA. Nagase (2022), for instance, identifies structures in the Pfizer and Moderna vials that resemble biological entities, yet which contain neither nitrogen nor phosphorus, two of the six "building blocks of life," implying that they cannot be biological (cf. Hughes, 2022c, p. 460). Kirsch (2022b) claims that an unnamed colleague conducted mass spectrometry on two Pfizer and two Moderna vials and found phosphorus in none of them, again implying no mRNA.

Because of the known variability between batches, failure to find mRNA in some vials by no means precludes the possibility that it will be found in others. Yet, one batch in every 200 is over 50 times more deadly than the rest (Hill, 2022; Wilson, 2022; cf. Schmeling et al., 2023), which is too radical a discrepancy to be attributed to bad manufacturing processes, as per D4CE's (2023, p. 1) analysis. It seems likely that we are dealing here with a worldwide experiment without informed consent, in which certain batches were more toxic than others *by design*, perhaps to calibrate the tolerance of different groups of people to different levels of whatever is in the shots. At any rate, the deaths of "bad batch" victims cannot be attributed to a general theory of mRNA toxicity.

D4CE (2023, Chap. 4) utilises histology, in particular based on autopsy reports and the work of the late Arne Burkhardt, to claim the circulation of the spike protein throughout the body. Yet, using a non-specific antigen test to infer infection with "SARS-CoV-2" offers a weak standard of proof; the alleged spike proteins are not assayed for directly (Cowan, 2023).

DNA Contamination in the Vials?

At least three genomics scientists claim to have discovered extremely high levels of plasmid DNA contamination in the Pfizer/BioNTech vials, namely, Kevin McKernan (McKernan et al., 2023), Phillip Buckhaults (see Demasi, 2023), and Jürgen O. Kirchner (see Kogon, 2023). If what they claim is true, then debates about whether mRNA from the "vaccines" can be reverse-transcribed and integrated into the genome of human cells recede in significance, because DNA was already present in the vials.

Pfizer/BioNTech used two different production methods for its "vaccine": the first, in clinical trials, used PCR to amplify the DNA template used for production of the mRNA ("a highly pure mRNA product"), and the second, for purposes of large-scale manufacturing, used bacteria to make large quantities of DNA plasmid which, in turn, were used to provide the blueprint for the mRNA (Demasi, 2023). The DNA should, at that stage, have been removed to "safe" levels (if there is such a thing), yet, if McKernan, Buckhaults, and Kirchner are correct, preliminary indications are that the DNA contamination level is at least ten times the "safe" level set by the EMA (Jones, 2023), or perhaps 188–509 times higher (Speicher et al., 2023, p. 3). Normally, bacterial DNA does not survive long enough to enter cells, but if present in the "vaccines" will allegedly be packaged in lipid nanoparticles that are taken up by cells. Widespread biodistribution then implies the risk of foreign DNA interfering with cell function throughout the body, potentially accounting for the extremely wide range of reported serious adverse reactions (Hodgkinson, 2023). Unlike mRNA, DNA implies genetic changes that may be permanent and passed down to the next generation.

Not unlike the Vanden Bossche open letter about the potential for the "Covid-19 vaccines" to lead to immune escape (see Chap. 4), we are faced here with some alarmist claims unsupported by reliable scientific evidence. McKernan et al. (2023) admit: "These vials were sent to us anonymously in the mail without cold packs" and "All of the monovalent vaccines [but not the bivalent vaccines] in this study are past the expiration date listed on the vial," implying no adequate chain of custody and tests conducted on vials which would not have been administered to patients. McKernan's second preprint (Speicher et al., 2023, p. 3), released in October 2023, notes that its findings need to be "replicated under forensic conditions." As of December 2023, neither preprint had passed peer review.

The Kirchner data (as in Kogon, 2023) derive from an *open letter* to the German medical regulator (the Paul Ehrlich Institute) and have not been independently verified. Testimony by the triple- "vaccinated" Buckhaults to the South Carolina Senate Medical Affairs Ad-Hoc Committee is gushing in its praise for "mRNA vaccines," pointing to their "revolutionary" future benefits (Demasi, 2023), much as Vanden Bossche's (2021) ultimate solution is more and better "vaccines."

It would be interesting to know why no one in the world detected DNA contamination in the "Covid-19 vaccines" for the whole of 2021 and 2022, and then suddenly it became a narrative in 2023. Are we looking here at science or propaganda? As with the focus on mRNA in the previous section, the focus on DNA here encourages us to think in strictly biological terms. Although the "vaccines" may well involve an attempt to manipulate cell biology (though not necessarily to produce viral spike protein), as military products they may also involve other technologies (see next section).

A legal case filed in the Australian Federal Court in July 2023, for which McKernan provides expert testimony, alleges that both DNA contamination and the mRNA in lipid nanoparticles fall under the legal definition of a GMO, with both allegedly being able to enter the cell nucleus and integrate into the human genome (Barnett, 2023). The case argues that the Office of Gene Technology Regulator, and not the Therapeutic Goods Administration, should have been the appropriate regulator of the "mRNA vaccines."

The intellectual foundations of the case are laid out by Gillespie (2023). Aside from the unverified claims of McKernan, Gillespie's argument rests mainly on just two peer-reviewed studies. One of them (Domazet-Lošo, 2022) is purely theoretical, arguing that a longstanding literature on the biology of retroposition was ignored in the development of "Covid-19 vaccines." This tells us nothing, however, about whether the "vaccines" do, in fact, induce retroposition, hence Domazet-Lošo's call for experimental studies to find out. The other paper (Aldén et al., 2022) claims that Pfizer's BNT162b2 can be reverse-transcribed into human DNA using a human liver cell line, but this is a single in vitro finding that is yet to be independently replicated. A third peer-reviewed study, which claims that mice pre-exposed to a mRNA-LNP platform can pass down acquired immunity to influenza to their offspring, is also cited, yet its authors note that it is unknown "whether any such immune inheritance may be observed in humans vaccinated with mRNA vaccines" (Qin et al., 2022). Gillespie (2023, p. 944) additionally cites an unnamed "PhD in Molecular and Cellular Biology," who "consulted with several similarly qualified colleagues," including a "Ph.D. in Genomics," who in turn cites a 2022 preprint and claims "it has been suggested that [...]." Who are these mystery figures, and where is their peer-reviewed evidence? In sum, the scientific evidence base for the Australian court case is not robust.

According to a headline by the self-styled World Council for Health (WCH, 2023), "WCH Expert Panel Finds Cancer-Promoting DNA Contamination in Covid-19 Vaccines." The panel, however, "found" no such thing: rather, these are McKernan's claims (who sits on the panel), and to a lesser extent those of Brigitte König (who worked with Kirchner). The other panel members (Sucharit Bhakdi, Peter McCullough, Byram Bridle, Jessica Rose, Alexandra Henrion-Caude, and Janci

Lindsay) merely endorse the claims. Consensus is not the same as proof of scientific discovery.

Evidence of Undisclosed Technologies in the "Covid-19 Vaccines"

Accounts which take for granted that "mRNA vaccines" are what they appear to be necessarily ignore/suppress/dismiss evidence to the contrary. Much of that evidence is collected in Hughes (2022c), which summarises the findings of 26 independent researchers and research teams who conducted microscopic and spectroscopic analysis of the contents of "Covid-19 vaccine" vials and "vaccinated" blood. Surprise findings include sharp-edged geometric structures, fibrous or tube-like structures, crystalline formations, "microbubbles," and possible self-assembling nanotechnology. Published literature on vaccine contaminants before "Covid-19" does not feature such artefacts, which experienced doctors and scientists claim never to have seen before in their professional experience (Hughes, 2022c, pp. 464, 470, 488, 567–8, 575).

Studies by a team of Australian scientists (in Hughes, 2022c, p. 549), Taylor (see Hughes, 2023, 50:25), and Nixon (see Mangiaracina, 2022) point towards EMF-responsive components in the "Covid-19 vaccines." Nixon has uniquely recorded videos of what happens to the "vaccine" contents under the microscope over extended periods of time (see the "Key Videos" section on drdavidnixon.com); the results show structures and processes too advanced/complex to be naturally occurring crystals (cf. also the imagery in Hughes, 2022c, pp. 510–514, 535). Some structures visibly resemble electronic circuitry, according to electrical engineers (see Hughes, 2022c, pp. 534, 555). Based on the resemblance of certain items found within the vials to published literature on (bio)nanotechnology, Andersen (2021) proposes that the "vaccines" enable an intracorporeal nanonetwork. It has been claimed, based on experimental findings, that "vaccinated" people emit hexadecimal MAC addresses (Sarlangue et al., 2021), although adequately powered studies are needed to determine the truth of such claims (Hughes, 2023, 1:18:00; cf. Taylor, 2023).

Even before "Covid-19," it was known that most vaccines contain a large array of undisclosed inorganic (typically metallic) contaminants, which are neither biocompatible nor biodegradable and are "capable of stimulating the immune system in an undesirable way," around the time of injection or much later, even more so as their number and synergic effect increase (Gatti & Montanari, 2017). Spectroscopic analysis of the "Covid-19 vaccine" contents reveals the presence of undisclosed exotic/toxic metals, including the highly toxic antimony (in Moderna only), caesium, barium, titanium, cerium, gadolinium, aluminium, silicon, bismuth, and vanadium (Vaccines Education Working Group, 2022; Young, 2021). The possible presence of graphene oxide, which is key to bio-nano engineering, has also been identified (Campra, 2021; UNIT, 2022; Young, 2021).

Countless online videos emerged in 2021 of people who had become magnetic at the injection site and sometimes elsewhere ("Magnetgate 3," 2021). Contrary to "fact checkers'" breathless reassurances that this was a "hoax" or an online "challenge" and that none of the "vaccines'" disclosed ingredients contain anything magnetic, most of the evidence appears genuine and requires explanation.

Especially in the context of the IT/Bio/Nano era (see Chap. 8), this is a lot of empirical evidence to write off, yet commentators hesitate to entertain the possibility of undisclosed technologies in the "Covid-19 vaccines" for several reasons. For starters, it sounds preposterous—the stuff of sci-fi—and falls too far outside the spectrum of socially acceptable opinion. This, however, merely reflects the limitations of human psychology and groupthink; it is not evidence-based science. Military-grade propaganda means that the public's perceptual parameters remain limited to the virus, the spike protein, mRNA/DNA, and dangers deriving from the *disclosed* "vaccine" ingredients. Most doctors, virologists, microbiologists, etc., know very little about bio-nanotechnology, so are unqualified to comment and understandably prefer to stick to their fields of expertise. Fear of reprisal (e.g. hit pieces by the media, attacks by colleagues, withdrawal of medical licences, harassment, and threats to life) disincentivise scientists/doctors from publicly challenging orthodoxy. Pied pipers for the intelligence agencies (widely promoted "controlled opposition" figures) are deployed to win the trust of sceptics and steer them away from the truth.

We need to be open to the possibility of black technology (i.e. classified military technology) within the "Covid-19" injectables, because we are dealing here with a deep state military operation. Galison (2004, p. 231) estimates that classified scientific research is "on the order of five to ten times larger than the open literature that finds its way to our libraries." Thus, it is "we in the open world [...] who are living in a modest information booth facing outwards, our unseeing backs to a vast and classified empire we barely know." In other words, the public has no idea of the full extent of what is technologically possible behind the scenes. In the undeclared Omniwar against humanity, black technology constitutes an ideal weapon, as not only can it be deployed by stealth, but the public would not believe it to be real even if presented with the evidence (cf. Wood, 2011).

Cognitive Dissonance

Origins of the Concept

Despite the saturation of the official "Covid-19" narrative with deceit, most people cannot and will not see it. The reason for this has to do with "cognitive dissonance," a term coined by Festinger (1957). Today, that term is often applied to those who are psychologically incapable of challenging official narratives because of the propaganda and other brainwashing techniques to which they have been subjected. "Exposure to new information may create cognitive elements that are dissonant with existing cognition," Festinger writes, and the greater the dissonance, the greater the pressure to reduce it (1957, pp. 261, 263). *Weltanschauungskrieg*, or "worldview warfare" is the Nazi term from which the phrase "psychological warfare" is derived (Simpson, 1994, p. 24). When someone whose worldview has been shaped by propaganda encounters contrary information, they will automatically find ways of disregarding it. For example, the information may not register, it may be ignored, it may be denied, it may be denigrated as "conspiracy theory," the topic of conversation may be instantly changed, or the source of the information may be attacked—anything to avoid confronting evidence that undermines the programming.

The totalitarian origins of cognitive dissonance are seldom discussed, yet the collective social dimension of what Festinger (1957) presents primarily in terms of individual psychology is extremely important. For once the Big Lie has been used to deceive the masses, "Even though the facts which prove this to be so may be brought clearly to their minds, they will still doubt and waver and will continue to think that there may be some other explanation" (Hitler, 1939, p. 183). The Big Lie thus persists. "In totalitarian surroundings," Meerloo (1956, p. 204) writes, hardly anyone keeps his thinking free of contagion, and nearly everyone becomes, albeit temporarily, the victim of delusion." In other words, indoctrination/brainwashing is contagious: the greater the number of people who believe something to be true (or who remain silent in the face of lies), the more pressure there is on non-believers to conform to the majority opinion.

This insight was weaponised by the Rockefellers using Reesian methods: "any Reesian form of social organisation will tend to cause mass brainwashing in the members of such a group if the stress applied is sufficient and sufficiently prolonged," and, in such a state, "the members of the group will effectively brainwash one another" (Marcus, 1974, p. 26). A heavily propagandised society subjected to induced stress can, therefore, be left to police itself, with the indoctrinated majority keeping the minority of free thinkers in check by attacking their views as "unpatriotic," "fringe," "conspiracy theory," "crazy," "dangerous," "extremist," etc.

Particularly interesting is Festinger's (1957, 262) claim that "Identical dissonance in a large number of people may be created when an event occurs which is so compelling as to produce a uniform reaction in everyone. For example, an event may occur which unequivocally invalidates some widely held belief." Prior to "9/11," the widely held belief was that the United States, as the "sole superpower" in a world free from "great power" conflict, was immune to attack. After that event, the uniform reaction was support for the United States' "War on Terror," and anyone who dared question either the event or its consequences was a "conspiracy theorist." The lesson is that traumatising events can be used to manufacture cognitive dissonance on a mass scale. "Information learned in the context of trauma," Kyrie and Broudy (2022b) observe, drawing on Howie & Ressler's (2021) insights into the "neurobiology of fear learning," becomes "neurologically hardwired, and resistant to change, including from subsequent factual, logical disconfirmation and evidence."

No Longer Open to Argument

In a totalitarian society, once a fearful citizen has "accepted the 'logic' of [their] leaders," they are "no longer open to discussion or argument" (Meerloo, 1956, pp. 136–7). Similarly, Arendt (1962, p. 308) writes of totalitarianism that "within the organizational framework of the movement, so long as it holds together, the fanaticized members can be reached by neither experience nor argument."

The inability to deal with evidence-based counter-arguments has been a defining feature/weakness of "Covid-19" true believers. As Hopkins (2021b) observes, "You can show [them] the facts all you like"—e.g. around fake reports of people dropping dead in the streets in March 2020, hyperbolic projected death rates, the PCR test scam, studies on mask ineffectiveness, manipulated death statistics, hospital propaganda, the survival rates for people under 70, the unnecessary risk of injecting children, etc.—yet "none of this will make the slightest difference." In the "Covid-19" context, Harradine (2020) observes, "People react to discrediting evidence not by acknowledging reality but by entrenching their beliefs even further." They will not listen to reason. Or perhaps they will listen politely, and then continue as though the conversation never happened.

For many victims of psychological operations, the gulf between what they have been indoctrinated to believe and the dark nature of sociopolitical reality (the power of evil) is too much to bear. For example, realising that the events of "9/11" were not what the public was indoctrinated to believe can generate a profound sense of ontological insecurity, at least to begin with (Hughes, 2020, p. 73). Or take the inhumane logic of Big Pharma, which generates profit by keeping people sick (Gøtzsche, 2013). Big Pharma has repeatedly incurred gigantic fines for experimenting upon, injuring, and killing people with its products, which it accepts as the cost of doing business. Yet, before the horror show of the "Covid-19 vaccines," most people blindly believed the mantra that vaccines are "safe and effective." Tragically, many still do, and for them, challenging their indoctrination could "shatter their fragile delusions, leaving them lost and bewildered in a frightening world they cannot face" (Davis, 2019).

Bertrand Russell once wrote that "Collective fear stimulates herd instinct, and tends to produce ferocity toward those who are not regarded as members of the herd" (2009, p. 106). For members of totalitarian societies and cults, "nothing is more threatening [...] "than those who challenge their fundamental beliefs, confront them with facts, or otherwise demonstrate that their 'reality' isn't reality at all, but, rather, a delusional, paranoid fiction" (Hopkins, 2021a). Particularly when the facts threaten to expose deep state criminality and the psychological operations that provide cover for it, "the more deep the criticism, the more visceral the reaction" (de Lint, 2021, pp. 221–22).

Anyone tactfully asking evidence-based questions about "Covid-19 countermeasures" risked incurring a visceral (over)reaction from traumatised victims of the "Covid-19" operation. As Cullen observes, "what happens is they get angry! And it's from 0 to 60," i.e. perfectly calm one moment, furious the next (Anthony & Cullen, 2021). "It's almost as if the propaganda in their mind, the virus of their mind, so to speak [...] has [a] security system in place, which puts up a wall," Cullen adds. Scott (2021a) observes the "mask rage, vaccine rage, social distancing rage—when violations/non-compliance/refusal of these occurs." McDonald (2022, p. 21) references "countless videos [...] showing angry, hysterical [people] screaming at others for not wearing a mask, often chasing them and even physically attacking them." In March 2021, when comedian Alex Lasarev sarcastically used a megaphone to congratulate pedestrians for "following the narrative and trusting the news and not questioning anything," a triggered cyclist used his bicycle to smash in Lasarev's car window at a junction (Macmichael, 2021).

A striking manifestation of cognitive dissonance among "vaccinated" people was the tendency to respond to getting "Covid-19" (in their view) by insisting how much worse it would have been had they not taken the injections and continuing to urge everyone else to take them. The illogical mindset here is that the "vaccines" are protecting them against the very thing ("Covid-19") that is making them ill. There is no criticising the "vaccines" for their obvious ineffectiveness in preventing infection, no thought to inquire into the frequency of "breakthrough cases" in case there is a pattern, and no consideration of what proportion of "unvaccinated" people remain uninfected and healthy. Tragically, some "vaccine"-injured individuals continued to defend and advocate for the very injections that, by their own admission, had caused harm to them and their loved ones.

Societal Implications

Behavioural psychology teaches that the more someone has invested into something (time, money, effort, personal identity), the harder it becomes to admit they were wrong and to change course (the sunk cost fallacy). This is associated with the idea of loss aversion, i.e. that "we dislike losses more than we like gains of an equivalent amount" (Dolan et al., 2010, p. 20). Consider, then, how many sunk costs there are for those who bought into the official "Covid-19" narrative; who were tricked into publicly virtue-signalling their loyalty to a raft of deeply sinister agendas; who sought to marginalise, ostracise, and otherwise persecute those seeking to defend freedom (including for them); and who surrendered their bodily autonomy to the point of making themselves (and their children) test subjects for unlicensed, experimental injections with no adequate safety data. Given such a high level of buy-in, there are powerful psychological reasons why large numbers of people may not be willing to admit the error of their ways.

This has left society fractured. There are those whose worldviews are fundamentally determined by whatever the government and the media tell them—and those who, for whatever reason, see through the calculated attempts at manipulating public perception by whatever means possible to serve ruling-class agendas. It comes as a heavy burden to those in the latter camp to realise that rational communication is barely possible with those whose unconscious mind has been so thoroughly manipulated and abused that they would rather attack those standing up for truth, freedom, justice, and love than engage in any kind of evidence-based discussion around issues that challenge their programming.

Such fractures run deep and have criss-crossed family relationships, friendships, and even intimate relationships. Consequently, the key questions about what is really going on in the world risk becoming taboo: the indoctrinated refuse to ask them (and may turn on those who do), while those whose critical facilities have remained intact through the psychological operation often do not wish to jeopardise close relationships by asking those questions.

The implications of this psychological schism in society are profound. A year *before* "Covid-19," Davis (2019) wrote:

> On the back of their ignorance, intolerance, and refusal to even look at the mountain of evidence that justifies some scepticism, it appears the rest of us may very well face compulsory injection at the hands of ruthless multinational corporations based upon research partly funded by the military industrial complex.

This is an accurate, and powerful, assessment of the situation. For as long as enough people can be kept in a mind-controlled stupor, blindly believing the propaganda that "vaccines" are "safe and effective," they contribute to a situation in which *anything*, regardless of the contents (Hughes, 2022c), could be injected into our bodies, without our informed consent—and, for most people, has been already.

Total Deception

It is dawning on more and more people that The Science™ which they were told to follow was fraudulent. Bell (2022), for instance, provides a "short list of Really Big Lies," including:

- Banning students from school for a year protects the elderly;
- Cloth and surgical masks stop aerosolised virus transmission;
- Post-infection immunity to respiratory viruses is expected to be poor and short-lived, while vaccines to a single viral protein will somehow produce much stronger immunity;
- Immunity to viruses is best measured by antibody concentrations rather than T-cell response or clinical outcomes;
- It is appropriate to give a new gene-based pharmaceutical class in pregnancy that crosses the placenta without any pregnancy trial data, toxicology studies, or long-term outcomes data (in anyone) [in England, perinatal mortality rates "increased across the UK in 2021 after 7 years of year-on-year reduction" (Draper et al., 2023)];
- It is appropriate to inject children with drugs lacking long-term safety data in order to protect the elderly;
- Pandemics are becoming more frequent and more deadly, despite the historical record, and the progress of modern medicine, indicating quite the opposite.

Referring to the "industrial-scale fraud" perpetrated by Big Pharma and state-aligned media, as well as by governments against their own citizens, Chuter (2021) alleges a psychological warfare operation "built on a litany of these Big Lies, one of which is that universal vaccination is our only way out of the pandemic."

Seemingly everything the public was told to believe in the name of following The Science™ has turned out to be false. Knightly (2023) provides a crib sheet of 40 facts debunking some of the main lies regarding death counts, testing, "lockdowns," "vaccines," etc. Hudson (2021) debunks 20 lies on which The Science™ is premised. Atlas (2023) lists the "10 biggest falsehoods—known for years to be false, not recently learned or proven to be so—promoted by America's public health leaders, elected and unelected officials, and now-discredited academics." In Blaylock's (2022) opinion, the public was fed an "unending series of lies, distortions and disinformation by the media, the public health officials, medical bureaucracies (CDC, FDA and WHO) and medical associations."

In terms of the "Covid-19" operation, we are dealing, not merely with errors in The Science™, but, rather, with Big Lies in the totalitarian sense. Ultimately, unless scientists have more to show, particularly in demonstrating beyond reasonable doubt that "SARS-CoV-2" exists, then it is reasonable to deduce, as Devlin (2021, p. 2) does, that "every single aspect of the official narrative beaten into the consciousness of the public has been laden with fraud." There was no "pandemic," there was no "virus," and there were no "vaccines." Instead, there was a highly advanced psychological operation initiating the war for technocracy.

References

Agamben, G. (1998). *Homo sacer*. Stanford University Press.

Agamben, G. (2021). *Where are we now?* Rowman and Littlefield.

Aldén, M., Falla, F. O., Yang, D., Barghouth, M., Luan, C., Rasmussen, M., & De Marinis, Y. (2022). Intracellular reverse transcription of Pfizer BioNTech COVID-19 mRNA vaccine BNT162b2 in vitro in human liver cell line. *Current Issues in Molecular Biology, 44*(3), 1115–1126. https://doi.org/10.3390/cimb44030073.

Altman, P., Rowe, J., Hoy, W., Brady, G., Lefringhausen, A., Cosford, R., & Wauchope, B. (2023, January 5). Did national security imperatives compromise COVID-19 vaccine safety? *Brownstone Institute*. https://brownstone.org/articles/did-national-security-imperatives-compromise-covid-19-vaccine-safety/.

Andersen, M. (2021, December 10). *Intracorporeal nanonetwork. Brief summary*. https://everydayconcerned.net/wp-content/uploads/2021/12/12-intracorporal_nanonetwork.pdf.

Anthony, J., & Cullen, D. (2021, January 6). Breaking the Covid trance: How the Irish people were psychologically manipulated [Speech transcript]. *UK Column*. https://www.ukcolumn.org/article/breaking-covid-trance-how-irish-people-were-psychologically-manipulated.

Arendt, H. (1962). *The origins of totalitarianism*. The World Publishing Company.

Atlas, S. W. (2023, March 6). America's Covid response was based on lies. *Newsweek*. https://www.newsweek.com/america-covid-response-was-based-lies-opinion-1785177.

Bailey, M. (2022, March 24). Rapid antigen tests—making "viruses" real again. *Dr. Sam Bailey*. https://drsambailey.com/rapid-antigen-tests-making-viruses-real-again/.

Barnett, R. (2023, September 25). Scientists "shocked" and "alarmed" at what's in the mRNA shots. *Spectator Australia*. https://www.spectator.com.au/2023/09/scientists-shocked-and-alarmed-at-whats-in-the-mrna-shots/.

Bell, D. (2022, November 4). Global health and the art of really big lies. *Propaganda in Focus*. https://propagandainfocus.com/global-health-and-the-art-of-really-big-lies/.

Bill Gates says COVID is "kind of like the flu," and that the vaccines are "imperfect." (2022, May 5). *KUSI News*. https://www.kusi.com/bill-gates-says-covid-is-kind-of-like-the-flu-and-that-the-vaccines-are-imperfect/.

Billionaire Warren Buffett predicts new pandemic worse than Covid-19. (2021, July 3). *SFGATE*. https://www.sfgate.com/business/article/Billionaire-Warren-Buffett-Predicts-New-Pandemic-16290384.php.

Blair, T. (2002, September 24). Foreword to the dossier on Iraq. *The Guardian*. https://www.theguardian.com/world/2002/sep/24/iraq.speeches.

Blaylock, R. L. (2022). Covid update: What is the truth? *Surgical Neurology International*, *13*, Article 167. https://doi.org/10.25259/SNI_150_2022.

Borger, P., Malhotra, B. R., Yeadon, M., Craig, C., McKernan, K., Steger, K., McSheehy, P., Angelova, L., Franchi, F., Binder, T., Ullrich, H., Ohashi, M., Scoglio, S., Doesburg-van Kleffens, M., Gilbert, D., Klement, R., Schruefer, R., Pieksma, B. W., Bonte, J., Dalle Carbonare, B. H., Corbett, K.P., & Kämmerer, U. (2020, November 27). *Corman-Drosten review report*. Retrieved 13 June, 2023, from https://www.medicdebate.org/node/1183.

Boyd, C. (2021, April 1). Chris Whitty says Britain will treat Covid "like the flu" in future but warns we will be vulnerable to the disease for another two years and says a vaccine-resistant variant will emerge. *Daily Mail*. https://www.dailymail.co.uk/news/article-9427169/Chris-Whitty-warns-Britain-vulnerable-Covid-two-years.html.

Broudy, D., & Hoop, D.K. (2021). Messianic mad men, medicine, and the media war on empirical reality: Discourse analysis of mainstream Covid-19 propaganda. *International Journal of Vaccine Theory, Research, and Practice*, *2*(1), 365–388. https://doi.org/10.56098/ijvtpr.v2i1.22.

Brunson, E. K., Chandler, H., Gronvall, G. K., Ravi, S., Sell, T. K., Shearer, M. P., & Schoch-Spana, M. (2020). The SPARS pandemic 2025–2028: A futuristic scenario to facilitate medical countermeasure communication. *Journal of International Crisis and Risk Communication Research*, *3*(1), 71–102. https://doi.org/10.30658/jicrcr.3.1.4.

Brzezinski, Z. (1970). *Between two ages: America's role in the technetronic era*. Viking Press.

Bujard, M., & Andersson, G. (2022). Fertility declines near the end of the Covid-19 pandemic: Evidence of the 2022 birth declines in Germany and Sweden. Preprint retrieved from https://su.figshare.com/articles/preprint/Fertility_declines_near_the_end_of_the_COVID-19_pandemic_Evidence_of_the_2022_birth_declines_in_Germany_and_Sweden/20975611.

Campra, P. (2021, November 2). *Detection of Graphene in COVID19 Vaccines by Micro-Raman Spectroscopy. Technical Report*. https://www.dropbox.com/s/tnnq4ftw818chmx/FINAL_VERSI%C3%93N_CAMPRA_REPORT_DETECTION_GRAPHENE_IN_COVID19_VACCINES.pdf?dl=0Cam.

Cancryn, A., Cook, N., & Diamond, D. (2020, April 25). White House weighing plan to replace Azar. *Politico*. https://www.politico.com/news/2020/04/25/white-house-replace-alex-azar-208151.

Cassol, C. A., Gokden, N., Larsen, C. P., & Bourne, T. D. (2020). Appearances can be deceiving—viral-like inclusions in Covid-19 negative renal biopsies by electron microscopy. *Kidney360*, *1*(8), 824–828. https://doi.org/10.34067/KID.0002692020.

Centre for Research on Population and Security. (1972). *Population and the American future*. https://www.population-security.org/rockefeller/001_population_growth_and_the_american_future.htm.

Centres for Disease Control and Prevention. (2020, October 6). *U.S. influenza surveillance system: Purpose and methods*. https://www.cdc.gov/flu/weekly/overview.htm.

Centres for Disease Control and Prevention. (2021, January 27). *Similarities and differences between flu and Covid-19*. https://www.cdc.gov/flu/symptoms/flu-vs-covid19.htm#table.

Children's Health Defence. (2020, November 18). Leading Canadian health expert outraged at government response to COVID. *The Defender*. https://childrenshealthdefense.org/defender/health-expert-outraged-government-response-covid/.

Chomsky, N. (2003). *Hegemony or survival: America's quest for global dominance*. Metropolitan Books.

Chossudovsky, M. (2021). *The 2020 worldwide corona crisis: Destroying civil society, engineered economic depression, global coup d'état, and the "great reset."* Centre for Research on Globalization.

Chudov, I. (2022a, November 6). Association between vaccines and excess mortality getting stronger—and is discussed in UK parliament. *Igor's Newsletter*. https://igorchudov.substack.com/p/association-between-vaccines-and.

Chudov, I. (2022b, December 22). Is depopulation we are seeing, planned or incidental? December births and deaths update. *Igor's Newsletter*. https://igorchudov.substack.com/p/is-depopulation-we-are-seeing-planned.

Chuter, R. (2021, October 14). Another big Covid lie bites the dust. *Empowered!* https://robynchuter.substack.com/p/another-big-covid-lie-bites-the-dust.

Corman, V. M., Bleicker, T., Brünink, S., Drosten, C., Landt, O., Koopmans, M., Zambon, M., & Peiris, M. (2020a, January 13). Diagnostic detection of Wuhan coronavirus 2019 by real-time RT-PCR. *World Health Organisation.* https://www.who.int/docs/default-source/coronaviruse/wuhan-virus-assay-v1991527e5122341d99287a1b17c111902.pdf.

Corman, V. M., Landt, O., Kaiser, M., Molenkamp, R., Meijer, A., Chu, D., Daniel, K. W., Bleicker, T., Brünink, S., Schneider, J., Schmidt, M. L., Mulders, D. G. J. C., Haagmans, B. L., van der Veer, B., van den Brink, S., Wijsman, L., Goderski, G., Romette, J., Ellis, J., Zambon, M., Peiris, M., Goossens, H., Reusken, C., Koopmans, M. P. G., & Drosten, C. (2020b). Detection of 2019 novel coronavirus (2019-nCoV) by real-time RT-PCR. *Eurosurveillance, 25*(3). https://doi.org/10.2807/1560-7917.ES.2020.25.3.2000045.

Cowan, T. (2020, October 15). *Only poisoned monkey kidney cells "grew" the virus*. https://drtomcowan.com/blogs/blog/only-poisoned-monkey-kidney-cells-grew-the-virus.

Cowan, T. (2023, June 10). *Circulating spike protein?* [Video]. Odysee. https://odysee.com/@shortXXvids:e/Dr-Tom-Cowan---SP-Issues--3,-Circulating-SPs:1?r=FABHJRisWD1S4JYWmGeKjZit5KmmZfyX.

Davidsson, E. (2013). *Hijacking America's mind on 9/11: Counterfeiting evidence*. Algora.

Davidsson, E. (2020). *America's betrayal confirmed. 9/11: Purpose, cover-up and impunity*. Toost Publishing.

Davis, I. (2019, May 6). The evisceration of Dr. Andrew Wakefield. *Iain Davis*. https://iaindavis.com/wakefield/.

Davis, I. (2021). *Pseudopandemic*. Independently published.

Demasi, M. (2023, September 20). Researchers alarmed to find DNA contamination in Pfizer vaccine. *Brownstone Institute*. https://brownstone.org/articles/researchers-alarmed-to-find-dna-contamination-in-pfizer-vaccine/.

Devlin, M. (2021). *Musical truth, volume 3*. aSys Publishing.

Digital Citizen. (2003, September 25). 9/11 official theory. Are you brainwashed? *Phil Taylor's Papers*. https://universityofleeds.github.io/philtaylorpapers/vp01eff8.html.

Doctors for Covid Ethics. (2023). *mRNA Vaccine Toxicity*. https://doctors4covidethics.org/mrna-vaccine-toxicity/.

Dolan, P., Hallsworth, M., Halpern, D., King, D., & Vlaev, I. (2010). *MINDSPACE: Influencing behaviour through public policy*. Cabinet Office and Institute for Government. https://www.instituteforgovernment.org.uk/sites/default/files/publications/MINDSPACE.pdf.

Dolgin, E. (2015). Business: The billion-dollar biotech. *Nature 522*, 26–28. https://www.nature.com/articles/522026a.

Domazet-Lošo, T. (2022). mRNA vaccines: Why is the biology of retroposition ignored? *genes*, *13*(5), Article 719. https://doi.org/10.3390/genes13050719.

Draper, E. S., Gallimore, I. D., Smith, L. K., Matthews, R. J., Fenton, A. C., Kurinczuk, J. J., Smith, P. W., & Manktelow, B. N. (2023). UK perinatal deaths for births from 1 January 2021 to 31 December 2021. *MBRRACE-UK*. https://timms.le.ac.uk/mbrrace-uk-perinatal-mortality/surveillance/.

Dyer, C. (2021). Pandemic preparedness: UK government kept coronavirus modelling secret. *BMJ*, *373*, Article n1501. https://doi.org/10.1136/bmj.n1501.

Dymond, G. (2020, December 13). Why this campaign of terror? *OffGuardian*. https://off-guardian.org/2020/12/13/why-this-campaign-of-terror/.

Engdahl, F. W. (2004). *A century of war. Anglo-American oil politics and the new world order* (2nd ed.). Pluto Press.

Engelbrecht, T., & Köhnlein, C. (2020, October 1). Covid-19 (excess) mortalities: Viral cause impossible—drugs with key role in about 200,000 extra deaths in Europe and the United States alone. *Real News Australia*. https://realnewsaustralia.com/2020/10/01/covid-19-excess-mortalities-viral-cause-impossible-drugs-with-key-role-in-about-200000-extra-deaths-in-europe-and-the-us-alone/.

EvidenceNotFear. (2020, April 20). *Communication and public engagement—Marc Van Ranst, Belgian Flu Commissioner*. https://evidencenotfear.com/communication-and-public-engagement-marc-van-ranst-belgian-flu-commissioner/.

Farber, C. (2020, December 3). Ten fatal errors: Scientists attack paper that established global PCR driven lockdown. *uncoverdc.com*. https://www.uncoverdc.com/2020/12/03/ten-fatal-errors-scientists-attack-paper-that-established-global-pcr-driven-lockdown/.

Festinger, L. (1957). *A theory of cognitive dissonance*. Stanford University Press.

Fitts, C. A., & Betts, C. (2022, December 1). Missing money part 2 [Video]. *CHD.TV*. https://live.childrenshealthdefense.org/chd-tv/shows/financial-rebellion-with-catherine-austin-fitts/the-missing-money-part-2/.

Fleetwood, J. (2023, April 7). Fauci says "there will absolutely be an outbreak of another pandemic": "It may be next year." *American Faith*. https://americanfaith.com/fauci-says-there-will-absolutely-be-an-outbreak-of-another-pandemic-it-may-be-next-year/.

Fleming, S. (2021, February 28). EU must prepare for "era of pandemics," von der Leyen says. *Financial Times*. https://www.ft.com/content/fba558ff-94a5-4c6c-b848-c8fd91b13c16.

Florko, N. (2020, September 28). New document reveals scope and structure of Operation Warp Speed and underscores vast military involvement. *STAT*. https://www.statnews.com/2020/09/28/operation-warp-speed-vast-military-involvement/.

Food and Drug Administration. (2020). *Briefing document. Vaccines and related biological products advisory committee meeting October 22, 2020*. https://www.fda.gov/media/142723/download.

Fumento, M. (2010, February 5). Why the WHO faked a pandemic. *Forbes Magazine*. https://web.archive.org/web/20201011163656if_/https://www.forbes.com/2010/02/05/world-health-organization-swine-flu-pandemic-opinions-contributors-michael-fumento.html.

Galison, P. (2004). Removing knowledge. *Critical Inquiry, 31*(1), 229–243. https://doi.org/10.1086/427309.

Ganser, D. (2005). *NATO's secret armies. Operation Gladio and terrorism in Western Europe*. Frank Cass.

Garde, D. (2017, January 10). Lavishly funded Moderna hits safety problems in bold bid to revolutionize medicine. *STAT*. https://www.statnews.com/2017/01/10/moderna-trouble-mrna/.

Gates, B. (2020b, December 22). These breakthroughs will make 2021 better than 2020. *GatesNotes*. https://www.gatesnotes.com/About-Bill-Gates/Year-in-Review-2020.

Gates, B. (2020, April 23). The first modern pandemic. *GatesNotes*. https://www.gatesnotes.com/Health/Pandemic-Innovation.

Gates, B., & Gates, M. (2021, January 27). The year global health went local. *GatesNotes*. https://www.gatesnotes.com/2021-Annual-Letter.

Gates, B. (2021, December 7). Reasons for optimism after a difficult year. *GatesNotes*. https://www.gatesnotes.com/About-Bill-Gates/Year-in-Review-2021.

Gatti, A. M., & Montanari, S. (2017). New quality-control investigations on vaccines: Micro- and nanocontamination. *International Journal of Vaccines and Vaccination*, 4(1), 7–14. https://doi.org/10.15406/ijvv.2017.04.00072.

Gilchrist, K. (2022, February 18). Bill Gates says Covid risks have "dramatically reduced" but another pandemic is coming. *CNBC*. https://www.cnbc.com/2022/02/18/bill-gates-covid-risks-have-reduced-but-another-pandemic-will-come.html.

Gillespie, J. (2023). The canaries in the human DNA mine. *International Journal of Vaccine Theory, Practice, and Research, 3*(1), 929–956. https://doi.org/10.56098/ijvtpr.v3i1.83.

Glaberman, M., & Faber, S. (2002). Back to the future: The continuing relevance of Marx. *Critique: Journal of Socialist Theory, 30*(1), 167–177. https://doi.org/10.1080/03017600508413479.

Goldsmith, C. S., Tatti, K. M., Ksiazek, T. G., Rollin, P. E., Comer, J. A., Lee, W. W., Rota, P. A., Bankamp, B., Bellini, W. J., & Zaki, S. R. (2004). Ultrastructural characterization of SARS coronavirus. *Emerging Infectious Diseases, 10*(2), 320–326. https://doi.org/10.3201/eid1002.030913.

Gøtzsche, P. (2013). *Medicines and organised crime: How Big Pharma has corrupted healthcare*. CRC Press.

Gourley, J. (2012). *The 9/11 Toronto report*. International Centre for 9/11 Studies.

Griffin, D. R. (2005). *The 9/11 Commission report: Omissions and distortions*. Olive Branch.

Griffin, D. R., & Scott, P. D. (Eds.). (2006). *9/11 and American empire: Intellectuals speak out*. Olive Branch.

Griffin, D. R., & Woodworth, E. (2018). *9/11 unmasked: An international review panel investigation*. Olive Branch.

Harari, Y. N. (2017, February 27). *Workplace automation and the "useless class"* [Video]. Carnegie Council for Ethics in International Affairs. https://www.carnegiecouncil.org/media/series/39/20170222-homo-deus-a-brief-history-of-tomorrow.

Harcourt, J., Tamin, A., Lu, X., Kamili, S., Sakthivel, S. K., Murray, J., Queen, K., Tao, Y., Paden, C. R., Zhang, J., Li, Y., Uehara, A., Wang, H., Goldsmith, C., Bullock, H. A., Wang, L., Whitaker, B., Lynch, B., Gautam, R., … Thornburg, N. J. (2020). Severe acute respiratory syndrome coronavirus 2 from patient with coronavirus disease, United States. *Emerging Infectious Diseases, 26*(6), 1266–1273. https://doi.org/10.3201/eid2606.200516.

Harradine, K. (2020, October 23). Why so many believe in the Covid cult. *TCW*. https://www.conservativewoman.co.uk/why-so-many-believe-in-the-covid-cult/.

Harsanyi, D. (2022, March 4). Ron DeSantis was entirely right to close the curtain on Covid theater. *New York Post*. https://nypost.com/2022/03/04/ron-desantis-was-right-to-close-the-curtain-on-covid-theater/.

Hatchard, G. (2023, September 1). Deaths up 14%. Births down 28%. Disability up 37%. Wake up, politicians! *TCW*. https://www.conservativewoman.co.uk/deaths-up-14-births-down-28-disability-up-37-wake-up-politicians/.

Hattersley, M., Brown, G. D. A., Michael, J., & Ludvig, E. A. (2022). Of tinfoil hats and thinking caps: Reasoning is more strongly related to implausible than plausible conspiracy beliefs. *Cognition, 218*, Article 104956. https://doi.org/10.1016/j.cognition.2021.104956.

Hayward, A. C., Fragaszy, E. B., Bermingham, A., Wang, L., Copas, A., Edmunds, W. J., Ferguson, N., Goonetilleke, N., Harvey, G., Kovar, J., Lim, M. S. C., McMichael, A., Millet, E. R. C., Nguyen-Van-Tam, J. S., Nazareth, I., Pebody, R., Tabassum, F., Watson, J. M., Wurie, F. B., Zambon, M., et al. (2014). Comparative community burden and severity of seasonal and pandemic influenza: Results of the flu watch cohort study. *The Lancet, 2*(6), 445–454. https://doi.org/10.1016/S2213-2600(14)70034-7.

Health and Human Services Department. (2020, April 15). Amendment to Declaration under the Public Readiness and Emergency Preparedness Act for Medical Countermeasures against COVID-19. *Federal Register*. https://www.federalregister.gov/documents/2020/04/15/2020-08040/amendment-to-declaration-under-the-public-readiness-and-emergency-preparedness-act-for-medical.

Hill, J. (2022, January 10). Researchers confirm highly variable vaccine batch toxicity despite VAERS data artifacts: Latypova. *James Hill MD's Newsletter*. https://hillmd.substack.com/p/researchers-confirm-highly-variable.

Hitler, A. (1939). *Mein Kampf* (J. Murphy, Trans.). Hurst and Blackett.

Hodgkinson, M. (2023, June 30). Contaminated vaccines – how much longer can the 'safe and effective' narrative survive? *TCW*. https://www.conservativewoman.co.uk/contaminated-vaccines-how-much-longer-can-the-safe-and-effective-narrative-survive/.

Hoffmann, S., Huntington, S. P., May, E. R., Neustadt, R. N., & Schelling, T. C. (1981). Vietnam reappraised. *International Security, 6*(1), 3–26. https://doi.org/10.2307/2538527.

Hoover, J. E. (1956, August). Communist "new look." *Elks Magazine*. https://www.metabunk.org/images/1956%20Elks%20Hoover%20OCR.pdf.

Hope-Simpson, R. E. (1992). *The transmission of epidemic influenza*. Springer.

Hopkins, C. J. (2021a, April 21). The Covidian cult (part II). *Consent Factory, Inc*. https://consentfactory.org/2021/04/21/the-covidian-cult-part-ii/.

Hopkins, C. J. (2021b, June 21). Manufacturing (new normal) "reality." *OffGuardian*. https://off-guardian.org/2021/06/21/manufacturing-new-normal-reality/.

Hopkins, C. J. (2021c, November 22). Pathologized totalitarianism 101. *Consent Factory, Inc*. https://consentfactory.org/2021/11/22/pathologized-totalitarianism-101/.

Howie, H., & Ressier, K. J. (2021). The neurobiology of trauma memory consolidation: Implications for preventing PTSD. In E. Vermetten, I. Frankova, L. Carmi, O. Chaban, & J. Zohar (Eds.), *Risk management of terrorism induced stress* (pp. 33–40). IOS Press.

Hudson, N. (2021, December 23). 20 lies. *PANDA*. https://www.pandata.org/20-lies/.

Hughes, D. A. (2020). 9/11 truth and the silence of the IR discipline. *Alternatives, 45*(2), 55–82. https://doi.org/10.1177/0304375419898334.

Hughes, D. A. (2021, October 12). Questions not asked: 9/11 and the academy [Video]. *UK Column*. https://www.ukcolumn.org/video/propaganda-and-the-911-global-war-on-terror-dr-david-hughes.

Hughes, D. A. (2022b, July 29). Wall Street, the Nazis, and the crimes of the deep state. *Propaganda in Focus*. https://propagandainfocus.com/wall-street-the-nazis-and-the-crimes-of-the-deep-state/.

Hughes, D. A. (2022c). What is in the so-called Covid-19 "vaccines"? Part 1: Evidence of a global crime against humanity. *International Journal of Vaccine Theory, Practice, and Research*, *2*(2), 455–586. https://doi.org/10.56098/ijvtpr.v2i2.52.

Hughes, D. A. (2022a). "Covid-19 vaccines" for children in the UK: A tale of establishment corruption. *International Journal of Vaccine Theory, Practice, and Research*, *2*(1), 209–247. https://doi.org/10.56098/ijvtpr.v2i1.35.

Hughes, D. A. (2023, April 14). We are in a global class war [Video]. Bitchute. https://www.bitchute.com/video/ZPHbyPe04Yc0/.

Hughes, D. A., Broudy, D., & Kyrie, V. (2023, February 22). Global class war and the politics of a hatchet job: A reply to John Waters. *The Solari Report*. https://constitution.solari.com/global-class-war-and-the-politics-of-a-hatchet-job-a-reply-to-john-waters/.

International Schiller Institute. (2021, May 25). *WHO director denounces "scandalous" vaccine inequity, warns the pandemic is not over*. https://schillerinstitute.com/blog/2021/05/27/who-dir-denounces-scandalous-vaccine-inequity-warns-the-pandemic-is-not-over/.

Ioannidis, J. P. A. (2020a, March 17). A fiasco in the making? As the coronavirus pandemic takes hold, we are making decisions without reliable data. *STAT*. https://www.statnews.com/2020/03/17/a-fiasco-in-the-making-as-the-coronavirus-pandemic-takes-hold-we-are-making-decisions-without-reliable-data/.

Ioannidis, J. P. A. (2020b). The infection fatality rate of Covid-19 inferred from seroprevalence data. Preprint retrieved from https://www.medrxiv.org/content/https://doi.org/10.1101/2020.05.13.20101253v2.

Ioannidis, J. P. A. (2021). Infection fatality rate of Covid-19 inferred from seroprevalence data. *Bulletin of the World Health Organisation, 99*, 19–33. https://doi.org/10.2471/BLT.20.265892.

Jones, W. (2023, March 13). mRNA vaccine contamination much worse than thought: Jabs "up to 35%" DNA that turns human cells into long-term spike protein factories. *The Daily Sceptic*. https://dailysceptic.org/2023/03/13/mrna-vaccine-contamination-much-worse-than-thought-jabs-up-to-35-dna-that-turns-human-cells-into-long-term-spike-protein-factories/.

Kean, T. H., & Hamilton, L. H. (2004). *The 9/11 Commission report*. National Commission on Terrorist Attacks upon the United States.

Keil, U. (2010, January 26). Introductory statement to Social, Health and Family Affairs Committee of the Parliamentary Assembly of the Council of Europe hearing: The handling of the H1N1 pandemic: More transparency needed? Retrieved June 13, 2023, from http://assembly.coe.int/CommitteeDocs/2010/20100126_ContributionKeil.pdf.

Kendrick, M. (2022, September 14). Covid-19 – so many questions, so few real answers. *Dr. Malcolm Kendrick*. https://drmalcolmkendrick.org/2022/09/14/covid19-so-many-questions-so-few-real-answers/.

Kennedy Jr., R.F. (2021). *The real Anthony Fauci. Bill Gates, big pharma, and the global war on democracy and public health*. Skyhorse.

Kheriaty, A. (2022, May 24). The WHO treaty is tied to a global digital passport and ID system. *Brownstone Institute*. https://brownstone.org/articles/who-treaty-tied-to-digital-passport-id-system/.

Kim, J., Chung, Y., Jo, H. J., Lee, N., Kim, M. S., Woo, S. H., Park, S., Kim, J. W., Kim, H. M., & Han, M. (2020). Identification of coronavirus isolated from a patient in Korea with Covid-19. *Osang Public Health and Research Perspectives, 11*(1), 3–7. https://doi.org/10.24171/j.phrp.2020.11.1.02.

Kingston, K. (2022, October 12). Part 1: Dismantling Covid-19 deceptions: The "novel" coronavirus & "spike protein." *The Kingston Report*. https://karenkingston.substack.com/p/part-1-dismantling-the-the-deceptions.

Kingston, K. (2023, January 3). How Florida can bring criminal charges against Pfizer and the FDA under Title 46 Ch. 790. *The Kingston Report*. https://karenkingston.substack.com/p/how-florida-can-bring-criminal-charges.

Kirsch, S. (2022a, May 5). New UK Government data shows the Covid vaccines kill more people than they save. *Steve Kirsch's Newsletter*. https://kirschsubstack.com/p/uk-government-data-shows-nobody-should.

Kirsch, S. (2022b, August 1). Want to know what's inside the vaccine vials? *Steve Kirsch's Newsletter*. https://kirschsubstack.com/p/want-to-know-whats-inside-the-vaccine.

Knightly, K. (2021, September 11). Covid, 9/11 & forever war. From the war on terror to the "pandemic," the elite are constructing fake threats to start wars that never have to end. *OffGuardian*. https://off-guardian.org/2021/09/13/covid-9-11-forever-war/.

Knightly, K. (2022, April 19). "Pandemic treaty" will hand WHO keys to global government. *OffGuardian*. https://off-guardian.org/2022/04/19/pandemic-treaty-will-hand-who-keys-to-global-government/.

Knightly, K. (2023, March 24). 40 facts you need to know: The real story of "Covid." *OffGuardian*. https://off-guardian.org/2023/03/24/40-facts-you-need-to-know-the-real-story-of-covid/.

Kogon, R. (2023, September 23). German whistleblower finds DNA contamination up to 354 times recommended limit in BioNTech-Pfizer vaccine. *The Daily Sceptic*. https://dailysceptic.org/2023/09/23/german-whistleblower-finds-dna-contamination-up-to-354-times-recommended-limit-in-biontech-pfizer-vaccine/.

Kottasová, I., Cassidy, A., Diab, S., & Kolirin, L. (2022, April 12). Boris Johnson fined by police over lockdown-breaking parties at UK government premises. *CNN*. https://edition.cnn.com/2022/04/12/uk/boris-johnson-uk-pm-coronavirus-fine-intl-gbr/index.html.

Kyrie, V., & Broudy, D. (2022a, May 22). Hiding in plain sight: Technocratic tyranny behind a medical mask. *Propaganda in Focus*. https://www.propagandainfocus.com/hiding-in-plain-sight-technocratic-tyranny-behind-a-medical-mask/.

Kyrie, V., & Broudy, D. (2022b, September 22). The Covid-19 concoction: A recipe for successful psychological operations. *Propaganda in Focus*. https://propagandainfocus.com/the-covid-19-concoction-a-recipe-for-successful-psychological-operations/.

Kyrie, V., & Broudy, D. (2022c). Cyborgs R us: The bio-nano panopticon of injected bodies? *International Journal of Vaccine Theory, Practice, and Research*, 2(2), 355–383. https://doi.org/10.56098/ijvtpr.v2i2.49.

Latham, J. (2017, December 4). Gates Foundation hired PR firm to manipulate UN over gene drives. *Independent Science News*. https://www.independentsciencenews.org/news/gates-foundation-hired-pr-firm-to-manipulate-un-over-gene-drives/.

Latypova, S. (2022a, December 2). Intent to harm – Evidence of the conspiracy to commit mass murder by the US DOD, HHS, pharma cartel [Video]. *Bitchute*. https://www.bitchute.com/video/8ftbShzrkjl9/.

Latypova, S. (2022b, December 13). Intent to harm. *Due Diligence and Art*. https://sashalatypova.substack.com/p/intent-to-harm.

Lena, T. (2023). How real is our reality? An old interview with ex agent John Stockwell. *Tessa Fights Robots*. https://tessa.substack.com/p/john-stockwell-old-interview.

Lewandowsky, S., Oberauer, K., & Gignac, G. E. (2013). NASA faked the moon landing—therefore, (climate) science is a hoax: An anatomy of the motivated rejection of science. *Psychological Science, 24*(5), 622–634. https://doi.org/10.1177/0956797612457686.

de Lint, W. B. (2021). *Blurring Intelligence Crime: A Critical Forensics*. Springer.

Lovett, S. (2021, February 25). Not a single case of flu detected by Public Health England this year as Covid restrictions suppress virus. *The Independent*. https://www.independent.co.uk/news/health/flu-cases-covid-england-phe-latest-b1805124.html.

Lupkin, S. (2020, September 29). How Operation Warp Speed's big vaccine contracts could stay secret. *NPR*. https://www.npr.org/sections/health-shots/2020/09/29/917899357/how-operation-warp-speeds-big-vaccine-contracts-could-stay-secret?t=1601459337006.

Macmichael, S. (2021, April 2). Cyclist uses bike to smash Covid conspiracy theorist's car window. *Road.cc* https://road.cc/content/news/cyclist-may-be-charged-over-covid-conspiracy-theorist-row-282273.

Magnetgate 3. (2021, June 1). *Bitchute* [Video]. https://www.bitchute.com/video/rfFai2Bpkgpi/.

Mangiaracina, E. (2022, December 2). Australian doctor finds chips, "self-assembling" structures forming in Pfizer vaccine contents. *LifeSite News*. https://www.lifesitenews.com/news/australian-doctor-finds-chips-self-assembling-structures-forming-in-pfizer-vaccine-contents/.

Marcus, L. (1974). The real CIA—the Rockefellers' fascist establishment, a polemic. *The Campaigner, 7*(6), 5–34.

Massey, C. (2022). FOIs reveal that health/science institutions around the world (211 and counting!) have no record of SARS-COV-2 isolation/purification, anywhere, ever. *Fluoride Free Peel*. https://www.fluoridefreepeel.ca/fois-reveal-that-health-science-institutions-around-the-world-have-no-record-of-sars-cov-2-isolation-purification/.

Matsuyama, S. N. N., Shirato, K., Kawase, M., Saito, S., Takayama, I., Nagata, N., Sekizuka, T., Katoh, H., Kato, F., Sakata, M., Tahara, M., Kutsuna, S., Ohmagari, N., Kuroda, M., Suzuki, T., Kageyama, T., & Takeda, M. (2020). Enhanced isolation of SARS-CoV-2 by TMPRSS2-expressing cells. *PNAS, 117*(13), 7001–7003. https://doi.org/10.1073/pnas.2002589117.

Matters, R. (2020, September 19). A bigger perspective highlights Covid-19 scam and fraudulent data. *NewBraveWorld*. https://www.newbraveworld.org/a-bigger-perspective-highlights-covid-19-scam-and-fraudulent-data/.

McCrae, N. (2023, March 24). Did Boris Johnson fake his Covid-19 illness? *21st Century Wire*. https://21stcenturywire.com/2023/03/24/did-boris-johnson-fake-his-covid-19-illness/.

McDonald, M. (2022). *United States of Fear*. Bombardier Books.

McKernan, K., Helbert, Y., Kane, L. T., & McClaughlin, S. (2023). Sequencing of bivalent Moderna and Pfizer mRNA vaccines reveals nanogram to microgram quantities of expression vector dsDNA per dose. Preprint retrieved from https://doi.org/10.31219/osf.io/b9t7m.

McLovincraft, H.C. (2020). Did CIA director William Casey really say "we'll know our disinformation program is complete when everything the American public believes is false"? *Hellbound and Down*. https://hellboundanddown.com/2020/12/26/did-cia-director-william-casey-really-say-well-know-our-disinformation-program-is-complete-when-everything-the-american-public-believes-is-false/.

Meadows, D. H., Meadows, D. L., Randers, J., & Behrens III, W. W. (1972). *The Limits to Growth*. Potomac Associates.

Medicines and Healthcare products Regulatory Agency. (2019). *Yellow card: please help to reverse the decline in reporting of suspected adverse drug reactions*. https://www.gov.uk/drug-safety-update/yellow-card-please-help-to-reverse-the-decline-in-reporting-of-suspected-adverse-drug-reactions.

Medicines and Healthcare products Regulatory Agency. (n.d.). *COVID-19 vaccine analysis overview* . https://yellowcard.ukcolumn.org/yellow-card-reports.

Meerloo, J. A. (1956). *The rape of the mind. The psychology of thought control, menticide, and brainwashing*. World Publishing Company.

Melton, H. K., & Wallace, R. (2009). *The official CIA manual of trickery and deception*. William Morrow.

Menage, J. (2020, October 22). Re: Covid-19: Ignoring the knowns. *BMJ*, *371*, Article m3979. https://doi.org/10.1136/bmj.m3979.

Meserve, J. (2003, February 11). Duct tape sales rise amid terror fears. *CNN*. http://edition.cnn.com/2003/US/02/11/emergency.supplies/.

Meyssan, T. (2002). *9/11: The big lie*. Carnot Publishing.

Mike Pompeo we're in a live exercise here. (2020, March 20). *C-SPAN*. https://www.c-span.org/video/?c4875167/user-clip-mike-pompeo-live-exercise.

Mikovits, J., & Heckenlively, K. (2020). *Plague of corruption*. Skyhorse.

Minnicino, M. (1974). Low intensity operations: The Reesian theory of war. *The Campaigner, 7*(6), 37–55.

Myers, F. (2021, June 14). The G7 and the arrogance of Covid theatre. *Spiked!* https://www.spiked-online.com/2021/06/14/the-g7-and-the-arrogance-of-covid-theatre/.

Nagase, D. (2022, April 18). Dr. Nagase reviews images from COVID vaccines, shows no "elements of life." *Western Standard*. https://rumble.com/v11go0d-watch-dr.-nagase-reviews-images-from-covid-vaccines-shows-no-elements-of-li.html.

Naked Emperor. (2023, March 4). Number of births in England falls by 11.9% in 2022. *The Daily Sceptic*. https://dailysceptic.org/2023/03/04/number-of-births-in-england-falls-by-11-9-in-2022/.

Nance, K. D., & Meier, J. L. (2021). Modifications in an emergency: The role of N1-methylpseudouridine in Covid-19 vaccines. *ACS Central Science, 7*(5), 748–756. https://doi.org/10.1021/acscentsci.1c00197.

National Security Council (1974). *National security study memorandum 200*. https://pdf.usaid.gov/pdf_docs/PCAAB500.pdf.

National Institutes of Health. (2008, August 19). Bacterial pneumonia caused most deaths in 1918 influenza pandemic. https://www.nih.gov/news-events/news-releases/bacterial-pneumonia-caused-most-deaths-1918-influenza-pandemic.

Neil, M., Engler, J., and Fenton, N. (2023, May 11). Sensors set to off. *Where Are The Numbers?* https://wherearethenumbers.substack.com/p/sensors-set-to-off.

Nolte-'t Hoen, E., Cremer, T., Gallo, R. C., & Margolis, L. B. (2016). Extracellular vesicles and viruses: Are they close relatives? *PNAS*, *113*(33), 9155-9161. https://doi.org/10.1073/pnas.1605146113.

O'Toole, T., Mair, M., & Inglesby, T. V. (2002). Shining light on "dark winter." *Clinical Infectious Diseases, 34*(7), 972–983. https://doi.org/10.1086/339909.

Office for National Statistics. (2021). *Average age of those who had died with Covid-19*. https://archive.ph/uFLe5#selection-713.1-713.48.

Oller, J., & Santiago, D. (2022). All cause mortality and Covid-19 injections: Evidence from 28 weeks of Public Health England Covid-19 "vaccine surveillance reports. *International Journal of Vaccine Theory, Practice, and Research*, *2*(2), 301–319. https://doi.org/10.56098/ijvtpr.v2i2.42.

OpenVAERS. (n.d.). *VAERS Covid vaccine adverse event reports*. Retrieved June 17, 2023, from https://openvaers.com/covid-data.

Park, W. B., Kwon, N. -J., Choi, S. –J., Kang, C. K., Choe, P. G., Kim, J. Y., Yun, J. Y, Lee, G. -W., Seong, M. -W., Kim, N. J., Seo, J. -S., & Oh, M. -D. (2020). Virus isolation from the first patient with SARS-CoV-2 in Korea. *Journal of Korean Medical Science*, *35*(7), Article e84. https://doi.org/10.3346/jkms.2020.35.e84.

Parry, P. I., Lefringhausen, A., Turni, C., Neil, C. J., Cosford, R., Hudson, N. J., & Gillespie, J. (2023). "Spikeopathy": COVID-19 spike protein is pathogenic, from both virus and vaccine mRNA. *Biomedicines*, *11*(8), Article 2287. https://doi.org/10.3390/biomedicines11082287.

Pezzullo, A. M., Axfors, C., Contopoulos-Ioannidis, D. G., Apostolatos, A., & Ioannidis, J. P. A. (2023). Age-stratified infection fatality rate of Covid-19 in the non-elderly population. *Environmental Research*, *216*(3), Article 114655. https://doi.org/10.1016/j.envres.2022.114655.

Pfeiffer, M.B. (2022, November 28). The missing babies of Europe. *RESCUE with Michael Capuzzo*. https://rescue.substack.com/p/the-missing-babies-of-europe?utm_campaign=post.

Pijl, K. van der. (2022). *States of emergency. Keeping the global population in check*. Clarity Press.

Ponton, F. (2023a, February 1). Are Covid-19 "vaccines" a military biodefense response gone terribly wrong? *21st Century Wire*. https://21stcenturywire.com/2023/02/01/covid-19-vaccine-a-military-response-to-a-public-health-threat/.

Ponton, F. (2023b, March 8). NATO's Trojan horse behind Europe's Covid-19 response—part 1: Vaccinating Europe with a military experimental biodefense countermeasure. *21st Century Wire*. https://21stcenturywire.com/2023/03/08/nato-trojan-horse-behind-europes-covid-19-response-part-1-vaccinating-europe-with-a-military-experimental-biodefense-countermeasure/.

Public Health England. (2020). *Weekly coronavirus disease 2019 (Covid-19) surveillance report, Week 40*. https://assets.publishing.service.gov.uk/government/uploads/system/uploads/attachment_data/file/923668/Weekly_COVID19_Surveillance_Report_week_40.pdf.

Public Health England. (2021a). *Emergency department syndromic surveillance system: England*. https://assets.publishing.service.gov.uk/government/uploads/system/uploads/attachment_data/file/950352/EDSSSBulletin2020wk53.pdf.

Public Health England. (2021b). *Weekly national influenza and Covid-19 surveillance report, Week 8*. https://assets.publishing.service.gov.uk/government/uploads/system/uploads/attachment_data/file/964754/Weekly_Flu_and_COVID-19_report_w8.pdf.

Public Health England. (2021c). *Reply to FOIA request re: isolation of SARS-COV-2*. https://www.whatdotheyknow.com/request/isolation_of_sars_cov_2_covid_19.

Qin, Z., Bouteau, A., Herbst, C., & Igyártó, B. Z. (2022). Pre-exposure to mRNA-LNP inhibits adaptive immune responses and alters innate immune fitness in an inheritable fashion. *PLOS Pathogens, 18*(9), e1010830. https://doi.org/10.1371/journal.ppat.1010830.

Rancourt, D., Baudin, M., & Mercier, J. (2021). *Nature of the Covid-era public health disaster in the USA, from all-cause mortality and socio-geo-economic and climatic data*. https://denisrancourt.ca/uploads_entries/1635189453861_USA%20ACM%20into%202021%20-%20article----12d.pdf.

Rancourt, D., Baudin, M., Hickey, J., & Mercier, J. (2023, September 23). COVID-19 vaccine-associated mortality in the Southern Hemisphere. *CORRELATION*. https://correlation-canada.org/covid-19-vaccine-associated-mortality-in-the-southern-hemisphere/.

Rockefeller Foundation and Global Business Network. (2010, May). *Scenarios for the future of technology and international development*. https://archive.org/details/scenarios-for-the-future-of-technology-and-international-development-rockefeller-foundation-2010.

Ruechel, J. (2021, July 17). The emperor has no clothes: Finding the courage to break the spell. https://www.juliusruechel.com/2021/07/the-emperor-has-no-clothes-finding.html.

Roscoe, M. (2022, July 20). Podcaster and Hollywood actor spark mass Twitter debate over "the Great Reset." *EuroWeekly News*. https://euroweeklynews.com/2022/07/20/hollywood-actor-twitter-debate-the-great-reset/.

Russell, B. (2009). *Unpopular essays*. Routledge.

Sabra, R., & Branch, R. A. (1990). Amphotericin B nephrotoxicity. *Drug Safety, 5*(2), 94–108. https://doi.org/10.2165/00002018-199005020-00003.

Santiago, D. (2022a). A partial answer to the question posed by David A. Hughes, Ph.D., in the article: "What is in the so-called Covid-19 'vaccines'? Part 1: evidence of a global crime against humanity." *International Journal of Vaccine Theory, Practice, and Research*, *2*(2), 587–594. https://doi.org/10.56098/ijvtpr.v2i2.56.

Santiago, D. (2022b). Playing Russian roulette with every Covid-19 injection: The deadly global game. *International Journal of Vaccine Theory, Practice, and Research*, *2*(2), 619–650. https://doi.org/10.56098/ijvtpr.v2i2.36.

Santiago, D., & Oller, J. (2023). Abnormal clots and all-cause mortality during the pandemic experiment: Five doses of Covid-19 vaccine are evidently lethal to nearly all medicare participants." *International Journal of Vaccine Theory, Practice, and Research*, *3*(1), 847–890. https://doi.org/10.56098/ijvtpr.v3i1.73.

Sarlangue, G., Devilleger, J., Trillaud, P., Fouchet, S., Taillasson, L., & Catteau, G. (2021, November 30). *Project Bluetooth Expérience X*. http://www.nakim.org/israel-forums/download.php?id=920.

Schmeling, M., Manniche, V., & Hansen, P. R. (2023, March 30). Batch-dependent safety of the BNT162b2 mRNA COVID-19 vaccine. *European Journal of Clinical Investigation*, *53*(8), Article 13998. https://doi.org/10.1111/eci.13998.

Schraer, R. (2020, July 7). Coronavirus: majority testing positive have no symptoms. *BBC News*. https://www.bbc.co.uk/news/health-53320155.

Schwab, K., & Malleret, T. (2020). *Covid 19: The Great Reset*. World Economic Forum.

Scott, P. D. (2017). *The American deep state. Big money, Big Oil, and the struggle for U.S. democracy*. Rowman and Littlefield.

Scott, B. (2021a, May 2). We are all Pavlov's dogs now. *UK Column*. https://www.ukcolumn.org/article/we-are-all-pavlovs-dogs-now.

Scott, B. (2021b, October 13). Beyond a state of fear: Menticide and schizogenesis. *Borderline*. https://dr-bruce-scott.com/2021/10/13/beyond-a-state-of-fear-menticide-and-schizogenesis/.

Scott, P. D., & Marshall, J. (1991). *Cocaine politics: Drugs, armies, and the CIA in Central America*. University of California Press.

Shayler, D. (2022). *From 9/11 to 'Covid-19': Fakery & the war waged on mankind*. https://www.bookofthelaw.org/downloads/911_to_covid19_fakery_and_the_war_waged_on_mankind.pdf.

Simpson, C. (1994). *Science of coercion: Communication research and psychological warfare, 1945–1960*. Oxford University Press.

Smith, L. (2020, May 16). Trump compares coronavirus vaccine search to the Manhattan Project. *Newsweek*. https://www.newsweek.com/trump-coronavirus-vaccine-operation-1504551.

Speicher, D. J., Rose, J., Gutschi, L. M., Wiseman, D. M., & McKernan, K. (2023). DNA fragments detected in monovalent and bivalent Pfizer/BioNTech and Moderna modRNA COVID-19 vaccines from Ontario, Canada: Exploratory dose response relationship with serious adverse events. Preprint retrieved from https://osf.io/preprints/osf/mjc97.

Steinbuch, Y. (2020, December 29). WHO warns Covid-19 Pandemic is "not necessarily the big one." *New York Post*. https://nypost.com/2020/12/29/who-warns-covid-19-pandemic-is-not-necessarily-the-big-one/.

Sunde, M. G. (2021, January 17). The unexpected case of the disappearing flu. *Medium*. https://medium.com/illumination-curated/the-unexpected-case-of-the-disappearing-flu-64fd1fa5e909.

Swami, V., Pietschnig, J., Tran, U. S., Nader, I. W., Stieger, S., & Voracek, M. (2013). Lunar lies: The impact of informational framing and individual differences in shaping conspiracist beliefs about the moon landings. *Applied Cognitive Psychology, 27*(1), 71–80. https://doi.org/10.1002/acp.2873

Swiss Policy Research. (2022, June). *Covid vaccines and fertility (2022)*. https://swprs.org/covid-vaccines-and-fertility/.

Taylor, M. (2023). *Bluetooth deep dive anyone? Calling all monkey wrenchers!* [Video]. Bitchute. https://www.bitchute.com/video/7G4kHfIfAkKr/.

UK Government. (2021). *New global partnership launched to fight future pandemics*. https://www.gov.uk/government/news/new-global-partnership-launched-to-fight-future-pandemics.

UK Health Security Agency. (2022). *Weekly national influenza and Covid-19 surveillance report, week 27*. https://assets.publishing.service.gov.uk/government/uploads/system/uploads/attachment_data/file/1088929/Weekly_Flu_and_COVID-19_report_w27.pdf.

UK Health Security Agency. (2023). *COVID-19: non-pharmaceutical interventions to reduce transmission*. https://www.gov.uk/government/publications/covid-19-non-pharmaceutical-interventions-to-reduce-transmission.

UNIT. (2022). *Project CUNIT-2–112Y6580 Qualitative Evaluation of Inclusions In Moderna, AstraZeneca and Pfizer Covid-19 vaccines*. http://www.ukcitizen2021.org/Case_Briefing_Document_and_lab_report_Ref_AUC_101_Report%20.pdf.

United Nations. (2020). *Declare war on this virus—U.N. chief on the coronavirus COVID-19 (13 March 2020)*. https://www.unon.org/file/394.

Vaccines Education Working Group. (2022). *Collection of Preliminary Findings*. https://www.aerzte-fuer-aufklaerung.de/wp-content/uploads/2022/07/Sammlung_erster_Ergebnisse_der_AG_Impfstoffe_Aufkla%CC%88rung_20220706.pdf.

Valentine, D. (2017). *The CIA as organized crime*. Clarity Press.

Vanden Bossche, G. (2021, March 6). *To all authorities, scientists and experts around the world, to whom this concerns: The entire world population*. https://mcusercontent.com/92561d6dedb66a43fe9a6548f/files/bead7203-0798-4ac8-abe2-076208015556/Public_health_emergency_of_international_concert_Geert_Vanden_Bossche.01.pdf.

Watt, K. (2023, November 8). Sasha Latypova and Katherine Watt discussing non-regulation of non-medicines known as "vaccines," and other US military biochemical weapons. *Bailiwick News*. https://bailiwicknews.substack.com/p/sasha-latypova-and-katherine-watt.

Webb, W. (2020, October 6). Operation Warp Speed is using a CIA-linked contractor to keep Covid-19 vaccine contracts secret. *The Last American Vagabond*. https://www.thelastamericanvagabond.com/operation-warp-speed-is-using-a-cia-linked-contractor-to-keep-covid-19-vaccine-contracts-secret/.

White House. (2022, September 12). *Executive order on advancing biotechnology and biomanufacturing innovation for a sustainable, safe, and secure American bioeconomy*. https://www.whitehouse.gov/briefing-room/presidential-actions/2022/09/12/executive-order-on-advancing-biotechnology-and-biomanufacturing-innovation-for-a-sustainable-safe-and-secure-american-bioeconomy/.

Wilford, H. (2008). *The mighty Wurlitzer: How the CIA played America*. Harvard University Press.

Wilson, R. (2022, January 11). Dr Mike Yeadon: The variability in serious adverse events by vaccine lot is the "calibration of a killing weapon." *Daily Exposé*. https://expose-news.com/2022/01/11/mike-yeadon-the-variability-in-serious-adverse-events/.

Wodarg, W., Baselga, F. A., Ayva, L., Bajen, A. C., Czinege, I., Flynn, P., Grozdanova, D., Hancock, M., Huss, J. A., Marquet, B., McCafferty, C. A., Ohlsson, C., Ünal, M., & Volonte, L. (2009, December 18). *Faked pandemics—a threat for health. Motion for a recommendation*. Council of Europe Parliamentary Assembly. http://whale.to/vaccine/EDOC12110.pdf.

Wood, J. (2011). *Where did the Towers go? Evidence of Directed Free-energy Technology on 9/11*. The New Investigation.

Wood, P. (2018). *Technocracy: The hard road to world order*. Coherent Publishing.

World Council for Health (2023, October 10). *WCH Expert Panel Finds Cancer-Promoting DNA Contamination in Covid-19 Vaccines*. https://worldcouncilforhealth.org/news/news-releases/dna-contamination-covid-19-vaccines/.

World Health Organisation. (n.d.-a). *VigiAccess*. Retrieved June 17, 2023, from https://vigiaccess.org/.

World Health Organisation. (n.d.-b). *Influenza laboratory surveillance information*. Retrieved June 17, 2023, from https://app.powerbi.com/view?r=eyJrIjoiZTkyODcyOTEtZjA5YS00ZmI0LWFkZGUtODIxNGI5OTE3YjM0IiwidCI6ImY2MTBjMGI3LWJkMjQtNGIzOS04MTBiLTNkYzI4MGFmYjU5MCIsImMiOjh9.

World Health Organisation. (n.d.-c). Coronavirus (COVID-19) Dashboard: Cumulative confirmed COVID-19 cases per million people . Retrieved

December 23, 2023, from https://ourworldindata.org/explorers/coronavirus-data-explorer?tab=map&facet=none&country=IND~USA~GBR~CAN~DEU~FRA&hideControls=true&Interval=Cumulative&Relative+to+Population=true&Color+by+test+positivity=false&Metric=Confirmed+cases.

World Health Organisation. (2019a). *Non-pharmaceutical public health measures for mitigating the risk and impact of epidemic and pandemic influenza*. https://apps.who.int/iris/bitstream/handle/10665/329438/9789241516839-eng.pdf?ua=1.

World Health Organisation. (2019b, March 11). *WHO launches new global influenza strategy*. https://www.who.int/news/item/11-03-2019-who-launches-new-global-influenza-strategy.

World Health Organisation. (2020, January 21). *Novel coronavirus (2019-nCoV) situation report—1*. https://apps.who.int/iris/bitstream/handle/10665/330760/nCoVsitrep21Jan2020-eng.pdf.

World Health Organisation. (2021). *FluNet Summary*. https://www.who.int/influenza/gisrs_laboratory/updates/flunet_globalviruscirculation_20210212.pdf?ua=1.

Yeadon, M. (2023, March 22). Why I don't believe there ever was a Covid virus. *TCW*. https://www.conservativewoman.co.uk/why-i-dont-believe-there-ever-was-a-covid-virus/.

Young, R. O. (2021, February 5). *Scanning & transmission electron microscopy reveals graphene oxide and parasites in CoV-19 vaccines*. https://www.drrobertyoung.com/post/transmission-electron-microscopy-reveals-graphene-oxide-in-cov-19-vaccines.

Zaks, T. (n.d.). The disease-eradicating potential of gene editing [Video]. *TEDx*. https://www.ted.com/talks/tal_zaks_the_disease_eradicating_potential_of_gene_editing.

Zarembka, P. (Ed.). (2008). *The hidden history of 9/11*. Seven Stories.

Zhou, P., Yang, X.-L., Wang, X.-G., Hu, B., Zhang, L., Zhang, W., Si, H.-R., Zhu, Y., Li, B., Huang, C.-L., Chen, H.-D., Chen, J., Luo, Y., Guo, H., Jiang, R.-D., Liu, M.-Q., Chen, Y., Shen, X.-R., Wang, X., … Shi, Z.-L. (2020). A pneumonia outbreak associated with a new coronavirus of probable bat origin. *Nature, 579*, 270–273. https://doi.org/10.1038/s41586-020-2012-7.

Zhu, N., Zhang, D., Wang, W., Li, X., Yang, B., Song, J., Zhao, X., Huang, B., Shi, W., Lu, R., Niu, P., Zhan, F., Ma, X., Wang, D., Xu, W., Wu, G., Gao, G. F., & Tan, W. (2020). A novel coronavirus from patients with pneumonia in China, 2019. *The New England Journal of Medicine, 382*, 727–733. https://doi.org/10.1056/NEJMoa2001017.

CHAPTER 7

Mass Paranoia and Hysteria: Turning Society Against Itself

In keeping with totalitarianism, Covid-era psychological warfare worked to turn people against one another, to prevent them from uniting against their oppressors. Mass paranoia was inculcated through the lie that "anyone can spread it." Guilt was weaponised to blame and shame those not following the "rules" and "protecting others." Mask mandates segregated society. Dissenters were scapegoated. A new form of hate speech was introduced: "anti-maskers," "anti-vaxxers," etc. Members of the public were encouraged to police one another. The public was primed for violence against dissenters misleadingly framed as "fringe." The "pandemic of the unvaccinated" myth styled the outgroup as vectors of disease, like Jews in Nazi propaganda. The "vaccinated" were turned on the "unvaccinated" through mechanisms of blame, medicalised apartheid, incitement of hatred by the media, and lies that hospitals were filling up with "unvaccinated" patients. Society is now divided between those who can see through psychological operations and those who cannot.

The Production of Mass Paranoia

Tavistock's John Rawlings Rees was inspired by British imperialist methods that enabled limited regular military forces to maintain control over foreign populations that were, in principle, capable of defeating them. This required finding sociological and psychological means of dividing the population against itself, so that the regular military forces

D. A. Hughes, *"Covid-19," Psychological Operations, and the War for Technocracy*, https://doi.org/10.1007/978-3-031-41850-1_7

never faced more than a hard core of resistance fighters (Marcus, 1974, p. 14). Similar means can be used against domestic populations. According to Versluis (2006, p. 143), for instance, "The totalitarian system is predicated upon paranoia and division [...] Society turns on itself, urged on by the ruling authorities. The effect of such a collective psychosis is to strengthen the power of the authorities [...]." Similar principles were followed by the "Covid-19" operation.

"Anyone Can Spread It"

The first step in turning society against itself was to create mass paranoia (extreme irrational mistrust) by terrorising the public into believing that *anyone* can be a vector of deadly disease. Thus, in late March and early April of 2020, UK Government/NHS posters urged, "ANYONE CAN GET IT. ANYONE CAN SPREAD IT" and "ACT LIKE YOU'VE GOT IT. ANYONE CAN SPREAD IT." The public was instructed not to come within two metres of another human being and soon people were swerving to avoid one another, displaying what Lacter (2007), in the context of ritual abuse victims, calls a "global distrust of humanity." Kidd and Ratcliffe (2020) observed at the time: "People we might once have passed on the street with a smile or a nod are now experienced as potential disease carriers, to be met with suspicion or avoided."

Kevin Corbett (2020) notes that the government's list of "very generic and non-Covid-specific symptoms," which includes such mundane symptoms as a sore throat, temperature, and dry cough, "weaponises the everyday experience of people and instils contagion-fear, loathing and ultimately paranoia." If "anyone can spread it," then asymptomatic transmission, too, poses an existential threat. Inculcating paranoia was the name of the game: "Almost every decision now comes with a paranoid new calculus: How do you minimize your risk of contracting or spreading COVID-19?" (Gates & Gates, 2021).

"ANYONE CAN SPREAD IT" propaganda in the UK was put out in late March 2020. Yet, on April 2, 2020, the WHO was still claiming that there was no evidence of asymptomatic transmission, according to later testimony provided by Health Secretary Hancock, and there was "a global scientific consensus" at that time that "coronaviruses do not transmit from people who don't have symptoms" (Science and Technology Committee and Health and Social Care Committee, 2021, p. 21). On July 5, 2020, Hancock claimed that in the month leading up to

April 16 (when blanket testing of all patients discharged from hospital was introduced), "it was not known about the asymptomatic transmission of this disease, because no other coronavirus transmits asymptomatically" ("Hancock: Asymptomatic coronavirus transmission 'was not known,'" 2020). If there was no knowledge of asymptomatic transmission of "SARS-CoV-2" as late as mid-April, why was UK Government/NHS propaganda premised on that very concept? The only plausible answer is to create mass paranoia and hysteria.

There is a connection in the epidemiology literature between asymptomatic transmission and justification of quarantine measures. For example, "the use of quarantine will be most beneficial only when there is significant asymptomatic transmission [...]" (Day et al., 2006, p. 484). Or "If asymptomatic individuals transmit at a rate that is at least 20% that of symptomatic individuals, quarantine is always more effective" (Podder et al., 2007, p. 185). In the "Covid-19" context, the idea of asymptomatic transmission is needed to justify "lockdowns," for if the virus were only (or predominantly) spread by those with symptoms, there would be no need to place the whole of society under "a form of house arrest" (Sumption, 2020, p. 1). As in the past, the sick could isolate, leaving the rest of society to get on with life.

The WHO's Maria Van Kerkhove claimed in a press briefing on June 8, 2020, that asymptomatic transmission of "SARS-CoV-2" is "very rare" (cited in Perez, 2020). The following day, however, having apparently been disciplined for going off message, she changed her position to "there is a subset of people who don't develop symptoms and to truly understand how many people don't have symptoms, we don't actually have that answer yet" (cited in Joseph, 2020). The *Guardian* misreported this as "Maria Van Kerkhove says she accepts models show up to 40% of infections come from asymptomatic people" (Boseley, 2020). Widespread asymptomatic transmission of "SARS-CoV-2" was part of a *narrative* rather than a scientific fact.

What was the scientific evidence of asymptomatic transmission of "SARS-CoV-2" in 2020? According to Craig and Engler (2020), a high volume of CCP-approved studies appeared in the early days, and the most frequently cited Western meta-analyses of those studies, even after excluding most of them for not meeting the qualifying criteria for scientific significance, are based on studies which all come back to the same "surprisingly small number of cases (six in total globally)," involving alleged asymptomatic transmission to a total of just seven other people.

In other words, the scientific evidence base for asymptomatic transmission was practically non-existent.

A new propaganda offensive by the UK Government in winter 2020/21 sought to reinforce the threat of asymptomatic transmission. Everyone was urged to stay at home and "act like you've got it," with the Department of Health and Social Care (2021) claiming that "Around 1 in 3 people with COVID-19 don't have any symptoms and can pass it on without realising." "Act like you've got it" turns "Covid-19" into a perverse performance, with otherwise healthy people acting as though they are diseased in a kind of mass hypochondriasis. The disease need not even exist in an objective scientific sense for its performance to make it real as a pervasive social phenomenon. The "1 in 3" claim, which was aggressively pushed for months, was incompatible with ONS data; a more accurate estimate, after adjusting for false positive PCR tests, was 1 in 19 (Fenton et al., 2021), assuming the disease exists.

Fauci claimed in January 2020 that "In all the history of respiratory-born viruses of any type, asymptomatic transmission has never been the driver of outbreaks [...] Even if there is a rare asymptomatic person that might transmit, an epidemic is not driven by asymptomatic carriers" (cited in Ballan, 2021). There are obvious reasons for this: viral spread requires viral replication and shedding, and in immune individuals, the virus is prevented from replicating rapidly (Craig & Engler, 2020). The chance of asymptomatic carriers spreading the virus is therefore low. Some people may be presymptomatic, but in the case of "SARS-CoV-2" even this accounts for a "very small proportion of transmission [< 7%)]" (Craig & Engler, 2020). Corroborating this figure, laboratory-confirmed "cases" in which no symptoms were reported were consistently between 1 and 7% in 2020/21 according to Fig. 12 of the UK *Weekly National Influenza and COVID-19 Surveillance Report* (e.g., Public Health England, 2021). Some of those "cases," however, will involve detection of non-viable RNA fragments rather than live virus because PCR and lateral flow tests are incapable of distinguishing between the two (Pollock & Lancaster, 2020). Thus, asymptomatic transmission of "SARS-CoV-2" did not pose a major threat and the paranoia induced by "ANYONE CAN SPREAD IT" was morally and scientifically unjustifiable.

"Protecting Others"

With society having been induced into a state of mass paranoia, a new moral order was introduced under which following orders ("government guidelines") was equated with virtue ("civic duty," "protecting others," "doing the right thing"), while non-compliance (resisting tyranny) was associated with vice ("selfishness," "irresponsibility," "putting other people's lives at risk").

The "Covid-19" moral order elevates the collective above the individual and represents an attack on liberty. According to Schwab and Malleret (2020, p. 87), "The pandemic has forced all of us, citizens and policy-makers alike, willingly or not, to enter into a philosophical debate about how to maximize the common good in the least damaging way possible." Maximising the common good is a totalitarian principle. As per Point 10 of the Nazi *25-Point Plan*, "The activities of the individual must not clash with the general interest, but must proceed within the framework of the community and be for the general good." It is worth remembering that when individual rights and due process were suspended the day after the Reichstag fire—very likely a false flag event (Hett, 2014; Sutton, 2016, pp. 118–19)—this was done in the name of "protecting" the public, via the Decree for the Protection of People and State.

In the "Covid-19" context, the Scientific Pandemic Insights Group on Behaviours, a UK body tasked with using behavioural psychology to help create behaviour change in line with SAGE recommendations, immediately pointed to the need to "emphasise and explain the duty to protect others" and added that wearing face masks outdoors "could complement existing government messaging of social responsibility if communicated alongside the effectiveness of masks in protecting others who are not infected" (SPI-B, 2020a, p. 2, 2020b, p. 1). The NHS contact tracing app was promoted using the slogan, "Protect your loved ones." Seeking to justify mask mandates on public transport, Transport Secretary Grant Shapps claimed: "a face covering helps protect our fellow passengers. It's something we can each do to help each other" (cited in Wright, 2020).

Face masks were a powerful tool for promoting the idea of "protecting others." As early as April 9, 2020, WEF agenda contributor Trisha Greenhalgh made the case for wearing masks to protect others in a *BMJ* comment piece (Greenhalgh et al., 2020). This was followed three days later by a preprint by WEF Young Global Leader Jeremy Howard, who founded the #Masks4All "movement" and got 100 academics to co-sign an open letter calling for U.S. states to mandate the wearing of cloth masks (Howard et al., 2020). On April 16, Cheng et al. (2020) argued that face mask mandates "shifts the focus from self-protection to altruism." Stutt et al. (2020) argue that "my mask protects you, your mask protects me." All four pieces recognise the lack of scientific research on the efficacy of the public wearing of face masks during a pandemic, yet are willing to set aside basic evidentiary standards, based on the *perception* of an existential threat (and public perception is easily manipulated through propaganda). The "precautionary principle," in this instance an anti-scientific moral imperative based on exploitation of a state of fear, is also invoked by these authors, and SAGE's recommendations, too, "are based on a precautionary approach" (2021, p. 8). The worst can always happen, but there must be some sensible cost–benefit analysis involved—a risk assessment of the kind that the UK Government failed to conduct when introducing mask mandates. Even cloth masks were recommended, by SAGE (2021) and others, despite the admission of at least one author that "Wearing a cloth face mask is less about science and more about solidarity" (Kolstoe, 2020), i.e., is politically rather than scientifically motivated.

A UK Government and NHS advertisement from September 2020 featured a diverse range of people, speaking in a range of local accents, all reciting the mantra of protecting others:

> "I wash my hands to protect my family"; "I wear a face covering to protect my mates"; "I make space to protect my Nan"; "Hands, face, space"; "I wash my hands to protect my colleagues"; "I wear a face covering to protect strangers"; "I make space to protect you"; "Hands, face space." (James, 2021)

On November 3, 2020, the CDC (2020) released a video titled, "I wear a mask because." In it, a range of characters meeting the necessary diversity requirements each deliver a line beginning with "I wear a mask because [...]," followed by a formulation of the "protecting others" motif ("I want *you* to stay healthy"; "I want to keep others safe"; "I want to protect everybody," etc.).

The media conveyed the same message: "The main purpose of face coverings is to protect other people from coronavirus, rather than yourself" (Whitfield, 2021). According to the *Daily Mail* in November 2020,

"Face masks do NOT protect the wearer from coronavirus, but will stop them from infecting other people, Danish study finds" (Kekatos, 2020). In fact, the Danish study finds no such thing. It finds that face masks make no statistically significant difference to the likelihood of the wearer contracting "SARS-CoV-2" but remains agnostic with respect to the role of masks in source control of SARS-CoV-2 infection (Bundgaard et al., 2021). This is yet another example of the media twisting the truth for propaganda purposes.

The "protect others" motif was also applied to "vaccination." For example, Matt Hancock claimed in November 2020: "Getting a vaccine—whether it's for flu or hopefully for coronavirus—is something that not only protects you but protects the people around you. So it's a really important step" (cited in Zeltman, 2020b).

"Protecting others" is a powerful propaganda device. For one thing, who would not want to protect others? It is very hard to resist unless one is willing to go so far as to argue that "government guidelines" were never fundamentally about protecting others—but that is not something that can be dropped into casual conversation or grasped without extensive prior research. "Protecting others" removes the possibility of saying, "I will take my chances" with a disease whose infection fatality rate is 0.5–1% according to the WHO (2020) and 0.23%, falling to 0.05% (corrected median) for the under-70s, according to Ioannidis (2021). Even though 99.95% of under-70s, therefore, survive "Covid-19," "protecting others" creates a moral imperative to obey instructions that overshadow scientific evidence and common sense. As former Israeli health minister Yoram Lass reasons, "For the sake of a few people who anyways don't have a long life expectancy, you don't ruin a country. You don't ruin the world" (cited in Magen, 2020). It is doubtful that the over-70s wanted the rest of society, including the young, to sacrifice their freedoms on their behalf.

Weaponising Guilt

The deliberate exploitation of guilt as part of psychological warfare is nothing new. Meerloo (1956, p. 81) refers to "the method of systematically exploiting unconscious guilt to create submission"; by such means were the Nazis "able to convert courageous resistance fighters into meek collaborators." The CIA torture manuals propose inducing feelings of guilt in order to break the prisoner's will: "Frequently the subject will experience a feeling of guilt. If the 'questioner' can intensify these guilt feelings, it will increase the subject's anxiety and his urge to cooperate as a means of escape" (CIA, 1983, § J-2). For Ellul (1965, p. 312), a key objective of propaganda is to induce guilt feelings.

Guilt is also used as a control mechanism in cults. As "ultimate judges of good and evil within their world," cult leaders use "universal tendencies toward guilt and shame as emotional levers for their controlling and manipulative influences" (Lifton, 1989, p. 424). They set up standards of absolute purity for membership of the cult and wage an "all-out war upon impurity," demanding that cult members "strive permanently and painfully for something which not only does not exist but is in fact alien to the human condition." Every deviation from these impossible standards is used to shame the deviant, who is taught to expect punishment, humiliation, and ostracism. This guilt attachment to the cult serves as a powerful form of emotional bondage.

One way of leveraging guilt is to make the victim feel responsible for their own suffering: "[...] it should always be implied that the subject himself is to blame by using words such as, 'You leave me no other choice but to...' He should never be told to comply 'or else!'" (CIA, 1983, § I-8). In domestic abuse situations, the abuser typically blames the victim for their own suffering, claiming, for instance: "Look at all I have done for you—and you repay me like this!" (Anthony & Cullen, 2021). The victim may internalise the blame: "He only hits me because he loves me. It was my fault really." Responsibility for the abuse gets inverted when abusers paint themselves as victims: "See what you made me do?".

During the "Covid-19" era, the state assumed the role of the abuser, victimising the public. The chief mechanism of abuse was "lockdowns," which caused catastrophic psychological, economic, and social damage (Dettmann et al., 2022; Bhattacharya & Packalen, 2020; Green & Bhattacharya, 2021; Rancourt et al., 2021; Bardosh, 2023; Harrison, 2023), while doing nothing to reduce excess mortality (Agrawal et al., 2023). The "lockdowns" were the result, not of a "virus" with a 0.05% IFR for the under-70s (Ioannidis, 2021), but of government policy, with governments acting in lockstep at the behest of the transnational ruling class.

Yet, the UK Government blamed the public for its own degradation, in line with advice from behavioural scientists. "The public must understand," according to SPI-B (2020b), that "tighter restrictions will be immediately re-imposed if there is an increase in risky behaviour or infection rates—but that good adherence will provide the basis for further resumption of activity if infection rates remain well controlled." Beneath the pseudoscience, this amounts to a form of victim blaming: if the public does as it is told, the abuse will lessen; if it breaks the "rules," the abuse will get worse.

The effect was multiplied by ghoulish propaganda showing "patients" (most likely actors hired by the PR companies responsible) wearing oxygen masks, with the slogan "LOOK [X] IN THE EYES" being variously followed by "AND TELL HIM YOU ALWAYS KEEP A SAFE DISTANCE," "AND TELL HER YOU NEVER BEND THE RULES," "AND TELL HIM THE RISK ISN'T REAL"—exactly the "hard-hitting emotional messaging" called for by SPI-B (2020a, pp. 1–2). Television "news" items also showed patients in oxygen masks, although concerns were raised that many of those patients turned out to be actors. Perhaps hiring actors is deemed more ethical than interviewing genuine sick patients, but it only adds to the impression that the "pandemic" was simulated. The aim of the propaganda was to guilt-trip people into complying with the "measures." It also stoked the desire for retributive justice by showing the alleged victims of outgroup behaviour (cf. Drolet et al., 2016).

On July 15, 2020, the Government announced the "eat out to help out" scheme. Five days later, the *Independent* ran a piece titled "Boris Johnson says it's our own fault if we face a second coronavirus lockdown" (O'Grady, 2020). This is consistent with narcissistic abuse: first encourage members of the public to get out and about, then blame them for doing so.

When thousands of holidaymakers flocked to British beaches in the spring and summer of 2020, they were portrayed as selfishly risking the health of others ("The weekend's coastal visitors were irresponsible and selfish," 2020). Yet, hospitalisation and death rates did not surge in Devon & Cornwall, a key "hotspot." On the contrary, this was one of the few areas to be placed into Tier 1 (fewest restrictions) on November 26, 2020. Mark Woolhouse, an epidemiologist at the University of Edinburgh, told the House of Commons Science and Technology Committee on February 17, 2021: "There were no outbreaks linked to crowded beaches. There's never been a Covid-19 outbreak linked to a beach, ever, anywhere in the world, to the best of my knowledge" (cited in J. Davies, 2021).

On October 4, 2020, with the new regional tier system of "lockdowns" imminent, SPI-B's Susan Michie told LBC Radio that the public had been "complacent" in not following the "Covid-19" regulations. The abusive relationship between the authorities and the public was established: "We were good, we did our best, but now we have been told we are complacent, and we are now trapped, just like a victim of abuse" (Scott, 2021). The pattern was obvious: "lockdowns are blamed on 'the selfish' who aren't observing 'The Rules'" (Harradine, 2020).

The authorities narcissistically refused to admit responsibility for their actions. For example, when Boris Johnson announced new "Tier 4" restrictions on December 20, 2020, which threatened to spoil Christmas for millions of people in London and surrounding areas, he claimed in a Downing Street press conference that although he was taking the decision with a "heavy heart," the scientific evidence had left him with no choice (Cordon, 2020). Thus, the government is never to blame; it is always The Science™ which compels it to abuse the public. In classic abuser fashion, the government in fact blamed the public, as when Matt Hancock branded the huge number of people crowding into London's railway stations to escape the restrictions in time as "totally irresponsible" (cited in Jones, 2020).

In the run-up to Christmas 2020, Public Health England director, Susan Hopkins, warned that for each day of relaxation on restrictions, five days of tighter restrictions would be needed (Roach, 2020). By wanting to enjoy Christmas, the public was made to feel guilty about spreading the virus and complicit in harsher measures to come. Rising "case" numbers were invoked as the pretext for asking families to reconsider their plans to meet up at Christmas, and a third national "lockdown" was threatened should "infections" continue to rise after Christmas (Rayner, 2020). On December 14, 2020, the 77th Brigade's Tobias Ellwood told Parliament, "Let's not begin the New Year with a 3rd Wave. Letting down our guard for 5 days over Xmas could be very dangerous indeed." The following evening, Ellwood was caught, in the words of Home Secretary Priti Patel, "having dinner outside of the rules with a large number of people" ("Tory MP Tobias Ellwood broke Covid rules," 2020). The third national "lockdown" in England duly began on January 5, 2021, even though UEA's Paul Hunter saw no convincing evidence that Christmas did anything to make things worse (cited in Butcher, 2021).

Meanwhile, the "Zero Covid" agenda pushed by Independent SAGE (2020) (and more influential still in other island countries such as Australia and New Zealand) presented an impossible standard, reminiscent of Lifton's (1989, p. 423) "standards of absolute purity for membership of the cult" that are "alien to the human condition." Nothing the public can do, on this agenda, is ever good enough; single "cases" are enough to "lock down" entire societies; and ultimately, only complete surrender to authority will suffice.

Creating the Outgroup

Scapegoating the "Enemy Within"

Meerloo (1956, 132) writes that totalitarianism "needs the images of outside enemies—imaginary cruel monsters who spread plague and disease—to justify its own internal troubles." No less dangerous is the "enemy within," for in totalitarian societies, "there is only a pervasive atmosphere of terror, and a projection of 'the enemy,' imagined to be 'in our midst'"; in such an atmosphere, "no one knows any longer whom to trust"; there is "paranoia society-wide" (Versluis, 2006, p. 143).

Such tactics are not the sole preserve of totalitarian regimes. During the Cold War, similar tactics were deployed by the West, e.g. during the Second Red Scare using the communist "contagion" metaphor. Post-communism, the Club of Rome sought a new "common enemy against whom we can unite" and proposed "humanity itself" for its disastrous inference in natural processes (King & Schneider, 1991, p. 115). When this failed to gain traction, "terrorism" became the new "enemy within" after 9/11, and when that narrative started to wear thin after almost two decades (Hughes, 2022), it was replaced by the Covid-era conception of human beings as potentially deadly disease vectors.

According to Meerloo (1956, pp. 130, 122), "The more fear there is in a society, the more guilt each individual member of the society feels, [and] the more need there is for internal scapegoats and external enemies" against which to direct "the individual's inner fury and rage." A "pandemic" represents the ideal vehicle for generating scapegoats: "Throughout history, the important and recurring pattern [in pandemics] has been to search for scapegoats and place the blame firmly on the outsider" (Schwab & Malleret, 2020, p. 9). Befitting of a totalitarian society, Sumption (2020, p. 10) observes, fear "promotes intolerant conformism. It encourages abuse directed against anyone who steps out of line, including many responsible opponents of this government's measures and some notable scientists who have questioned their empirical basis." The mass fear propaganda in the spring of 2020 (see Chap. 4) had predictable and deliberate effects. Lass, for instance, observes: "we have become monstrously hysterical and in the past fascist regimes have come to power. It's the same type of craziness" (cited in Magen, 2020).

"Lockdowns" are an effective way of creating scapegoats, because they utilise a well-worn tactic of punishing an entire group (in this case, all of society) for the alleged misdemeanours of a minority. For POWs in the Korean War, brainwashing made it hard to observe comrades objectively: "In such surroundings, it is easy to make an innocent scapegoat for all the suffering of the group—and facts can easily be hallucinated in such an atmosphere of mass contagion" (Meerloo, 1956, p. 203). In the Stanford prison experiment, when one of the guards made the other prisoners repeatedly shout, "Because of the bad things that Prisoner 819 did, your cells are a mess," 819 began shaking out of fear of retribution and immediately became more conformist (Perlstadt, 2018, p. 53). In applied behavioural psychology, a successful tactic has been "to make one gang member's actions affect all his/her peer group," e.g. by targeting the entire gang for an offence committed by a single member (Dolan et al., 2010, p. 31).

A well-known concept in psychology is the "fundamental attribution error": "When things go well in our lives, we attribute it to ourselves; when they go badly, it's the fault of other people, or the situation we were put in" (Dolan et al., 2010, p. 27). Those tricked into believing that they were behaving virtuously by "following government guidelines" naturally blamed the ongoing restrictions on those who refused to comply, rather than on those instigating them. As Sidley (2020) writes, "the altruistic majority who are openly conforming with the diktats will blame any subsequent increase in coronavirus cases or deaths on those who didn't comply, while themselves taking the credit for any positive change in the statistics."

Masks as Symbols of Social Segregation

On April 5, 1968, the day after Martin Luther King Jr. was assassinated, elementary school teacher Jane Elliott gave a famous lesson on discrimination in which she privileged blue-eyed schoolchildren over brown-eyed ones, who were made to wear special collars (Bloom, 2022). The following day, Elliott reversed the roles: now brown-eyed people were superior, while the blue-eyed had to wear collars. The children who were privileged performed better in learning tasks, while those made to wear collars became miserable. A class of previously happy and friendly children was quickly divided into two antagonistic groups; on one occasion, physical violence ensued. Reflecting on their experiences on the third day, the class unanimously rejected discrimination based on eye colour or skin colour. Whatever one thinks about the ethics of Elliott's lesson in hindsight or its failure to get at the root causes of racial discrimination, it demonstrates how easy it is to divide people and turn them against one another based on arbitrary markers.

In the "Covid-19" context, mask mandates served as an instrument of social segregation, forcing the public to display outwardly who was willing to comply with the "measures" and who was not. In an interesting twist on the collars in Elliot's lesson, face masks were likened by critics to muzzles, putting the wearer "in a state of humiliation, like dogs not trusted off our leads" (Wright, 2020)—only now they served as symbols of belonging to the ingroup rather than the outgroup. "Virtue" and self-degradation were wickedly conflated.

In the view of Holocaust survivor Vera Sharav, "Mandatory masks are an insidious psychological weapon. They demean our dignity as free human beings. They do not work in this or any epidemic and they are the symbolic equivalent of the yellow star" (in Wolfe, 2021). A *Telegraph* reader expresses similar forebodings: "I would no more support masks than I would the dehumanising label of the Star of David forced on Jews in Nazi Germany to separate some people from others based on race marking them as dirty and unsafe to be near" (see InProportion2, 2021). The yellow star marked out Jewish victims of Nazi persecution, whereas the face mask signals compliance with the regime; both are instruments of segregation. Farringtons School in Kent, though, left little to the imagination when it made mask-exempt pupils wear yellow badges (Lewis, 2021).

Hate Speech

According to Meerloo (1956, pp. 137, 203), totalitarian regimes must "fabric a hate language in order to stir up the mass emotions" and the "enemy who is attacked by vituperative slogans is merely the scapegoat and substitute for all the anger and anxiety that lives inside the threatened people." Intergroup psychology lends itself to this: outgroup members are derogated as inferior/defective, meaning that smears and aspersions are "readily adopted and deployed along group lines, turning citizens into propaganda multipliers, and stoking divide and conquer tactics and discouraging dissent" (Kyrie & Broudy, 2022).

Hate speech deployed against dissidents in the "Covid-19" context included such terms as "Covidiots," "Covid deniers" (based on "Holocaust denial"), "anti-maskers," and "anti-vaxxers," as well as tired pre-existing pejoratives such as "dangerous conspiracy theorists," "antisemites," and "far right extremists" (cf. Fleet Street Fox, 2021; "Hardcore vaccine refuseniks could need deradicalising like terrorists," 2021). The idea is that citizens themselves will amplify this propaganda, as after "9/11," when the "conspiracy theorist" *ad hominem* proved sufficient to suppress critical questioning of the official narrative among the wider population for the better part of two decades.

In seeking to stir hate by appealing to the emotions, the trick is to present political problems in moral, rather than scientific terms, such that facts come to be discussed "in the language of indignation, a tone which is almost always the mark of propaganda" (Ellul, 1965, p. 58, n. 9). The attempt to repackage matters of scientific fact in moral terms was a feature of the "Covid-19" operation. Since The Science™ was supposedly beyond question, "questions about the adequacy of evidence [were] often reinterpreted in moral terms and dismissed as irresponsible acts of 'covidiocy'" (Kidd & Ratcliffe, 2020). Meanwhile, truthful speech which challenges emergent technocracy is rebranded as "harmful" and gets censored.

As a means of subliminal manipulation, "persuasion-by-association" operates by linking a certain idea, person, cause, etc. with another idea/image that is automatically regarded as either good or bad in a given culture, depending on whether the intended association is to be positive or negative (Huxley, 1958, p. 81). In "War on Terror" propaganda, for instance, ideas about Islam were routinely paired with negative concepts (e.g. "Islamic fundamentalism," "Islamic extremism," "religious terrorism") (Jackson, 2007) to win public support for U.S. interference in a string of Muslim-majority countries. In "Covid-19" propaganda, the idea that is automatically to be regarded as good is The Science™ and the outgroup then appears in negative terms: "anti-masker," "anti-vaxxer," "science denier," etc.

Snitching

Totalitarian societies get the citizenry to police itself: "each citizen is continually watched [...] His neighbors watch him, his postman, his children, and they all represent the punishing state, just as he himself must represent the state and watch others. Not betraying them is a crime" (Meerloo, 1956, p. 121). With everyone a potential asymptomatic killer under "Covid-19" propaganda, citizens were similarly "enlisted in policing and punishing each other, adding an extra layer of division and fear between members of populations" and corroding popular resistance to abuses of power (Kyrie & Broudy, 2022).

In March 2020, SPI-B (2020a, p. 2) was already proposing strategies for getting community members to police one another: "Communication strategies should provide social approval for desired behaviours and promote social approval within the community"; conversely, "social disapproval from one's community can play an important role in preventing anti-social behaviour or discouraging failure to enact pro-social behaviour." Legislation, "with community involvement," should be used to "compel key social distancing measures" (SPI-B, 2020a, p. 2). This came with the caveat that such measures need to be "carefully managed to avoid victimisation [and] scapegoating," but the door to scapegoating was nevertheless opened.

British Home Secretary Priti Patel claimed in September 2020 that she would "call the police" if her neighbours broke the "rule of six," thus giving the green light for the public to do the same (Heffer, 2020). Three weeks later, "Covid marshals" were introduced (Aitken, 2020). The fact that "Covid marshals" had no legal power to enforce any rules was beside the point: their psychological function was to create the impression of a society that must police itself, as well as to "impress pretended central authority upon local people and structures" (Thomson, 2020). Nazi Germany "institutionalized rewards for children spying on and informing against parents" (Zimbardo, 2005, p. 133); in January 2021, a *Telegraph* headline read: "Children can be used as undercover spies to report on parents," according to a covert intelligence bill (Hymas, 2021). By December 2020, the enforcement mechanisms were clear: as psychiatrist Mark McDonald observes, "It's actually coming from us, our parents, our children, our neighbors; it's coming from businesses, corporations" (cited in Tapscott, 2020).

The enforcement was driven, not out of ideological conviction, but by fear. It was carried out in myriad small ways, not by ideological fanatics, but by ordinary people seeking to avoid ostracism and punishment (Hopkins, 2021c). Ostracism activates the same pain centres as physical pain and can be "one of the most aversive experiences for human beings" (Kyrie & Broudy, 2022). It can therefore be used as a deterrent against dissent and opposition, because most people prefer the comparative safety of belonging to the ingroup (hence the metaphor of "following the herd").

Fear of being accused promotes conformity and the betrayal of once close relationships (Meerloo, 1956, pp. 131, 103). In totalitarian societies, Hopkins observes, "It isn't usually the Gestapo that comes for you. It's usually your friends and colleagues" (2021a). This was certainly witnessed in the "Covid-19" era, with nonconformists unexpectedly, and to their horror, finding themselves discriminated against by those whom they had known their whole lives. Academics who spoke out against the "Covid-19" narrative were discriminated against by their own colleagues, as cases from Yale, NYU, and Stanford illustrate (Abaluck et al., 2020; Miller, 2020; Bhattacharya, 2023).

History teaches that "Institutionalized spying by friends, family, and neighbors" destroys social bonds and relations of trust, creating socially atomized 'locked loneliness'" (Zimbardo, 2005, p. 134). In totalitarian societies where merit is gauged by denunciation of comrades, it follows that most people will keep to themselves for fear of being accused, creating an "atomized and individualized society" (Arendt, 1962, p. 323). This, surely, was a key purpose of the "lockdowns," i.e. to atomise society and make people fearful of one another. An atomised society is unable to unite against the predator class that holds it in subjugation.

Priming the Public for Violence

Manipulation of Base Instincts

Fromm (1960, p. 5) realised during the Hitler years that totalitarianism is "a political system which, essentially, does not appeal to rational forces of self-interest, but which arouses and mobilizes diabolical forces in man which we had believed to be non-existent, or at least to have died out long ago." Meerloo (1956, pp. 133–4) notes that totalitarianism seeks to manufacture hysteria in order to "awaken the brute Neanderthal psyche in man," which it can then exploit through the "systematic organization of the lower passions in man" to produce "violent and criminal" behaviour. According to Huxley (1958, p. 45), the demagogue makes his appeal to "subhuman mindlessness" and "moral imbecility," qualities which are found, not in individuals, but in crowd-intoxicated masses, as "symptoms of herd-poisoning."

In the Stanford prison experiment (1971), a simulated prison environment led to unexpectedly sadistic outcomes. Even though participants were selected for their "normal" psychological profile, "episodes of deprivation, bullying, and humiliation emerged unplanned," guard aggression continued to escalate even after most prisoners had ceased resisting, and the experiment had to be prematurely terminated for ethical reasons (Perlstadt, 2018, pp. 45, 55). "Lockdown" is a prison term, and the "Covid-19 lockdowns" acted as "a form of house arrest" (Sumption, 2020, p. 1), during which everyone was expected to "perform" the "pandemic" (see Chap. 6). Thus, the "lockdowns" produced a simulated prison environment and may have been designed with the Stanford prison experiment in mind, to bring out the worst in people. Like the guards in Zimbardo's experiment, those who felt they had the power of the state behind them must have felt emboldened in their attacks on dissenters.

Two other experiments carried out by Zimbardo in the late 1960s and early 1970s found that anonymity leads to a greater propensity towards violence, and according to anthropological research, "societies that prepare young men for war by first changing their appearance through painted faces or masks tend to kill, mutilate, and torture their captives significantly more" than those which do not (Zimbardo, 2005, p. 138). One is reminded of *Lord of the Flies*: "[Jack] began to dance and his laughter became a bloodthirsty snarling. He capered towards Bill and the mask was a thing on its own, behind which Jack hid, liberated from shame and self-consciousness" (Golding, 2012, p. 63). The anonymity and deindividuation provided by masks diminishes empathy and accountability and frees hostile impulses. It is for similar reasons that armies give soldiers identical uniforms and haircuts, and why paramilitary organisations often wear balaclavas or cloth coverings to hide the face. A deindividuated persona—someone out of touch with their true self—can commit violent acts without hesitation or remorse. As Zimbardo (2005, p. 131) puts it, "anything that makes us feel anonymous perverts the human spirit into not caring for others—and makes vandalism and violence more probable."

It is impossible in this context to overlook the role of face masks in the "Covid-19" operation. Among their many evil functions, face masks perform a deindividuating function. The face is traditionally where personal identity is expressed, yet the face mask hides half of it, including most of the muscles through which emotion is expressed (Fischer et al., 2012, p. 266). Worn with sunglasses and perhaps a hat or cap, the face vanishes almost entirely—and with it nearly all expression of personal identity and indeed humanity. Face masks help to create the anonymity that is known to prime people for violence.

But what unleashes that violence? According to Zimbardo, "anonymity promotes destructive behaviour—*when permission is also given to behave in aggressive ways that are ordinarily prohibited*. War provides the institutionally approved permission to kill or wound one's adversaries" (2007, p. 304, my emphasis). In that respect, recall the role of the British authorities in giving permission for mask wearers to behave aggressively towards non-mask wearers, viz. the injunction by the head of the London Metropolitan Police, Cressida Dick, on July 22, 2020, that mask wearers should "shame" non-wearers into compliance ("London Police to enforce Face Masks," 2020). On October 8, 2020, the BBC's Stephen Nolan ambushed a man who had gone into a store without a mask (perhaps legitimately, for all Nolan knew), harassed him, and was subsequently accused of "shaming ordinary citizens" (Zeltman, 2020a). In January 2021, Matt Hancock called on supermarkets to ban non-mask wearers (Merrick, 2021). Such actions greenlighted a witch hunt against those not visibly signalling compliance.

The actions of Dick, Nolan, and Hancock are consistent with a totalitarian regime under which citizens "no longer [have] to suppress or reject some of [their] own primitive [and sadistic] impulses. The system assumes the full burden of [their] guilt." Civilised standards, Meerloo (1956, p. 133) continues, are corrupted as "flowery catchwords, such as 'historical necessity,' help the individual to rationalize immorality and evil into morality and good." The flowery catchwords of the "Covid-19" operation included "stop the spread," "flatten the curve," and "protect others." In their name, civilised standards of behaviour were corroded. Some people became giddy at the opportunity to force their irrational beliefs on others, safe in the knowledge that they had the backing of the state.

The results were appalling to behold, and the media were only too keen to report on them. For example, in July 2020, a 24-year-old disabled woman and her 16-year-old sister were verbally attacked on a train after the latter removed her mask to enable lip reading (Rampen, 2020). In September 2020, a policeman pepper sprayed a man who refused to wear a mask for medical reasons (Hodge, 2020). In Barcelona in July 2021, masked passengers attacked a young man and ejected him from a train for not wearing a mask ("Masked Train Passengers attack Man for not wearing Mask," 2021). In December 2021, a row over face masks on a train sparked a brawl that left children in tears (Coleman, 2021). One woman, with a mask around her chin, attacked an 80-year-old man in a plane, repeatedly yelling "put your f***ing mask on!" (Bradford, 2021).

Framing Dissenters as "Fringe"

One way of enhancing group-based identification is to "create the perception that the majority of people hold the official view and frame dissenters as minority/fringe/ 'other'" (Kyrie & Broudy, 2022). A good example is the media's misreporting of protests against the "Covid-19" countermeasures. Common tactics include: claiming that far fewer people were present than there were in reality; painting the protestors, rather than the police, as violent; not reporting on the protest at all; and giving disproportionate attention to other, astroturfed protests.

For example, when Berlin's Straße des 17. Juni filled with revellers/ fans in 2001 and 2006, the BBC reported 1.3 million and 1 million people, respectively ("No love for Berlin Parade," 2001; "Germany 1–1 Argentina," 2006), yet when anti-lockdown protestors twice packed the same boulevard in August 2020 (see the photograph in Manancourt, 2020), the BBC reported "about 20,000 people" and "18,000 people" ("Thousands protest in Germany against Restrictions," 2020; "Germany coronavirus: Protests call for end of Restrictions," 2020)—at least 50 times lower than the actual figure—providing minimal coverage and smearing the protestors as "far right conspiracy theorists." When hundreds of thousands, possibly half a million, people took to the streets of London on April 24, 2021, the BBC failed to cover it; then, a day late, it reported on it in terms of "senseless violence against police" ("Hyde Park: Police Attacks at anti-lockdown Protest condemned," 2021), even though footage from the event clearly shows the police provoking the crowd (UK Column, 2021, 06:00–25:00). Note that the BBC articles do not provide author names, so that no individuals can be held responsible for these distortions.

Opinion polls offer a powerful means of manipulating public perception. YouGov, for instance, which was founded by Nadeem Zahawi, later the UK Minister for Covid Vaccine Deployment, produced findings that consistently supported the official "Covid-19" narrative. For example: 54% of the public supports limiting air travel to "vaccinated" people (7/12/20); 75% supports Tier 4 coronavirus restrictions (20/12/20); 62% opposes reopening primary schools" (4/1/21); 82% supports requiring secondary school pupils in England to wear masks (23/2/21); 79% supports mask wearing on public transport (76% in shops), with 65% supporting "social distancing" in pubs/restaurants and 55% anywhere outside (4/8/21); 64% supports 16–17-year-olds getting injected without their parents' consent (4/8/21); 59% supports masking schoolchildren aged 12 and over (3/9/21); 81% supports mask mandates for public transport (76% for shops), with further support for "social distancing" in pubs/restaurants (67%) and the "2m rule" (59%) (26/10/21); 71% supports mandating a Covid booster jab for high-risk groups (64% for the general public) (22/11/21); and 80% supports showing a Covid pass in order to attend large events (15/12/21).

These results, which suggest that most Britons repeatedly support having their freedoms taken away, their lives made considerably harder, and their children's lives spoiled, are simply not credible, and they diverge sharply from those of the World Vaccine Poll, where selection bias works in the opposite direction. As Dodsworth (2021) recognises, "When you see a result such as 76% of Britons want to see the return of compulsory face masks in shops and on public transport (YouGov), you are meant to identify with the group and imagine yourself in the majority—'ah yes, that is what I think too!'" Opinion polls can also be used to collect real information on public opinion while concealing the truth from the public, generating an asymmetry of information that gives social engineers the advantage (much as investment bankers and hedge fund managers principally rely on asymmetrical information to outperform the market).

Matt Hancock claimed in a press briefing on November 30, 2020 (two days before MHRA approval of the Pfizer "vaccine"): "We think that by encouraging the uptake of the vaccine, we will get a very high proportion of people in this country to take up the vaccine [...]" (cited in Hayes et al., 2020). Hancock was attempting to set a social norm, whereby only a "fringe" group would be perceived as refusing the injection. In December 2021, the *Mail* pointed to "Britain's five million vaccine refuseniks" (Neil, 2021), yet UKHSA data published in July 2022 show that 18.9 million Brits remain "unvaccinated," including 12.4 million adults (UKHSA, 2022b, Table 5).

Dehumanisation

According to Huxley (1936, p. 99), "The purpose of propaganda is to make one set of people forget that other sets of people are human," thereby putting them "outside the pale of moral obligation" and helping to legitimise their persecution. Zimbardo (2007, p. 307) concurs: "By identifying certain individuals or groups as being outside the sphere of humanity, dehumanizing agents suspend the morality that might typically govern reasoned action toward their fellows." New recruits in the army are called names such as "maggot" and "worm" by the drill sergeant to dehumanise them, because without a dehumanised perspective, "there is a direct relationship between the empathic and physical proximity of the victim and the resultant difficulty and trauma of the kill" (Grossman, 1995, p. 97).

Dehumanisation can involve portraying a particular group of people as subhuman. For example, the 1937 Rape of Nanking was made possible, in the words of a Japanese general, "because we thought of them [Chinese civilians] as *things*, not people like us" (cited in Zimbardo, 2007, p. 307). Nazi propaganda that led to the Holocaust depicted Jews as vermin or voracious rats. The stigmatisation of black people as "niggers" was a necessary condition for lynchings in the United States. In the Rwandan genocide, Hutus regarded Tutsis as "insects" and "cockroaches." According to Hassan and Shah (2019), "every genocide on record has the perpetrators referring to their victims as sub-human, or as vermin."

The "Covid-19" operation was dehumanising insofar as it primed people to think of one another as disease-ridden biohazards rather than humane participants in a civilised society. Hopkins refers to this as "the pathologization of society," manifesting "a morbid obsession with disease and death" (2021a). For the first time in history, and against basic standards of epidemiology and medicine, human beings were presumed sick until proven healthy, even if they displayed no symptoms of disease. This flawed assumption led to dehumanising measures such as telling people to stay away from and not hug their loved ones (recalling flawed advice in the 1980s not to touch those with HIV), barring people from seeing their dying relatives in care homes, and use of floor stickers to get people to face away from each other in lifts.

Propaganda played a crucial role in promoting the image of human beings as repositories of disease. In autumn 2020, the government/NHS released a sinister ad campaign which used CGI to animate "SARS-CoV-2" particles coming out of people's mouths. As Yeadon (2020) wryly comments, "It seems not to be understood that in the 'hierarchy of medical evidence,' the results of a well-conducted, randomized clinical trial is not superseded by someone showing you a video of vapour moving around a person's head." A year later, the government and NHS released a similar video in conjunction with the Universities of Cambridge and Leeds (including SAGE's Catherine Noakes), showing two dummies in an eery green light "exhaling" a mist that steadily fills the room (Baynes, 2021). The advert encouraged people to open their windows over the winter at a time when energy bills were soaring. The Cambridge/Leeds scientists appear not to have considered the role of natural immunity against a virus that had been in circulation for over 20 months, or the alleged protection offered by "vaccination," or the fact that asymptomatic transmission does not drive disease outbreaks, according to Fauci (cited in Ballan, 2021).

Another aspect of the dehumanising propaganda involved British morning television presenters Holly Willoughby and Phillip Schofield hugging each other through a plastic sheet (Gillibrand, 2020). One company manufactured a plastic "hugging coat." An expression of affection was, thus, twisted into an act of potential harm. As restrictions were gradually lifted, outrageous headlines appeared, such as "When can we hug again? When can I hug my grandchildren?" (Langton, 2021a, 2021b) and "People in England will soon be allowed to officially hug and kiss again" (Kwai, 2021)—as though the state ever had any right to interfere in ordinary people's personal relationships. Feeding the propaganda, London mayor Sadiq Khan claimed: "I know people are ready for me to be hugging again. The first person I'm going to hug is my mum" (cited in Kwai, 2021). SAGE's Noakes claimed it would worry her "if we were advocating we can hug all of our friends every time we meet them again" (cited in Shukman & O'Connor, 2021). The BBC provided "five ways to make hugging safer, from the experts," namely: "be selective," "make it quick," "avoid face-to-face contact," "do it outside," and "get tested" (Gillett, 2021). This represents a diabolical attack on human affection.

"Social distancing" is dehumanising because it instils a learned distrust of human contact. Like all the other "Covid countermeasures," its scientific basis is dubious. As recently as 2018, there was "a paucity of well-designed epidemiological studies" on social distancing in non-healthcare workplaces (Ahmed et al., 2018). The two metres social distancing rule was scientifically arbitrary: NERVTAG's Robert Dingwall claimed in April 2020 that it had been "conjured up out of nowhere" (cited in Gant, 2020). A report by Rancourt (2021) finds "social distancing" and mask mandates "arbitrary and nonsensical, in light of actual knowledge about transmission of viral respiratory diseases, including COVID-19." According to Martin (2021, p. 25), "To date, not a single study has confirmed that social distancing of any population prevented the transmission of, or the infection by SARS CoV-2." In July 2021, the UK Government (2021) published a "social distancing review" that cites no peer-reviewed scientific literature, only organisations such as SAGE, the WHO, the CDC, and the European Centre for Disease Prevention, whose credibility since 2020 lies in tatters. "Social distancing" in fact goes back to computer scientist Robert Glass' quasi-autistic model of disease control based on forced human separation (Glass et al., 2006); Glass was part of a network, established in 2005, which addressed "infectious disease modelling and *military readiness*" (Feighner et al., 2009, my emphasis). "Social distancing" is a *military* measure.

The face mask serves as an instrument of dehumanisation. "There is something hideous about the suffocating mask," notes Potts (2020), for masked people "don't look human. The lower part of their face is disguised by a grotesque protuberance" that prevents expressions of their humanity from being read. A *Telegraph* reader concurs: "I find masks utterly dehumanising. To cover someone's identity and human expression is to separate us from others, to remove the deeply human aspect of social interaction through our face and facial expression [...]" (cited in InProportion2, 2021). In Fagan's (2020) view, "The point of face masks is not to protect humans, but to diminish humanity—to rob people of their ego, their identity, and their autonomy. Masks are worn by disposable horror movie villains and ignorable background dancers; they make people less-than-human." Indeed, when one thinks of masks in popular culture, the examples tend to be horrific, e.g. Hannibal Lecter, Bane, or the masked handmaids in the 2017 television adaptation of Margaret Atwood's *The Handmaid's Tale*. Gimp masks, too, create a "sense of dehumanization and degradation" and are "likely to suggest and embody horrific qualities" (Lunning, 2013, p. 100; Needham, 2014, p. 152). The dehumanising aspect of masks may explain why the euphemism "face coverings" is often used instead (Wright, 2020).

Extensive use was made of dehumanising infographics, either online or in physical signage, telling people how to behave. Such infographics never show flesh and blood human beings; instead, they typically show cartoon characters, sometimes with eyes, nose, and mouth (i.e. facial expression/personal identity) removed for good measure (CDC, 2021; Gillett, 2021). From March 2020 until February 2022, the main BBC News website included a "Coronavirus" or "Coronavirus Explained" bar featuring five articles. Although the articles changed, the thumbnails for articles 1,2,3, and 5 tended to be chosen from a repository of blue and white infographic images—cold, sterile, dehumanised.

SS *Reichsführer* Heinrich Himmler claimed in 1943 that "Antisemitism is exactly the same as delousing. Getting rid of lice is not a question of ideology. It is a matter of cleanliness" (cited in Westermann, 2015, p. 488). In November 2020, 1000 Northern Ireland fans were made to pass through a "disinfecting pod" in order to watch their team play football (Arnold, 2020). In May 2021, a pub owner advocated for the "Steripod," which sprays a light disinfectant mist onto customers for ten seconds, as a means of helping business get back to normal. These pseudoscientific propaganda stunts, which obviously would not prevent an infectious person from spreading the virus, call to mind how pest control companies treat vermin and are faintly reminiscent of Zyklon B in the showers of Nazi concentration camps. Writing from Germany, Hopkins (2021b) was only half-joking when he claimed, "At this point, I'm just sitting here waiting for the news that mass 'disinfection camps' are being set up to solve the 'Unvaccinated Question.'".

The propaganda term "pandemic of the unvaccinated," coined by CDC director Rochelle Walensky, paints those refusing the dangerous injections as disease spreaders, much as Jews were treated in Nazi Germany: "the Jewish population was framed as a constant danger to the average German citizen's health, inspiring disgust as an aversion response [and] maliciously recruiting the basic human revulsion of filth and pestilence into a force for dehumanizing Jews" (Haque et al., 2012, p. 475).

The "vaccination" campaign in Britain was couched in the dehumanising language of "getting jabs into arms," a phrase repeatedly used by ministers. Human beings are a lot more than just their arms, however: they are sovereign individuals with the final say over what goes into their bodies.

Turning the "Vaccinated" on the "Unvaccinated"

Blaming the "Unvaccinated"

In Nazi Germany, a "new moral order" meant that "principles of exclusion and enmity such as antisemitism and anti-Bolshevism reigned supreme" (Westermann, 2015, p. 488). The "Covid-19" new moral order sought to exclude a new category of person, known as "the unvaccinated," which bears quasi-biblical overtones of being "unclean." What started small—temperature guns fired at foreheads, encouraging people to report one another for not obeying the "rules," masks as a visible symbol of division between the rule takers and the rule breakers, etc.—escalated into "vaccine" apartheid in 2021.

First, the minority of "vaccine" refusers was blamed for keeping the UK in "lockdown." A *Mail* article from February 2021, for example, asks "Why should the whole country be held hostage by the one in five who refuse a vaccine?" (Lee, 2021). Note the use of language: "held hostage," as though the "lockdowns" were the fault, not of the criminal masterminds behind them, but, rather, of responsible adults concerned for the principle of bodily autonomy. The media also encouraged "vaccinated" people to put pressure on their counterparts. Former Chancellor of the Exchequer, George Osborne, for instance, wrote in the *Evening Standard*: "Whatever Whitehall decides, the vaccinated public is going to demand that those around them are vaccinated too" (Osborne, 2021). The *Guardian* produced a sinister op-ed, titled "It is only a matter of time before we turn on the unvaccinated" (Cohen, 2021).

Sardi (2021) predicted on March 26, 2021, that "deaths will quickly be blamed, not on the vaccinated, but on the unvaccinated. They must be spreading the disease." The authorities did indeed try to pin "Covid-19" deaths on "the unvaccinated." In July 2021, the "pandemic of the unvaccinated" concept was propagated by the corporate media. German Health Minister Jens Spahn, a former WEF Young Global Leader, used the same term ("Germany experiencing 'Pandemic of the unvaccinated,'" 2021). The "pandemic of the unvaccinated," McDonald argues, has no scientific credibility, but is "full of coercive psychological power": it is "an expression of propaganda meant to provoke anger toward those who exercise medical choice in deferring or refusing the experimental vaccine

[…] It intentionally divides [the public] against one another" (cited in Hayen, 2021).

Contradicting the propaganda, scientific studies revealed "little to no difference between the COVID vaccinated and unvaccinated in terms of becoming infected, harboring the virus (viral load in the oral and nasopharynx), and transmitting it" (Alexander, 2021). In fact, the "Covid-19 vaccines" did such a poor job of preventing infection and transmission that the CDC was forced to change its definition of vaccination on September 1, 2021, to remove all reference to immunity (Stieber, 2021). Increases of "Covid-19 cases" in the United States proved "unrelated to levels of vaccination across 68 countries and 2947 counties" (Subramanian & Kumar, 2021). Kampf (2021) is, therefore, correct to argue that "stigmatising the unvaccinated is not justified" given "increasing evidence that vaccinated individuals continue to have a relevant role in transmission."

"New variants," too, were blamed on "the unvaccinated." A CNN headline from July 4, 2021, reads: "Unvaccinated People are 'Variant Factories,' Infectious Diseases Expert Says" (Fox, 2021). According to the *New York Times* on July 25, 2021, "Were a wider swath of the population vaccinated, there would be no resurgence—of the Delta variant, or Alpha variant, or any other version of the coronavirus" (Mandavilli, 2021). Yet, those who do not get the flu vaccine are not blamed for new flu variants every year. Again, there was no scientific evidence for such claims; on the contrary, one study found that "the vaccine effect on reducing transmission is minimal in the context of delta variant circulation" (Wilder-Smith, 2021).

"Vaccine" Apartheid

In a bitter historical twist, the very state that was founded in response to Jewish persecution was the first to institute a two-tier system distinguishing between "vaccinated" and "unvaccinated" people. Israel's "Green Pass" programme, announced in late February 2021, required people to show proof of "Covid-19 vaccination" to gain entrance to registered venues (shopping centres, restaurants, sports venues, etc.) (Jaffe-Hoffmann, 2021). A document from the 1942 Nazi occupation of France that was circulating online at the time shows that Jews were prohibited from going to restaurants, concerts, cafes, museums, libraries, and other public venues.

In March 2021, the European Union announced its own "Digital Green Certificate" (note the "green" language, creating continuities with "green" agendas, perhaps in preparation for "climate lockdowns"), the legislation for which was finalised in June. The NHS app was made to function as a "vaccine passport" and in July the European Union and the United Kingdom began work on integrating their two systems (Nuki, 2021). It became increasingly clear that participation in everyday life was to be made conditional upon submission to routine injections and biometric IDs—the biodigital version of a checkpoint society all too familiar from the history of totalitarianism.

Tony Blair claimed on June 6, 2021, that "It is time to distinguish for the purposes of freedom from restriction between the vaccinated and unvaccinated," granting the former the maximum freedom possible within constraints imposed by "new variants" (cited in Doherty, 2021). The idea that freedom is something that can be given is itself the hallmark of authoritarianism. A BBC headline from July 6, 2021, reads "Covid: Fully jabbed people to be treated differently—Javid"; the headline was later changed, but the original intention is clear enough. In the United States, Anthony Fauci claimed: "It's almost like it's going to be two Americas," namely, "under-vaccinated regions" and the rest of the country (da Silva, 2021). CNN called for "the unvaccinated" to be segregated and made to pay for daily tests (Watson, 2021).

Common shop window signs in Nazi Germany included "*Juden werden hier nicht bedient*" (Jews not served here) and "*Juden sind hier unerwünscht*" (Jews not welcome here). Similar signs were once erected in the United States: "NO: DOGS, NEGROES, MEXICANS" (in that order). Separate shop entrances and rest rooms for "whites" and "coloreds" were commonplace. In Britain, it was "No blacks, No Irish, No dogs" (in varying configurations). Similar discriminatory signage appeared in the "Covid-19" context, e.g. in Ireland: "Covid Passport and ID (for all members of your group) Use Front Door"; "Non-vaccinated Guests use Beer Garden Entrance." A sign seen on the office door of a French MP in July 2021 read: "*La permanence est interdite aux: animaux; personnes sans pass sanitaire*": no entry to animals and unvaccinated people, the latter ranking below animals. In Germany of all places, "*Ungeimpfte unerwünscht*" (unvaccinated not welcome) appeared on shop windows on December 1, 2021 ("Ungeimpfte unerwünscht," 2021). The following week, it was "*Kauft nicht bei Ungeimpften*" (don't buy from the unvaccinated) (Reitschuster, 2021), recalling "*Kauft nicht bei Juden*" (don't buy from Jews) on Jewish shop windows during the Third Reich.

By the autumn of 2021, signs of vaccine apartheid were commonplace. For example, Vancouver International Airport introduced separate lanes for "unvaccinated passengers" and "fully-vaccinated passengers." In Estonia, "the unvaccinated" were segregated behind metal fences in town squares. In Britain, Suffolk County Council introduced different rules for "vaccinated" and "unvaccinated" children (Turner, 2021), first-year university students were given wristbands to signify their "vaccination" status (Somerville, 2021), and businesses such as Morrisons, Ikea, Next, and Ocado cut sick pay for "unvaccinated" staff (Rodgers, 2022). In Germany, it was announced in late October that "the unvaccinated" would be banned from Berlin's Christmas market (Bunyan, 2021), and by early December, supermarket shoppers in Berlin were divided by metal fences according to their vaccination status. In Canada, the Royal Canadian Legion (Montgomery branch) denied access to "unvaccinated" veterans, showing how the "Covid-19" operation works to undermine patriotism. When New Zealand Prime Minister Jacinda Ardern was asked in October 2021 if the vaccine passport system was creating two classes of people, "the vaccinated" and "the unvaccinated," she brazenly replied: "That is what it is, so, yep" (cited in Laila, 2021).

Discriminatory "lockdowns of the unvaccinated," or calls for similar measures, were issued across a range of European countries, including Austria, Germany, Slovakia, the Czech Republic, the Netherlands, Greece, Romania, and Ukraine (Langton, 2021b). It is telling that Austria, Italy, and Germany—formerly fascist states—were among the first to call for "lockdowns of the unvaccinated" (cf. Ibbetson & Pleasance, 2021). In a referendum in early December, 60% of Swiss voted for the "Covid pass"—"essentially lockdown of the unvaccinated"—following a campaign which "pitted the old against the young, the vaccinated against the unvaccinated, the rural areas [...] against urban areas and even neighbour against neighbour" (Morgan Edwards, 2021). With the UK government remaining silent on "lockdowns of the unvaccinated" instead of condemning them, Deputy Prime Minister Dominic Raab refused to rule out such a policy (Pearson, 2021), and the *Express* planted the idea that the "UK could follow Germany on unvaccinated rules" (Phillips, 2021).

"No jab, no job" policies forced millions of principled people out of work for refusing to surrender their bodily autonomy to the state, while others reluctantly took the shot to be able to keep a roof over their heads and provide for their families. While the bravest opponents of medicalised tyranny were forced to sacrifice their livelihoods, injection mandates for military and intelligence agency personnel in the United States meant that those left working for those organisations had proven their loyalty by allowing an unknown experimental substance into their bodies amidst enormous safety concerns (Seneff & Nigh, 2021).

As Tucker (2021) wrote at the time, "This is no longer about scientific confusion. This is starting to look like an old-fashioned political purge [...], an intensification of the mask mandate to become a needle mandate as a means of ferreting out dissidents." The biosecurity paradigm ultimately demands that the state exercise power directly over biological bodies, the rights of citizenship no longer applying (Agamben, 1998, p. 148). In such a totalitarian system, there can be no room for dissidents. The abortive "vaccine mandates" were a first step towards what is to come if the global technocratic coup is not put down.

Incitement of Hatred Against "the Unvaccinated"

In religious and political fanaticism, Versluis (2006, p. 142) observes, "'Our' side is always right; 'their' side is of the devil, so fundamentally wrong that one can only detest them. Once one acquiesces in such a view, one is well on the way to becoming a persecutor [...]" In modern societies, however, this does not happen naturally or spontaneously. Rather, it relies upon *instigators* whose role is to "tune and transmit the messages that will effectively motivate others to cause harm" (Mandel, 2002, p. 102). The British media played that role when it came to inciting hatred against "the unvaccinated" (and it was hardly alone, as the infamous *Toronto Star* front page from August 26, 2021, illustrates). For example, ITV's *Good Morning Britain* in April 2021 featured Edwina Currie claiming: "I don't want them next to me or anywhere near me or even in the same carriage on the train [...] They can exercise their freedom by staying at home" (cited in McCormack, 2021).

On May 6, 2021, the *Guardian* irresponsibly advertised the fact that, owing to a loophole in NHS Digital's "vaccine" booking system, "anyone who possesses basic personal details of a friend, colleague or stranger" could find out that person's "vaccination" status, even explaining how to do so (Hern, 2021). Then, on May 17–18, 2021, the British media unleashed a coordinated campaign of vilification against those not wanting to take the "Covid-19 vaccine." The *Sun* implored "Jab them up" (an apparent call for forced injections), taking aim at "anti-vax conspiracy theory clowns" ("Adults of all ages in hotspots should now be jabbed as fast as possible," 2021). *Sky News* did an interview with Rachel Johnson, the Prime Minister's sister, who claimed that the government's priority should be "not allowing anybody not to have the vaccine" (a call for mandatory injections) (see Delingpole, 2021). LBC's Shelagh Fogarty appeared to issue an incitement to violence on air: "I would literally be in fights with these people. How do you see them at work without wanting to poison their coffee?" (in Delingpole, 2021). Sarah Vine (2021), Michael Gove's then wife, wrote in the *Mail*: "We can't let selfish idiots who don't want free Covid vaccines" (whom she calls "vaccine refuseniks") "hold us hostage" following "months in lockdown." A *Mail* + headline reads: "Now vaccine refuseniks threaten freedom [….]" (Groves & Martin, 2021). Historically, "refuseniks" were Soviet Jews denied permission to emigrate to Israel, therefore, the media's appropriation of the term to stigmatise those unwilling to take the "Covid-19 vaccine" could be construed as antisemitic.

In June 2021, the British media continued its campaign of ostracisation, shaming, and calumny against those not willing to take an unlicensed, experimental drug with no long-term safety data while official reports of serious adverse reactions went off the charts (OpenVAERS, n.d.; MHRA, n.d.; WHO, n.d. [search "COVID-19 vaccine" for over 5.2 million reports]). The *Telegraph*, for instance, ran a callous piece whose author claimed to be willing to sacrifice her "unvaccinated friends" (Mulvey, 2021). Freelance journalist Angela Epstein claimed on Jeremy Vine's Channel 5 show: "Vaccine refusers are selfish, morally repugnant, irresponsible people who are enjoying their freedom because the rest of us are being vaccinated" (Galpin, 2021).

In the autumn of 2021, a rabid British media establishment engaged in a coordinated hate campaign against those who had refused the "vaccine." Newspaper headlines appeared such as: "The unvaccinated have become a lethal liability we can ill-afford" (McElvoy, 2021); "It's time to punish Britain's five million vaccine refuseniks: They put us all at risk of more restrictions. So why shouldn't we curb some of their freedoms?" (Neil, 2021); "I'm fed up with the unvaccinated rump who risk pushing us back into lockdown" (Johnston, 2021); "Make the unjabbed face their own lockdown so we can live our lives" (Brady, 2021); "It's time for London's unvaccinated to pay with their freedoms, not ours" (Sheffield, 2022); and "Antivaxxers are dumb as breeze blocks—It's time we stopped tolerating them" (Baldwin, 2022). "Reserve the harshest restrictions for the 5 million people who have declined to be vaccinated," Mason (2021) urges. "The unvaccinated must become social pariahs," writes Hudson (2022): "They shouldn't be allowed into indoor communal spaces like restaurants, cinemas, shops, gigs and [...] pubs [...] Get jabbed, or else." Thus, tabloids and broadsheets alike all delivered the same incitement of hatred against "unvaccinated" people.

On mainstream British television, the following views were expressed on the *Jeremy Vine Show*. Vine himself claimed: "We either allow this [vaccine refusal] or we end up holding people down and jabbing them by force" (cited in Investment Watch, 2021). Lucy Beresford claimed: "You have to start taking away freedoms, you have to start putting some kind of punishment in place" ("Watch: UK pundit Lucy Beresford's deranged plan to take freedoms away from the unvaccinated," 2021). According to Yasmin Alihai-Brown, "Those who haven't had jabs but could have jabs need to have a badge saying 'unjabbed'" (cited in Gantzer, 2022). Carole Malone claimed: "Giving up your human rights is justifiable when you're in a global pandemic" (cited in Bembridge, 2021).

Benjamin Butterworth opined on TalkRadio that "a lockdown of the unvaccinated isn't a bad idea" (in Schiavone, 2021). Nick Ferrari on LBC Radio proposed an escalating series of fines for "vaccine refusers." Piers Morgan produced a stream of vitriol against those who had refused the "vaccine" (see Sherman, 2022).

The media barrage of hate against "the unvaccinated" led seamlessly into political leaders, past and present, becoming openly abusive towards the same group. Tony Blair stated: "If you're not vaccinated and you're eligible, and you've not got a health reason for not being vaccinated, you're not just irresponsible, you're an idiot" (cited in Grylls, 2021). The White House (2021) announced that, "For the unvaccinated, you're looking at a winter of severe illness and death for yourselves, your families, and the hospitals you may soon overwhelm." Emmanuel Macron claimed that he really wanted to "piss off" those who had refused the "vaccine" by banning them from public places ("French president Macron vows to 'piss off' unvaccinated," 2022). Justin Trudeau claimed of "the unvaccinated": "They don't believe in science or progress and are very often misogynistic and racist," asking, "do we tolerate these people?" (in Schiavone, 2022). Boris Johnson claimed that "antivax campaigners, the people who are putting this mumbo-jumbo on social media, they are completely wrong"

(Penna, 2022). All five remarks were made within a 16-day period and were obviously part of a transnationally coordinated propaganda strategy.

Were Hospitals Filling Up with "the Unvaccinated"?

Another way of discriminating against those who had declined the "vaccine" was to claim that they took up a disproportionate number of hospital beds. According to the *Guardian* in November 2021, for instance, "In hospital, Covid-19 has largely become a disease of the unvaccinated"—this based on the unverifiable word of an anonymous "secret consultant" (Secret Consultant, 2021). A *Sunday Times* headline a week later reads: "Intensive care beds filled with unvaccinated Covid patients" (Spencer & Calver, 2021). Health Secretary Sajid Javid claimed on December 19, 2021: "In fact, if we look at those most ill in hospital, needing the most care and attention, around 9 out of 10 of them are unvaccinated" (cited in Bosotti, 2021).

UK Health Security Agency data contradicts these claims. For Weeks 49–52 of 2021 (December 6, 2021, to January 2, 2022), "COVID-19 cases presenting to emergency care" numbered 4056 "unvaccinated" and 5791 "vaccinated" (of which 5283 double- "vaccinated") (UKHSA, 2022a, Table 11), meaning that "unvaccinated" cases accounted for 41% of the total, not 90%. A UKHSA report for data up to December 29, 2021, estimates that the "Proportion of hospitalised cases with confirmed or probable (SGTF +) Omicron who are unvaccinated" is 25% across England (UKHSA, 2021b), however, all regions outside London register 22.6% or lower (as low as 10%, for a mean average of 17.6%). UKHSA data from December 12, 2021, indicates that 19.3% of UK adults had refused the shot, with the total percentage of the population "unvaccinated" rising to 32.1% including children (UKHSA, 2021a, Table 10). Therefore, the proportion of "unvaccinated" people in hospital outside London is *lower* than one would expect given the proportion of "unvaccinated" people overall, and quite why London is such an outlier (39.3% of "Omicron" hospitalisations being "unvaccinated" vs. the 17.6% average elsewhere) requires explanation.

On December 29, 2021, Boris Johnson claimed: "I've talked to doctors who say the numbers are running up to 90% of people in intensive care, who are not boosted," and "If you're not vaccinated, you're eight times more likely to get into hospital altogether" (cited in Morris, 2021). The latter claim is an obvious whopper, judging by the UKHSA data above, but note also how the former claim shifts Javid's 90% "unvaccinated" claim ten days earlier (Bosotti, 2021) to 90% "not boosted," now ignoring most intensive care patients who had taken 1–2 shots. Evidently, figures were being plucked out of thin air to push agendas, something previously seen in lies that the Mater hospital in Belfast was "full with young (in 20/30s) critically unwell, UNvaccinated COVID patients on ventilators" (exposed by Citizen Journalists, 2021) and NHS England Chief Executive Amanda Pritchard's claim that "We have had 14 times the number of people in hospital with COVID-19 than we saw this time last year" (G. Davies, 2021). Far from "vaccinated" people being healthier than "unvaccinated" people, it turns out that age-standardised mortality rates for January to May 2022 were lowest among the unvaccinated population in *every* age group ("Pfizergate," 2022).

The full ONS dataset on deaths involving "Covid-19" by vaccination status in England between April 1, 2021, and May 31, 2023, shows that only 5% of those deaths involve "unvaccinated" people, vs. 78.7% who took four shots (ONS, 2023). Those who took one dose account for 0.7% of the deaths, two doses 3.8%, and three doses 11.8%. The ONS is at pains to point out that the fourth dose was targeted at the clinically vulnerable and older adults in care homes (i.e. two demographics most likely to die anyway). Even ignoring the fourth dose, however, we see that 5% of deaths involve "unvaccinated" people and 16.3% of deaths accrue among those who had taken 1–3 shots. "Unvaccinated" deaths, then, account for 23.5% of the revised total, which is in line with the 23% of adults who remained "unvaccinated" as of July 2022 (UKHSA, 2022b, Table 5). This correlation only holds, however, if it is assumed that everyone who took a fourth dose would have died anyway ***and*** that there is no difference in the death rate between "vaccinated" and "unvaccinated" people (a primary purpose of "vaccination" being to reduce the risk of dying). Therefore, judging by ONS data, "Covid-19 vaccines" are at best ineffective in preventing deaths involving "Covid-19," or—far more likely—they *increase* the risk of death.

The Road to Genocide?

There has been a deliberate, premeditated, and finely tuned attempt on the part of the transnational ruling class to divide society and to turn it against itself as part of an attempt to destroy democracy and institute a novel, technocratic form of totalitarianism. In certain respects, the operation was successful. Citizens were made to turn on one another, at times with a "[terrifying] level of cruelty" signifying "the collapse of a moral, decent, and compassionate society" (Blaylock, 2022). Many people imagine they would have been in the resistance in Nazi Germany, Christine Anderson MEP noted in a 2023 interview, yet they need only look at their conduct over the previous three years for an answer. The brute fact is that most of society participated, in some cases fanatically, in the tyranny, not because of inherent character flaws, but because it had been psychologically manipulated into doing so by the orchestrators of the "Covid-19" operation.

The mechanisms of division analysed in this chapter are consistent with the first four stages of Stanton's (2016) "ten stages of genocide," i.e. classification (imposing "us" vs. "them" identity categories), symbolisation (naming groups, imposing symbols on them), discrimination (use of power to deny groups their rights and create segregation/apartheid), and dehumanisation (painting outgroup members as subhuman so as to overcome the normal human revulsion against murder). Although "genocide," defined by Article II of the United Nations Genocide Convention as any of five "acts committed with intent to destroy, in whole or in part, a national, ethnical, racial or religious group" (United Nations, 1948), is not the correct term for what is happening today (because the targeted group is defined by dissidence), we should be on our guard. There are only four intervening stages before Stage 9 (extermination), i.e. organisation (using secret police and arming and training armies and militias), polarisation (arrest and murder of leaders of targeted groups, use of emergency laws/decrees against those groups, e.g. requiring their disarmament), preparation (perhaps disguising genocide as self-defence or counterinsurgency), and persecution (death lists drawn up, property expropriated, victims deported to concentration camps, deprivation of food/water, forced sterilisation, extrajudicial killings, torture, forced displacement). The digital surveillance infrastructure for advanced counterinsurgency is already in place (see Chap. 8).

Preventing the descent into barbarism from going any further requires unified class consciousness. The "Covid-19" operation, however, has sowed deep division between families, friends, and communities. Nearly everyone has lost friends or fallen out with people they thought they were close to since 2020. An atmosphere of distrust pervades society. A minority can see through the psychological operation, but the majority cannot. One side, indoctrinated by propaganda and brainwashed by psychological warfare, believes in The Science™, trusts the authorities, and mindlessly caricatures the other side as "conspiracy theorists." Conversely, those who, for whatever reason, have remained immune to the largest psychological warfare operation in history see their counterparts as unwitting victims, trapped in an artificial reality in which their mind is controlled in ways they cannot begin to imagine.

Yet, to borrow Vernon Coleman's sign-off, more and more people are "waking up," and, once awake, they stay awake. The real question, as in 1938, is whether subjective consciousness will catch up with objective conditions fast enough. "The objective prerequisites for the proletarian revolution have not only 'ripened,'" Trotsky (1938) warned: "they have begun to get somewhat rotten. Without a socialist revolution, in the next historical period at that, a catastrophe threatens the whole culture of mankind." We know what followed between 1939 and 1945. What, then, will be the outcome of World War III?

References

Abaluck, J., Cohen, T., Desir, G. V., D'Onofrio, G., Forman, H. P., Gonsalves, G., Grubaugh, N. D., Hines, R., Horsley, V., Iwasaki, A., Kapczynski, A., Kershaw, T., Ko, A. I., Latham, S. R., Morton, F. S., Omer, S. B., Paltiel, A. D., Parikh, S., Santucci, K., Smith, M. N., & Weinberger, D. (2020, August 4). Statement from Yale faculty on hydroxychloroquine and its use in Covid-19. *Counterpunch*. https://www.counterpunch.org/2020/08/04/statement-from-yale-faculty-on-hydroxychloroquine-and-its-use-in-covid-19/.

Adults of all ages in hotspots should now be jabbed as fast as possible. (2021, May 17). *The Sun*. https://www.thesun.co.uk/news/14986764/sun-says-hotspots-jabbed/.

Agamben, G. (1998). *Homo sacer*. Stanford University Press.

Agrawal, V., Cantor, J., Sood, N., & Whaley, C. (2023). The impact of COVID-19 shelter-in-place policy responses on excess mortality. *Health Economics, 32*(11), 2499–2515. https://doi.org/10.1002/hec.4737.

Ahmed, F., Zviedrite, N., & Uzicanin, A. (2018). Effectiveness of workplace social distancing measures in reducing influenza transmission: A systematic review. *BMC Public Health, 18,* Article 518. https://doi.org/10.1186/s12889-018-5446-1.

Aitken, A. (2020, October 8). Coronavirus: Who are the covid marshals and do they have any powers? *BBC News*. https://www.bbc.co.uk/news/explainers-54105672.

Alexander, P. E. (2021, December 14). Must we segregate the unvaccinated from the vaccinated? *Brownstone Institute*. https://brownstone.org/articles/must-we-segregate-the-unvaccinated-from-the-vaccinated/.

Anthony, J. & Cullen, D. (2021, January 6). Breaking the Covid trance: How the Irish people were psychologically manipulated [Speech transcript]. *UK Column*. https://www.ukcolumn.org/article/breaking-covid-trance-how-irish-people-were-psychologically-manipulated.

Arendt, H. (1962). *The origins of totalitarianism*. The World Publishing Company.

Arnold, B. (2020, November 13). Watch: fans go through "disinfecting pod" ahead of Northern Ireland clash. *Extra.ie*. https://extra.ie/2020/11/13/sport/soccernews/northern-ireland-fans-disinfecting-pod.

Baldwin, P. (2022, January 11). Antivaxxers are dumb as breeze blocks—it's time we stopped tolerating them. *The Express*. https://www.express.co.uk/comment/expresscomment/1547968/anti-vaxxers-covid-19-vaccine-deniers-pfizer-astra-zeneca-covid-deaths-today.

Ballan, A. (2021, July 15). Covid—start at the beginning and question everything. *TCW*. https://www.conservativewoman.co.uk/covid-start-at-the-beginning-and-question-everything/.

Bardosh, K. (2023). How did the Covid pandemic response harm society? A global evaluation and state of knowledge review (2020–21). Preprint retrieved from https://doi.org/10.2139/ssrn.4447806.

Baynes, M. (2021, November 5). "Stop Covid-19 hanging around": Campaign encourages people to open windows over Christmas. *Sky News*. https://news.sky.com/story/stop-covid-19-hanging-around-campaign-encourages-people-to-open-windows-over-christmas-12460028.

Bembridge, J. (2021, November 26). Fear and fascism growing on the Vine. *TCW*. https://www.conservativewoman.co.uk/fear-and-fascism-growing-on-the-vine/.

Bhattacharya, J. (2023, January 11). How Stanford failed the academic freedom test. *Tablet*. https://www.tabletmag.com/sections/arts-letters/articles/stanford-failed-academic-freedom-test.

Bhattacharya, J., & Packalen, M. (2020, May 16). Lives vs lives—the global cost of lockdown. *The Spectator*. https://www.spectator.co.uk/article/lives-vs-lives-the-global-cost-of-lockdown.

Blaylock, R. L. (2022). Covid update: What is the truth? *Surgical Neurology International*, *13*, Article 167. https://doi.org/10.25259/SNI_150_2022.

Bloom, L. (2022, November 22). Blue eyes, brown eyes: On race and Jane Elliott's famous experiment on prejudice. *Skeptic*. https://www.skeptic.com/reading_room/blue-eyes-brown-eyes-jane-elliott-prejudice-experiment/.

Boseley, S. (2020, June 9). WHO expert backtracks after saying asymptomatic transmission "very rare." *The Guardian*. https://www.theguardian.com/world/2020/jun/09/who-expert-backtracks-after-saying-asymptomatic-transmission-very-rare.

Bosotti, A. (2021, December 19). Sajid Javid launches in brutal rant at unvaccinated Brits over "huge damage" caused to UK. *The Express*. https://www.express.co.uk/news/politics/1538300/Sajid-Javid-rant-unvaxxed-Britain-coronavirus-damage-Covid-19-vn.

Bradford, C. (2021, December 28). Baywatch star and ex-Playboy model Patricia Cornwall "hit 80-year-old Delta passenger in argument over masks on flight." *The Sun*. https://www.the-sun.com/news/4351299/baywatch-ex-playboy-model-patricia-cornwall-delta-masks/.

Brady, K. (2021, December 11). Make the unjabbed face their own lockdown so we can live our lives. *The Sun*. https://www.thesun.co.uk/news/17011353/make-unnjabbed-face-lockdown-so-we-can-live-lives/.

Bundgaard, H., Bundgaard, J. S., Raaschou-Pedersen, D. E. T., von Buchwald, C., Todsen, T., Norsk, J. B., Pries-Heje, M. M., Vissing, C. R., Nielsen, P. B., Winsløw, U. C., Fogh, K., Hasselbalch, R., Kristensen, J. H., Ringgaard, A., Andersen, M. P., Goecke, N. B., Trebbien, R., Skovgaard, K., Benfield, T., … Iversen, K. (2021). Effectiveness of adding a mask recommendation to other public health measures to prevent SARS-CoV-2 infection in Danish mask wearers. *Annals of Internal Medicine, 174*(3), 335–343. https://doi.org/10.7326/M20-6817.

Bunyan, R. (2021, October 27). Unvaccinated people are set to be banned from Berlin's Christmas market after officials approved shutting them out in latest example of two-tier post-Covid society. *Daily Mail*. https://www.dailymail.co.uk/news/article-10135427/Unvaccinated-people-set-BANNED-Berlins-Christmas-market.html.

Butcher, B. (2021, January 16). Did we see a Christmas coronavirus spike? *BBC News*. https://www.bbc.co.uk/news/55669736.

Central Intelligence Agency. (1983). *Human resource exploitation training manual*. https://nsarchive2.gwu.edu/NSAEBB/NSAEBB122/#hre.

Centres for Disease Control and Prevention. (2020, November 3). *I wear a mask because*. https://www.cdc.gov/coronavirus/2019-ncov/prevent-getting-sick/i-wear-a-mask-because.html.

Centres for Disease Control and Prevention. (2021, January 7). *Masks protect you and me*. www.cdc.gov/coronavirus/2019-ncov/prevent-getting-sick/masks-protect-you-and-me.html.

Cheng, K. K., Lam, T. H., & Leung, C. C. (2020). Wearing face masks in the community during the Covid-19 pandemic: Altruism and solidarity. *The Lancet, 399*, E39–E40. https://doi.org/10.1016/S0140-6736(20)30918-1

Citizen Journalists. (2021, October 6). *Confirmed: The Mater hospital was not full of unvaccinated 20/30-year-olds on ventilators on the 22nd July*. https://citizenjournos.com/2021/10/06/confirmed-the-mater-hospital-was-not-full-of-unvaccinated-20-30-year-olds-on-ventilators-on-the-22nd-july/.

Cohen, N. (2021, February 27). It is only a matter of time before we turn on the unvaccinated. *The Guardian*. https://www.theguardian.com/commentisfree/2021/feb/27/it-is-only-a-matter-of-time-before-we-turn-on-the-unvaccinated.

Coleman, L. (2021, December 16). Face mask row sparks brawl on train as furious passengers come to blows—leaving kids in tears. *The Sun*. https://www.thesun.co.uk/news/uknews/17057039/face-mask-row-brawl-on-train-furious-passengers/.

Corbett, K.P. (2020, May 26). *The Covid Nazification of the National Health Service*. https://kevinpcorbett.com/onewebmedia/Nazification%20of%20the%20National%20Health%20Servicev1.rtf.

Cordon, G. (2020, December 20). Update: Tier 4 restrictions may be needed in UK for "couple of months." *London South East*. https://www.lse.co.uk/news/update-tier-4-restrictions-may-be-needed-in-uk-for-couple-of-months-jvf9arff3v3chqa.html.

Craig, C., & Engler, J. (2020, December 19). Has the evidence of asymptomatic spread of Covid-19 been significantly overstated?" *Lockdown Sceptics*. https://lockdownsceptics.org/has-the-evidence-of-asymptomatic-spread-of-covid-19-been-significantly-overstated-2/.

da Silva, C. (2021, June 30). Fauci warns Delta variant will produce 'two Americas' for vaccinated and unvaccinated. *The Independent*. https://www.independent.co.uk/news/world/americas/fauci-delta-variant-covid-america-b1875572.html.

Davies, J. (2021, February 17). No Covid outbreaks have ever been linked to crowded beaches, government adviser claims. *Daily Mail*. https://www.dailymail.co.uk/news/article-9270359/Staycation-hope-SAGE-expert-claims-no-Covid-outbreak-world-linked-beach.html.

Davies, G. (2021, November 10). NHS must be "careful" with numbers, warns health secretary in wake of Amanda Pritchard error. *The Telegraph*. https://www.telegraph.co.uk/news/2021/11/10/nhs-must-careful-numbers-warns-health-secretary-wake-amanda/.

Day, T., Park, A., Madras, N., Gumel, A., & Wu, J. (2006). When is quarantine a useful control strategy for emerging infectious diseases? *American Journal of Epidemiology, 163*(5), 479–485. https://doi.org/10.1093/aje/kwj056.

Delingpole, J. (2021, May 20). UK media and celebs gang up to vilify vaccine 'refuseniks.' *Breitbart*. https://www.breitbart.com/europe/2021/05/20/uk-media-and-celebs-gang-up-to-vilify-vaccine-refuseniks/.

Department of Health and Social Care. (2021). *New TV advert urges public to stay at home to protect the NHS and save lives*. https://www.gov.uk/government/news/new-tv-advert-urges-public-to-stay-at-home-to-protect-the-nhs-and-save-lives.

Dettmann, L. M., Adams, S., & Taylor, G. (2022, February 9). Investigating the prevalence of anxiety and depression during the first COVID-19 lockdown in the United Kingdom: Systematic review and meta-analyses. *British Journal of Clinical Psychology, 61*(3), 757–780. https://doi.org/10.1111/bjc.12360.

Dodsworth, L. (2021, December 18). *A week of life under the ministry of fear*. https://lauradodsworth.substack.com/p/a-week-of-life-under-the-ministry.

Doherty, C. (2021, June 6). "Time to distinguish" between vaccinated and unvaccinated, says Tony Blair. *The Standard*. https://www.standard.co.uk/news/uk/tony-blair-labour-nhs-london-twitter-b938975.html.

Dolan, P., Hallsworth, M., Halpern, D., King, D., & Vlaev, I. (2010). *MINDSPACE: Influencing behaviour through public policy*. Cabinet Office and Institute for Government. https://www.instituteforgovernment.org.uk/sites/default/files/publications/MINDSPACE.pdf.

Drolet, C. E., Hafer, C. L., & Heuer, L. (2016). The role of perceived deservingness in the toleration of human rights violations. *Social Justice Research, 29*, 429–455. https://doi.org/10.1007/s11211-016-0273-y.

Ellul, J. (1965). *Propaganda: The formation of men's attitudes*. Knopf.

Fagan, P. (2020, July 28). Face masks make you stupid. *The Critic*. https://thecritic.co.uk/face-masks-make-you-stupid/.

Feighner, B. H., Eubank, S., Glass, R. J., Davey, V. J., Chrétien, J. -P., & Gaydos, J. C. (2009). Infectious disease modeling and military readiness. *Emerging Infectious Diseases, 15*(9). https://doi.org/10.3201/eid1509.090702.

Fenton, N., Neil, M., & McLachlan, S. (2021). *What proportion of people with Covid-19 do not get symptoms?* http://www.eecs.qmul.ac.uk/~norman/papers/asymptomatics.pdf.

Fischer, A. H., Gillebaart, M., Rotteveel, M., Becker, D., & Vliek, M. (2012). Veiled emotions: The effect of covered faces on emotion perception and attitudes. *Social Psychological and Personality Science, 3*(3), 266–274. https://doi.org/10.1177/1948550611418534.

Fleet Street Fox. (2021, September 20). Anti-vaxxers want to kill your babies, stage a coup and cause another lockdown. *Daily Mirror*. https://www.mirror.co.uk/news/politics/anti-vaxxers-kill-your-babies-25025422.

Fox, M. (2021, July 4). Unvaccinated people are "variant factories," infectious diseases expert says. *CNN Health*. https://edition.cnn.com/2021/07/03/health/unvaccinated-variant-factories/index.html.

French president Macron vows to "piss off" unvaccinated amid record Covid-19 cases. (2022, January 5). *Statecraft*. https://www.statecraft.co.in/article/french-president-macron-vows-to-piss-off-unvaccinated-amid-record-covid-19-cases.

Fromm, E. (1960). *Fear of freedom*. Routledge and Kegan Paul.
Galpin, J. (2021, June 17). Hundreds complain to Ofcom over Covid rant on Jeremy Vine show. *Joe*. https://www.joe.co.uk/coronavirus/hundreds-complain-to-ofcom-over-covid-rant-on-jeremy-vine-show-276695.
Gant, J. (2020, April 25). Is there any science behind two-metre social distancing rule...? Government adviser says guidelines on keeping apart was "conjured out of nowhere." *Daily Mail*. https://www.dailymail.co.uk/news/article-8256109/Social-distancing-two-metres-apart-based-figure-says-government-adviser.html.
Gantzer, O. (2022, February 3). Jeremy Vine backlash: Channel 5 show sparks Ofcom complaints over Covid jab row. *The Express*. https://www.express.co.uk/showbiz/tv-radio/1559986/Jeremy-Vine-backlash-Ofcom-complaints-Covid-jab-debate.
Gates, B., & Gates, M. (2021, January 27). The year global health went local. *GatesNotes*. https://www.gatesnotes.com/2021-Annual-Letter.
Germany 1–1 Argentina. (2006, June 30). *BBC Sport*. http://news.bbc.co.uk/sport1/hi/football/world_cup_2006/5122640.stm.
Germany coronavirus: Protests call for end of restrictions. (2020, August 29). *BBC News*. https://www.bbc.co.uk/news/av/world-europe-53958428.
Germany experiencing "pandemic of the unvaccinated." (2021, November 3). *RTE*. https://www.rte.ie/news/coronavirus/2021/1103/1257602-coronavirus-germany/.
Gillett, F. (2021, May 14). Covid-19: Five ways to make hugging safer, from the experts. *BBC News*. https://www.bbc.co.uk/news/uk-57083571.
Gillibrand, A. (2020, September 1). Holly Willoughby hugs Phillip Schofield through plastic sheet as they reunite on This Morning. *Metro*. https://metro.co.uk/2020/09/01/holly-willoughby-reunites-phillip-schofield-hugs-plastic-sheet-morning-13205646/.
Glass, R. J., Glass, L. M., Beyeler, W. E., & Min, J. (2006). Targeted social distancing designs for pandemic influenza. *Emerging Infectious Diseases, 12*(11), 1671–1681. https://doi.org/10.3201/eid1211.060255.
Golding, W. (2012). *Lord of the flies*. Faber and Faber.
Green, T., & Bhattacharya, J. (2021, July 22). Lockdowns are killers in the Global South. *Unherd*. https://unherd.com/thepost/lockdowns-are-killers-in-the-global-south/.
Greenhalgh, T., Schmid, M.B., Czypionka, T., Bassler, D., & Gruer, L. (2020). Face masks for the public during the Covid-19 Crisis. *BMJ*, *369*, Article m1435. https://doi.org/10.1136/bmj.m1435.
Grossman, D. (1995). *On killing: The psychological cost of learning to kill in war and society*. Little, Brown and Company.
Groves, J., & Martin, D. (2021, May 18). Now vaccine refuseniks threaten freedom: Tory MPs warn Boris not to delay unlocking over the few who

won't have jab. *Mail+*. https://www.mailplus.co.uk/edition/news/coronavirus/70780/now-vaccine-refuseniks-threaten-freedom-tory-mps-warn-boris-not-to-delay-unlocking-over-the-few-who-wont-have-jab.

Grylls, G. (2021, December 22). Tony Blair: If you're eligible and refuse the Covid vaccine, you're an idiot. *The Times*. https://www.thetimes.co.uk/article/tony-blair-if-youre-eligible-and-refuse-the-covid-vaccine-youre-an-idiot-sz97xhkdq.

Hancock: Asymptomatic coronavirus transmission "was not known." (2020, July 5). *BBC News*. https://www.bbc.co.uk/news/av/uk-53298369.

Haque, O. S., De Freitas, J., Viani, I., Niederschulte, B., & Bursztajn, H. J. (2012). Why did so many German doctors join the Nazi Party early? *International Journal of Law and Psychiatry, 35*(5–6), 473–479. https://doi.org/10.1016/j.ijlp.2012.09.022.

Hardcore vaccine refuseniks could need deradicalising like terrorists—expert. (2021, December 8). *ITV News*. https://www.itv.com/news/2021-12-08/hardcore-vaccine-refuseniks-could-need-deradicalising-like-terrorists-expert.

Harradine, K. (2020, October 23). Why so many believe in the Covid cult. *TCW*. https://www.conservativewoman.co.uk/why-so-many-believe-in-the-covid-cult/.

Harrison, N. (2023, December 7). Lockdowns: A study of the harms. *UK Column*. https://www.ukcolumn.org/article/lockdowns-a-study-of-the-harms.

Hassan, S. A., & Shah, M. J. (2019). The anatomy of undue influence used by terrorist cults and traffickers to induce helplessness and trauma, so creating false identities. *Ethics, Medicine, and Public Health, 8*, 97–107. https://doi.org/10.1016/j.jemep.2019.03.002.

Hayen, T. (2021, September 12). Covid's willing executioners. *OffGuardian*. https://off-guardian.org/2021/09/12/covids-willing-executioners/.

Hayes, G., Carpani, J., & Global Health Security Team. (2020, November 30). Virus "back under control" after lockdown, Matt Hancock says. *The Telegraph*. https://www.telegraph.co.uk/global-health/science-and-disease/coronavirus-news-tiers-covid-lockdown-oxford-vaccine-christmas/.

Heffer, G. (2020, September 15). Coronavirus: Home Secretary Priti Patel "would call the police" if neighbours broke "rule of six." *Sky News*. https://news.sky.com/story/coronavirus-home-secretary-priti-patel-would-call-the-police-if-neighbours-broke-rule-of-six-12072281.

Hern, A. (2021, May 6). NHS Covid jab booking site leaks people's vaccine status. *The Guardian*. https://www.theguardian.com/world/2021/may/06/nhs-covid-jab-booking-site-leaks-peoples-vaccine-status.

Hett, B. C. (2014). *Burning the Reichstag: An investigation into the Third Reich's enduring mystery*. Oxford University Press.

Hodge, M. (2020, September 4). "I've done nothing wrong." Moment cop "pepper-sprays train passenger who refuses to wear mask claiming medical condition." *The Sun*. https://www.thesun.co.uk/news/12578596/train-pas senger-face-mask-cop-spray/.

Hopkins, C. J. (2021a, April 21). The Covidian cult (part II). *Consent Factory, Inc*. https://consentfactory.org/2021/04/21/the-covidian-cult-part-ii/.

Hopkins, C. J. (2021b, May 26). *Greetings from "new normal" Germany!* https://cjhopkins.substack.com/p/greetings-from-new-normal-germany.

Hopkins, C. J. (2021c, November 2). (New normal) winter is coming. *OffGuardian*. https://off-guardian.org/2021/11/02/new-normal-winter-is-coming/.

Howard, J. (2020, May 14). Masks help stop the spread of coronavirus—the science is simple and I'm one of 100 experts urging governors to require public mask-wearing. *The Conversation*. https://theconversation.com/masks-help-stop-the-spread-of-coronavirus-the-science-is-simple-and-im-one-of-100-experts-urging-governors-to-require-public-mask-wearing-138507.

Hudson, P. (2022, January 25). As Covid restrictions ease, it's time to get tough on anti-vaxxers. *The Mirror*. https://www.mirror.co.uk/news/uk-news/as-covid-restrictions-ease-its-26046616.

Hughes, D. A. (2022, July 29). Wall Street, the Nazis, and the crimes of the deep state. *Propaganda in Focus*. https://propagandainfocus.com/wall-street-the-nazis-and-the-crimes-of-the-deep-state/.

Huxley, A. (1936). *The olive tree and other essays*. Chatto and Windus.

Huxley, A. (1958). *Brave new world revisited*. Harper and Row.

Hyde Park: Police attacks at anti-lockdown protest condemned. (2021, April 25). *BBC News*. https://www.bbc.co.uk/news/uk-england-london-56878486.

Hymas, C. (2021, January 6). Children can be used as undercover Spies to report on Parents, covert intelligence bill reveals. *The Telegraph*. https://www.telegraph.co.uk/news/2021/01/06/children-can-used-undercover-spies-report-parents-covert-intelligence/.

Ibbetson, R., & Pleasance, C. (2021, November 17). Now Italy is set for "lockdown of the unvaccinated": Five regions demand Rome follows Austria in imposing medical apartheid amid ferocious fourth wave of Covid as Merkel calls for tougher curbs in Germany. *Daily Mail*. https://www.dailymail.co.uk/news/article-10212701/Angela-Merkel-warns-Germanys-Covid-situation-dramatic.html.

Independent Sage. (2020). *A better way to go: towards a zero Covid UK*. https://www.independentsage.org/wp-content/uploads/2020/07/202 00717-A-Better-Way-To-Go.pdf.

InProportion2. (2021). *Scrapbook: Dissent, democracy and disease*. https://inp roportion2.talkigy.com/scrapbook_2021-02-24.html.

Investment Watch. (2021, October 4). *On UK news channel: We either allow this or we end up holding people down and jabbing them by force*. https://www.investmentwatchblog.com/on-uk-news-channel-we-either-allow-this-or-we-end-up-holding-people-down-and-jabbing-them-by-force/.

Ioannidis, J. P. A. (2021). Infection fatality rate of Covid-19 inferred from seroprevalence data. *Bulletin of the World Health Organisation, 99*, 19–33. https://doi.org/10.2471/BLT.20.265892.

Jackson, R. (2007). Constructing enemies: "Islamic terrorism" in political and academic discourse. *Government and Opposition, 42*(3), 394–426. https://doi.org/10.1111/j.1477-7053.2007.00229.x.

Jaffe-Hoffman, M. (2021, February 28). Everything you need to know about Israel's green passport program. *The Jerusalem Post*. https://www.jpost.com/israel-news/everything-you-need-to-know-about-israels-green-passport-program-659437.

James, M. (2021, March 25). Highlights of NHS comms campaigns through Covid-19. *Communicate*. https://www.communicatemagazine.com/news/2021/highlights-of-nhs-comms-campaigns-through-covid-19/.

Johnston, P. (2021, December 21). I'm fed up with the unvaccinated rump who risk pushing us back into lockdown. *The Telegraph*. https://www.telegraph.co.uk/news/2021/12/21/fed-unvaccinated-rump-risk-pushing-us-back-lockdown/.

Jones, H. (2020, December 20). Matt Hancock slams "totally irresponsible" Brits trying to leave tier 4 London. *Metro*. https://metro.co.uk/2020/12/20/matt-hancock-slams-totally-irresponsible-brits-trying-to-leave-tier-4-london-13779575/.

Joseph, A. (2020, June 9). "We don't actually have that answer yet": WHO clarifies comments on asymptomatic spread of Covid-19. *STAT*. https://www.statnews.com/2020/06/09/who-comments-asymptomatic-spread-covid-19/.

Kampf, G. (2021). Covid-19: Stigmatising the unvaccinated is not justified. *The Lancet, 398*(1871), Article 10314. https://doi.org/10.1016/S0140-6736(21)02243-1.

Kekatos, M. (2020, November 18). Face masks do not protect the wearer from coronavirus, but will stop them from infecting other people, Danish study finds. *Daily Mail*. https://www.dailymail.co.uk/health/article-8962397/Danish-study-finds-face-masks-provide-limited-protection-wearer.html.

Kidd, I. J., & Ratcliffe, M. (2020, November). Welcome to Covidworld. *The Critic*. https://thecritic.co.uk/issues/november-2020/welcome-to-covidworld/.

King, A., & Schneider, B. (1991). *The first global revolution: A report by the Council of the Club of Rome*. Pantheon Books.

Kolstoe, S. (2020, May 20). "Coronavirus: Wearing a cloth face mask is less about science and more about solidarity." *The Conversation*. https://theconversation.com/coronavirus-wearing-a-cloth-face-mask-is-less-about-science-and-more-about-solidarity-138461.

Kwai, I. (2021, May 10). People in England will soon be allowed to officially hug and kiss again. *New York Times*. https://www.nytimes.com/live/2021/05/10/world/covid-19-coronavirus#people-in-england-will-soon-be-allowed-to-officially-hug-and-kiss-again.

Kyrie, V., & Broudy, D. (2022, September 22). The Covid-19 concoction: A recipe for successful psychological operations. *Propaganda in Focus*. https://propagandainfocus.com/the-covid-19-concoction-a-recipe-for-successful-psychological-operations/.

Lacter, E. P. (2007, June 29). Relationships between mind control programming and ritual abuse. *End Ritual Abuse*. http://www.whale.to/b/lacter2.html.

Laila, C. (2021, October 24). New Zealand PM Jacinda Ardern happily admits she created two classes of people: The vaccinated and the unvaccinated. *The Gateway Pundit*. https://www.thegatewaypundit.com/2021/10/new-zealand-pm-jacinda-ardern-happily-admits-created-two-classes-people-vaccinated-unvaccinated-video/.

Langton, K. (2021a, April 9). When can we hug again? When can I hug my Grandchildren? *The Express*. https://www.express.co.uk/news/uk/1401275/when-can-we-hug-again-when-can-I-hug-my-grandchildren-EVG.

Langton, K. (2021b, November 21). Unvaccinated lockdowns: Which European countries have unvaccinated lockdowns? Full list. *The Express*. https://www.express.co.uk/news/world/1524493/unvaccinated-lockdown-Europe-countries-full-list-EVG.

Lee, J. (2021, February 24). Why should the whole country be held hostage by the one in five who refuse a vaccine? *Daily Mail*. https://www.dailymail.co.uk/debate/article-9293147/Dr-JOHN-LEE-country-held-hostage-one-five-refuse-vaccine.html.

Lewis, L. (2021, November 24). £34,050-a-year Kent private school that makes children wear yellow badges if they are exempt from wearing masks is slammed for the "inappropriate" similarity to yellow stars Nazis forced condemned Jews to display." *Daily Mail*. https://www.dailymail.co.uk/news/article-10236627/34-050-year-Kent-school-makes-children-wear-yellow-badges-exempt-wearing-masks.html.

Lifton, R. J. (1989). *Thought reform and the psychology of totalism*. University of North Carolina Press.

London police to enforce face masks "as last resort." (2020, July 22). *BBC News*. https://www.bbc.co.uk/news/uk-england-london-53498100.

Lunning, F. (2013). *Fetish Style*. Bloomsbury.

Magen, H. (2020, March 22). Lockdown lunacy. *Globes*. https://en.globes.co.il/en/article-lockdown-lunacy-1001322696.

Manancourt, V. (2020, August 1). Thousands protest against coronavirus measures in Berlin. *Politico*. https://www.politico.eu/article/coronavirus-berlin-protest/.

Mandavilli, A. (2021, July 25). The Delta variant is the symptom of a bigger threat: Vaccine refusal. *The New York Times*. https://www.nytimes.com/2021/07/25/health/coronavirus-vaccine-refusal.html.

Mandel, D. R. (2002). Evil and the instigation of collective violence. *Analyses of Social Issues and Public Policy, 2*(1), 101–108. https://doi.org/10.1111/j.1530-2415.2002.00030.x.

Marcus, L. (1974). The real CIA—the Rockefellers' fascist establishment, a polemic. *The Campaigner, 7*(6), 5–34.

Martin, D. (2021). *The Fauci/COVID-19 Dossier*. https://foreignaffairsintelligencecouncil.files.wordpress.com/2021/02/the-fauci-covid-19-dossier.pdf.

Masked train passengers attack man for not wearing mask. (2021, July 15). *Infowars* https://www.newswars.com/watch-masked-train-passengers-attack-man-for-not-wearing-mask/.

Mason, R. (2021, December 28). What to do about the UK's unvaccinated? No 10's Covid dilemma. *The Guardian*. https://www.theguardian.com/world/2021/dec/28/unvaccinated-uk-covid-dilemma-vaccine-refusers.

McCormack, K. (2021, April 5). Edwina Currie says non-vaccinated people "can exercise their freedom by staying at home." *The Mirror*. https://www.mirror.co.uk/tv/tv-news/edwina-currie-says-non-vaccinated-23853785.

McElvoy, A. (2021, December 14). The unvaccinated have become a lethal liability we can ill-afford. *Evening Standard*. https://www.standard.co.uk/comment/covid-unvaccinated-omicron-vaccine-passports-b971877.html.

Medicines and Healthcare products Regulatory Agency. (n.d.). *COVID-19 vaccine analysis overview* [Dataset]. https://yellowcard.ukcolumn.org/yellow-card-reports.

Meerloo, J. A. (1956). *The rape of the mind. The psychology of thought control, menticide, and brainwashing*. World Publishing Company.

Merrick, R. (2021, January 12). Ban non-mask wearers, Health Secretary tells supermarkets. *The Independent*. https://www.independent.co.uk/news/uk/politics/face-mask-ban-supermarket-matt-hancock-b1785625.html.

Miller, M. C. (2020, November 30). Just sent my petition in defence of academic freedom, with its 17,700+ signatories, to President Andrew Hamilton at NYU. *News From Underground*. https://markcrispinmiller.com/2020/11/just-sent-my-petition-in-defense-of-academic-freedom-with-its-17700-signatories-to-president-andrew-hamilton-at-nyu/.

Morgan Edwards, L. (2021, December 6). The Swiss need the spirit of William Tell. *TCW*. https://www.conservativewoman.co.uk/the-swiss-need-the-spirit-of-william-tell/.

Morris, S. (2021, December 29). Covid-19: Boris Johnson says "up to 90%" in intensive care have not had a booster and urges people to get jabbed. *Sky News*. https://news.sky.com/story/covid-19-boris-johnson-says-up-to-90-in-intensive-care-have-not-had-a-booster-and-urges-people-to-get-jabbed-12505590.

Mulvey, K. (2021, June 2). Why I'm disinviting my unvaccinated friends from my dinner parties. *The Telegraph*. https://www.telegraph.co.uk/women/life/wont-have-vaccine-no-friend-mine/.

Needham, G. (2014). Bringing out the Gimp: Fashioning the SM imaginary. *Fashion Theory, 18*(2), 149–168. https://doi.org/10.2752/175174114X13890223974506.

Neil, A. (2021, December 9). It's time to punish Britain's five million vaccine refuseniks: They put us all at risk of more restrictions. So why shouldn't we curb some of their freedoms?" *Daily Mail*. https://www.dailymail.co.uk/debate/article-10294225/Its-time-punish-Britains-five-million-vaccine-refuseniks-says-ANDREW-NEIL.html.

No love for Berlin parade. (2001, April 4). *BBC News*. http://news.bbc.co.uk/1/hi/entertainment/1260784.stm.

Nuki, P. (2021, September 24). UK on brink of joining EU Covid vaccine passport scheme. *The Telegraph*. https://www.telegraph.co.uk/global-health/science-and-disease/uk-brink-joining-eu-passport-scheme-sources-confirm-nhs-system/.

Office for National Statistics. (2023). *Deaths involving COVID-19 by vaccination status, England: deaths occurring between 1 April 2021 and 31 May 2023*. https://www.ons.gov.uk/peoplepopulationandcommunity/birthsdeathsandmarriages/deaths/bulletins/deathsinvolvingcovid19byvaccinationstatusengland/deathsoccurringbetween1april2021and31may2023.

O'Grady, S. (2020, July 20). Boris Johnson says it's our own fault if we face a second coronavirus lockdown. *The Independent*. https://www.independent.co.uk/voices/boris-johnson-coronavirus-second-lockdown-test-and-trace-blackburn-outbreak-a9627791.html.

OpenVAERS. (n.d.). *VAERS Covid vaccine adverse event reports*. Retrieved June 17, 2023, from https://openvaers.com/covid-data.

Osborne, G. (2021, February 9). To lead a normal life you'll need a Covid passport—here's why. *Evening Standard*. https://www.standard.co.uk/comment/george-osborne-covid-passports-normal-life-b919119.html.

Pearson, C. (2021, November 19). Dominic Raab refuses to fully rule out a "lockdown for the unvaccinated." *Unity News Network*. https://unitynewsnetwork.co.uk/dominic-raab-refuses-to-fully-rule-out-a-lockdown-for-the-unvaccinated/.

Penna, D. (2022, January 6). Boris Johnson hits out at anti-vaxxers spouting "mumbo jumbo" on social media. *The Telegraph*. https://www.telegraph.co.uk/politics/2022/01/06/boris-johnson-energy-crisis-travel-testing-rules-isolation/.

Perez, M. (2020, August 8). WHO says asymptomatic spread of coronavirus "very rare," but experts raise questions. *Forbes*. https://www.forbes.com/sites/mattperez/2020/06/08/who-says-asymptomatic-spread-of-coronavirus-very-rare-but-experts-raise-questions/.

Perlstadt, H. (2018). How to get out of the Stanford prison experiment: Revisiting social science research ethics. *Current Research Journal of Social Sciences*, *1*(2), 45–59. https://doi.org/10.12944/CRJSSH.1.2.01.

PfizerGate: Official government reports prove hundreds of thousands of people are dying every single week due to covid-19 vaccination. (2022, August 14). *The Exposé*. https://expose-news.com/2022/08/14/gov-reports-prove-hundreds-thousands-dying-covid-vaccine/.

Phillips, A. (2021, November 18). Lockdown warning for millions of Britons: UK could follow Germany on unvaccinated rules. *The Express*. https://www.express.co.uk/news/uk/1523105/lockdown-news-uk-warning-Germany-unvaccinated.

Podder, C., Gumel, A. B., Bowman, C. S., & McLeod, R. G. (2007). Mathematical study of the impact of quarantine, isolation, and vaccination in curtailing an epidemic. *Journal of Biological Systems, 15*(2), 185–202. https://doi.org/10.1142/S0218339007002180.

Pollock, A., & Lancaster, J. (2020). Asymptomatic transmission of Covid-19. *BMJ*, 371, Article m4851. https://doi.org/10.1136/bmj.m4851.

Potts, S. C. (2020, June 9). The cult of the mask. *The Remnant*. https://remnantnewspaper.com/web/index.php/articles/item/4927-the-cult-of-the-mask#_ftnref1.

Public Health England. (2021). *Weekly national influenza and Covid-19 surveillance report, Week 8*. https://assets.publishing.service.gov.uk/government/uploads/system/uploads/attachment_data/file/964754/Weekly_Flu_and_COVID-19_report_w8.pdf.

Rampen, J. (2020, July 24). Disabled woman abused by stranger on train over face mask in sickening attack. *Liverpool Echo*. https://www.liverpoolecho.co.uk/news/liverpool-news/disabled-woman-abused-stranger-train-18660291.

Rancourt, D. (2021, February 6). *Analysis of the scientific basis for Ontario, Canada's mandatory face masking and physical distancing law,*

2020. https://ocla.ca/wp-content/uploads/2021/02/OCLA-Report-2021-1-4th-science-review-for-covid-policy-Reg-364-20-7f.pdf.

Rancourt, D., Baudin, M., & Mercier, J. (2021). *Nature of the Covid-era public health disaster in the USA, from all-cause mortality and socio-geo-economic and climatic data*. https://denisrancourt.ca/uploads_entries/1635189453861_USA%20ACM%20into%202021%20-%20article----12d.pdf.

Rayner, G. (2020, December 17). Third national lockdown looms after Christmas. *The Telegraph*. https://www.telegraph.co.uk/politics/2020/12/17/third-national-lockdown-possible-coronavirus-infections-keep/.

Reitschuster, B. (2021). *"Kauft nicht bei Ungeimpften."* https://reitschuster.de/post/kauft-nicht-bei-ungeimpften/.

Roach, A. (2020, November 18). Public Health England director says every day of "relaxed" restrictions around Christmas will need five days of tighter measures. *Evening Standard*. https://www.standard.co.uk/news/uk/relaxed-covid-restrictions-christmas-five-days-tighter-measures-b73392.html.

Rodgers, L. (2022, January 17). Firms are cutting sick pay for the unvaccinated—what does employment law say? *The Conversation*. https://theconversation.com/firms-are-cutting-sick-pay-for-the-unvaccinated-what-does-employment-law-say-174985.

Sardi, B. (2021, March 26). *The coming witch hunt against anti-vaxxers*. https://www.lewrockwell.com/2021/03/bill-sardi/the-coming-witch-hunt-against-anti-vaxxers/.

Schiavone, A. (2021, November 23). Unvaccinated Britons should face consequences of their actions "Send them home!" *The Express*. https://www.express.co.uk/news/uk/1525598/covid-news-benjamin-butterworth-lockdown-vaccine-jab-non-vaccinated-uk-europe-vn.

Schiavone, A. (2022, January 6). Justin Trudeau savaged over "polarising" rant at "misogynistic and racist" anti-vaxxers. *The Express*. https://www.express.co.uk/news/world/1545278/Justin-Trudeau-Tonia-Buxton-antivaxxers-racist-mysogynistic-Emmanuel-Marcon-VN.

Schwab, K., & Malleret, T. (2020). *Covid 19: The Great Reset*. World Economic Forum.

Science and Technology Committee and the Health and Social Care Committee. (2021). *Oral evidence: coronavirus: Lessons learnt, HC 95*. https://committees.parliament.uk/oralevidence/2318/pdf#page=22.

Scientific Pandemic Insights Group on Behaviours. (2020a). *Options for increasing adherence to social distancing measures*. https://assets.publishing.service.gov.uk/government/uploads/system/uploads/attachment_data/file/882722/25-options-for-increasing-adherence-to-social-distancing-measures-22032020.pdf.

Scientific Pandemic Insights Group on Behaviours. (2020b). *Theory and evidence base for initial SPI-B recommendations for phased changes in activity restrictions*. https://assets.publishing.service.gov.uk/government/uploads/system/uploads/attachment_data/file/892031/S0470_Theory_and_evidence_base_for_initial_SPI-B_recommendations_for_phased_changes_in_activity_restrictions.pdf.

Scientific Advisory Group for Emergencies. (2021). *Application of physical distancing and fabric face coverings in mitigating the B117 variant SARS-CoV-2 virus in public, workplace and community settings*. https://assets.publishing.service.gov.uk/government/uploads/system/uploads/attachment_data/file/957010/s1029-emg-face-coverings-distancing.pdf.

Scott, B. (2021, January 3). Psychological attack on the UK. *UK Column*. https://www.ukcolumn.org/article/psychological-attack-uk.

Secret Consultant. (2021, November 21). ICU is full of the unvaccinated—my patience with them is wearing thin. *The Guardian*. https://www.theguardian.com/world/2021/nov/21/icu-is-full-of-the-unvaccinated-my-patience-with-them-is-wearing-thin.

Seneff, S., & Nigh, G. (2021). Worse than the disease? Reviewing some possible unintended consequences of the mRNA vaccines against Covid-19. *International Journal of Vaccine Theory, Practice, and Research*, *2*(1), 38–79. https://doi.org/10.56098/ijvtpr.v2i1.23.

Sheffield, E. (2022, January 7). It's time for London's unvaccinated to pay with their freedoms, not ours. *Evening Standard*. https://www.standard.co.uk/comment/unvaccinated-lockdowns-novak-djokovic-london-covid-b975487.html.

Sherman, Y. (2022, October 18). Piers Morgan tries to whitewash "violent and vicious" remarks against unvaccinated. *Frontline News*. https://frontline.news/post/piers-morgan-tries-to-whitewash-violent-and-vicious-remarks-against-unvaccinated.

Shukman, D., & O'Connor, M. (2021, May 9). Coronavirus: expert urges caution over hugs as lockdown eases. *BBC News*. https://www.bbc.co.uk/news/uk-57047525.

Sidley, G. (2020, October 24). How the mean psychologists got us to comply with coronavirus restrictions. *Coronababble*. https://www.coronababble.com/post/how-the-mean-psychologists-induced-us-to-comply-with-coronavirus-restrictions.

Somerville, E. (2021, September 28). Anger on campuses as freshers given wristbands to signify Covid vaccination. *The Telegraph*. https://www.telegraph.co.uk/news/2021/09/28/anger-campuses-freshers-given-wristbands-signify-covid-vaccination/.

Spencer, B., & Calver, T. (2021, November 28). Intensive care beds filled with unvaccinated Covid patients. *The Sunday Times*. https://www.thetimes.co.uk/article/intensive-care-beds-filled-with-unvaccinated-covid-patients-9m0qbx03h.

Stanton, G. (2016). The ten stages of genocide. *Genocide Watch*. http://genocidewatch.net/genocide-2/8-stages-of-genocide/.

Stieber, Z. (2021, November 26). CDC changed definition of "vaccine" because of Covid-19 vaccines: Emails. *[your]News*. https://yournews.com/2021/11/04/2248400/cdc-changed-definition-of-vaccine-because-of-covid-19-vaccines-emails/.

Stutt, R. O. J. H., Retkute, R., Bradley, M., Gilligan, C. A., & Colvin, J. (2020). A modelling framework to assess the likely effectiveness of facemasks in combination with "lock-down" in managing the Covid-19 pandemic. *Proceedings of the Royal Society A*, *476*(2238), Article 20200376. https://doi.org/10.1098/rspa.2020.0376.

Subramanian, S. V., & Kumar, A. (2021). Increases in Covid are unrelated to levels of vaccination across 68 countries and 2,947 counties in the United States. *European Journal of Epidemiology, 36*, 1237–1240. https://doi.org/10.1007/s10654-021-00808-7.

Sumption, J. (2020, October 27). *Government by decree: Covid-19 and the constitution*. Cambridge Freshfields Annual Law Lecture. https://resources.law.cam.ac.uk/privatelaw/Freshfields_Lecture_2020_Government_by_Decree.pdf.

Sutton, A. C. (2016). *Wall Street and the rise of Hitler*. Clairview.

Tapscott, M. (2020, December 2). Americans are suffering "delusional psychosis" about CCP virus, psychiatrist claims. *The Epoch Times*. https://www.theepochtimes.com/california-psychiatrist-claims-americans-are-suffering-a-delusional-psychosis-about-ccp-virus_3601044.html.

The weekend's coastal visitors were irresponsible and selfish. (2020, March 25). *Lincolnshire World*. https://www.lincolnshireworld.com/news/opinion/columnists/column-the-weekends-coastal-visitors-were-irresponsible-and-selfish-we-need-to-adjust-to-a-new-kind-of-normal-2517263.

Thomson, A. (2020, September 15). What is a Covid-19 marshal? *UK Column*. https://www.ukcolumn.org/article/what-covid-19-marshal.

Thousands protest in Germany against restrictions. (2020, August 1). *BBC News*. https://www.bbc.co.uk/news/world-europe-53622797.

Tory MP Tobias Ellwood broke Covid rules, says Home Secretary. (2020, December 17). *BBC News*. https://www.bbc.co.uk/news/uk-politics-55343187.

Tucker, J. A. (2021, September 28). The purges have begun. *Brownstone Institute*. https://archive.ph/231ns.

Turner, C. (2021, October 7). Fury as council creates "vaccine apartheid" among schoolchildren. *The Telegraph*. https://www.telegraph.co.uk/news/2021/10/07/council-accused-creating-vaccine-apartheid-among-schoolchildren/.

UK Column. (2021, May 3). *UK Column news—26th April 2021*. https://www.ukcolumn.org/ukcolumn-news/uk-column-news-26th-april-2021.

UK Government. (2021). *Social distancing review: Report*. https://assets.publishing.service.gov.uk/government/uploads/system/uploads/attachment_data/file/999413/Social-Distancing-Review-Report.pdf.

UK Health Security Agency. (2021a). *Weekly national influenza and COVID-19 surveillance report, Week 50*. https://assets.publishing.service.gov.uk/government/uploads/system/uploads/attachment_data/file/1041447/Weekly_Flu_and_COVID-19_report_w50.pdf.

UK Health Security Agency. (2021b). *Omicron daily overview: 31 December 2021*. https://assets.publishing.service.gov.uk/government/uploads/system/uploads/attachment_data/file/1044522/20211231_OS_Daily_Omicron_Overview.pdf.

UK Health Security Agency. (2022a). *Covid-19 vaccine surveillance report, week 1*. https://assets.publishing.service.gov.uk/government/uploads/system/uploads/attachment_data/file/1045329/Vaccine_surveillance_report_week_1_2022.pdf.

UK Health Security Agency. (2022b). *Weekly national influenza and Covid-19 surveillance report, week 27*. https://assets.publishing.service.gov.uk/government/uploads/system/uploads/attachment_data/file/1088929/Weekly_Flu_and_COVID-19_report_w27.pdf.

"Ungeimpfte unerwünscht": Ladenbesitzer wird für Schriftzug angefeindet—und entschuldigt sich. (2021, December 1). *Stern*. https://www.stern.de/panorama/weltgeschehen/-ungeimpfte-unerwuenscht---ladenbesitzer-wird-fuer-schriftzug-angefeindet-30976262.html.

United Nations. (1948). *Convention on the Prevention and Punishment of the Crime of Genocide*. https://www.un.org/en/genocideprevention/genocide.shtml.

Versluis, A. (2006). *The new inquisitions: Heretic-hunting and the intellectual origins of modern totalitarianism*. Oxford University Press.

Vine, S. (2021, May 18). We can't let selfish idiots who don't want free Covid vaccines that scientists worked around the clock to develop hold us hostage. *Daily Mail*. https://www.dailymail.co.uk/debate/article-9593417/SARAH-VINE-let-selfish-idiots-dont-want-free-Covid-vaccines-hold-hostage.html.

Watch: UK pundit Lucy Beresford's deranged plan to take freedoms away from the unvaccinated. (2021, October 29). *Daily Telegraph NZ*. https://dailytelegraph.co.nz/covid-19/lucy-beresfords-deranged-plan-to-take-away-freedoms-from-the-unvaccinated/.

Watson, S. (2021, July 23). CNN: Segregate unvaccinated, make them pay for tests every day. *Summit News*. https://summit.news/2021/07/23/cnn-segregate-unvaccinated-make-them-pay-for-tests-every-day/.

Westermann, E. B. (2015). Political soldiers. In P. Hayes (Ed.), *How was it possible? A Holocaust reader* (pp. 481–494). University of Nebraska Press.

White House. (2021, December 17). *Press briefing by White House Covid-19 response team and public health officials*. https://www.whitehouse.gov/briefing-room/press-briefings/2021/12/17/press-briefing-by-white-house-covid-19-response-team-and-public-health-officials-74/.

Whitfield, K. (2021, May 17). When can we stop wearing masks? Government guidance update. *The Express*. https://www.express.co.uk/news/uk/1435545/when-can-we-stop-wearing-masks-government-guidance-update-evg.

Wilder-Smith, A. (2021). What is the vaccine effect on reducing transmission in the context of the SARS-CoV-2 Delta variant? *The Lancet, 22*(2), 152–153. https://doi.org/10.1016/S1473-3099(21)00690-3.

Wolfe, R. (2021, June 17). Holocaust survivor warns against Covid mandates, new "fascist dictatorship." *LifeSite News*. https://www.lifesitenews.com/news/holocaust-survivor-warns-against-covid-mandates-new-fascist-dictatorship/.

World Health Organisation. (n.d.). *VigiAccess*. Retrieved June 17, 2023, from https://vigiaccess.org/.

World Health Organisation. (2020, August 4). *Estimating mortality from Covid-19*. https://www.who.int/news-room/commentaries/detail/estimating-mortality-from-covid-19.

Wright, R. (2020, June 23). Saving face. *The Critic*. https://thecritic.co.uk/saving-face/.

Yeadon, M. (2020, October 16). What SAGE has got wrong. *Lockdown Sceptics*. https://lockdownsceptics.org/what-sage-got-wrong/.

Zeltman, B. (2020a, October 8). Mask row: BBC presenter slammed for chasing and confronting shoppers for not wearing face masks at petrol station. *The Sun*. https://www.thesun.co.uk/news/12879305/bbc-nolan-slammed-chasing-shoppers-mask/.

Zeltman, B. (2020b, November 16). Deadly conspiracy: NHS workers join anti-vax Facebook group that claims coronavirus vaccine is a 'poison' to be 'unleashed' on the world. *The Sun*. https://www.thesun.co.uk/news/13208307/nhs-workers-anti-covid-vaccine-facebook-group/.

Zimbardo, P. (2005). Mind control in Orwell's *Nineteen eighty-four*: Fictional concepts become operational realities in Jim Jones's jungle experiment. In A. Gleason, J. Goldsmith, & M. C. Nussbaum (Eds.), *On* Nineteen eighty-four*: Orwell and our future* (pp. 127–154). Princeton University Press.

Zimbardo, P. (2007). *The Lucifer effect: Why good people turn evil*. Random House.

CHAPTER 8

The Coming Unrest

The transnational ruling class has no choice but to keep pushing for global technocracy, and the rest of humanity has no choice but to fight back. Knowing since 1968 at least that this moment was coming, the former has developed the CIA's information-liquidation model used in Indonesia and Vietnam in the 1960s into a global digital surveillance dragnet. The "Covid-19 vaccines," shot into as many people as possible for no sound medical reason, could form part of an advanced weapons system, not least in the context of the emergent "IT/Bio/Nano era" envisaged by NASA in 2001, involving the use of nanotechnologies to connect human beings to an external network. If the brain is the twenty-first-century battlescape, and given that syringe-injectable neural nets were a reality by 2018, the evil potential of weaponised neurotechnology knows no bounds. History teaches that as the old social order breaks down, a moment of revolutionary potential arises. Lest unimaginable horrors be allowed to manifest, as in previous world wars, that moment must be seized.

The Coming Unrest

Physical War Becomes Inevitable

As Sun Tzu (1963, p. 77) teaches, "To subdue the enemy without fighting is the acme of skill." So far, this has largely been achieved. There have been no major battles for history to record, only the insidious infiltration of governments and institutions with technocrats, of human minds

D. A. Hughes, *"Covid-19," Psychological Operations, and the War for Technocracy*, https://doi.org/10.1007/978-3-031-41850-1_8

with psychological programming (see Volume 2 of this book), and of human bodies with substances of an undisclosed nature (Hughes, 2022c). Before "Covid-19," van der Pijl (2022, p. 77) argues, the IT revolution allowed the transnational ruling class to "evade a physical war against the population via the alternative of permanent surveillance and information warfare."

Yet, now that all possibility of class compromise has been removed by a transnational ruling class that would sooner escalate to World War III than maintain its post-1968 strategy of low-intensity operations against the public, physical war becomes inevitable. As van der Pijl (2022, p. 268) argues, "It has been the governments, operating under the auspices of the internationalized state and ultimately, the capitalist oligarchy, which, by their declaration of war on society, have created a potentially revolutionary situation." That situation may not have been created by the working classes, but it can only be resolved by them. Recall Minnicino's (1974, p. 51) insight half a century ago that "the only war that is left [is] the world revolution." We appear to be nearing that point.

In the final analysis, Minnicino (1974, p. 37) writes, it is "'the armed body of men' upon which class rule depends," and "someday such armies [will] have to exercise their true function openly." The warning signs are becoming ever more visible. Hedge fund manager Ed Dowd, for instance, seeing just one part of the bigger picture, thinks that the "emergence of global totalitarianism" is to "control the masses when they realise the economy is collapsing," the ramifications of which may be the loss of pensions and social security income (Hope, 2022). The goal, in Dowd's view, is to "prevent the riots that are going to ensue once this thing all unwinds." Sri Lanka provides an island test case of the kind of social unrest that could follow (Sicetsha, 2022).

So far, the role of the military has remained largely covert, e.g. in information warfare (Webb, 2022). The military has been presented in a benign way, viz. its role in "assisting" with the "vaccine" rollout, even though it was behind it (see Chapter 6). The only overt physical violence to speak of has been police and paramilitary violence against those protesting the so-called "Covid-19 countermeasures" (Broudy et al., 2022), although there has been mass *covert* violence wrought by the effects of "lockdowns" and "vaccines," disguised as public health measures (see Chapter 6). Keeping recognised physical violence to a minimum for as long as possible is strategically important from a deep state perspective, "because the facade of democracy must remain intact until the very end, even during the seizure of power. An unbridled assault on the population carries great risks and can even lead to a general political collapse" (van der Pijl, 2022, p. 76). If the public gets wise to what is happening before it is too late, then the controlled demolition of liberal democracy will spin out of control and the likelihood of revolution will increase exponentially.

The "Covid-19" operation was intended to blindside the public and render it incapable of mounting significant resistance to the transition to technocracy. Historically, a key function of psychological warfare has been to weaken target populations before the main fighting begins. During World War II, for example, OSS director William "Wild Bill" Donovan (a former Wall Street lawyer) saw propaganda as "the arrow of initial penetration," to be followed by sabotage and subversion, commando raids, guerrilla action, and behind-the-lines resistance movements—all representing the "softening-up process of an area prior to invasion by friendly armed forces" (Paddock, 1979, p. 9).

Military-grade propaganda, as well as other means of psychological warfare deployed against the public during the "Covid-19" operation, acted as the "arrow of initial penetration." But numerous developments since the winding down of that operation in 2022 pose cause for alarm. For example, should the WHO Pandemic Treaty and amendments to the 2005 International Health Regulations be ratified, the door is opened to a global health dictatorship able to decree compulsory "lockdowns," "vaccinations," and the centralisation of health data surveillance tied to a global digital passport and ID system (Kheriaty, 2022). Central bank digital currencies are being heavily pushed by governments: they amount to a form of biodigital enslavement (Davis, 2023; Hughes, 2022a, p. 234). So-called "15-minute cities" are being phased in, against the will of the people, using physical bollards and licence plate recognition cameras to impose significant restrictions on freedom of movement. Those measures are meeting with civil disobedience (in terms of infrastructure destruction), protests (such as that in Oxford in February 2023), and interventions at the local political level (such as against Colchester City Council in March 2023). The rapid rollout of 5G, despite failure to address serious safety concerns (Burdick, 2023; Jamieson, 2023), is another highly troubling development.

Concerns have been raised about the 51,000 migrants being housed in 400 hotels throughout the United Kingdom at a reported cost to the taxpayer of £6.8 million a day (Young et al., 2023). Such a policy has no precedent or convincing justification, and, under the circumstances, it is reasonable to suspect an ulterior agenda for reasons that have nothing to do with far-right ideology. Since 1994, annual net migration to the UK fell mostly within the 170,000–330,000 range (Office for National Statistics, 2023). Following a dip during the "pandemic," that figure suddenly spiked in Q3 of 2021 to 443,000, and rose every quarter until Q4 of 2022, when it reached 745,000; the latest available figure, for Q2 of 2023, is 672,000. Virtually the whole of this massive increase has been driven by non-EU immigration, with EU immigration turning negative. Along with everything else in the unfolding Omniwar, migration appears to have been weaponised, either to stoke social division and tensions through the sudden surge, or worse. Stage 5 of Stanton's (2016) ten stages of genocide involves the training and arming of special army units or militias, and it is now a brute fact that tens of thousands of fighting-age males with no patriotic loyalty have been stationed throughout the UK, despite Brexit.

By now, global technocratic agendas and deep state military operations are obvious for anyone with eyes to see: they represent an attack on human freedom, dignity, and humanity itself. The transnational ruling class continues to erect various (largely invisible) architectures of oppression, while the public awakens at an ever faster rate to the Omniwar being waged against it. In this context, it seems possible that physical conflict could be about to break out as we enter the next stage of World War III, instigated not by the people, but, rather, by a transnational ruling class willing to go to any lengths to prevent its own demise.

Ultimately, human freedom depends on defeating a tiny cabal whose evil methods act like a cancer against the body politic, creating a "disease of inter-human relations," as Meerloo (1956, p. 108) refers to totalitarianism. Unfortunately, while this solution is only now starting to dawn on a relatively small segment of the population, the ruling class has understood the logic of the coming global class confrontation for well over half a century and has spent that time carefully scheming its plan of attack.

The "Information-Liquidation" Model

As argued in Chapters 1 and 2, low-level counterinsurgency techniques have been deployed against Western populations since 1968, with the Strategy of Tension becoming globalised and turned into a permanent state of exception after "9/11." However, we know where Anglo-American counterinsurgency operations in the so-called "Third World" ultimately led: namely, to what van der Pijl (2022, p. 59) calls "the information-liquidation model," which involves "sending agents to penetrate the resistance and then, on the basis of centralized information, moving to take out the leadership." The British did this in Malacca and Kenya; the Americans did it in Indonesia and Vietnam. In Indonesia, hundreds of thousands (possibly rising to over two million) were killed (van der Pijl, 2014, p. 174); in Vietnam, Operation Phoenix killed tens of thousands.

In Vietnam, everyone aged 15 and over had to carry an identity card, enabling a "computerized [...] means of generating 1,800 names a month for the target list, coordinating the information on suspects from 30,000-plus informants" (Thomas, 2007, p. 27). Operation Phoenix represented "a "template for systemic domination," which involved "targeting civilians with Einsatzgruppen-style 'special forces' [i.e. death squads] and Gestapo-style secret police" (Valentine, 2017, pp. 55–63). The victims, in Valentine's view, were "patriots resisting foreign aggression and seeking to take back their country, but they were considered spies and terrorists," and it was on this basis that laws were written allowing the U.S. military to "torture and kill them by every means possible."

The information-liquidation model was transnationalised—in Italy, Lebanon, Israel/Palestine, Guatemala, El Salvador, and elsewhere (van der Pijl, 2022, p. 59). Under Operation Condor, intelligence agencies in the Southern Cone shared information about dissidents using "a state-of-the-art computer system provided by Washington—and then gave each other's agents safe passage to carry out cross-border kidnappings and torture"—a prefiguration of the CIA's "extraordinary rendition" network (Klein, 2007, p. 91). Domestically, meanwhile, the ARPANET was used to share files with intelligence agencies on 7 million U.S. citizens involved in anti-war and civil rights movements (van der Pijl, 2018, p. 13). Preventing social revolution, van der Pijl (2022, p. 73) infers, was always the fundamental purpose of the new information technology.

After 9/11, Operation Phoenix became the "template for policing the empire and fighting its eternal War on Terror," with the CIA and U.S. military conducting joint Phoenix-style operations worldwide, most prominently in Afghanistan and Iraq (Valentine, 2017, pp. 25, 64). But domestically, too, "Homeland Security" was advertised as protecting people against terrorism, just as in the Phoenix programme, raising a troubling question: "What is to stop [the CIA and military] applying the full systematic extent of Phoenix-style operations to include political dissidents, immigrants, and despised minorities in America, just as they did in Vietnam?" (Valentine, 2017, p. 64). And not just in the United States. The Edward Snowden leaks in 2013 revealed a global surveillance programme being run by intelligence agencies and communications corporations in the USA, UK, Germany, the Netherlands, France, Sweden, Canada, and Australia. Its presumptive purpose: to ensure that "everything is known about the population before it might even think of revolt" (van der Pijl, 2022, p. 60).

In Algeria in the 1950s, the French used a system of military aid to the civilian community to get "right under the skin of the population," before introducing identity cards (Kitson, 1971, p. 80). Silicon Valley, it might be argued, has performed a similar clandestine function of getting the military right under the skin of populations, provided one understands that "the Big Tech giants *are* the Pentagon and the intelligence community" (Corbett, 2019a). Dating at least as far back as the development of the ARPANET, the CIA and ARPA (later DARPA) have spent decades working on "a worldwide signals intelligence operation, directed not only at the militaries of foreign countries, but at the population of the world as a whole," with all the Big Tech giants (e.g., Oracle, Sun Microsystems, Google, and Facebook) originating with those very agencies (Corbett, 2019a). Big Tech essentially serves as a global dragnet hoovering up personal data about everyone so that the intelligence agencies can analyse it (e.g., using Peter Thiel's Palantir) and use it for social control purposes. It is no accident that figures such as Regina Dugan have moved seamlessly between DARPA, Google, and Facebook: they are all part of one and the same project. "The internet was never intended as a tool of liberation," Corbett (2019a) concludes. "It was from its very inception intended to be a tool for tracking, surveilling and, ultimately, controlling a target population." With such an infrastructure in place, Valentine (2017, p. 66) contends, "it is only a matter of time until we enter the next Phoenix phase of explicit terror here at home."

Writing just before the "Covid-19" operation was launched, Mikovits asks: "How far will our government go to attack members of what it perceives to be its domestic opposition? In other words, what measures will the United States government employ against its own citizens?" (Mikovits & Heckenlively, 2020, p. 46). This was in reference to the known history of harsh repression, up to and including murder, of outspoken critics of Big Pharma, an issue that was soon to intensify as medical professionals worldwide lost their licences for speaking out against the "Covid-19" narrative in a growing climate of censorship, persecution, and intimidation.

Robert F. Kennedy Jr., in April 2020, told a rally: "We are in a guerilla war" against a broken system. If so, there are serious reasons for concern, given van der Pijl's (2022, p. 35) contention that "The information warfare model developed in counterinsurgency operations in Southeast Asia and Central America is now being applied to the home front in the West." So far, this has mainly been applied to rooting out and censoring dissidents in cyberspace (Fisher & Smyth, 2020), but if dissidents can be targeted virtually, they can also, in principle, be targeted physically.

Injections No Matter What

Global power brokers made it very clear that they intend to see *everyone* (apart from their own class) injected with the novel technologies now known to contain all manner of undisclosed ingredients (Hughes, 2022c). According to Gates (2020a), "we need to make the vaccine available to almost every person on the planet," such that "normalcy only returns when we have largely vaccinated the entire global population." "You don't have a choice," Gates threatens. "People act like you have a choice" ("Transcript: Bill Gates speaks to the FT about the Global Fight against Coronavirus," 2020). Boris Johnson at the 2021 G7 summit called on wealthy countries to "commit to vaccinating the world against Covid-19" (cited in Shearing, 2021). Justin Trudeau claimed: "the way to get through this pandemic is for everyone to get vaccinated" (cited in Connolly, 2021). According to European Commission President Ursula von der Leyen, the EU must consider mandatory "vaccination" (Boffey & Smith, 2021). According to UNICEF (2021), "no one is safe until everyone is safe," and the accompanying UNICEF advertisement threatened: "Nobody gets out of the Covid-19 pandemic until we get everyone protected around the world." This is echoed by Schwab's (2022) threat that "nobody will be safe if not everyone is vaccinated." In that respect, "global public health" resembles a mafia protection racket.

Once the "Covid-19" narrative collapsed in late 2021, especially regarding the absurdity of pro-"vaccination" arguments (see Chapter 5), and with the emergent harms of the injections becoming ever more obvious, one might reasonably have expected the "Covid-19 vaccination" agenda to disappear altogether. As van der Pijl (2022, p. 281) wrote at the time, "The absurdity of pressing on with the vaccination campaign in spite of growing signs it poses severe health risks, with gene therapies that do not work, all that against a virus that for most poses no risk whatsoever, is rapidly eroding popular acceptance."

But instead, after a half-year hiatus, the "vaccine" pushers were back for more. In July 2022, the *Lancet* published a "viewpoint," whose authors include Chelsea Clinton, advocating for mandatory "vaccination" (Mello et al., 2022). In August 2022, the Rockefeller Foundation (2022) announced its Mercury Project to "boost Covid-19 vaccination rates and counter public health mis- and disinformation in 17 countries." The outgoing Anthony Fauci in September 2022 anticipated "annual updated COVID-19 shots matched to the currently circulating strains for most of the population" (White House, 2022b).

In May 2023, the MHRA (2023) approved a new "Covid-19 vaccine," called SKYCovion, which was developed with funding from CEPI and the Bill & Melinda Gates Foundation. The proposed UK "New Bill of Rights" could conceivably be used to pretend that inalienable rights, such as the right to bodily sovereignty, can be overridden in the name of "safeguarding the broader public interest" (Davis, 2022a). Claiming that an estimated 10–15 million people have already been killed by "Covid-19 vaccines"—Rancourt et al., (2023, p. 3) calculate 17 million—Yeadon (2023) warns: "these are but the first of many mRNA injections to come," based on the number of doses that governments have already agreed to purchase.

Especially given the inexorable rollout of the WHO Pandemic Treaty, proposed amendments to the 2005 International Health Regulations, and "vaccine passports" (Wailzer, 2023), it may only be a matter of time before "the next pandemic" repeatedly touted by Gates (2021), or "the second pandemic" let slip by Joe Biden (White House, 2022a), is used as the pretext for mandatory "vaccination," despite there being no such thing as an unusually deadly pandemic in the post-antibiotics era (see Chapter 6).

The irrational, anti-scientific, and immoral drive to force dangerous experimental products into everyone cannot possibly have anything to do with public health. Rather, the so-called "Covid-19 vaccines" are potential military technologies intended to give the oligarchy the decisive advantage should mass violence erupt when social order finally breaks down (as it must for the desired remaking of society to occur). As Schwab and

Malleret (2020, p. 21) write, "It is far from certain that the COVID-19 crisis will tip the balance in favour of labour and against capital. For political and social reasons, it could, but technology changes the mix." What technology, exactly?

The Covert Installation of Military Hardware into Human Bodies?

The IT/Bio/Nano Era

The Clinton administration threw its weight behind nanotechnology research with the foundation of the National Nanotechnology Initiative in 2000, claiming that nanotechnology research goals "may take twenty or more years to achieve" (i.e. by 2020) (White House, 2000).

A July 2001 NASA Langley Research Centre report on "Future Warfare," which aims to provide a "Heads Up" for the "Intel Community," expects "ongoing worldwide technological revolutions" and "economic trends" to lead to a new warfighting paradigm by "circa 2025" (Bushnell, 2001, pp. 1, 5, 109). With a "Bio/NANO" era beginning around "2020-?," an "IT/Bio/Nano" warfare paradigm will involve "everyone" and utilise "key future [nano]technologies" such as "carbon nanotubes" and "assemblers/living factories." Moreover, a "takedown of the US" involving, among other things, "selective anti-personnel RF/MW [radio frequency and microwave] (Towers)" will be "ACCOMPANIED BY SERIOUS PSYWAR" (Bushnell, 2001, pp. 7, 13, 35, 98, 107).

In light of all that has happened since 2020, including massive psychological warfare, the erection of 5G towers in densely populated areas, and the discovery of apparent carbon nanotubes and self-assembling structures (possibly synthetic biology) in the blood of "vaccinated" patients (Hughes, 2022c), it seems hard to avoid the impression that the "Covid-19" operation was planned since at least the turn of the millennium, much as "pandemic preparedness" exercises—in which "CIA involvement was a consistent feature" (Kennedy Jr., 2021, p. 385)—date at least as far back as Operation Dark Winter in June 2001 (O'Toole et al., 2002).

A 2002 U.S. National Science Foundation and Department of Commerce report on "convergent technologies" in "nanotechnology, biotechnology, [and] information technology" argues that "within twenty years' time" (i.e. by 2022), there could occur a "turning point in the evolution of human society" and the "transformation of civilization" (Roco & Bainbridge, 2002, pp. ix–x). The report envisages "bionano processors" and "fast broadband interfaces directly between the human brain and machines" that would take a further decade or so (by ca. 2030) to implement "in new technologies, industries, and ways of life" (2002, p. 3). It should be noted that Charles Lieber had already, by this point, developed self-assembling nano-biosensors, analogous to "a computer, suspended in a flask of liquid, which assembles itself when the liquid is poured onto a desktop" (Shaw, 2001). One comment in the NSF/ Department of Commerce report from W.A. Wallace stands out: "If the Cognitive Scientists can think it, the Nano people can build it, the Bio people can implement it, and the IT people can monitor and control it" (2002, p. 11). Wallace neglects to mention that whoever controls the IT people rules society.

Kurzweil (2005, Chapter 5) writes of "three overlapping revolutions": in genetics, nanotechnology, and robotics, creating intersections between information, biology, and the physical world. This is very similar to the claim of the founder of Sun Microsystems, paraphrased by van der Pijl (2022, p. 256), that "nanotechnology, genetics and information science would merge and might be able to begin to make self-replicating nanorobots."

The RAND Corporation (2006) envisages a "Global Technology Revolution to 2020" involving "biotechnology trends," "nanotechnology trends," "materials trends," and "information and communications technology trends" (i.e. IT/BIO/Nano convergence). So-called "wildcard" technologies would have "broad and substantial impacts" should "unlikely breakthroughs" occur (RAND, 2006, p. 4). Nanotechnology is one such "wildcard," promising "self-assembly methods," "carbon nanotubes or semiconducting and metallic nanowires as individual (designed) functional elements in electronic circuits," "manufacturing using molecular or biological methods," "implants that connect directly to the brain and nervous system," and "therapeutic delivery of DNA and RNA and the creation of multifunctional delivery systems" (2006, pp. 4, 12, 14, 201–2).

From Neuroscience to Neurotechnology

The "wildcard" breakthrough was made in 2010, when Lieber and his colleagues used nanowires to create transistors so small that they can "enter and probe cells without disrupting the intracellular machinery," enabling "two-way communication with individual cells" (Shaw, 2011)—perhaps the first example of the IT/Bio/Nano convergence in practice. According to Pentagon neuroscientist James Giordano (2018), neuroscience and neurotechnology became "viable for operational use in NSID [National Security Investigations Division]" in 2010, were considered for "military operational use" in 2013, and were "in operational NSID use" by 2014. The timing fits with Lieber's breakthrough, as well as with developments in graphene-based technology (see below).

In January 2013, the Rockefeller Foundation and the Peking Union Medical College held a summit in Beijing titled "Dreaming the Future of Health for the Next 100 Years" (Rockefeller Foundation, 2013). That imagined future, as summarised by Kyrie and Broudy (2022a), involves

> the "re-engineering of humans through genetic engineering or mixed human-robots," nanobots and nanotechnology, synthetic biology and "human-designed life," optogenetics, or remote brain monitoring and control using light signals, tissue-implantable sensors that interact with big data, self-replicating A.I., delivery of medical and health services through telemedicine and A.I., and a future in which the "abundance of data, digitally tracking and linking people may mean the 'death of privacy' and may replace physical interaction with transient, virtual connection."

Health here is just a guise for rolling out IT/Bio/Nanotechnology that will facilitate eugenics (redirecting the course of human evolution), mind control, and ultra-surveillance.

In April 2013, President Obama launched the BRAIN Initiative, whose stated purpose is to "unlock the mysteries of the brain" by making extraordinary scientific advances in a short time frame under the "Grand Challenges" framework (White House, 2013). The Human Brain Project in Europe, also launched in 2013, served a similar function. Research funding for the BRAIN Initiative was disbursed through DARPA ($50 million), the NIH ($40 million), and the National Science Foundation ($20 million), beginning in FY 2014. Four private sector partners were named: the Allen Institute for Brain Science, the Howard Hughes Medical Institute, the Rockefeller-affiliated Kavli Foundation, and the Salk Institute for Biological Studies. The BRAIN initiative working group, which outlined the scope of the project, was co-chaired by Rockefeller

University's Cori Bargmann. One early project to be funded was a Rockefeller University (2014) initiative to find a "new way to remotely control brain cells" using radiogenetics, which "combines the use of radio waves or magnetic fields with nanoparticles to turn neurons on or off." This was successfully achieved in rats, enabling what Rockefeller University (2016) calls "magnetic mind control." A WEF article from 2018 (since deleted) is titled "Mind Control using Sound Waves?" (Jérusalem, 2018). The in-house references to mind control give the game away. Optogenetics (using pulses of light), sonogenetics (ultrasound waves), magnetogenetics (magnetic fields), and chemogenetics (engineered proteins, viz. DREADDS, or "Designer Receptors Exclusively Activated by Designer Drugs") were all explored for purposes of remotely controlling brain activity.

We should not lose sight of the hubristic nature of attempts to "unlock the mysteries of the brain" (White House, 2013). No one, for instance, has ever managed to explain human consciousness. In fact, human beings are still so far away from being able to explain the Majesty of Creation, that Caltech professor Christof Koch, chief scientific officer at the Allen Institute for Brain Science in Seattle, admits: "The roundworm has exactly 302 neurons, and we still have no frigging idea how this animal works" (cited in Keats, 2013). Although the goal of communicating with *one million* neurons sounds lofty, according to Phillip Alvelda, DARPA's Neural Engineering System Design programme manager, "A million neurons represents a miniscule percentage of the 86 billion neurons in the human brain. Its deeper complexities are going to remain a mystery for some time to come" (DARPA, 2017). The EU Horizon 2020 BrainCom project aimed to develop "biocompatible and high bandwidth neural interfaces" with an "ultra-high-count of sensors" to begin addressing the problem that the brain contains 100 billion (!) neurons (BrainCom, 2020). This goes to show how far researchers really are from "unlocking the brain with novel graphene technology," to quote BrainCom's strapline.

DARPA has been investing in brain-computer interface technology since at least 2002. Its known programmes include (by year of initiation): the Brain Machine Interface (BMI) and Human Assisted Neural Devices (HAND) programmes (2002), the Neurotechnology for Intelligence Analysts (NIA) programme (2005), the Revolutionizing Prosthetics programme (2006), the Cognitive Technology Threat Warning System (CT2WS) programme (2007), the Accelerated Learning programme

(2007), the Restorative Encoding Memory Integration Neural Device (REMIND) programme (2009), the Reorganization and Plasticity to Accelerate Injury Recovery (REPAIR) programme (2010), the Reliable Neural Interface Technology (RE-NET) programme (2010), the Reliable Central nervous system Interfaces (RCI) programme (2011), the Reliable Peripheral Interfaces (RPI) programme (2011), the Narrative Networks (N2) programme (2011), the Neuro Function, Activity, Structure, and Technology (Neuro-FAST) programme (2014), the Systems-Based Neurotechnology for Emerging Therapies (SUBNETS) programme (2014), the Restoring Active Memory (RAM) programme (2014), the Hand Proprioception and Touch Interfaces (HAPTIX) programme (2015), the Electrical Prescriptions (ElectRx) programme (2015), the Neural Engineering System Design (NESD) programme (2015), the Targeted Neuroplasticity Training (TNT) programme (2016), and the Next-Generation Nonsurgical Neurotechnology (N3) programme (2019).

With all these developments underway since around the turn of the millennium, Klaus Schwab seems late to the party with his dubious "Fourth Industrial Revolution," a concept coined in December 2015, premised on a "fusion of technologies across the physical, digital and biological worlds" (Schwab, 2016, p. 7). If anything, Schwab (2016, p. 13) seems to be opportunistically positioning himself, pointing to the need for an "institutional framework [no doubt with the WEF at the heart] to govern the diffusion of innovation and mitigate the disruption" caused by the new technologies and the inevitable "popular backlash" to them. Interestingly, Schwab's physical/digital/biological triad does not include nano (as in IT/Bio/Nano). Instead, Schwab has repeatedly mooted the possibility of implantable microchips in the brain, as when he asked Sergey Brin: "Can you imagine that in ten years, twenty years, sitting here, we have an implant in our brains, and [...] I can immediately tell you how the people react to your answers?" (WEF, 2017; cf. Schwab, 2016, p. 110). Elon Musk's Neuralink similarly involves a microchip robotically implanted "in a person's skull" (Asher Hamilton, 2022), although in an early interview, Musk claimed "You could go through the veins and arteries" (cited in Jiminez, 2017). It seems possible that the public is being fed the image of brain-implantable microchips as some kind of emergent futuristic technology, when self-assembling bionanotechnologies capable of communicating with an external network may already be a reality.

Giordano (2018) tells West Point recruits: "The brain is, and will be, the twenty-first-century battlescape." Clearly, by this point, neuroscience and neurotechnology had entered military operational use. Weaponised neurotechnology, Giordano (2017) teaches, can be used to:

> 1) assess, predict, and control particular cognitions, emotions, and behaviours; 2) mitigate aggression and foster cognitions, emotions, and/or behaviours of affiliation or passivity; 3) incur burdens of morbidity, disability, or suffering and in this way "neutralise" potential opponents, or 4) induce mortality.

In other words, it can be used to control subjective experience and behaviours and to leave a target sick, disabled, or dead. The way it works is to "put minimal sized electrodes in a network within a brain through only minimal intervention to be able to read and write into the brain function, in real time, remotely" (Giordano, 2018).

This, again, is consistent with Lieber's research, this time involving a 1 cm-squared neural net comprised of superfine "nanowire [field effect transistors] as general biological nanosensors" syringe-injected into the brains of rats, where it seamlessly integrates with neural tissue and remains intact for at least a year (Hong et al., 2018, pp. 34–5). "Looking into the future," Lieber and his co-authors write, nanowire technology could be "incorporated into other platforms, such as syringe-injectable mesh electronics [….] perhaps eventually bringing 'cyborgs' to reality" (Zhang et al., 2019, p. 3). Kyrie and Broudy's (2022b) "Cyborgs R Us" article presents a large amount of circumstantial evidence that this is indeed the plan. Policy Horizons Canada (2020) has a chilling document on "biodigital convergence" that points to the end of *homo sapiens* and "synthetic biology machines that can be programmed to create entirely new organisms." The UK Ministry of Defence (2021) has a similar document on "human augmentation."

"mRNA Vaccines" as Cover for Military Technologies?

If the aim of the deep state (Hughes, 2022b) is to use public health as the disguise under which to introduce military technology into the bodies of the population, then traditional forms of vaccine must be replaced. This, it seems, is the purpose of so-called "mRNA vaccines." In addition to camouflaging the true nature of their contents, "mRNA vaccines" can allegedly be produced at speed, anywhere, based on computer code rather than a physical sample of a virus. With governments, regulators, and the media all captured, the public has no reliable way of knowing what these new products contain (Hughes, 2022c).

Former DARPA Director Regina Dugan recalls "a pivotal moment in 2010" (the breakthrough year above), when Dan Wattendorf asked: "What if we have a global pandemic and it's a novel pathogen? That will be catastrophic. We can't wait the normal 3–10 years for a vaccine. And what if instead we could use mRNA to create a vaccine in days and weeks [...]?" ("How DARPA Seeded the Ground for a Rapid Covid-19 Cure," 2020). The context for Wattendorf's question is not provided, but it is easy to imagine a DARPA brainstorming session on how to provide for injecting as many people as possible, at speed, with a revolutionary new military technology whose proof of concept had just been established. In December 2013, DARPA awarded Pfizer $7.7 million for research to "cut response times to pandemic or bioterrorism threats by eliminating several of the steps currently needed to confer immunity," though "details of the research are scarce" (Taylor, 2013).

Moderna was founded in September 2010 and operationalised in 2011. In 2012, "despite being years away from testing its science in humans," and with no scientific publications to its name, $40 million of venture capitalist funding flowed into the company (Crunchbase, n.d.), plus $240 million from AstraZeneca for the rights to mRNA drugs that did not yet exist (Garde, 2020). On October 2, 2013, DARPA awarded Moderna $25 million of research funding (Moderna, 2013). On October 24, 2013, Moderna was named a WEF "global growth company" and heralded as "an industry leader in innovative mRNA therapeutics." In 2014, the company achieved the rare "unicorn" status (a $1 billion stock valuation for a private startup), even though it was offering a "fledgling drug technology" that had still not been tested in humans (Dolgin, 2015). None of this makes any sense from a commercial perspective, and the fingerprints of the deep state are not difficult to detect.

In a panel called "Making Influenza History: The Quest for a Universal Flu Vaccine," held at the Milken Institute's Future of Health Summit (October 28–30, 2019), the panellists repeatedly stressed the urgency of abandoning traditional methods of vaccine production in favour of what BARDA Director Rick Bright calls "synthetic-based vaccines," specifically "messenger RNA-based" vaccines that could be produced remotely based on the RNA sequence of the virus—say, if a novel virus escaped from China ("Clip of Universal Flu Vaccine," 2019). The "novel coronavirus" was sequenced in Wuhan about eleven weeks later. Fauci, at the 21-minute mark, proposes "not growing the virus at all, but getting the sequences, getting the appropriate protein and sticking it on a self-assembling nanoparticle that is much more immunogenic." Thus, not only was the public health groundwork for novel "vaccines" being laid directly after the World Military Games in Wuhan (October 18–27, 2019)—to which one narrative ascribes the outbreak of "SARS-CoV-2"—and directly before the "coronavirus pandemic," but the idea of injecting self-assembling nanotechnologies was being openly discussed.

Moderna's 10-Q Q2 2020 filing with the SEC states: "*We have incurred significant losses since our inception and anticipate that we will continue to incur significant losses for the foreseeable future*" (Moderna, 2020). Moderna only had one viable commercial product, i.e. mRNA-1273 (its "Covid-19 vaccine"). All other products remained "years" away from commercialisation, with the company admitting it "may never achieve profitability." Then, as if by magic, the "Covid-19 pandemic" allowed for emergency use authorisation that bypassed the need for animal trials and long-term safety data. $1 billion of U.S. taxpayer money flowed into research for mRNA-1273, a $1.5 billion advance purchase arrangement was made through Operation Warp Speed, and further support came from CEPI (Dearden, 2022). Moderna achieved its first ever quarterly profit in Q1 of 2021 and finished 2021 with pre-tax profits of $13 billion ($36 million of profit per day). Moderna executives become multi-millionaires and billionaires through suspiciously timed selling of shares (Egan & Isidore, 2020; Webb, 2021). Canada, Australia, and the United Kingdom announced new contracts with Moderna for mRNA "vaccine" manufacturing plants in the first half of 2022. None of this is believable without treating Moderna as part of a transnational deep state operation to inject "mRNA vaccines" into as many people as possible.

In the "race" for a "Covid-19 vaccine" in 2020, traditional types of vaccine were never in the running, and of the novel types of "vaccine" that were, the mRNA kind soon established dominance. According to CDC data, 97% of all "Covid-19 vaccines" administered in the United States by August 3, 2022, were either Pfizer (59%) or Moderna (38%); Johnson & Johnson's adenovirus vector injection and the protein-based Novavax (granted EUA in July 2022) barely register (CDC, n.d.). In the UK, one of the two main "Covid-19 vaccines," Oxford-AstraZeneca (viral vector)—which, according to MHRA (n.d.) data, was responsible for the lion's share of "Covid-19 vaccine" injuries and deaths following a Wimbledon Centre Court standing ovation for their pioneer, Dame Sarah Gilbert—was quietly phased out in 2021 as Moderna was phased in. The "vast majority" of UK third doses were Pfizer (30.1 million) and Moderna (9.4 million), vs. just 56,000 for AstraZeneca (Head, 2022). In the EU/EEA, of the 1.26 billion doses distributed by July 21, 2022, mRNA types accounted for 80% (Comirnaty 63%, Spikevax 17%) (European Centre for Disease Prevention and Control, n.d.). Similar data can be found in virtually every Western country (Official Data collated by Our World in Data, n.d.). An attempted "coup" appears to be underway in which traditional vaccines are to be replaced by "mRNA vaccines."

We must remember that we are dealing with a camouflaged military operation, saturated in deceit (cf. Chapter 6). It is possible that "mRNA" (Moderna trading as MRNA) is a decoy to disguise other components/functions of the injectables. We know, for instance, that the ultra-cold storage requirements for "Covid-19 mRNA vaccines"—"as low as -80 degrees C" for Pfizer (Gates, 2020a)—above which the mRNA and combined nanoparticles were said to lose their integrity, were quickly rescinded in favour of fridge temperatures (Vedmore, 2020) or "normal freezer" temperatures (DHS Science & Technology Directorate, 2021, p. 11). There are serious quality issues with industrial-scale mRNA "vaccine" production, as Maria Gutschi explains (NZDSOS, 2022), and the European Medicines Agency had "major concerns over unexpectedly low quantities (around 55%) of intact mRNA in batches of the vaccine developed for commercial production" (BMJ, 2021). Moderna refused to share its mRNA vaccine knowledge to boost production of COVID-19 vaccines (Meyer, 2022), consistent with its trademark furtiveness (Dearden, 2022). The "mRNA vaccine" narrative thus seems questionable on several levels. What if "mRNA" is cover for something else?

Graphene

Graphene, first discovered in 2004 by University of Manchester researchers, is a "2D," i.e. "one-atom thick, layer of carbon atoms in a honeycomb crystal lattice" that possess "unique electronic and optical properties" (Jornet & Akyildiz, 2014, p. 685).

In 2010, DARPA Director Regina Dugan testified that nanotechnologies hitherto had "resisted practical implementation in systems," but that graphene promised to "break through the 50-year old limitations of traditional silicon microelectronic devices" (Dugan, 2010). DARPA's CERA (carbon electronics for radiofrequency applications) programme looked to use graphene to create components for nanoscale circuitry, e.g. "graphene channel RF-transistors and key amplifier components such as LNAs [low noise amplifiers, used to amplify very low power signals]" (Albrecht, 2010). By February 2012, DARPA (2012, pp. 47–8, 218) had produced "graphene mechanical transistors with single-layer graphene sheets successfully transferred onto a silicon substrate"; "semiconducting nanowires, graphene ribbons, quantum dots, Kane q-bits, carbon nanotubes and other structures using tips-based nano-manufacturing (TBN) for specific device applications"; and "a low power, low noise amplifier (LNA) using graphene-field effect transistors (FETs) as the channel material."

In 2014, DARPA announced it had developed "graphene sensors that are electrically conductive but only 4 atoms thick," allowing "nearly all light to pass through across a wide range of wavelengths." This provided "proof-of-concept" for a technology that could "measure and stimulate neural tissue [...] by applying programmed pulses of electricity or light to temporarily activate neurons," there being "causal linkages between neural activity and behavior" (DARPA, 2014). Thus, DARPA was proposing a graphene-based means of neurological manipulation that can be used to control human behaviour. DARPA deleted the 2014 announcement from its website, and the last available access to it on the Wayback Machine is April 20, 2015. There appear to be no further mentions of graphene on DARPA's website, suggesting the agency went dark on the subject in April 2015.

Far more visible has been the EU Graphene Flagship, founded in 2013 with €1 billion of funding from the European Commission, EU member states, and associated states. Its stated goal is "bringing together academic and industrial researchers to take graphene from the realm of academic laboratories into European society in the space of 10 years [i.e. by 2023]" (Graphene Flagship, n.d.). The Flagship's "core consortium" consists of ca. 170 academic and industrial research groups (roughly evenly divided) in 22 countries; there are also around 100 associate members. By November 2021, the Graphene Flagship had published over 4000 peer-reviewed studies, attracting hundreds of citations a year. It hosts an annual Graphene Week to showcase its innovations, which cover a staggering array of applications, mostly outside neuroscience.

The Graphene Flagship is, thus, the public face of graphene research. As the "flagship" metaphor is intended to suggest, the public is meant to think that this is where the most important graphene research is being done. Attention is thereby drawn away from military research organisations such as DARPA, which has an annual budget of ca. $4 billion and was investigating potential graphene applications years before the Flagship existed.

Here is what we know about graphene from non-classified research. Graphene can "easily enter biological systems and interact with them physically and electromagnetically," making it potentially useful as a "nanotag" (Tian et al., 2011). Graphene solves the problem of communication between nano-devices via tuneable nano-antennae operating in the Terahertz band (Jornet & Akyildiz, 2014). It is paramagnetic (Zhang et al., 2021) and can be made ferromagnetic (Marquardt, 2015). Graphene-based substrates can interface directly with neurons without impairing their signalling properties, promising to "pave the way for better deep brain implants to both harness and control the brain" (Fabbro et al., 2016; University of Cambridge, 2016). A graphene skin patch is in use for monitoring diabetics' glucose levels and delivering drugs through microneedles (Cuthbertson, 2016). Graphene nanostructures are being developed for use in bioelectronic devices to "enable real-time monitoring or control of physiological processes" (Huang et al., 2019; San Roman et al., 2020). "Flexible solid-state electrical double layer supercapacitors" exist, based on graphene hydrogel electrodes (Lee et al., 2020). Graphene sheets aligned at precisely the right angle can form an "unconventional superconductor," which is "highly integrative with neuron cells in the brain" (Chu, 2021). Graphene nanostructures can "morph from conductor to semiconductor and back again," potentially facilitating "high performance computing and nanoscale quantum devices" able to "interact with electrons, light, and even magnetism" (Brown & Crommie, 2021). Mobile phone signals can be used to trigger the delivery of drugs via a graphene oxide platform (Sahoo et al., 2022).

In sum, we know that DARPA was excited in 2014 about the prospects of graphene to create a novel form of neurological manipulation that can be used to control human behaviour. Based on subsequent research, we also know that it is theoretically possible to create a graphene-based nano-operating system within the human body that is capable of monitoring and controlling physiological processes, and which can be controlled remotely. We could be looking here at a highly advanced weapons system, as Andersen (2021) proposes in a study that compares items found in the "Covid-19 vaccines" to components found in the nanotechnology literature.

The Evil Potential of Weaponised Neurotechnology

The above considerations make the covert transnational military campaign (see Chapter 6) to inject as many people as possible with substances containing undisclosed ingredients, apparently including self-assembling EMF-responsive nanotechnology (Hughes, 2022c, 2023, 50:25), extremely worrying, especially in the context of an undeclared Omniwar in which the public is the enemy. Moreover, with the rapid rollout of 5G technology capable of targeting individuals, plus projects such as Elon Musk's Starlink, Amazon's Project Kuiper, and OneWeb all vying to provide internet coverage to every part of the world from low earth orbit, there could, potentially, be no escape from a wireless technocratic control grid.

Steele proposes that the metallic components found in the "Covid-19 vaccines" (cf. Hughes, 2022c, pp. 461, 572) make their recipients radio-traceable for directed energy weapons kill missions ("Mark Steele on 5G," 2023); in the military context described above, we have to take such possibilities seriously. The exotic technologies apparently contained within the "Covid-19" injectables (Hughes, 2022c) have been linked to MAC addresses (Sarlangue et al., 2021); if proven, this would make human bodies identifiable components of the Internet of Things and thus directly targetable on the information-liquidation model.

Nanotechnology within the body capable of communicating with an external network is sold as a positive development in terms of healthcare (e.g. nanorobots can explore within the body and deliver precision payloads of medicine without the need for invasive surgery). Those funded to do this kind of research probably justify their activities in such terms. However, it can also be dual-use technology, much like the "'dual use' vaccine and weapon technologies" developed since the anthrax attacks of 2001 (Kennedy Jr., 2021, p. 384). "The problem of dual-use science research and technology," Miller (2018) argues, is that "such research and technology has the potential to be used for great evil as well as for great good." Sonogenetics, for example, "is not without its risks of misuse. It could be a revolutionary healthcare technology for the sick, or a perfect controlling tool with which the ruthless control the weak" (Jérusalem, 2018).

Consider the potential for evil if the deep state's aim is to connect human bodies to a technocratic control grid. For one thing, there are the health implications of injecting exotic technologies into the human body, which could explain the very high level of serious adverse reactions to the "Covid-19 vaccines" (OpenVAERS, n.d.; MHRA, n.d.; WHO, n.d. [search "COVID-19 vaccine"]). Graphene oxide, for instance, a non-degradable substance 100 times stronger than steel with a melting temperature approximately 80% as hot as the sun's surface, is suspected of being present in the "Covid-19 vaccines" (Campra, 2021; UNIT, 2021), yet is known to be toxic (Newman, 2020; Ou et al., 2016; Pumera, 2016).

Why did WEF ideologue Yuval Noah Harari (2020), as early as March 20, 2020, refer to "under-the-skin surveillance"? Was the insider, Harari, anticipating "the mass injection of intrabody components for a Bio-Nano Internet of Things" (Kyrie & Broudy, 2022b, p. 368)? Certainly, "the technology, protocols, industry intentions, and government plans to connect human bodies to the internet, and deploy nanorobots inside the body, using a combination of nanotechnology and 'smart' technology exist." So too does the military motivation in a global class war.

Through IT-Bio-Nanotechnologies, human beings could in principle be surveilled "from the inside out," down to the level of bodily activity and thought patterns. Researchers at a DARPA-funded laboratory at UC Santa Cruz, for instance, have been working on nano sensors the size of a single viral particle that can traverse the blood–brain barrier: "Once inside the brain they would act like a kind of antenna, turning neural activity into optical signals that could be wirelessly sent to an external device" (Taylor, 2021).

Microsoft patent WO/2020/060606 (awarded March 26, 2020) is for a device that will "award cryptocurrency to the user whose body activity data is verified" via a "mining process" (Abramson et al., 2020). Human bodies thereby become part of the financial system, trainable via cryptocurrency rewards. This has to be understood in the context of the move towards CBDC (a centralised form of blockchain), whereby all money must be digital and it must be tied reliably to human beings via a biometric ID system such as the AADHAR system trialled in India, which was set up by N.R. Narayana Murthy, the billionaire father-in-law of British Prime Minister and former Chancellor of the Exchequer, Rishi

Sunak (Hughes, 2022a, p. 234). Why else would IMF chief Kristalina Georgieva make the extraordinary claim in 2021 that "This year, next year, vaccine policy is economic policy, and it is an even higher priority than the traditional tools of fiscal and monetary policy. Why? Because without it, we cannot turn the fate of the world economy around" (cited Australian Voice, 2021). The aim seems to be to make human bodies part of a revolutionised global financial system.

Conversely, two-way communication with human bodies via an external network could, in principle, allow intracorporeal technologies to be programmed/manipulated "from the outside in." This opens onto the possibility of remote-control human beings, dating back to MKULTRA Subproject 119 in the early 1960s, which explored "techniques of activation of the human organization by remote electronic means" but did not result in any device for doing so (Miyamoto, 2018).

In 1966, Rodríguez Delgado, funded by the CIA through the Office of Naval Intelligence, was able to halt a charging bull using remote-controlled electrical stimulation of the brain. He was also able to make a chimpanzee become "quieter, less attentive and less motivated" by using a stimoceiver to cause a sensation of pain when certain amygdala signals were detected (Coates, 2008, p. 36). In *Physical Control of the Mind*, Delgado (1969, p. 91) predicts that the new technology will "provide the essential link from man to computer to man, with a reciprocal feedback between neurons and instruments which represents a new orientation for the medical control of neurophysiological functions." In the 1970s, Delgado placed brain transponders in humans, and in the 1980s, he claimed that brainwave patterns and physiology could be altered using electromagnetic broadcasting from up to three kilometres away (Thomas, 2007, pp. 32–33).

Today, the possibility of "vaccination as neurological remote-control" must be taken seriously, for "after achieving access by vaccination to the biomass of the 7 to 8 billion individuals who have to be controlled, remote-controlling them is no longer an absurd fantasy" (van der Pijl, 2022, pp. 249, 256). Just as the central bankers want to "go direct" in their control of people's money (BlackRock, 2020), so the military and intelligence agencies seem to want to "go direct" in their control of people's bodies. According to Harari (2017, p. 289), human beings can be manipulated like rats by stimulating relevant areas of the brain, and "the U.S. military has recently initiated experiments on implanting computer chips in people's brains." To see where this could go in the hands of psychopaths, one need only consider the remote-control beetle (Bolton, 2016).

According to Doug Weber, DARPA's ElectRx programme manager, "the peripheral nervous system is the body's information superhighway" (DARPA, 2015). As the Edward Snowden leaks in 2013 revealed, however, the internet allowed the NSA backdoor access into everyone's personal computers. An Internet of Bodies could allow the deep state (Hughes, 2022b) backdoor access to everyone's bodies. The implications do not bear thinking about. "Imagine a dictatorial regime," Jérusalem (2018) cautions, "with access to the tricks and tools to change the way its citizens think or behave." The control would be total. More terrifyingly still, individuals, made radio-identifiable by the technologies inside their bodies, could be remotely assassinated via a 5G network capable of targeting individuals with specific frequencies capable of interacting with intracorporeal nanotechnology. This would be the perfect murder weapon: targeted, asymmetrical, and traceless. All dissidents could be quickly and efficiently eliminated in the ultimate version of the information-liquidation model.

INBRAIN Neuroelectronics was spun off from the Catalan Institute of Nanoscience & Nanotechnology (ICN2), a partner of the Graphene Flagship, in 2019. It describes itself as "scientists, doctors, techies and humanity lovers, with the mission of building neuroelectronic interfaces to cure brain disorders" (INBRAIN, n.d.). INBRAIN's promotional video boasts that its Graphene Brain Interface "enables perfect brain surface contact," "real-time brain mapping," and is "easily coupled with modern electronics, contributing to the huge momentum of connected and smart devices." Here is a technology that is laudable if it helps to cure brain disorders or allows physically disabled people to control smart devices by the power of their mind. However, the flip side is that it could be used to connect human brains to a technocratic control grid. In July 2021, INBRAIN and Merck announced a partnership to co-develop the next generation of graphene bioelectronic vagus nerve therapies. In the wrong hands, such technologies could be used as weapons to target the heart, lungs, and digestive tract remotely. In view of the widespread abandonment of medical ethics since 2020 ("first do no harm" vs. coerced injection of entire populations with dangerous experimental substances), there is no reason to think that such technologies will be responsibly used.

Alternatively, dissidents could be tortured by remote control. As explained in Chapter 3, torture goes hand in hand with the logic of the shock doctrine. During Operation Condor, for instance, many "saw a direct connection between the economic shocks that impoverished millions and the epidemic of torture that punished hundreds of thousands of people who believed in a different kind of society" (Klein, 2007, p. 7). The torture techniques described in Chapter 3, stomach-churning as they are, by no means exhaust the available repertoire. In 2019, United Nations Special Rapporteur on Torture, Nils Melzer, received various reports of gang stalking, electronic torture, the use of cybertechnologies to intimidate, harass, surveil, shame, and defame, and even forms of torture involving "medical implants, and, conceivably nano- or neurotechnological devices" (Phelan, 2020). Given concerns about such devices potentially being present in the "Covid-19 vaccines," the implications do not bear thinking about.

Prospects for Revolution

Socialism or Barbarism

As capitalism once more enters a period of acute crisis, we are, yet again, faced with the stark choice posed by Rosa Luxemburg (1915), i.e. socialism or barbarism.

Barbarism currently has the upper hand. The "lockdowns" left behind a "legacy of harm for hundreds of millions of people in the years ahead" owing to

> a rise in non-Covid excess mortality, mental health deterioration, child abuse and domestic violence, widening global inequality, food insecurity, lost educational opportunities, unhealthy lifestyle behaviours, social polarization, soaring debt, democratic backsliding and declining human rights. (Bardosh, 2023)

There is clear evidence of democide (Rancourt, 2020; Rancourt et al., 2021, 2023), state-sponsored euthanasia, and experimentation on human beings (Hughes et al., 2022). Patterns of sadism and cruelty have been deliberately instigated, from locking elderly people up in care homes and not allowing relatives to visit (HART, 2022a), to forcing children to wear masks in schools all day, to persecuting those not complying with tyranny (see Chapter 7). Constitutional rights and the centuries-old social contract, whereby the government's first responsibility is to protect its citizens, have gone to the shredder, as Agamben (1998) foresaw, meaning that "the social and political system of the original liberal West has run its historic course and after 300 years has dropped all pretence of a social contract other than the state of emergency" (van der Pijl, 2020). Those who protest this orchestrated breakdown of civilised society have been met with police brutality, riot squads, and water cannon (Broudy et al., 2022).

A reported 5.55 billion people (as of March 2023) have been injected with dangerous experimental substances containing a devil's brew of undisclosed ingredients (Holder, 2023; Hughes, 2022c). Huge numbers of people, including previously fit and healthy people, have suffered serious adverse reactions to those injections, including severe disability and death, viz. Yellow Card (MHRA, n.d.) and VAERS data (OpenVAERS, n.d.) (with most deaths accruing towards the time of injection), which may only account for between 1% and 10% of the total (Ross et al., 2010; MHRA, 2019). Strange, rubbery "clots," often huge, are being pulled out of dead "vaccinated" bodies by embalmers such as Richard Hirschmann (Tice, 2022); they do not appear to be natural blood clots, and are possibly caused by hydrogel polymers (Mihalcea, 2023). "Died suddenly" and "vaccine genocide" trend routinely on social media. Websites such as www.instagram.com/jab_injuries_global/ collect testimonials from "vaccine"-injured people and are quickly shut down. Highly distressing videos are all over the internet of people suffering horrific adverse reactions to the "vaccine" and/or collapsing and dying in public (some collected in Broudy et al., 2022). The "vaccine" rollout to children and young people was premised wholly on corruption and not science, as I warned *before* the rollout reached 5–11-year-olds in Britain (Hughes, 2022a), and since then, children, young adults, and athletes have been collapsing and having heart attacks at a historically unprecedented rate (Dowd, 2022).

For reasons unknown, but consistent with war conditions, excess mortality rates prove most consistent among the working-age population. According to the UK Office for Health Improvements and Disparities (n.d.), the 50–64 age range (as at December 1, 2023, search by age range) experienced excess mortality *every week* bar five since March 2020, i.e. 187/192 weeks, or 97.4% of all weeks. For the 25–49 age range, the figure is 164/192 weeks (85.4% of all weeks). These figures are higher than for any other age range. For the 15–44 age range in the UK, excess deaths from cardiovascular diseases rose by 13% in 2020, 30% in 2021, and 44% in 2022, vis-à-vis the 2010–2019 average, and Personal

Independent Payment (disability) claims for cardiovascular diseases were "more than double the equivalent rises in deaths" (Phinance Technologies, 2023, pp. 3–5). Since the start of the "pandemic," according to the Office for National Statistics (2022), "the number of people out of work because of long-term sickness has risen by 363,000"; the trend began in early 2019 and accounts for a 25% increase.

In the United States, the baseline number of deaths for the 15–34 age range since 2020 displays "a permanent (1.5 years and counting) step-wise time-independent increase in mortality" in both males and females, accounting for ca. 400 additional deaths per week (Rancourt et al., 2021, pp. 139, 111). An increased baseline mortality can also be seen in the 35–54 age range, but not in older-age groups. This was *before* the "Vietnam War equivalent" event identified by Dowd that occurred for the 25–44 age range in Q4 of 2021 (cited in Kennedy Jr., 2022).

Despite all the unfolding horrors, there is no sign of any significant political or legal resistance in sight, as is consistent with the idea of a global class war in which all institutions aligned with the ruling class, including the legislature and the judiciary, must unite against the general population. Politicians, the world over, repeatedly voted in favour of "lockdowns" and other "Covid countermeasures," moving liberal democracies ever further in the direction of police states (see Chapter 3). Under these conditions, all major legal challenges to tyranny can be expected to fail. In Ireland, for instance, the Supreme Court effectively ruled that "lockdown" measures were constitutional, dismissing the idea that "there is a burden on the State to justify legislative measures that interfere with constitutional rights" (O'Faolain, 2022).

The professions have failed in spectacular fashion to challenge the lurch towards totalitarianism since 2020. The medical profession is the primary culprit, with its removal of licences from dissenting doctors and its threats to remaining members not to speak out against medical fascism (Blaylock, 2022) and criminal medical negligence (Dalgleish, 2023). Mary Holland argues that events 2020 have exposed "the degree of rot and subversion of medicine in all its aspects – medical science, clinical medicine, and public health" (D4CE, 2023a, p. xvii). Academia, too, has had precious little to say about the tyranny enveloping our world and the methods used to facilitate it; in fact, it has tried to silence dissenting academics (Bhattacharya, 2023), through open letters (Abaluck et al., 2020) and other means, in contravention of academic freedom (Miller, 2020). The psychology profession has remained largely silent on the menticidal methods deployed against the public (Sidley, 2022; Scott, 2021).

Where does this leave us? Forming new political parties seems an exercise in futility given that the political system itself is captured by vested interests. Recourse to the legal system can only be expected to end in failure, the higher up the system one goes. Ultimately, the only resolution to the crisis that has unfolded since 2020 lies at the social level. An inhumane and rapacious global capitalist system that is now metastasizing into a global technocracy intent on human enslavement through whatever means necessary must be removed. Objectively, the conditions are present for worldwide revolution.

Prospects for Revolution

Politically, we live now, as Lenin did in May 1917, in an age of war and revolution (Lenin, 1964). With the old social order (in our time, liberal democracy) being dissolved under war conditions, the future is pregnant with revolutionary potential. In that respect, history has lessons to teach. The two world wars were

> partly intended as a response to the sharp increase in social unrest, especially labour unrest, and to the political organization of the working population and the intellectuals associated with it. However, they were followed by social explosions that were even more violent: after WWI the Russian revolution, after WWII, the Chinese, Korean, and Vietnamese revolutions and the decolonization of Asia and Africa, the Cuban Revolution, etcetera. (van der Pijl, 2022, p. 269)

What will be the social response to the mass atrocities and crimes against humanity that have been committed since 2020 in a desperate effort to keep the global population in check (Hughes et al., 2022; Hughes, 2022c)? Or, as van der Pijl (2022, p. 281) asks: "Given that governments, acting for the oligarchy and the internationalized state, will not let go, the question is: will there be a revolutionary response?"

If there is not, then we should recall Huxley's (1958, p. 118) warning that the "scientific dictatorship" could prove permanent, there being "no good reason" why it "should ever be overthrown." Such a dictatorship is now being attempted at the global level and, if allowed to happen, even if only by a narrow margin, like the NSDAP election victory in 1933 with only 44% of the vote, it could prove irreversible. Critics of the "Covid-19" narrative have expressed concern that "humanity's event horizon is close to hand" (Yeadon, cited in Forte, 2021) and that "humanity is now at its most critical inflection point" (Henningsen, 2021). For Altman et al. (2023), "The fate of humanity and all future generations is literally at a critical tipping point."

On the other hand, the real power structures in the world have come into much sharper focus since 2020 and look very much like the "global public–private partnership" described by Davis (2021), with governments acting as mere enforcers of policies formulated and distributed at higher levels. The key actors are becoming ever more visible to the global population, including:

- the major investment banks, central banks, and Bank for International Settlements;
- the intelligence agencies (in particular the CIA, MI5, MI6, and Mossad, as well as military intelligence);
- the major tax-exempt foundations used by powerful families to advance their interests (the Rockefeller Foundation, the Ford Foundation, the Bill and Melinda Gates Foundation, the Soros Open Society Foundations, the Carnegie Endowment for International Peace, the Wellcome Trust, etc.);
- the major think tanks used to formulate policy and "strategic narratives" (e.g. Chatham House, the Council on Foreign Relations, the Club of Rome);
- coordinators of transnational capital such as the World Economic Forum, the Trilateral Commission, and the Bilderberg Group;
- international organisations that are increasingly coming to set policy at a global level, e.g. the WHO (via the Pandemic Treaty) and the UN (via the IPCC);
- the biggest institutional investors, such as BlackRock, Vanguard, and State Street;
- Establishment-aligned media, without which propaganda and psychological warfare against the public would not be possible;
- Big Tech companies responsible for the technocratic control grid; and
- the heads of Big Pharma and the regulators, which facilitated the experimental injection of billions of people.

Phillips (2018) lists the few hundred individuals who control nearly all of world affairs: the list needs updating, but this "global power elite" seems to be acting in ways that are ever more at odds with the interests of humanity.

It is hard to say what worldwide revolution in the twenty-first century would look like. There is no central Party to provide leadership and organisation, and that is probably a good thing, given what the Party became in the twentieth century, and given that the information-liquidation model is specifically designed to identify and target key organisers. Rather, the model has to be decentralised and relies on a surge in class consciousness (which today goes by the name of the Great Awakening) that will result in mass rejection of all aspects of technocracy. There is no requirement, and certainly no desirability, that this process be violent, despite Omniwar being waged in the opposition direction by deep state actors too cowardly to show their faces. Mass non-compliance renders technocratic agendas unenforceable. Non-compliance at the individual level and civil disobedience at the social level can soon spread, as we are already seeing in Britain and elsewhere in response to the attempted rollout of 15-minute cities.

A simple but extremely powerful tactic—a mass disabling event from the perspective of technocracy—would be for a new social norm to cascade, whereby as many people as possible got rid of their "smart" (slave) devices by which they voluntarily hook themselves up to the control grid and feed it information on all areas of their lives. There is a reason why those devices are designed to be highly addictive; notifications, for instance, create "short-term, dopamine-driven feedback loops," as Chamath Palihapitiya, Facebook's vice-president for user growth until 2011, admitted (cited in Wong, 2017). In that respect, society urgently needs to kick its habit.

We have to hope that smart surveillance technologies have not already gone "under the skin" of 5.55 billion people, to quote Harari (2020). This is why adequately powered studies urgently need to be carried out into claims that "vaccinated" individuals emit hexadecimal MAC addresses when exposed to EMF radiation. In principle, this should be simple to test using a faraday cage to isolate test subjects from background EMF radiation and then introducing specific frequencies from within the cage (or by some other protocol that scientists should be able to design, cf. Taylor, 2023). Given the seriousness of this issue, and the fact that it is empirically testable, it is frustrating that scientists and academics around the world are *not* doing the work to get to the bottom of it. Even if the MAC address phenomenon is disproven, we still need satisfactory answers as to why 5G technology—which has not passed adequate safety tests (Frank, 2021), is known to be harmful to human health (Burdick, 2023; Jamieson, 2023), and allows for potentially "limitless power to surveil and control a target population" (Corbett, 2019b)—is being rolled out.

We are in a race against time. Technocracy's biodigital gulag is at an advanced stage of construction, with its CBDC, Internet of Bodies, smart cities, social credit scoring, ESGs, 5G networks, etc. starting to materialise around us. Will enough people, in the wake of the "Covid-19" operation, be able to see what is happening and take decisive action to stop it, before it is too late?

Ruling-Class Desperation

As close as the transnational ruling class may appear to be to achieving its war aim, i.e. the rollout of technocracy, the "Covid-19" operation was also a sign of incredible desperation. As Wolff (2021) puts it, "What we are experiencing at this time is a gigantic act of desperation, probably the biggest that has ever occurred in the whole history of mankind," necessary for the ruling class to maintain control as the old paradigm of rule collapses. It has all been seen before. Trotsky (1938), one year before the outbreak of World War II, describes how the ruling class, forced to "stake its last upon the card of fascism, [...] now toboggans with closed eyes toward an economic and military catastrophe."

On the one hand, the planning for global technocracy goes back to the early 1970s (see Chapter 1), the "IT/Bio/Nano" paradigm and "pandemic preparedness" exercises date at least as far back as 2001 (Bushnell, 2001; O'Toole et al., 2002), and Gates' "Decade of the Vaccine" (2010–2019) led seamlessly into "Covid-19" (with China first notifying the WHO of a "pneumonia of unknown cause" on December 31, 2019). As argued in Chapter 1, the planning behind the "Covid-19" operation must have taken years, such was its complexity and transnational coordination.

But, on the other hand, the proximate triggers for the initiation of the "Covid-19" operation (described in Chapter 1) appear to have come sooner than anticipated. "Too much has been set in motion too early, too disjointedly," observes van der Pijl (2022, p. 2), "and the contradictions between the different interests and institutions, only apparently in agreement, are bound to turn into overt conflict." The enormity of the events that have taken place since 2020 has blown the cover hitherto meticulously maintained by the transnational deep state (Hughes, 2022b) and was entirely out of keeping with its preferred method of introducing social change gradually, over long periods of time, so that the population does not notice the encroaching tyranny and global centralisation of power. Brzezinski (1970, pp. 253, 260), for instance, envisages the "piecemeal transformation of the United States into a highly controlled society," with "the needed change" being "more likely to develop incrementally and less overtly."

For whatever reason, an 18-month window (the same length of time between "9/11" and the U.S. invasion of Iraq, incidentally) seems to have been identified by the ruling class at the start of the "Covid-19" operation. For example, 18 months is the timeframe used in the Event 201 simulation. Neil Ferguson, following CEPI, puts the development of a new "vaccine" at 18 months (Ferguson et al. 2020, p. 1). Zeke Emmanuel, who later became part of President Biden's Covid-19 Advisory Board, claimed on April 7, 2020, that "Covid-19 will be here for the next 18 months or more" (cited in Olson, 2020). The Minneapolis Federal Reserve Bank president, Neel Kashkari, warned in April 2020 that 18 months of lockdowns would follow (cited in Titus, 2021). Gates (2020a) put the time frame for the development of a "Covid-19 vaccine" at 18 months.

During this 18-month window, a note of urgency was detectable in the pronouncements of Establishment mouthpieces. The WEF partnered with the WHO on March 11, 2020, to launch a "COVID Action Platform" to move at "scale and speed [so as] to help end the global emergency [for them, the spectre of revolution] as soon as possible" (Vanham, 2020). According to Gates (2020a), "We need to make billions of doses, we need to get them out to every part of the world, and we need all of this to happen as quickly as possible." The name "Operation Warp Speed" says it all. According to Schwab (2020), "the pandemic represents a rare but narrow window of opportunity [to] reset our world." Prince Charles, announcing the WEF's "Great Reset" on the same day, claimed, "We have a unique but rapidly shrinking window of opportunity to learn lessons and reset ourselves on a more sustainable path. It is an opportunity we have never had before and may never have again. So, we must use all the levers at our disposal [...]" (Prince of Wales, 2020). On November 10, 2020, Charles pleaded at the Green Horizon Summit, "I'm afraid we are literally at the last hour. And there is real urgency for action [...] We know now what we have to do to rescue the situation, rather than going on talking about it" ("Prince Charles says Firms must prioritise Climate Change Fight," 2020). On December 22, 2020, Blair (2020) called for vaccination efforts to be "radically accelerated." According to the Good Health Pass Initiative (2021, p. 13), "we do not have the luxury of time" when it comes to rolling out "vaccine passports."

The "vaccination" agenda did not go according to plan, however. As of July 2022, 18.9 million Brits (30% of a NIMS cohort of 63.4 million) had not taken a first dose of a "Covid-19 vaccine" by July 2022 (UKHSA, 2022, Table 5). This includes 12.4 million responsible adults (20% of the cohort, or 23% of the adult population of 54 million). Thus, even according to official data, almost a quarter of the UK adult population successfully withstood the prolonged assault on their bodily sovereignty. The proportion is likely higher when one factors in routine manipulation of official "Covid-19" statistics (Crawford, 2022), creating "one of the most manipulated infectious disease events in history" (Blaylock, 2022).

This non-conformist segment of the population roughly corresponds to the "fifth of the population" that "cannot be hypnotized at all"; another fifth "can be hypnotized very easily"; and the remaining 60% of the population falls somewhere in the middle (Huxley, 1958, pp. 94–5). This shows how finely poised the balance of social forces really is. If the 23% of "unvaccinated" UK adults wins over another 27% of the adult population, the balance is even. Fascinatingly, in that respect, the "injection rejection" (HART, 2022b) grew with each new dose. 21.5 million people did not receive the second dose, and 30.4 million (48% of the NIMS cohort) did not receive the third; in terms of adults, 40% refused a "booster shot" (see UKHSA, 2022b, Table 5). In most parts of the world, people stopped coming forward for "Covid-19 vaccination" during 2022 (HART, 2022b).

Once the 18-month window closed in September 2021, concern set in among the ruling class. Ngaire Woods, speaking at a WEF event in November 2021, claimed: "in every single country [polled], the majority of people trusted their elite less. So, we can lead, but if people aren't following, we're not going to get to where we want to go" (WEF, 2021, 39:20). Gates (2021) admits that he "underestimated how tough it would be to convince people to take the vaccine." Former New Zealand Prime Minister and WEF affiliate, Helen Clark, told Davos in 2022: "Popular support for measures is waning [...] We are in danger of losing this moment for transformative change" ("Helen Clark: 'Covid... we are in danger of losing this moment for transformative change,'" 2022). UCL professor Mariana Mazzucato asked:

> Did we actually manage to vaccinate everyone in the world? No. So, [we should highlight] water as a global commons [...] water is something that people understand. You know, climate change is a bit abstract [whereas...] every kid knows how important it is to have water [...] Can we actually deliver this time in ways that we have failed miserably other times? (World Economic Forum, 2022)

This appears to be an admission that the post-1968 project to manufacture global consciousness (see Chapter 6) is foundering, because not enough people buy into the technocrats' manufactured "climate change" and "pandemic" narratives (possibly even pointing to future water shortages as a means of compelling compliance). Clearly, all was not going according to plan.

Plan B: Ukraine

The almost surreal sudden disappearance of "Covid-19" from the top of the "news" agenda after two years of nothing but "Covid-19," and its replacement with the conflict in Ukraine as the 24/7 object of attention, indicates an obvious change of plan. Given that the global ruling classes fundamentally act as one, transnationally, against those layers of society not aligned with their interests, and have done so since 1968 at least, it makes sense that Vladimir Putin would be part of such a master plan (cf. Davis, 2022b, 2022c).

BlackRock (2019) knew before "Covid-19" that, "in the long run, the growth of money supply drives inflation." The inevitable high inflation resulting from record levels of quantitative easing in 2020 created a "cost-of-living crisis" that was then disingenuously blamed on Putin, even though the surge in UK inflation from 2 to 10% in a single year began in July 2021 (Rate Inflation, n.d.). We are looking here at a shift to economic warfare against Western populations following a period of shock, known from the CIA playbook: in the 1970s, for instance, "Not only were Chileans in a state of shock following Pinochet's violent coup, but the country was also traumatized by severe hyperinflation" (Klein, 2007, p. 7). This, in turn, was exploited by Milton Friedman to institute the original economic shock therapy, involving mass privatisation of public goods and services in the "most extreme capitalist makeover ever attempted anywhere."

It is impossible to predict exactly where the present crisis will lead, but with an estimated 700,000 UK households unable to afford the rent/mortgage payment in April 2023 ("Rent and mortgage payments are missed by 700,000 households," 2023), it does appear that poverty and debt are being used to demoralise sections of the working- and lower-middle classes ahead of the intended transition to CBDC, which could conceivably involve debt forgiveness and universal basic income for those willing to make the transition to a biodigital slavery system. One almost hears Aleister Crowley from beyond the grave: "In this way we shall have a contented class of slaves who will accept the conditions of existence as they really are, and enjoy life with the quiet wisdom of cattle" (Crowley, 1996, p. 131). Yet, things could also go the other way: the consequences of the economic depression being ushered in "cannot be foreseen and may in fact turn against" those responsible for it (van der Pijl, 2020)—should, for instance, disenfranchised populations rise up.

Although the Ukraine conflict is real in a geopolitical sense, it can also be used for psychological warfare purposes against Western populations. As the "Cold War" teaches, geopolitical conflict, or the threat of it, has long served as a weapon used to terrorise domestic populations, always requiring the surrender of liberty in exchange for the promise of security (Hughes, 2022b). Thus, it was no surprise to hear politicians and the media claiming that the Ukraine conflict is "the biggest war in Europe since 1945" (taking over seamlessly from "Covid-19" as the biggest peacetime threat since 1945) (Allegretti, 2022; Hirsh, 2022). The risk of a wider conflagration between NATO and Russia/China looms large in the minds of the public owing to propaganda about potential nuclear weapons usage (Brugen, 2023; Myre, 2022). Perhaps nuclear weapons (even if "only" tactical) *will* be used again in war—not to smash a state, but, rather, to create worldwide fear of nuclear Armageddon and thus yet more mass hysteria to be exploited through myriad psychological operations. What will not be seen is the kind of nuclear escalation feared by mid-twentieth-century thinkers, for in a post-1968 world, the ruling classes of all countries, even if nominal enemies, are as one when it comes to suppressing the working class.

World War III is a war for global technocracy; everything else, including different versions of the "biggest threat since 1945," up to and including alleged nuclear weapons usage, is a decoy. Plan A, involving the "Covid-19" operation, fell apart after the known 18-month window: ultimately, too many people were unwilling to submit to violations of their bodily autonomy and a biodigital version of the totalitarian "papers, please" society. Plan B, involving the Ukraine conflict, layered economic warfare and further psychological warfare onto Plan A, progressively demoralising a population struggling to make ends meet, having just been subjected to the most ferocious psychological warfare operation in history.

In *They Thought They Were Free* (first published in 1955), a German philologist recalls that ordinary Germans in the Third Reich were kept so "fascinated by the machinations of the 'national enemies,' without and within, that we had no time to think about these dreadful things that were growing, little by little, all around us" (Meyer, 2022, pp. 167–168). In our own time, while public attention has been focused on Russia/Ukraine and (since October 2023) Israel/Palestine, the cancer of technocracy continues to grow within Western societies. By such means, the ruling class continues to conceal its Omniwar manoeuvres, but the camouflage cannot be maintained indefinitely.

Towards Worldwide Revolution

With class consciousness rapidly rising, the day is fast approaching when the wider population starts to awaken to the undeclared Omniwar that is being covertly waged against it and begins to resist in large numbers. What that resistance will look like cannot be foreseen, but it begs the all-important question: "can the world population still be kept under control?" (van der Pijl, 2022, Chapter 2).

The U.S. Declaration of Independence asserts "the Right of the People to alter or to abolish" any form of government that becomes destructive of citizens' "unalienable Rights." Today, all rights are under attack from totalitarian technocracy, including the rights to free speech, freedom of movement, freedom of assembly, and bodily autonomy. If the Declaration still means anything to American patriots, then it is hard to see the status quo being maintained once they realise what is happening.

Any mass uprisings in the United States are almost certain to be met with an attempt to implement martial law. Planning for such an eventuality goes back to the Continuity of Government (COG) arrangements made in the early 1950s anticipating a possible nuclear attack, followed by the creation of the Federal Emergency Management Agency (FEMA) in 1978, the activation of COG provisions on "9/11," and the formation of a "shadow government that could take over from the formal, statutory agencies" in case of emergency (van der Pijl, 2022, pp. 39–41). FEMA's Federal Continuity Directive 1 (2017) states that the U.S. Government must provide "leadership visible to the Nation and the world [while] maintaining the trust and confidence of the American people"; if this fails, van der Pijl (2020) infers, then "a replacement, or military command, may take over," and thus there is "explicit provision for a seizure of power by the Deep State through the military." The transnational aspect of the deep state (Hughes, 2022b) means that similar measures will be attempted in multiple countries near-simultaneously.

There is no guarantee they will succeed, however. As the populations of affected countries come to understand that they have been viciously abused and lied to as part of a transnational deep state operation intended to lead to their technocratic enslavement, overwhelming numbers of people will join the resistance, shifting the balance of class forces decisively against the would-be global technocrats. The result will then be, not the passive acquiescence to tyranny witnessed during the "shock and awe" phase of the psychological warfare in 2020, but rather a global mass movement to defeat the actors and organisations behind the war for technocracy. Once victory is achieved, all collaborators, including those who pushed for "lockdowns," mandatory masks, testing, injections, and other assaults on human dignity and freedom, will need to be held to account.

References

Abaluck, J., Cohen, T., Desir, G. V., D'Onofrio, G., Forman, H. P., Gonsalves, G., Grubaugh, N. D., Hines, R., Horsley, V., Iwasaki, A., Kapczynski, A., Kershaw, T., Ko, A. I., Latham, S. R., Morton, F. S., Omer, S. B., Paltiel, A. D., Parikh, S., Santucci, K., Smith, M. N., & Weinberger, D. (2020, August 4). Statement from Yale faculty on hydroxychloroquine and its use in Covid-19. *Counterpunch*. https://www.counterpunch.org/2020/08/04/statement-from-yale-faculty-on-hydroxychloroquine-and-its-use-in-covid-19/.

Abramson, D., Fu, D., & Johnson Jr., J. E. (2020). Cryptocurrency system using body activity data. U.S. Patent No. Patent 16/138518. Washington, D.C.: U.S Patent and Trademark Office.

Agamben, G. (1998). *Homo sacer*. Stanford University Press.

Albrecht, J. (2010). Overview of DARPA carbon electronics for RF applications program (CERA). IEEE 68th device research conference. https://ieeexplore.ieee.org/document/5551913.

Allegretti, A. (2022, February 20). Boris Johnson says Russia has plans for "biggest war in Europe since 1945." *The Guardian*. https://www.theguardian.com/world/2022/feb/20/boris-johnson-says-russia-has-plans-for-biggest-war-in-europe-since-1945.

Altman, P., Rowe, J., Hoy, W., Brady, G., Lefringhausen, A., Cosford, R., & Wauchope, B. (2023, January 5). Did national security imperatives compromise COVID-19 vaccine safety? *Brownstone Institute*. https://brownstone.org/articles/did-national-security-imperatives-compromise-covid-19-vaccine-safety/.

Andersen, M. (2021, December 10). *Intracorporeal nanonetwork. Brief summary*. Retrieved June 13, 2023, from https://everydayconcerned.net/wp-content/uploads/2021/12/12-intracorporal_nanonetwork.pdf.

Asher Hamilton, I. (2022, July 7). The story of Neuralink: Elon Musk's AI brain chip company where he had twins with a top executive. *Insider*. https://www.businessinsider.com/neuralink-elon-musk-microchips-brains-ai-2021-2.

Australian Voice. (2021, August 27). IMF reveals jabs are not for your health: "This year, next year, vaccine policy is economic policy"! *Australian Voice*. https://australianvoice.livejournal.com/57270.html.

Bardosh, K. (2023). How did the Covid pandemic response harm society? A global evaluation and state of knowledge review (2020–21). Preprint retrieved from https://doi.org/10.2139/ssrn.4447806.

Bhattacharya, J. (2023, January 11). How Stanford failed the academic freedom test. *Tablet*. https://www.tabletmag.com/sections/arts-letters/articles/stanford-failed-academic-freedom-test.

BlackRock. (2019, August 15). Dealing with the next downturn. *BlackRock*. https://www.blackrock.com/corporate/insights/blackrock-investment-institute/publications/global-macro-outlook/august-2019.

BlackRock. (2020, March). Time for policy to go direct. *BlackRock*. https:/www.blackrock.com/corporate/literature/whitepaper/blackrock-bulletin-policy-going-direct-march-2020.pdf.

Blair, T. (2020, December 22). We are in a race against time and we must change our vaccine policy now. *The Independent*. https://www.independent.co.uk/voices/covid-vaccine-tony-blair-coronavirus-b1777845.html.

Blaylock, R. L. (2022). Covid update: What is the truth? *Surgical Neurology International*, 13, Article 167. https://doi.org/10.25259/SNI_150_2022.

BMJ. (2021, March 10). *Concerns over integrity of mRNA molecules in some Covid-19 vaccines*. https://www.bmj.com/company/newsroom/concerns-over-integrity-of-mrna-molecules-in-some-covid-19-vaccines/.

Boffey, D., & Smith, H. (2021, December 1). EU must consider mandatory covid jabs, says von der Leyen. *The Guardian*. https://www.theguardian.com/world/2021/dec/01/eu-must-consider-mandatory-covid-jabs-says-von-der-leyen.

Bolton, D. (2016, March 30). Remo Scientific Advisory Group for Emergencies te-control cyborg beetle developed by scientists. *The Independent*. https://www.independent.co.uk/news/science/cyborg-remote-control-beetle-nanyang-a6960301.html.

BrainCom. (2020). *Unlocking the brain with novel graphene technology*. https://www.braincom-project.eu/unlocking-the-brain-with-novel-graphene-technology/.

Broudy, D., Hughes, D. A., & Kyrie, V. (2022, December 10). The Psychology of Covid-19 Atrocities. *Doctors For Covid Ethics*. https://doctors4covidethics.org/session-iv-understanding-tactics-of-oppression-2/.

Brown, A. S., & Crommie, M. (2021, July 13). Reshaping graphene's future. *Kavli Foundation*. https://kavlifoundation.org/news/reshaping-graphenes-future.

Brugen, I. (2023, May 26). Russia's Medvedev threatens Ukraine with pre-emptive nuclear strike. *Newsweek*. https://www.newsweek.com/russia-medvedev-ukraine-nuclear-strike-weapons-west-putin-1802829.

Brzezinski, Z. (1970). *Between two ages: America's role in the technetronic era*. Viking Press.

Burdick, S. (2023, February 23). 5G towers can make healthy people sick, two case reports show. *The Defender*. https://childrenshealthdefense.org/defender/5g-cell-towers-microwave-syndrome/.

Bushnell, D. M. (2001, July). *Future strategic issues/future warfare [circa 2025]*. NASA Langley Research Centre. https://archive.org/details/future-strategic-issues-and-warfare_202011.

Campra, P. (2021, November 2). *Detection of Graphene in COVID19 Vaccines by Micro-Raman Spectroscopy. Technical Report*. https://www.dropbox.com/s/tnnq4ftw818chmx/FINAL_VERSI%C3%93N_CAMPRA_REPORT_DETECTION_GRAPHENE_IN_COVID19_VACCINES.pdf?dl=0Cam.

Centres for Disease Control and Prevention. (n.d.). *Covid data tracker*. Retrieved June 17, 2023, from https://covid.cdc.gov/covid-data-tracker/#vaccinations_vacc-total-admin-rate-total.

Chu, J. (2021, February 1). Physicists create tunable superconductivity in twisted graphene "nanosandwich." *MIT News*. https://news.mit.edu/2021/physicists-create-tunable-superconductivity-twisted-graphene-nanosandwich-0201.

Clip of universal flu vaccine. (2019, November 1). *C-SPAN*. https://www.c-span.org/video/?c4980377/user-clip-fauci-bright-universal-flu-vax-scenario-mrna-vax-covid.

Coates, S. D. (2008). *Neural interfacing*. Springer Cham. https://doi.org/10.1007/978-3-031-01640-0.

Connolly, A. (2021, August 18). Trudeau doubles down on mandatory Covid-19 vaccines for domestic travel. *Global News*. https://globalnews.ca/news/8122807/canada-election-covid-19-madatory-vaccination/.

Corbett, J. (2019a). Episode 359—The secrets of Silicon Valley: What big tech doesn't want you to know. *The Corbett Report*. https://www.corbettreport.com/siliconvalley/.

Corbett, J. (2019b, May 25). The 5G surveillance grid. *Steemit*. https://steemit.com/news/@corbettreport/the-5g-surveillance-grid.

Crawford, M. (2022, May 9). Proof of statistical sieves in VE data, Part 2: ONS data. *Rounding the Earth Newsletter*. https://roundingtheearth.substack.com/p/proof-of-statistical-sieves-in-ve.

Crowley, A. (1996). *The Law is for All: The Authorized Popular Commentary on Liber Al Vel Legis Sub Figura CCXX, the Book of Law* (3rd ed.). New Falcon.

Crunchbase. (n.d.). *List of Moderna's Investors*. Retrieved June 17, 2023, from https://www.crunchbase.com/search/principal.investors/field/organizations/num_investors/moderna-therapeutics.

Cuthbertson, A. (2016, March 22). Graphene "tattoo" tests diabetics' sweat and delivers drugs. *Newsweek*. https://www.newsweek.com/graphene-tattoo-diabetics-sweat-diabetes-skin-patch-439451.

Dalgleish, A. (2023, September 29). mRNA "vaccines" must be banned once and for all. *TCW*. https://www.conservativewoman.co.uk/mrna-vaccines-must-be-banned-once-and-for-all/.

Davis, I. (2021, October 6). What is the global public-private partnership? *Iain Davis*. https://iaindavis.com/what-is-the-global-public-private-partnership/.

Davis, I. (2022a, June 26). The UK's new bill of no rights. *UK Column*. https://www.ukcolumn.org/blogs/the-uks-new-bill-of-no-rights.

Davis, I. (2022b, July 5). Putin's false flag. *OffGuardian*. https://off-guardian.org/2022/07/05/putins-false-flag/.

Davis, I. (2022c, November 21). Who wants a multipolar world order?—part I. *UK Column*. https://www.ukcolumn.org/article/who-wants-a-multipolar-world-order-part-i.

Davis, I. (2023, March 7). Central bank digital currency is the endgame—part 1. *OffGuardian*. https://off-guardian.org/2023/03/07/central-bank-digital-currency-is-the-endgame-part-1/.

Dearden, N. (2022, March 16). Moderna's profits show why big pharma can't meet our health needs. *AlJazeera*. https://www.aljazeera.com/opinions/2022/3/16/modernas-profits-show-why-big-pharma-cant-meet-our-health-needs.

Defence Advanced Research Projects Agency. (2012). *Defense Advanced Research Projects Agency justification book volume 1: research, development, test & evaluation, defense-wide*. https://www.darpa.mil/attachments/(2G4)%20Global%20Nav%20-%20About%20Us%20-%20Budget%20-%20Budget%20Entries%20-%20FY2013%20(Approved).pdf.

Defence Advanced Research Projects Agency. (2014, October 20). *Atom-width graphene sensors could provide unprecedented insights into brain structure and function*. https://web.archive.org/web/20141023143904/https://www.darpa.mil/NewsEvents/Releases/2014/10/20.aspx.

Defence Advanced Research Projects Agency. (2015, October 5). *Work begins to support self-healing of body and mind*. https://www.darpa.mil/news-events/2015-10-05.

Defence Advanced Research Projects Agency. (2017, July 10). *Towards a high-resolution, implantable neural interface*. https://www.darpa.mil/news-events/2017-07-10.

Delgado, J. (1969). *Physical control of the mind*. Harper and Row.

DHS Science and Technology Directorate. (2021). *Master question list for covid-19 (caused by SARS-CoV-2) weekly report, 23 February 2021*. https://www.dhs.gov/sites/default/files/publications/mql_sars-cov-2_-_cleared_for_public_release_20210223.pdf.

Doctors for Covid Ethics. (2023). *mRNA Vaccine Toxicity*. https://doctors4covidethics.org/mrna-vaccine-toxicity/.

Dolgin, E. (2015). Business: The billion-dollar biotech. *Nature 522*, 26–28. https://www.nature.com/articles/522026a.

Dowd, E. (2022). *"Cause Unknown": The epidemic of sudden deaths in 2021 and 2022*. Skyhorse.

Dugan, R. (2010, March 23). *Statement submitted to the Subcommittee on Terrorism, Unconventional Threats and Capabilities, House Armed Services Committee, United States House of Representatives*. https://www.darpa.mil/attachments/TestimonyArchived%20(March%2023%202010).pdf.

Egan, M., & Isidore, C. (2020, May 22). Moderna unveiled encouraging coronavirus vaccine results. Then top execs dumped nearly $30 million of stock. *CNN Business*. https://edition.cnn.com/2020/05/22/investing/moderna-coronavirus-vaccine-stock-sales/index.html.

European Centre for Disease Prevention and Control. (n.d.). *Covid-19 vaccine tracker*. Retrieved June 17, 2023, from https://vaccinetracker.ecdc.europa.eu/public/extensions/COVID-19/vaccine-tracker.html#distribution-tab.

Fabbro, A., Scaini, D., León, V., Vázquez, E., Cellot, G., Privitera, G., Lombardi, L., Torrisi, F., Tomarchio, F., Bonaccorso, F., Bosi, S., Ferrari, A. C., Ballerini, L., & Prato, M. (2016). Graphene-based interfaces do not alter target nerve cells. *ACS Nano, 10*(1), 615–623. https://doi.org/10.1021/acsnano.5b05647.

Ferguson, N. M, Laydon, D., Nedjati-Gilani, G., Imai, N., Ainslie, K., Baguelin, M., Bhatia, S., Boonyasiri, A., Cucunubá, Z., Cuomo-Dannenburg, G., Dighe, A., Dorigatti, I., Fu, H., Gaythorpe, K., Green, W., Hamlet, A., Hinsley, W., Okell, L. C., van Elsland, S., Ghani, A. C., et al. (2020). *Report 9: Impact of non-pharmaceutical interventions (NPIs) to reduce Covid-19 mortality and healthcare demand*. https://www.imperial.ac.uk/media/imperial-college/medicine/sph/ide/gida-fellowships/Imperial-College-COVID19-NPI-modelling-16-03-2020.pdf.

Fisher, L., & Smyth, C. (2020, November 9). GCHQ in cyberwar on anti-vaccine propaganda. *The Times*. https://www.thetimes.co.uk/article/gchq-in-cyberwar-on-anti-vaccine-propaganda-mcjgjhmb2.

Forte, M.C. (2021, August 1). The pandemic narrative and the war against the people: Day 2 of an online interdisciplinary symposium. *Zero Anthropology*. https://zeroanthropology.net/2021/08/01/the-pandemic-narrative-and-the-war-against-the-people-day-2-of-an-online-interdisciplinary-symposium/.

Frank, J. W. (2021). Electromagnetic fields, 5G and health: What about the precautionary principle? *Journal of Epidemiology and Public Health, 75*(6), 562–566. https://doi.org/10.1136/jech-2019-213595.

Garde, D. (2017, January 10). Lavishly funded Moderna hits safety problems in bold bid to revolutionize medicine. *STAT*. https://www.statnews.com/2017/01/10/moderna-trouble-mrna/.

Garde, D. (2020, November 10). The story of mRNA: How a once-dismissed idea became a leading technology in the Covid vaccine race. *STAT*. https://www.statnews.com/2020/11/10/the-story-of-mrna-how-a-once-dismissed-idea-became-a-leading-technology-in-the-covid-vaccine-race/.

Gates, B. (2020a, April 30). What you need to know about the COVID-19 vaccine. *GatesNotes*. https://www.gatesnotes.com/Health/What-you-need-to-know-about-the-COVID-19-vaccine.

Gates, B. (2020b, December 22). These breakthroughs will make 2021 better than 2020. *GatesNotes*. https://www.gatesnotes.com/About-Bill-Gates/Year-in-Review-2020.

Gates, B. (2021, December 7). Reasons for optimism after a difficult year. *GatesNotes*. https://www.gatesnotes.com/About-Bill-Gates/Year-in-Review-2021.

Gates, B. & Gates, M. (2021, January 27). The year global health went local. *GatesNotes*. https://www.gatesnotes.com/2021-Annual-Letter.

Giordano, J. (2017, August 29). Brain science from bench to battlefield: The realities—and risks—of neuroweapons. *Centre for Global Security Research seminar, Lawrence Livermore National Laboratory*. https://cgsr.llnl.gov/event-calendar/2017/2017-06-12.

Giordano, J. (2018, September 25). The brain is the battlefield of the future. *Modern War Institute, West Point*. https://mwi.usma.edu/mwi-video-brain-battlefield-future-dr-james-giordano/.

Good Health Pass Initiative. (2021, February 9). *Good health pass: A safe path to global reopening*. https://www.goodhealthpass.org/wp-content/uploads/2021/02/Good-Health-Pass-Collaborative-Principles-Paper.pdf.

Graphene Flagship. (n.d.). *The Graphene Flagship*. https://graphene-flagship.eu/collaboration/about-us/the-graphene-flagship/.

Harari, Y. N. (2017). *Homo deus: A brief history of tomorrow*. HarperCollins.

Harari, Y. N. (2020, March 20). The world after coronavirus. *Financial Times*. https://www.ft.com/content/19d90308-6858-11ea-a3c9-1fe6fedcca75.

Head, M. (2022, May 23). What happened to the AstraZeneca vaccine? Now rare in rich countries, it's still saving lives around the world. *The Conversation*. https://theconversation.com/what-happened-to-the-astrazeneca-vaccine-now-rare-in-rich-countries-its-still-saving-lives-around-the-world-181791.

Health Advisory & Recovery Team. (2022a, February 25). *Care home isolation and neglect: An urgent crisis*. https://www.hartgroup.org/care-home-isolation-and-neglect-an-urgent-crisis/.

Health Advisory & Recovery Team. (2022b, November 20). *The Injection Rejection*. https://www.hartgroup.org/the-injection-rejection/.

Helen Clark: "Covid... we are in danger of losing this moment for transformative change. (2022, June 11). *SeeMoreRocks*. https://seemorerocks.is/helen-clark-covid-we-are-in-danger-of-losing-this-moment-for-transformative-change/.

Henningsen, P. (2021). Overcoming the noble lie: Great narratives and compelling futures. *New Dawn* 15(6). https://www.newdawnmagazine.com/articles/overcoming-the-noble-lie-great-narratives-compelling-futures.

Hirsh, M. (2022, February 24). Why Putin's war is the West's biggest test since World War II. *Foreign Policy*. https://foreignpolicy.com/2022/02/24/russia-ukraine-war-west-world-war-2/.

Holder, J. (2023, March 13). Tracking coronavirus vaccinations around the world. *New York Times*. https://www.nytimes.com/interactive/2021/world/covid-vaccinations-tracker.html.

Hong, G., Yang, X., Zhou, T., & Lieber, C. M. (2018). Mesh electronics: A new paradigm for tissue-like brain probes. *Current Opinion in Neurobiology, 50*, 33–41. https://doi.org/10.1016/j.conb.2017.11.007.

Hope, J. R. (2022, February 21). Pfizer and Moderna investors run for the exit. *The Desert Review*. https://www.thedesertreview.com/opinion/columnists/pfizer-moderna-investors-run-for-the-exits/article_f33832ce-9347-11ec-830c-6fe60d1a126b.html.

How DARPA seeded the ground for a rapid Covid-19 cure. (2020, December 17). *yahoo!* https://finance.yahoo.com/video/darpa-seeded-ground-rapid-covid-214655580.html.

Huang, H., Su, S., Wu, N., Wan, H., Wan, S., Bi, H., & Sun, L. (2019). Graphene-based sensors for human health monitoring. *Frontiers in Chemistry, 7*, Article 399. https://doi.org/10.3389/fchem.2019.00399.

Hughes, D. A. (2022a). "Covid-19 vaccines" for children in the UK: A tale of establishment corruption. *International Journal of Vaccine Theory, Practice, and Research, 2*(1), 209–247. https://doi.org/10.56098/ijvtpr.v2i1.35.

Hughes, D. A. (2022b, July 29). Wall Street, the Nazis, and the crimes of the deep state. *Propaganda in Focus*. https://propagandainfocus.com/wall-street-the-nazis-and-the-crimes-of-the-deep-state/.

Hughes, D. A. (2022c). What is in the so-called Covid-19 "vaccines"? Part 1: Evidence of a global crime against humanity. *International Journal of Vaccine Theory, Practice, and Research*, *2*(2), 455–586. https://doi.org/10.56098/ijvtpr.v2i2.52.

Hughes, D.A. (2023, April 14). *We are in a global class war* [Video]. Bitchute. https://www.bitchute.com/video/ZPHbyPe04Yc0/.

Hughes, D. A., Kyrie, V., & Broudy, D. (2022, November 29). Covid-19: Mass formation or mass atrocity? *Unlimited Hangout*. https://unlimitedhangout.com/2022/11/investigative-reports/covid-19-mass-formation-or-mass-atrocity/.

Huxley, A. (1958). *Brave new world revisited*. Harper and Row.

INBRAIN. (n.d.). *Decoding neural signals to restore patients' lives*. https://www.inbrain-neuroelectronics.com/.

Jamieson, G. (2023, February 1). How safe really is 5G? *The Daily Sceptic*. https://dailysceptic.org/2023/02/01/how-safe-really-is-5g/.

Jérusalem, A. (2018, November 7). Mind control using sound waves? We ask a scientist how it works. *World Economic Forum*. https://web.archive.org/web/20181107172700/https://www.weforum.org/agenda/2018/11/mind-control-ultrasound-neuroscience/.

Jiminez, A. (2017, February 27). Elon Musk says we'll have to become cyborgs to survive. *The American Genius*. https://theamericangenius.com/tech-news/elon-musk-cyborgs/.

Jornet, J.M., & Akyildiz, I.F. (2014). *Graphene-based plasmonic nano-transceiver for terahertz band communication*. https://unlab.tech/wp-content/uploads/2014/04/06901799.pdf.

Keats, J. (2013, May 14). The $1.3B quest to build a supercomputer replica of a human brain. *Wired*. https://www.wired.com/2013/05/neurologist-markam-human-brain/.

Kennedy Jr., R. F. (2021). *The real Anthony Fauci. Bill Gates, big pharma, and the global war on democracy and public health*. Skyhorse.

Kennedy, Jr., R. F. (2022, December 19). Ed Dowd's new book proves an undeniable and urgent reality. *Children's Health Defence*. https://childrenshealthdefense.org/defender/rfk-jr-ed-dowd-cause-unknown-book/.

Kheriaty, A. (2022, May 24). The WHO treaty is tied to a global digital passport and ID system. *Brownstone Institute*. https://brownstone.org/articles/who-treaty-tied-to-digital-passport-id-system/.

Kitson, F. (1971). *Low intensity operations*. Stackpole Books.

Klein, N. (2007). *The shock doctrine*. Metropolitan Books.

Kurzweil, R. (2005). *The singularity is near. When humans transcend biology*. Viking.

Kyrie, V., & Broudy, D. (2022a, May 22). Hiding in plain sight: Technocratic tyranny behind a medical mask. *Propaganda in Focus*. https://www.propagandainfocus.com/hiding-in-plain-sight-technocratic-tyranny-behind-a-medical-mask/.

Kyrie, V., & Broudy, D. (2022b). Cyborgs R us: The bio-nano panopticon of injected bodies? *International Journal of Vaccine Theory, Practice, and Research*, *2*(2), 355–383. https://doi.org/10.56098/ijvtpr.v2i2.49.

Lee, Y., Song, W. J., & Sun, J. -Y. (2020). Hydrogel soft robotics. *Materials Today Physics*, *15*, Article 100258. https://doi.org/10.1016/j.mtphys.2020.100258.

Lenin, V. I. (1964). War and revolution. In: *Lenin Collected Works* (I. Bernard, Trans.) (Vol. 24, pp. 398–421). Progress Publishers.

Luxemburg, R. (1915). *The Junius Pamphlet* (D. Hollis, Trans.). https://www.marxists.org/archive/luxemburg/1915/junius/index.htm.

Mark Steele on 5G, nanotechnology weapons in C19 Shots, use of heavy metals as weapons systems. (2023, February 5). *Dr. Ana's Newsletter*. https://anamihalceamdphd.substack.com/p/mark-steele-on-5g-nanotechnology.

Marquardt, M. (2015). Ferromagnetic thin film induces magnetism in graphene. *MRS Bulletin*, *40*, Article 202. https://doi.org/10.1557/mrs.2015.40.

Medicines and Healthcare products Regulatory Agency. (n.d.). *COVID-19 vaccine analysis overview* . https://yellowcard.ukcolumn.org/yellow-card-reports.

Medicines and Healthcare products Regulatory Agency. (2019). Yellow card: please help to reverse the decline in reporting of suspected adverse drug reactions. https://www.gov.uk/drug-safety-update/yellow-card-please-help-to-reverse-the-decline-in-reporting-of-suspected-adverse-drug-reactions.

Medicines and Healthcare products Regulatory Agency. (2023). *Regulatory approval of Covid-19 vaccine SKYCovion*. https://www.gov.uk/government/publications/regulatory-approval-of-covid-19-vaccine-skycovion.

Meerloo, J.A. (1956). *The rape of the mind. The psychology of thought control, menticide, and brainwashing*. World Publishing Company.

Mello, M. M., Opel, D. J., Benjamin, R. M., Callaghan, T., DiResta, R., Elharake, J. A., Flowers, L. C., Galvani, A. P., Salmon, D. A., Schwartz, J. L., Brewer, N. T., Buttenheim, A. M., Carpiano, R. M., Clinton, C., Hotez, P. J., Lakshmanan, R., Maldonado, Y. A., Omer, S. B., Sharfstein, J. M, & Caplan, A. (2023). Effectiveness of vaccination mandates in improving uptake of Covid-19 vaccines in the USA. *The Lancet*, *400*, Article 10351, 535–538. https://doi.org/10.1016/S0140-6736(22)00875-3.

Meyer, D. (2022, February 4). Moderna wouldn't share its vaccine technology, so South Africa and the WHO made a Covid jab based on it anyway. *Fortune*. https://fortune.com/2022/02/04/south-africa-afrigen-moderna-covid-vaccine-mrna-who-hotez-corbevax/.

Mihalcea, A. (2023, May 20). Visual inspection of C19 vaccinated live blood clots—rubber (hydrogel) like substance found—beware graphic images. *Dr. Ana's Newsletter*. https://anamihalceamdphd.substack.com/p/visual-inspection-of-c19-vaccinated.

Mikovits, J., & Heckenlively, K. (2020). *Plague of corruption*. Skyhorse.

Miller, S. (2018). *Dual use science and technology, ethics and weapons of mass destruction*. SpringerBriefs in Ethics. https://doi.org/10.1007/978-3-319-92606-3.

Miller, M.C. (2020, November 30). Just sent my petition in defence of academic freedom, with its 17,700+ signatories, to President Andrew Hamilton at NYU. *News From Underground*. https://markcrispinmiller.com/2020/11/just-sent-my-petition-in-defense-of-academic-freedom-with-its-17700-signatories-to-president-andrew-hamilton-at-nyu/.

Ministry of Defence. (2021). *Human augmentation—the dawn of a new paradigm*. https://assets.publishing.service.gov.uk/government/uploads/system/uploads/attachment_data/file/986301/Human_Augmentation_SIP_access2.pdf.

Minnicino, M. (1974). Low intensity operations: The Reesian theory of war. *The Campaigner, 7*(6), 37–55.

Miyamoto, K. (2018, November 11). *The CIA MKULTRA subproject 119 was their initial electromagnetic program, though not yielding any substantial methodologies*. https://ssrn.com/abstract=3284813.

Moderna. (2013, October 2). *DARPA awards Moderna Therapeutics a grant for up to $25 million to develop messenger RNA therapeutics™*. https://web.archive.org/web/20200131130511/https://investors.modernatx.com/news-releases/news-release-details/darpa-awards-moderna-therapeutics-grant-25-million-develop/.

Moderna. (2020). *Form 10-Q*. https://www.sec.gov/Archives/edgar/data/1682852/000168285220000017/mrna-20200630.htm.

Myre, G. (2022, October 4). How likely is a Russian nuclear strike in Ukraine? *NPR*. https://www.npr.org/2022/10/04/1126680868/putin-raises-the-specter-of-using-nuclear-weapons-in-his-war-with-ukraine.

Newman, L. (2020). Nose-to-brain translocation and cerebral biodegradation of thin graphene oxide nanosheets. *Cell Reports Physical Science*, *1*(9), Article 100176. https://doi.org/10.1016/j.xcrp.2020.100176.

NZDSOS. (2022, November 29). *Good manufacturing practices in Pfizer times: An independent analysis of vaccine quality issues*. https://nzdsos.com/2022/11/29/good-manufacturing-practices-in-pfizer-times/.

O'Faolain, A. (2022, July 5). Supreme Court dismisses Gemma O'Doherty and John Waters' action over Covid-19 laws. *The Irish Times*. https://www.irishtimes.com/crime-law/2022/07/05/supreme-court-dismisses-gemma-odoherty-and-john-waters-action-over-covid-19-laws/.

O'Toole, T., Mair, M., & Inglesby, T. V. (2002). Shining light on "dark winter." *Clinical Infectious Diseases, 34*(7), 972–983. https://doi.org/10.1086/339909.

Office for Health Improvements and Disparities. (n.d.). *Excess mortality in England*. Retrieved December 30, 2023, from https://app.powerbi.com/view?r=eyJrIjoiYmUwNmFhMjYtNGZhYS00NDk2LWFlMTAtOTg0OGNhNmFiNGM0IiwidCI6ImVlNGUxNDk5LTRhMzUtNGIyZS1hZDQ3LTVmM2NmOWRlODY2NiIsImMiOjh9.

Office for National Statistics. (2022, November 10). *Half a million more people are out of the labour force because of long-term sickness*. https://www.ons.gov.uk/employmentandlabourmarket/peoplenotinwork/economicinactivity/articles/halfamillionmorepeopleareoutofthelabourforcebecauseoflongtermsickness/2022-11-10.

Office for National Statistics. (2023). *Long-term international migration, provisional: year ending June 2023*. https://www.ons.gov.uk/peoplepopulationandcommunity/populationandmigration/internationalmigration/bulletins/longterminternationalmigrationprovisional/yearendingjune2023.

Official Data Collected by Our World in Data (n.d.). *Covid-19 vaccine doses administered by manufacturer* . https://ourworldindata.org/grapher/covid-vaccine-doses-by-manufacturer?country=.

Olson, T. (2020, April 8). Biden adviser, ObamaCare architect Zeke Emanuel says US should "prepare" for coronavirus measures to last 18 months. *Fox News*. https://www.foxnews.com/politics/biden-obamacare-architect-zeke-emanuel-says-u-s-should-prepare-ourselves-for-coronavirus-social-distancing-to-last-18-months.

OpenVAERS. (n.d.). *VAERS Covid vaccine adverse event reports*. Retrieved June 17, 2023, from https://openvaers.com/covid-data.

Ou, L., Song, B., Liang, H., Liu, J., Feng, X., Deng, B., Sun, T., & Shao, L. (2016). Toxicity of graphene-family nanoparticles: A general review of the origins and mechanisms. *Particle and Fibre Toxicology, 13*, Article 57. https://doi.org/10.1186/s12989-016-0168-y.

Paddock, A. H. (1979). *Psychological and unconventional warfare, 1941–1952: Origins of a "special warfare" capability for the United States Army*. U.S. Army War College.

Phelan, J. (2020, March 24). Media watch: Groundbreaking UN torture report shunned by mainstream. *Activist Post*. https://www.activistpost.com/2020/03/media-watch-groundbreaking-un-torture-report-shunned-by-mainstream.html.

Phillips, P. (2018). *Giants*. Seven Stories Press.

Phinance Technologies. (2023). *UK cause of death project:.Death and disability trends, ages 15–44: Cardiovascular Diseases*. https://phinancetechnologies.com/HumanityProjects/Resources/Project%20Brief%20-%20UK%20Cardiovascular%2015-44_091723.pdf.

Pijl, K. van der. (2014). *The discipline of Western supremacy*. Pluto Press.

Pijl, K. van der. (2018). *Surveillance capitalism and crisis*. https://www.academia.edu/35601607/Surveillance_Capitalism_and_Crisis.

Pijl, K. van der. (2020, April 27). Health emergency or seizure of power? The political economy of Covid-19. *New Cold War*. https://newcoldwar.org/health-emergency-or-seizure-of-power-the-political-economy-of-covid-19/.

Pijl, K. van der. (2022). *States of emergency. Keeping the global population in check*. Clarity Press.

Policy Horizons Canada. (2020). *Exploring biodigital convergence*. https://horizons.gc.ca/en/2020/02/11/exploring-biodigital-convergence/.

Prince Charles says firms must prioritise climate change fight. (2020, November 10). *Reuters*. https://www.reuters.com/article/uk-climate-change-britain-princecharles/prince-charles-says-firms-must-prioritise-climate-change-fight-idUSKBN27Q1DY/.

Prince of Wales. (2020, June 3). Remarks by HRH the Prince of Wales at a virtual roundtable event hosted by HRH's sustainable markets initiative and the World Economic Forum. https://www.princeofwales.gov.uk/speech/remarks-hrh-prince-wales-virtual-roundtable-event-hosted-hrhs-sustainable-markets-initiative.

Pumera, M. (2016). Graphene oxide stimulates cells to ruffle and shed plasma membranes. *Chem, 1*(2), 189–190. https://doi.org/10.1016/j.chempr.2016.07.008.

Rancourt, D. (2020). *All-cause mortality during Covid-19: No plague and a likely signature of mass homicide by government response*. https://denisrancourt.ca/entries.php?id=9&name=2020_06_02_all_cause_mortality_during_covid_19_no_plague_and_a_likely_signature_of_mass_homicide_by_government_response.

Rancourt, D., Baudin, M., & Mercier, J. (2021). *Nature of the Covid-era public health disaster in the USA, from all-cause mortality and socio-geo-economic and climatic data*. https://denisrancourt.ca/uploads_entries/1635189453861_USA%20ACM%20into%202021%20-%20article----12d.pdf.

Rancourt, D., Baudin, M., Hickey, J., & Mercier, J. (2023, September 23). COVID-19 vaccine-associated mortality in the Southern Hemisphere. *CORRELATION*. https://correlation-canada.org/covid-19-vaccine-associated-mortality-in-the-southern-hemisphere/.

RAND Corporation. (2006). *The global technology revolution 2020, in-depth analyses: Bio/nano/materials/information trends, drivers, barriers, and social implications*. The RAND Corporation. https://www.rand.org/pubs/technical_reports/TR303.html.

Rate Inflation. (n.d.). *United Kingdom inflation rate*. Retrieved June 17, 2023, from https://www.rateinflation.com/inflation-rate/uk-inflation-rate/.

Rent and mortgage payments are missed by 700,000 households in April as six in 10 renters report making changes to cover essential spending, survey finds. (2023, May 9). *Daily Mail*. https://www.thisismoney.co.uk/money/mortgageshome/article-12061213/Rent-mortgage-payments-missed-700-000-households-April-survey-finds.html.

Rockefeller Foundation. (2013). *Dreaming the future of health for the next 100 years*. https://www.rockefellerfoundation.org/report/dreaming-the-future-of-health-for-the-next-100-years/.

Rockefeller Foundation. (2022, August 23). *Mercury project to boost Covid-19 vaccination rates and counter public health mis- and disinformation in 17 countries worldwide*. https://www.rockefellerfoundation.org/news/mercury-project-to-boost-covid-19-vaccination-rates-and-counter-public-health-mis-and-disinformation-in-17-countries-worldwide/.

Rockefeller University. (2014, October 7). *Rockefeller neurobiology lab is awarded first-round BRAIN initiative grant*. https://www.rockefeller.edu/news/8772-rockefeller-neurobiology-lab-is-awarded-first-round-brain-initiative-grant/.

Rockefeller University. (2016, March 23). *Using magnetic forces to control neurons, study finds the brain plays key role in glucose metabolism*. https://www.rockefeller.edu/news/11045-using-magnetic-forces-to-control-neurons-study-finds-the-brain-plays-key-role-in-glucose-metabolism/.

Roco, M. C., & Bainbridge, W. S. (Eds.). (2002, June). *Converging technologies for improving human performance*. https://web.archive.org/web/20041026051927/wtec.org/ConvergingTechnologies/Report/NBIC_pre_publication.pdf.

Ross, L., Klompas, M., & Bernstein, S. (2010). Electronic support for public health—vaccine adverse event reporting system. https://digital.ahrq.gov/sites/default/files/docs/publication/r18hs017045-lazarus-final-report-2011.pdf.

Sahoo, D., Mitra, T., Chakraborty, K., & Sarkar, P. (2022). Remotely controlled electro-responsive on-demand nanotherapy based on amine-modified graphene oxide for synergistic dual drug delivery. *Materials Today Chemistry*, *25*, Article 100987. https://doi.org/10.1016/j.mtchem.2022.1009872468–5194/.

San Roman, D., Garg, R., & Cohen-Karni, T. (2020). Bioelectronics with graphene nanostructures. *APL Materials*, *8*(10), Article 100906. https://doi.org/10.1063/5.0020455.

Sarlangue, G., Devilleger, J., Trillaud, P., Fouchet, S., Taillasson, L., & Catteau, G. (2021, November 30). *Project Bluetooth Expérience X*. http://www.nakim.org/israel-forums/download.php?id=920--.

Schwab, K. (2016). *The Fourth Industrial Revolution*. World Economic Forum.

Schwab, K., & Malleret, T. (2020). *Covid 19: The Great Reset*. World Economic Forum.

Schwab, K. (2020, June 3). *Now is the time for a "great reset."* World Economic Forum. https://www.weforum.org/agenda/2020/06/now-is-the-time-for-a-great-reset/.

Schwab, K. (2022, April 10). Nobody will be safe if not everybody is vaccinated [Video]. *YouTube*. https://www.youtube.com/watch?v=cnajJ5N3Ifw.

Scott, B. (2021, October 13). Beyond a state of fear: Menticide and schizogenesis. *Borderline*. https://dr-bruce-scott.com/2021/10/13/beyond-a-state-of-fear-menticide-and-schizogenesis/.

Shaw, J. (2001, November-December). Liquid computing. *Harvard Magazine*. https://www.harvardmagazine.com/2001/11/liquid-computing.html.

Shaw, J. (2011, January-February). Virus-sized transistors. *Harvard Magazine*. https://www.harvardmagazine.com/2011/01/virus-sized-transistors.

Shearing, H. (2021, June 6). Covid: PM to push for world vaccination by end of 2022. *BBC News*. https://www.bbc.co.uk/news/uk-57373120.

Sicetsha, A. (2022, July 10). Watch: Sri Lanka rioters invade presidential palace. https://swisherpost.co.za/viral/sri-lanka-presidential-palace-invasion-video/.

Sidley, G. (2022, March 25). We need to talk about behavioural science – but the powers that be don't want to. *Laura Dodsworth*. https://lauradodsworth.substack.com/p/we-need-to-talk-about-behavioural.

Stanton, G. (2016). The ten stages of genocide. *Genocide Watch*. http://genocidewatch.net/genocide-2/8-stages-of-genocide/.

Taylor, I. (2021, July 24). The injectable nanosensor that will one day read your thoughts. *Science Focus*. https://www.sciencefocus.com/news/the-injectable-nanosensor-that-will-one-day-read-your-thoughts/.

Taylor, M. (2023). *Bluetooth deep dive anyone? Calling all monkey wrenchers!* [Video]. Bitchute. https://www.bitchute.com/video/7G4kHfIfAkKr/.

Taylor, N. P. (2013, December 9). Pentagon tasks Pfizer with radically rethinking vaccine development. *Fierce Pharma*. https://www.fiercepharma.com/r-d/pentagon-tasks-pfizer-radically-rethinking-vaccine-development.

Thomas, M. (2007). *Monarch: The new Phoenix program*. CreateSpace.

Tian, B., Wang, C., Zhang, S., Feng, L., & Liu, Z. (2011). Photothermally enhanced photodynamic therapy delivered by nano-graphene oxide. *ACS Nano*, *5*(9), 7000–7009. https://doi.org/10.1021/nn201560b.

Tice, A. (2022, July 30). "Concerned for humanity": Alabama embalmer discovers strange clots in people since release of Covid vaccine.

1819 News. https://1819news.com/news/item/embalmer-discovers-over-100-cases-of-strange-clots-in-people-since-release-of-covid-19-vaccine.
Titus, J. (2021). The going direct reset. *The Solari Report*. https://goingdirect.solari.com/the-going-direct-reset/.
Transcript: Bill Gates speaks to the FT about the global fight against coronavirus. (2020, April 9). *Financial Times*. https://www.ft.com/content/13ddacc4-0ae4-4be1-95c5-1a32ab15956a.
Trotsky, L. (1938). The death agony of capitalism and the tasks of the Fourth International. The transitional programme (S. Wilson, Ed.). https://www.marxists.org/archive/trotsky/1938/tp/tp-text.htm.
Tzu, S. (1963). *The art of war* (S.B. Griffith, Trans.). Oxford University Press.
UK Health Security Agency. (2022). *Weekly national influenza and Covid-19 surveillance report, week 27*. https://assets.publishing.service.gov.uk/government/uploads/system/uploads/attachment_data/file/1088929/Weekly_Flu_and_COVID-19_report_w27.pdf.
UNICEF. (2021, May 24). *No-one is safe until everyone is safe – why we need a global response to COVID-19*. https://www.unicef.org/press-releases/no-one-safe-until-everyone-safe-why-we-need-global-response-covid-19.
UNIT. (2021). *Project CUNIT-2–112Y6580. Qualitative evaluation of inclusions In Moderna, AstraZeneca and Pfizer Covid-19 vaccines*. http://www.ukcitizen2021.org/Case_Briefing_Document_and_lab_report_Ref_AUC_101_Report%20.pdf.
University of Cambridge. (2016, January 29). *Graphene shown to safely interact with Neurons in the Brain*. https://www.cam.ac.uk/research/news/graphene-shown-to-safely-interact-with-neurons-in-the-brain.
Valentine, D. (2017). *The CIA as organized crime*. Clarity Press.
Vanham, P. (2020, March 11). World Economic Forum launches Covid-19 action platform to fight coronavirus. *World Economic Forum*. https://www.weforum.org/agenda/2020/03/world-economic-forum-launches-covid-action-platform/.
Vedmore, J. (2020, November 18). Pfizer's experimental Covid-19 vaccine—what you're not being told. *Unlimited Hangout*. https://unlimitedhangout.com/2020/11/reports/pfizers-experimental-covid-19-vaccine-what-youre-not-being-told/.
Wailzer, A. (2023, July 5). WHO, EU announce partnership creating "global System" of digital vaccine passports. *LifeSite News*. https://www.lifesitenews.com/news/breaking-who-eu-announce-partnership-creating-global-system-of-digital-vaccine-passports/.
Webb, W. (2021, October 28). Covid-19: Moderna gets its miracle. *Unlimited Hangout*. https://unlimitedhangout.com/2021/10/investigative-reports/covid-19-moderna-gets-its-miracle/.

Webb, W. (2022, October 27). They may deplatform the truth, but their lies and distortions will never replace it. *The Defender*. https://childrenshealthdefense.org/defender/whitney-webb-government-truth-distortions/.

White House. (2000). *Remarks by the President at science and technology event*. https://clintonwhitehouse6.archives.gov/2000/01/2000-01-21-remarks-by-the-president-at-science-and-technology-event.html.

White House. (2013). *Fact Sheet: BRAIN Initiative*. https://obamawhitehouse.archives.gov/the-press-office/2013/04/02/fact-sheet-brain-initiative.

White House. (2022a, June 21). *Remarks by President Biden on Covid-19 vaccines for children under five*. https://www.whitehouse.gov/briefing-room/speeches-remarks/2022/06/21/remarks-by-president-biden-on-covid-19-vaccines-for-children-under-five/.

White House. (2022b, September 6). *Press briefing by White House Covid-19 response team and public health officials*. https://www.whitehouse.gov/briefing-room/press-briefings/2022/09/06/press-briefing-by-white-house-covid-19-response-team-and-public-health-officials-88/.

Wolff, E. (2021, September 20). The master plan behind the Covid crisis. *TCW*. https://www.conservativewoman.co.uk/the-master-plan-behind-the-covid-crisis/.

Wong, J. C. (2017, December 12). Former Facebook executive: Social media is ripping society apart. *The Guardian*. https://www.theguardian.com/technology/2017/dec/11/facebook-former-executive-ripping-society-apart.

Wood, J. (2011). *Where did the Towers go? Evidence of Directed Free-energy Technology on 9/11*. The New Investigation.

World Economic Forum. (2017, January 19). *An insight, an idea with Sergey Brin*. https://www.weforum.org/events/world-economic-forum-annual-meeting-2017/sessions/an-insight-an-idea-with-sergey-brin.

World Economic Forum. (2021, November 12). *The great narrative: A call to action* [Video]. https://www.weforum.org/events/the-great-narrative-2021/sessions/closing-plenary-03768dee1f.

World Economic Forum. (2022). Press conference: The new economics of water - Launch of global commission | Davos [Video]. *YouTube*. https://www.youtube.com/watch?v=1bw0gjFxu_w.

World Health Organisation. (n.d.). *VigiAccess*. Retrieved June 17, 2023, from https://vigiaccess.org/.

Yeadon, M. (2023, March 22). Why I don't believe there ever was a Covid virus. *TCW*. https://www.conservativewoman.co.uk/why-i-dont-believe-there-ever-was-a-covid-virus/.

Young, A., Fielding, J., & Kandohla, T. (2023, March 31). Asylum seekers say they are bored, the food is bad and it is 'like living in jail' in three and four-star hotels where taxpayers are footing their bill—as number of hotels filled with migrants nears 400 across Britain. *Daily*

Mail. https://www.dailymail.co.uk/news/article-11901377/Asylum-seekers-say-like-living-jail-hotels-taxpayers-footing-bill.html.

Zhang, X., Lia, G., Li, Q., Shaik, M. S., Li, Z. (2021). The pure paramagnetism in graphene oxide. *Results in Physics*, *26*, Article 104407. https://doi.org/10.1016/j.rinp.2021.104407.

Zhang, A., Zhaoa, Y., Youa, S. S., & Lieber, C. M. (2019). Nanowire probes could drive high-resolution brain-machine interfaces. *Nano Today, 31*, 1–3.

Index

D. A. Hughes, *"Covid-19," Psychological Operations, and the War for Technocracy*, https://doi.org/10.1007/978-3-031-41850-1

Q

R

SPRINGER NATURE

GPSR Compliance

The European Union's (EU) General Product Safety Regulation (GPSR) is a set of rules that requires consumer products to be safe and our obligations to ensure this.

If you have any concerns about our products, you can contact us on ProductSafety@springernature.com

In case Publisher is established outside the EU, the EU authorized representative is:

Springer Nature Customer Service Center GmbH
Europaplatz 3
69115 Heidelberg, Germany

The manufacturer's authorised representative in the EU is Springer Nature Customer Service Centre GmbH, Europaplatz 3, 69115 Heidelberg, Germany. If you have any concerns regarding our products, please contact ProductSafety@springernature.com

Printed and bound by CPI Group (UK) Ltd, Croydon, CR0 4YY
28/09/2026
02224060-0004